W9-BKX-827

SCHOOL LEADERSHIP

HANDBOOK • FOR • EXCELLENCE

Third Edition

Edited by

Stuart C. Smith

Philip K. Piele

Clearinghouse on Educational Management

University of Oregon

1997

Library of Congress Cataloging-in-Publication Data

School leadership : handbook for excellence / edited by Stuart C. Smith and Philip K. Piele ; foreword by Edwin M. Bridges. -- 3rd ed.
p. cm.
Includes bibliographical references.
ISBN 0-86552-134-4 (hardcover). -- ISBN 0-86552-135-2 (pbk.)
1. School management and organization--Handbooks, manuals, etc. 2. Educational leadership--Handbooks, manuals, etc. I. Smith, Stuart Carl, 1944- . II. Piele, Philip K. III. ERIC Clearinghouse on Educational Management.
LB2801.A1S34 1996
371.2--dc20 96-34636
CIP

Printed in the United States of America, 1996 (C145)
Reprinted January 1998
Reprinted June 2000 (G15)

Design: LeeAnn August
Type: 9.5/10.5 Palatino
Printer: Thomson-Shore, Inc.

ERIC Clearinghouse on Educational Management
1787 Agate Street
5207 University of Oregon
Eugene, OR 97403-5207
Telephone: (541) 346-5043 Fax: (541) 346-2334
ERIC/CEM Accession Number: EA 027 671

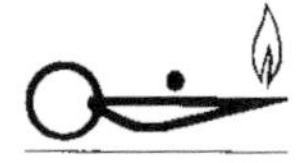

This publication was prepared in part with funding from the Office of Educational Research and Improvement, U.S. Department of Education, under contract no. OERI-RR 93002006. The opinions expressed in this report do not necessarily reflect the positions or policies of the Department of Education. No federal funds were used in the printing of this publication.

MISSION OF ERIC AND THE CLEARINGHOUSE

The Educational Resources Information Center (ERIC) is a national information system operated by the U.S. Department of Education. ERIC serves the educational community by disseminating research results and other resource information that can be used in developing more effective educational programs.

The ERIC Clearinghouse on Educational Management, one of several such units in the system, was established at the University of Oregon in 1966. The Clearinghouse and its companion units process research reports and journal articles for announcement in ERIC's index and abstract bulletins.

Research reports are announced in *Resources in Education* (*RIE*), available in many libraries and by subscription from the United States Government Printing Office, Washington, D.C. 20402-9371.

Most of the documents listed in *RIE* can be purchased through the ERIC Document Reproduction Service, operated by Cincinnati Bell Information Systems.

Journal articles are announced in *Current Index to Journals in Education. CIJE* is also available in many libraries and can be ordered from Oryx Press, 4041 North Central Avenue at Indian School, Suite 700, Phoenix, Arizona 85012. Semiannual cumulations can be ordered separately.

Besides processing documents and journal articles, the Clearinghouse prepares bibliographies, literature reviews, monographs, and other interpretive research studies on topics in its educational area.

CLEARINGHOUSE NATIONAL ADVISORY BOARD

ADMINISTRATIVE STAFF

Previous Editions

School Leadership: Handbook for Survival, edited by Stuart C. Smith, Jo Ann Mazzarella, and Philip K. Piele. 1981.

School Leadership: Handbook for Excellence, edited by Stuart C. Smith and Philip K. Piele. 1989.

Credits

Chapter 6 is adapted from Stephen Stolp and Stuart C. Smith. *Transforming School Culture: Stories, Symbols, Values and the Leader's Role.* Eugene, Oregon: ERIC Clearinghouse on Educational Management, 1995. 92 pages.

Chapter 7 is adapted and revised from Lori Jo Oswald. *School-Based Management: Rationale and Implementation Guidelines.* Eugene: Oregon School Study Council, March 1995. 66 pages. Reprinted by permission of Oregon School Study Council.

Chapter 8 is adapted from Lori Jo Oswald. *Quality Work Teams.* Eugene: Oregon School Study Council, November 1995. 44 pages. Reprinted by permission of Oregon School Study Council.

Portions of chapter 9 first appeared in Lynn Liontos. *Shared Decision-Making.* Eugene: Oregon School Study Council, October 1993. 42 pages. Reprinted by permission of Oregon School Study Council.

To

Christine, Mike, John,
and Anna Smith

Sandra, Melissa, and
Kathryn Piele

Contents

The Editors

Stuart C. Smith is associate director for publications, ERIC Clearinghouse on Educational Management, University of Oregon. He has led the Clearinghouse's publications program since 1967.

Philip K. Piele, director of the ERIC Clearinghouse on Educational Management since 1969, is professor of educational policy and management, College of Education, University of Oregon.

Contributors to This Edition

Karen Irmsher, a freelance writer residing in Eugene, Oregon, is also an instructor at Lane Community College. She has taught in grades K-12.

Larry Lashway is a writer and consultant who lives in Olympia, Washington. He is former director of the Teacher Leadership program at Silver Lake College, Manitowoc, Wisconsin.

Larry Nyland is an associate professor at Seattle Pacific University and resides in Seattle, Washington. He served as superintendent of the Pasco, Washington, school district from 1982 to 1992 and now directs the School Superintendent Program at SPU.

Lori Jo Oswald is a freelance writer who resides in Anchorage, Alaska. She received her doctor's degree in English at the University of Oregon in 1993.

David Peterson-del Mar is an associate professor at the University of Northern British Columbia, Prince George, B. C. He has written several synthesis papers for the Clearinghouse.

Jenny Waters is a freelance writer residing in Portland, Oregon, where she works as a social worker for the Veterans' Administration.

James Weber is Senior Technical Communication Specialist at Pacific Northwest National Laboratory, Richland, Washington. He is also adjunct professor of English at Washington State University, Tri Cities. He has written numerous syntheses of research on instructional leadership and other topics for the Clearinghouse.

Foreword

As a new century looms on the horizon, the changing context of public education poses a multitude of challenges for school leaders. Nationwide, revenues are not keeping pace with demands on school district budgets. Over the next few years, one-third of the current teaching force will need to be replaced, and the supply of teachers in some subject areas is projected to fall short of the demand. Enrollments are expanding as the student population is becoming increasingly diverse. In the near future, the public schools will be composed largely of minorities and a rising number of students who come from limited-English-speaking, poverty, single-parent, and transitional households.

School leaders, especially principals, will play a major role in determining how effectively public schools are able to respond to these challenges. The editors of *School Leadership: Handbook for Excellence* have anticipated this need and provided a valuable resource for those who are interested in preparing themselves to meet the challenges that lie ahead.

The essence of leadership is achieving results through people. Understandably, this book emphasizes these two aspects of leadership and provides the reader with informative and insightful treatments of a broad array of issues related to this important topic. If a leader is to accomplish results through others, he or she must be able to select teachers who can stand and deliver; to adopt leadership strategies and practices that capitalize on the talents and skills the new teachers bring to their roles; to promote a vision of excellence that is shared by all members of the school community; and to involve teachers in the creation of a sound instructional program.

Leaders must also be able to create organizational conditions under which people are motivated to do their best; to mobilize the resources and the support that they need in order to perform; and to make constructive use of the conflict that inevitably arises when people work together. These interrelated issues of school leadership are the very ones that the editors of this book have elected to underscore.

When discussing these and other issues, the authors provide a balanced perspective. They do not attempt to sell you on a particular way of thinking about an issue. Rather, the authors present the alternatives and the theory, research, and practical wisdom that speak to the soundness of these various options. They also recognize that there is a creative side of leadership where the leaders must assess the situation that they face and decide how to act in light of what they know about the particular situation and the relevant theory, research, and practical wisdom. There are no recipes to be found in this book, and rightfully so given the complexities inherent in being a school leader.

This book is also highly readable. Both the editors and the authors have striven to provide numerous examples of what a theory or a concept looks like in actual practice and to offer suggestions for translating theory and research into practice. Although I was familiar with much of the literature that formed the basis for the discussion of the various leadership issues that they treated, I found that their syntheses surfaced new questions and new insights.

For school leaders or aspiring leaders who desire to reach the fullest potential in their positions, I am confident that this book will be a valued resource, one to which they will turn and return as they confront the timely and timeless issues that this book addresses.

Edwin M. Bridges
Professor of Education and Director,
Prospective Principals' Program
Stanford University

Preface

School leadership has long been a priority topic for publications of the ERIC Clearinghouse on Educational Management. We published the first edition of this handbook in 1981 after many principals, superintendents, and other administrators told us of their need for practical information that would help them to be more effective leaders.

School leaders responded with eagerness to that handbook and to the second edition, published in 1989, confirming the need for a readable synthesis of research findings and current practices. Many administrators have told us they consult the handbook regularly, and the book also has been widely used as a text in the preservice and inservice training of school leaders throughout the country.

Of the fifteen chapters in this third edition, five are new. In response to school administrators' heightened interest in the ethical dimensions of leadership, we added to this edition a new part ("The Values") with three chapters on the foundation of ethics, vision, and values that guide the practice of school leadership. The last chapter in this part ("Cultural Leadership") replaces "School Climate."

Another new chapter ("Quality Work Teams") replaces "Team Management"; the emphasis shifts from how management can function as a team to teamwork as an essential strategy for a total-quality organization.

The other new chapter ("Shared Decision-Making," which replaces "Participative Decision-Making") reflects the wisdom that has been gained in recent years from both research and practice in this rapidly evolving model of school governance.

The other ten chapters have been revised, in varying degrees, to address new findings or issues that have come into prominence since the previous volume went to press. For example, chapter 2, previously devoted to leadership styles, now discusses as well the advantages and limitations of three leadership strategies: authoritative, transformational, and facilitative. And chapter 7, "School-Based Management," has been completely rewritten.

Several chapters that feature case studies of school or district practices rely on both written sources and interviews of practitioners. In such cases, followup interviews were conducted to bring the reports up to date.

One chapter in the previous volume, "Two Special Cases: Women and Blacks," was omitted from this edition; the themes of equity and diversity are now interwoven throughout the discussion of leadership characteristics, styles, training, recruitment, and hiring in the chapters of part 1.

This book exemplifies the philosophy of information analysis that had guided the publications program of the ERIC Clearinghouse on Educational Management for nearly three decades. Two key elements of that philosophy are *practicality* and *readability*.

In our view, the summary or analysis of research findings should not be an end in itself. Rather, keeping in mind that our main audience are school principals and superintendents, we have sought to point out the practical implications of the research findings—what they mean for the operation of schools and the day-to-day interactions of school leaders with other administrators, teachers, students, and the public. Hence, all the chapters in this volume include sections that spell out implications, recommendations, or guidelines for putting knowledge into practice. Adding to the book's practical focus are many examples or case studies of actual school programs or school leaders at work.

No matter how practical a book's content might be for school leaders, they will not find it useful if the prose is inaccessible. Again with our readers in mind, we have selected authors who write with clarity and precision. Each chapter is a simple yet detailed exposition of ideas and evidence on the topic, free of jargon and technical data. So as not to slow down the reader with a multitude of dates and page numbers, intext references to published materials cite only the authors' names. Dates are added only to distinguish among multiple works by the same author. For those readers who want to explore a topic further, each chapter's ample bibliography is an ideal starting place.

Edwin M. Bridges, whose foreword graces this edition, provided a fresh critique that strengthened each chapter's focus. We are deeply grateful to Professor Bridges for his energy in undertaking this project.

The chapters' authors are research analysts and writers with a special interest in education who were commissioned by the Clearinghouse. When an original chapter was updated by another writer or writers, all the authors' names appear. Appreciation is due all the authors for their skill in organizing and bringing clarity to the volumes of information that attended their topics.

We also thank LeeAnn Agost for designing the book, Linda Lumsden for editing the text and bibliography, and Meta Bruner for keyboarding the changes in succeeding drafts.

Leadership for Excellence

> "Leadership" is a word on everyone's lips. The young attack it and the old grow wistful for it. Parents have lost it and police seek it. Experts claim it and artists spurn it, while scholars want it. Philosophers reconcile it (as authority) with liberty and theologians demonstrate its compatibility with conscience. If bureaucrats pretend they have it, politicians wish they did. Everybody agrees there is less of it than there use to be.
>
> —Warren Bennis and Bert Nanus

Everyone knows how necessary and important leadership is. Why do some companies, teams, and schools succeed when others fail? The credit or blame most often goes to the manager, coach, or principal. After interviewing sixty corporate and thirty public-sector leaders, Bennis and Nanus concluded, "The factor that empowers the work force and ultimately determines which organizations succeed or fail is the leadership of those organizations."

What Is Leadership?

Literally hundreds of definitions of *leadership* have been offered. Some emphasize change or moving forward (implicit in the verb "to lead"), such as James Lipham's definition of leadership as "that behavior of an individual which initiates a new structure in interaction within a social system."

Other definitions differentiate between management and leadership. Carl Welte defined *management* as the "mental and physical effort to coordinate diverse activities to achieve desired results" and included in this process "planning, organization, staffing, directing, and controlling." In contrast, he saw *leadership* as "natural and learned ability, skill, and personal characteristics to conduct interpersonal relations which influence people to take desired actions." In simpler terms, John Pejza expresses the difference as follows: "You lead people; you manage things."

This emphasis on personal relations occurs in many definitions of leadership. Fred Fiedler, Martin Chemers, and Linda Mahar have noted that leadership includes "the ability to counsel, manage conflict, inspire loyalty, and imbue subordinates with a desire to remain on the job." Speaking more plainly, former President Harry Truman said, "My definition of a leader in a free country is a man who can persuade people to do what they don't want to do, or do what they're too lazy to do, and like it."

One of the best definitions of leadership was suggested by George Terry, who called it "the activity of influencing people to strive willingly for group goals." This is the definition of leadership on which this book is based. The purpose of the book is to suggest the knowledge, values, structure, and skills necessary for a leader to inspire all members of the school community to work together toward the goal of an excellent education for all students.

A simpler and yet somehow more elegant way of putting the same definition was offered by Scott Thomson when he was executive director of the National Association of Secondary School Principals: "Leadership is best defined as 'getting the job done through people'." This definition means that two things are necessary for effective leadership: accomplishment (getting the job done) and influencing others (through people). These two are intertwined. An ability to get things done makes leaders more influential.

Studies have shown that teachers are influenced most by principals who have "expert power," a term that simply means competence. Teachers are not influenced by the principal's power to punish, by his or her status or position, or even by the power to reward. They are influenced by their perception that the principal is an expert, is competent, can get the job done. One goal of this book is to give school administrators more "expert" power by helping them become more expert at what they do. A theme that recurs in many chapters of this book is that the leader's competence is most clearly manifest in the ability to empower and inspire others.

Competence alone, however, is not a sufficient qualification for leadership. Walter F. Ulmer, former president of the Center for Creative Leadership, advances the notion that leaders are able to gain, through ethical means, the followers' consent to be led:

> Leadership is an activity—an influence process—in which an individual gains the trust and commitment of others and without recourse to formal position or authority moves the group to the accomplishment of one or more tasks. (Quoted in Kenneth E. Clark and Miriam B. Clark)

Leaders' influence over others is a product of, in addition to competency, their integrity. By their behavior, leaders earn trust and inspire loyalty. This is a vital lesson in an age when scandals and broken trust in corporations, financial institutions, and government agencies make daily headlines. Schools, certainly as much as any other institution, deserve ethical leadership.

Assumptions about the Nature of Leadership

The exercise of leadership involves people: a leader or leaders, a follower or followers, and the interaction of their personalities, knowledge, skills, and moral predispositions. It also involves place: a group or organization, with its particular structure, culture, resources, and history. Because so many variables of personality and context go into the workings of leadership, it is not surprising that people have observed and studied leadership from many different perspectives. Theories and models of leadership abound.

So that the reader might know what to expect from this book, we set forth here our own assumptions about the nature of leadership.

Leadership Is Multidimensional

Good leaders operate out of a clear understanding of their values, goals, and beliefs and also those of their followers. Leaders both influence and are constrained by the organizational context. Leaders may, with good results, use any of a variety of styles and strategies of leadership, including hierarchical, transformational, and participative, depending on their reading of themselves, their followers, and the organizational context.

Schools Need To Be Both Managed and Led

Much of what passes for leadership in schools is really management. This should come as no surprise, because school administrators are trained primarily as managers, not leaders. Schools do need to comply with laws, establish consistent policies and procedures, and operate efficiently and on-budget. But schools also need, in the words of Lee Bolman and Terrence Deal, "purpose, passion, and imagination"—the products of a leader. "Particularly in times of crisis or rapid change," they say, "we look to leaders, not to managers, for hope, inspiration, and a pathway to somewhere more desirable." Here is how Scott Thomson defines the essential task of leadership in today's schools:

> As demands grow on schools for improved quality and broader services, a new leadership emerges. No longer managers of routines, school administrators need increasingly to take initiative. They must understand change as well as manage it. They must

> involve and motivate staff, create a positive culture, build a group vision, develop quality educational programs, provide a positive instructional environment, encourage high performance, apply evaluation processes, analyze and interpret outcomes, be accountable for results, and maximize human resources. They also must stimulate public support and engage community leaders. Finally, they must be certain that schools are persistent in getting students to understand the challenges they face, and what is required of them to compete on an equal footing in a global environment. In short, principals and superintendents must educate and lead.

Most school districts do not have the resources to hire for each school one person to manage, another to lead. So by necessity those who are trained to manage must also learn to lead, unless, of course, others in the school can be found to hold up the banner of leadership (more on this later).

Leadership Makes a Difference

Consider this statement by Kenneth E. Clark and Miriam B. Clark of the Center for Creative Leadership: "The exercise of leadership accomplishes goals more effectively than the usual management methods of trading rewards for performance." The power of leadership lies in its ability to inspire commitment, capture the imagination, earn trust.

The Clarks, summarizing propositions that have been derived from research on leadership in corporate, military, governmental, and educational settings, say "quality of leadership has been shown to have strong effects on (a) profitability of cost centers, (b) performance of work units, (c) quality of work output, (d) reduction of stress in the workplace, (e) worker satisfaction and morale, (f) reduced absenteeism, and (g) reduced accidents.... No wonder CEOs are paying attention to leadership issues."

The positive impact of principals' leadership gained validation in the 1970s when researchers found that instructionally effective schools were led by principals who set clear goals, participated in the instructional program, and made it clear to teachers and students that they were expected to excel.

One reviewer of the early studies done on effective schools, Ronald Edmonds, found leadership to be a key factor. In his summary of the "indispensable characteristics" of effective schools, Edmonds gave highest priority to "strong administrative leadership without which the disparate elements of good schooling can be neither brought together nor kept together."

"Principal leadership can make a difference in student learning," say Philip Hallinger and Ronald H. Heck, summarizing a decade and a half of empirical research. By influencing their schools' policies and norms, teachers' practices, and other school processes, principals indirectly affect student learning. Studies consistently point to one leadership behavior in particular that is tied to student achievement: "sustaining a schoolwide purpose focusing on student learning."

There Are No Substitutes for Leadership

Devolution of authority and responsibility remains a vibrant trend in the nation's school systems as well as in corporations and governments. We expect this trend to continue, as more schools establish site councils and more teachers, parents, and members of the community participate in school decision-making. As in past editions, several chapters of this book set forth recommended procedures for school-based management, shared decision-making, and teachers' coleadership of the instructional program.

None of these more inclusive governance processes, however, replaces the need for leadership. Granted, the leader's role might change, from a directive style to an enabling or facilitating style. But several essential tasks still must be performed by someone in a leadership position, presumably the principal. A leader or leaders must be able to create networks, build teams, resolve and creatively use conflicts, foster consensus on the school's vision, secure resources, and, especially important, focus attention on the goal: student learning.

But what about schools where teachers attain a high level of professionalism and form "self-renewing" learning communities? These teachers initiate their own improvement strategies, reflect upon their work, share their insights with one another, and collectively enforce high standards of performance. Such schools, it may be assumed, can operate on autopilot. They don't need a leader, only someone to manage the buses and bells. In our view, rather than having outgrown the need for leadership, strong professional communities require a commensurately higher caliber of leadership.

Self-renewing schools would appear to prosper with leaders who can "enhance the collective ability of a school to adapt, solve problems, and improve performance," which is the definition David T. Conley and Paul Goldman give for *facilitative leadership*. In addition to performing the tasks noted above, facilitative leaders possess the abilities to channel teachers' energy toward common goals and stimulate teachers' readiness for change.

Schools going through the process of restructuring seem to require this same kind of facilitative leadership. Paul V. Bredeson interviewed principals of twenty schools where teachers were taking on more responsibility in curriculum decisions, professional development programs, community outreach, and other school-improvement activities. Many of the principals experienced a transition in their roles from traditional manager-oriented leadership behaviors to group-centered leadership behaviors.

> These adjustments included increasing attention to group needs, relinquishing control and responsibility for task completion to others, becoming consultants and facilitators, providing a climate of support, modeling leadership behaviors, and entrusting group maintenance and process problems to members of the group. (Bredeson)

Worth noting is that this facilitative style fits precisely our definition of a *leader* as one who influences people to strive willingly for group goals. With shared governance and professional community, the group, not the individual, becomes the primary work unit. Group work places a premium on leadership; it is easier to manage the work of a collection of autonomous individuals than to lead a group.

Leadership Can Be Shared

Once it is understood that shared governance and professional community do not reduce the need for leadership but actually require a purer expression of it than a hierarchically run school does, the question becomes Who leads?

We find it hard to believe that a school could give birth to a vibrant professional community, self-initiating and self-renewing, without the active participation and encouragement of the principal. If teachers do take the initiative to form such a community, a principal who hasn't bought into the notion of faculty-as-change-agent is more likely than not to use his positional authority to sabotage the movement. The principal must actively support the process, either by taking a leadership role or by recruiting and supporting others who take that role.

The past decade's school-reform movement has given increased legitimacy to teacher leadership. Teachers engage in action research, perform staff development, serve as lead teachers, chair site councils, and so forth. Their craft knowledge is indispensable in the process of school renewal. When leadership is shared in this way, however, more might be involved than teachers' simply taking on leadership roles.

Marlene M. Johnson suggests that those who study and observe leadership have too readily assumed it is always the function of an individual. "The possibility of leadership as being a synergistic, interactive process created by numerous individuals within an ever-changing context has remained a 'blind spot'." Studies of facilitative leaders lend support to the idea that leadership can become an *organizational* function.

Facilitative leaders beget other facilitative leaders, say Conley and Goldman. Facilitative leadership by the principals they observed induced teacher leaders likewise to behave in a facilitative manner.

> Teachers who took advantage of new leadership opportunities tended to involve others rather than hoard personal power. There was less fear of being excluded from important decisions, or of needing to guard one's resources. The collegiality that occurred when many teachers interacted regularly and took leadership roles both reduced fears and presented many more forums for concerns to be raised. New leadership roles and structures were tools to solve problems, not merely maintain the status quo.

Facilitative leadership in these schools was contagious. Begun as an individual activity, it became collective practice and eventually characterized the manner in which the organization itself functioned. The synergy that occurs when leaders interact with and inspire other leaders is a topic meriting more attention than it has received.

Motive Matters

Our last assumption touches on a matter of the heart. It's important for school leaders to know *why* they want to lead. What do I hope to gain from holding this position, indeed, from *succeeding* in this position? Most individuals would readily answer, "To make a contribution to kids' learning." But honest reflection might yield other answers, too, some of which a leader might be reluctant to admit: to enjoy the prestige the principalship affords; to attain all the rewards that come from success, such as the approval of colleagues and possible advancement to a bigger school or the superintendency; and to earn more income than is available to a teacher.

Now, prestige, the esteem that accompanies success, and money (honestly earned) are not venal desires. But they are self-centered when compared to wanting simply that kids in your school *learn*.

Everyone performs a job for a mixture of selfish and altruistic reasons. In some careers, say driving a cement truck or playing cornerback on a professional football team, the motivation can be entirely selfish and probably not affect the quality of the job done. A leader, however, must set a higher standard by demonstrating a commitment to serve the organization and its members before self. Leadership theorists typically assume that leaders are motivated by their needs for varying amounts of affiliation, power, or achievement. We agree with Rabindra N. Kanungo and Manuel Mendonca, who argue that limiting the focus to these kinds of motivators ignores "the more profound motive of altruism, which is *the* critical ingredient of effective leadership."

The question is not whether leaders are motivated by the needs for affiliation, power, or achievement, but to what higher end? Does a leader seek warm relationships with followers out of a need for their approval, feeding on their affirmation of his importance, or is his goal to value them as partners in the enterprise so their ideas and skills can best be put to use in achieving the organization's mission? Does a leader seek power to aggrandize himself or does he regard it as an instrument to serve the needs of the institution and its members? In the quest for achievement, does a leader seek recognition and advancement primarily for herself, or does she find fulfillment in the group's accomplishment of its tasks?

These are fundamental questions that pierce to the core of a leader's character. How leaders—and more importantly, their followers—answer them ultimately governs the success or failure of their exercise of leadership. As Kanungo and Mendonca state, "Regardless of the need that operates as the motive, the leader's effectiveness will ultimately depend on whether the behavior manifested by that need is a reflection of and is guided by the overarching altruistic need." Altruism derives its power from the followers' perception that the leader is committed to their welfare. In reciprocal and paradoxical fashion, followers gladly bestow power on leaders who eschew it for themselves but use it to serve others.

Especially in education, where the product is knowledge, skills, and values instilled in young people, it matters a great deal whether the leader of a school or district seeks primarily to advance herself or to seek the highest good for those children in her care. Dale L. Brubaker collects the life stories of principals who attend his graduate education class at the University of North Carolina, Greensboro. Many of his students express dismay at the increasing politicization of their jobs, as Brubaker explains:

> In the minds of many principals, good ol' boy superintendents as politicians have been replaced by smoother but equally political "sharks" whose self-interest is still more important than student learning and teachers' welfare. Such superintendents, principals argue, set the stage for like-minded principals to behave in similar fashion. These are the principals who always have the media in their schools, have glitzy bulletin boards without substance, and insist on public relations events for parents that often distract students from the learning that should take place in classrooms.
>
> For such principals, test scores are more important than students receiving a solid education. These principals build a system of rewards for "the star teacher," thus passing down to the teachers self-serving norms of behavior.

The proposition that motive matters may be impossible to prove, because self-reports—the only way to establish motive—are of questionable validity. But if we assume a connection between a person's reason for doing something and the extent to which that "something" dominates the individual's thinking, we may be able to infer motive. Imagine, for example, two principals (Bob and Joan) who, during one day at their respective schools, each meets with a student who has been referred by a teacher for discipline.

During his meeting with the student, Bob reviews in his mind the steps spelled out in the school's discipline policy and remembers his promise at the last faculty meeting to enforce it more consistently than in the past. He must not be seen by the teachers, especially the two who complained at that meeting, as waffling in response to their referrals. Nor does he want to heed their suggestion that Bob invite the district's pupil-personnel coordinator to advise the school on its discipline procedures and thus risk the superintendent's finding out that his school has a problem. With these thoughts going through his mind, Bob informs the student that, this being his second referral this month, the school's discipline code requires a one-day suspension. He admonishes the student to improve his behavior and ushers him out the door.

Joan's school has also been struggling with enforcement of its discipline policy. As the student steps toward her desk for his third referral in six weeks, she recalls the school's mission and its motto, "Capture the potential in each child to excel." She searches for something positive about this student that she can say to encourage him and makes a mental note to follow up with him after his one-day suspension. She thinks he might benefit from a tutor and decides to assign one to him the day he returns to school. She plans to monitor his progress after two weeks.

Someone who was able to observe these two encounters between a principal and a misbehaving student might not notice any meaningful difference between them. Two principals and two students, meeting for an identical reason, follow a similar process that leads to the same result (suspension). The observer would have to get inside the heads of Bob and Joan to detect the difference in their thinking and motives and would still be left wondering whether even this difference mattered. Of course, it truly wouldn't matter unless Joan follows through with her intentions to find a tutor for her student and monitor his progress.

Is there any evidence that principals' thinking patterns influence their effectiveness as leaders? We find some support for this notion in the findings of a study reported by Samuel E. Krug. He and two colleagues examined the ways in which principals thought about—reflected on—their activities during five consecutive work days. Five times each day the principals responded to a pager that activated randomly. Each time the pager beeped, the principals recorded what they were doing, whether it was relevant to instructional leadership, and what they felt or thought about the activity. Then Krug and his associates, having used another instrument to evaluate each principal's instructional leadership, compared their thinking patterns with their performance as leaders.

"One of the most important conclusions of this study," Krug writes, "was that, while all the principals engaged in very similar kinds of activities, they did not all think about them in the same ways. Principals who are more effective perceive and use these activities as opportunities for exercising instructional leadership." Moreover, the principals' leadership scores showed a consistent relationship with student learning. "As leadership scores rose, student achievement scores rose; as leadership scores fell, student achievement scores fell."

The following statement by Krug, which inspired our stories of Joan and Bob, underscores the link between thought and action: "One principal saw a disciplinary meeting with a student as an opportunity to communicate the school's mission, monitor learning progress, and promote the instructional climate. A second principal saw the situation simply as an exercise in the management of discipline." What is it that explains why these principals thought as they did? Did they think and act differently because their motives differed, one burning with passion to see every child succeed, the other consumed with adult issues of school politics? Or, did they actually share the same passion to see their students excel, but one principal was simply quicker than the other to realize that any encounter with a student can serve an instructional purpose? We cannot definitively answer these kinds of questions from Krug and colleagues' data or, for that matter, from any research study. The answers will come only as these leaders search their own hearts to discern the pulse of their beliefs and commitments.

Leadership springs from an internal set of convictions, action following thought in the manner declared by this proverb: "As a man thinks in his heart, so is he." A principal whose thoughts center around bolstering his or her reputation will behave differently than a principal who passionately wants kids to learn and succeed. Outstanding school leaders start with a conviction about what schooling ought to be. This conviction gives birth to a vision, a mental image that guides these effective leaders in their daily routine activities and interactions with teachers, students, and communities.

We offer this book as food for the mind, nourishment for growth of the leader's conviction, passion, vision, and effectiveness.

How This Book Was Written

The purpose of this book is not to present new views or the authors' views of leadership. The authors of these chapters have attempted instead to summarize and explain a large body of literature with which educational leaders want and need to be familiar. Although readers are encouraged to refer to the original sources cited in the bibliographies, a perusal of them makes it apparent that no busy administrator or student has time to read all these books and articles. Nevertheless, the sources are important and contain many ideas useful to administrators. To make these important works easily accessible, we have tried to present the best ideas briefly and succinctly. This technique of distilling the most useful and important ideas is called "information analysis."

The authors of this book are more than mere "translators" of information and ideas, however. As well as analyzing information, they also attempt to synthesize information, to show how theories and ideas are connected, to resolve conflicting views.

Perhaps the most important kind of information synthesis in this book is the integration of theory and practice. Many books have been written on leadership theories and almost as many concern the "how to" of leadership practice. Practitioners complain that the theoretical writing is not useful in their everyday work, and researchers and theoreticians look askance at "practical" works whose ideas and suggestions are not empirically validated. Practitioners perceive that researchers and theoreticians are too isolated from the real problems of schools, that theories validated in laboratory settings may disintegrate in actual classrooms. Researchers and theoreticians argue that recommendations that are validated by only the experience of one administrator or one school are much too subjective to be useful to others.

Few books try to integrate these two conflicting views. This book tries to present the most useful aspects of theory along with the most thoughtful recommendations for action. A synthesis of the two, especially in areas where findings agree, can avoid many of the problems inherent in each single approach.

As well as presenting theories gleaned from educational literature and suggesting practices that might be derived from these theories, the book also contains ideas from practitioners within the field. These ideas are taken not only from written works, but, in many chapters, from interviews with administrators who are struggling with actual problems in schools.

Overview

This volume looks at leadership from four perspectives: the person, the values, the structure, and the skills. Chapters focusing on the person who holds a leadership position provide something of a theoretical background. These chapters answer the questions, Who is today's educational leader? What makes an effective leader different from a less effective leader? Which leadership styles and strategies seem to work best in which circumstances? How are school leaders trained, and what are the best methods for hiring them and inducting them into their positions?

The three chapters in part 2, new in this edition, deal with the foundation of ethics, vision, and values that give moral purpose and substance to the practice of school leadership. What are the leader's ethical responsibilities? Why is vision vital to the leader and how is it grasped? How can the leader help to create an effective work culture in his or her school?

The part of the volume focusing on the structure takes a look at the systems or support structures that underlie school leadership. It examines the balance of authority between the central office and the school site, the use of work teams in school improvement, and the context for making wise decisions. These chapters concern structures and management systems that can make good educational leadership possible—or impossible.

The chapters on leadership skills highlight the abilities needed by administrators to be effective leaders in education today. Foremost among those abilities is knowing how to lead the school's instructional program and manage the instructional staff. This part of the volume also looks at such knotty problems as how to communicate in today's more open, power-sharing organization, how to build coalitions of community groups for the support of schools, how to lead meetings more efficiently and effectively, and how to manage time, stress, and conflict.

This book is called a handbook because it is designed to be used as a reference when particular problems and concerns arise as well as to be read straight through. Those concerned about communication or decision-making or the advantages of different leadership strategies can turn directly to the appropriate chapters for the information they are seeking without reading the previous chapters. It is a book to be sampled, to be digested slowly, and to be turned to again and again as leaders grow in their leadership skills and effectiveness.

We hope that those charged with leading the nation's schools and those who aspire to this role will find the handbook useful as a source of encouragement and practical counsel.

PART 1

The Person

CHAPTER

1

Portrait of a Leader

Larry Lashway, JoAnn Mazzarella, Thomas Grundy

WANTED: Elementary principal for progressive suburban school district. Must have master's degree and relevant state certification, strong leadership qualities.

Ads like this appear thousands of times each year, symbols of every organization's search for leaders. What are these school districts looking for? How will they know when they've found it?

At a minimum, we can be sure they want someone who can carry out a long list of specific duties. The new principal will be expected to arrange class schedules, resolve discipline problems, administer a labor contract, evaluate teachers, and apply the oil of public relations to points of friction with the community. And that's just in the morning.

In short, school leaders must first of all be skillful managers—at worst, getting through the week without major disasters; at best, keeping the school humming with happy activity. Whatever else a district may want from its leaders, managerial skill is essential; without it, no school leader will last long.

But in asking for "strong leadership qualities," this district hints it may be looking for something beyond managerial competence. The search committee might have trouble defining this "something," but they undoubtedly hope to recognize it when they see it: a knack for inspiring trust, perhaps, or a talent for creating enthusiasm, or the ability to provide a sense of direction in a confusing world.

Most of us know people like that; if we're lucky, we work for them. But just what is it that we sense in them? Could we, on hearing a description of an utter stranger, recognize the qualities that make a leader? More to the point, could we work our way through a long list of applicants and be confident of making the right choice?

The Characteristics of Leaders

Scholars have been exploring this question for over a century, often with the assumption that leadership comes with the person, that certain individuals have some set of inherited or acquired traits that enable them to leave their mark on the world. Thomas Carlyle summed up an early version of this attitude with his claim "the history of the world is but the biography of great men."

For many years this belief led social scientists to concentrate almost solely on the personal traits of leaders. They studied the characteristics of corporate executives, football captains, or Girl Scout leaders and frequently came to different conclusions. Their research produced no shortage of candidates: intelligence, self-assurance, enthusiasm, good health, initiative, sociability—the list is almost endless. In fact, it became too large to be of any use.

Critics of the "trait" approach pointed to the unwieldy nature of the list and to the widely varied characteristics to substantiate their claim that there is no "essence" of leadership that will hold for all cases. As Warren Bennis remarked of the leaders he studied, other than demonstrating certain similar abilities, they were "tremendously diverse. They were tall, short, fat, thin . . . . They evinced no common pattern of psychological makeup or background."

Because of this disappointing result, researchers after World War II abandoned trait theories in favor of situational theories of leadership based on the belief there are no inherent leadership traits, just leader styles or behaviors that may change radically from one setting to another. "Situationists" believe that a person who is a leader in one situation may be a follower in another; traits useful in one situation may actually be disastrous in others. Hence, leaders are not born with any particular traits that determine leadership. Situationists have less interest in who a leader is than in what he or she does in a given situation.

A Role for Traits

It may be a bit premature, however, to throw out trait research. Edwin Locke and associates argue that while the situation plays an important role, "it now seems clear that certain traits and motives do indeed influence a leader's effectiveness." The difficulty is that certain traits are necessary, but not sufficient, for effective leadership; that is, they work in combination with other factors.

Thus, if a large number of trait studies yield modest generalizations, they may still point us in the right direction. One report that leadership is correlated with intelligence does not mean much; if twenty studies about twenty different types of leaders indicate a correlation, the findings are more convincing.

It also makes sense to use findings about a particular leader to make generalizations about this kind of leader alone. Each kind of leader has a number of unique characteristics. Studies about Girl Scout leaders are quite valuable to Girl Scout leaders—and those of school leaders most valuable to school leaders. Personal traits are part of any leader's resources—a kind of "human capital" on which he or she can draw. Focusing on these traits can simply make us aware of how a particular leader gets results.

And even if we fail to find any universal generalizations, knowledge of leader characteristics is useful. Just as our actions tell others much about "who we are" and "where we come from," so do our definitions. Daniel Duke puts it this way: "By identifying the properties associated with leadership, an understanding may be gained of prevailing structures of social meaning. How people make sense of leadership can tell us a great deal about how they regard themselves, their society, and the future."

This chapter explores the most significant findings of previous trait research as well as more recent research on educational leaders to paint a portrait of an effective leader.

Limiting Assumptions

As we sort through these findings, we should keep in mind some of the inherent limitations of this kind of research. "Leadership" is a broad abstraction, incorporating everything from Harry Truman's decision to drop the atomic bomb to a quiet parent's volunteering to be a room mother. Researchers can't measure it precisely without making a number of assumptions.

1. Many studies define a leader as anyone occupying a position with formal authority over others. If there is a difference between leadership and managerial competence, these studies may not capture it.

2. Many studies define leadership as whatever leaders do, without distinguishing between effective and ineffective actions.

3. Some studies define leadership by performance on short-term tasks in a laboratory setting (often using college students as subjects). But real-world leaders operate in real-world institutions, over long periods.

4. Some studies define leadership through peer ratings; that is, a leader is someone who is perceived to be a leader. While there is good reason to respect human judgment, there may be important differences between perceived leadership ability and objective leadership skills. (For example, a number of studies have shown that taller men are more likely to be

perceived as leaders. There is no reason to think this trait has anything to do with actual leadership skill.)

5. Finally, many generalizations are based on a leadership cadre that has never fully reflected society at large: No matter how the leadership portrait is drawn, it seems to include pale skin and a Y chromosome. Many studies may accurately describe the way these leaders behave but overlook the behavior of women and minority leaders simply because it is different. In other words, leadership as we have known it does not exhaust the possibilities of leadership as it might be.

It is also important to remember that none of this research reveals any single characteristic that *determines* leadership. Rather it suggests there are groups or constellations of qualities that appear to correlate with leadership. Not all leaders have these traits, and not even effective leaders have all of them. Many nonleaders have many of these characteristics, and still more have at least a few. Yet having many of these traits does appear to give one a better chance at leadership effectiveness.

Finally, it is important to remember the leader does not exist in a vacuum, but in an environment made up of people (subordinates and supervisors), who are acted upon by historical, philosophical, religious, cultural, social influences/assumptions/biases, and who in turn bring these influences and pressures to bear when they interact with the "leaders." Leadership is not simply the impersonal delegation of duties and responsibilities from machine to machine, and no matter how scientific our studies appear to be or how objective we try to be in our dealings with others, it remains a human activity, subject to all the complexities of human interaction.

What follows, then, is at best a picture, a still life, a portrait in time of what we now assume to be the qualities that make up a leader in our culture. Readers may want to accompany this chapter with an imaginary checklist to see how they compare with this portrait of an effective leader.

Energy and Involvement

Edmund Morris tells how the young Theodore Roosevelt approached his daily work as police commisioner of New York City. He would come striding briskly down the street, "goggling his spectacles enthusiastically at everything around, about, and behind him." Arriving at headquarters, he'd fly up the stairs, rush to his office, and, in one motion, sit down, take off his hat, and attack the nearest pile of documents, swiftly making decisions on major policies and minor details. After a day's worth of that, he'd prowl the streets at night, appearing like an apparition before malingering officers and sending them scurrying back to their posts.

Roosevelt was probably in a class by himself, but leadership has often been associated with high levels of energy and involvement. This energy may be physiological (the result of good health or lucky genes) or it may come from a desire to be at the center of things. This latter trait is sometimes called "dominance"; according to researchers like Harrison Gough, it correlates significantly with leadership.

Arthur Blumberg and William Greenfield describe effective principals this way:

> They appear to have a high need to control a situation and a low need to be controlled by others. They rather like being in charge of things, proposing ideas, and initiating action. They strongly dislike it, and tend to reject it, when constraints are put on their prerogatives or when their freedom of action and initiative are restricted in any way. They prefer to find their own solutions to ambiguous situations than to be told how to do it by others, particularly their organizational superiors.

Shirley M. Hord and Gene E. Hall likewise found that in facilitating instructional improvement, the most effective principals are those who are most actively involved. Labeling three styles in order of increasing effectiveness—responder, manager, initiator—they found that the principal who was most actively involved with teachers was the most effective.

One result is high visibility; involved principals walk the hallways and poke their noses in classrooms rather than sequestering themselves in their office. Blumberg provides a memorable example of one principal's five-minute trip to get a sandwich, during which she flushed smokers out of the washroom, asked a teacher how things were going in a particular program, chatted with a cafeteria worker, checked with a teacher about a discipline case, complimented a student on some work he had done, picked up pieces of paper from the floor, and hustled some lingering students off to class. The value of episodes like that is not just in their immediate practical results, but in the aura of leadership they create.

Competence

Having an aura of leadership is an obvious asset, but it quickly fades if the leader fails to deliver. People like their leaders to have energy, but they demand competence. Researchers have explored a number of types of competence; three are summarized here: intelligence, technical skill, and interpersonal skill.

Intelligence

Intelligence is such a fundamental human trait that researchers have often looked for a connection with leadership—and have usually found it. Bernard Bass, reviewing recent work in this area, reports a fairly high correlation (.5) between intelligence and the likelihood of being perceived as a leader. He also cites a number of earlier studies that found positive (but somewhat lower) correlations between intelligence and leadership.

These studies don't show *how* intelligence facilitates leadership, but we can make some reasonable guesses. Since most IQ tests contain a substantial verbal component, high scorers may have a mastery of the language that allows them to articulate ideas in a persuasive way, aiding in the essential task of communication.

Additionally, leadership of complex, dynamic organizations requires considerable abstract-thinking ability. Eliot Jaques, in his extensive studies of executive leadership, says the key variable is "cognitive complexity," the ability to handle many variables at different degrees of abstraction. At the highest level, for example, a leader can deal with multiple streams of information at a high level of abstraction. The higher the level of thinking, the more a leader can step back from the immediate situation and see long-term, large-scale patterns and trends.

Although the importance of intelligence is undeniable, its role needs to be qualified in several important ways. First, we may want to reserve judgment on how well the general findings on intelligence and leadership apply to schools—an issue that has not been much studied. Because school leaders have proved themselves capable of earning a master's degree, most of them are likely to have above-average intelligence. As a matter of simple statistics, correlations are likely to be lower when a trait has a narrow range. (It's a bit like examining the relationship between height and basketball success. If we study the whole population, height will obviously have a lot to do with it; if we study only NBA players, height will be less important in distinguishing superstars from everyday players.)

Second, the literature suggests there may be a point of diminishing returns. Bass notes a number of studies that suggest leaders who are far more intelligent than their followers are less likely to be successful. The reasons aren't clear, though one guess is that highly intelligent leaders use higher level concepts and vocabulary that may place a barrier between them and their followers.

Third, some researchers have challenged the validity of traditional intelligence tests for complex real-world environments. Richard Wagner and Robert Sternberg, for example, have suggested "street smarts" may be far more important in handling real problems. They note that unlike the problems encountered on tests, real dilemmas are typically ill-defined, don't come with all the information needed to solve them, and may not have one best answer.

Such problems are solved through the application of tacit knowledge—practical know-how that is usually learned informally on the job. Tacit knowledge includes such things as how to manage oneself (for example, avoiding procrastination); how to manage others (such as motivating); and how to manage tasks (such as communicating ideas clearly). While much of this knowledge is learned through experience, Wagner and Sternberg emphasize that some leaders are simply better than others in acquiring it. Their early studies (using simulated problems) have found that tacit knowledge is a better predictor of performance than intelligence.

Technical Knowledge and Skill

Every job requires mastery of certain ideas and processes. Research in a variety of fields indicates that those who master these core technical skills are more likely to be seen as leaders, and that subordinates readily accept "expert power" (Bass).

In education, this common-sense notion is embodied in certification requirements that require school leaders to have teaching experience. This experience provides the foundation for the role of "supervision," a term that implies principals will be closely monitoring teachers.

But expertise is a double-edged sword. On the one hand, principals need to demonstrate it to gain the respect of their staff, since teachers sometimes nurse a suspicion that administrators have lost touch with classroom realities. Some principals deliberately make periodic guest appearances in classrooms just to prove they haven't lost it.

On the other hand, teachers have traditionally operated in an isolated, semi-autonomous way, tailoring their approach to the particular students in their class. Detailed directives from above are seldom appreciated. The result, according to Blumberg, is a "territorial imperative" that makes principals reluctant to deal with curriculum and instruction in a top-down manner.

With the recent emphasis on teacher empowerment and facilitative leadership, this dilemma has sharpened. Nona Prestine, studying schools engaged in restructuring, found some principals frustrated at having their substantive ideas on curriculum ignored by a newly empowered faculty. Thus, it appears that while knowledge of teaching and learning are valuable assets for principals, this expertise has to be employed with tact and discretion.

Interpersonal Competence

School leadership is people-intensive; principals rarely go more than a few minutes without interacting with someone. Being friendly and outgoing isn't enough; getting along with others requires specific skills.

Communication

Most of the literature on school leadership agrees on the importance of communication. Richard Gorton and Kenneth McIntyre, in their study of the principalship, found that "significant others" (those knowledgeable about the principal's performance) see effective principals as strong in oral communication. Blumberg and Greenfield found "extremely well-developed expressive abilities" among the key characteristics of the eight outstanding principals they studied. "All of these principals had very well-developed interpersonal skills and were able to communicate effectively in face-to-face interaction with a diverse range of individuals and groups." Speaking and listening are also among the essential skills identified by experienced superintendents interviewed by Robert Crowson and Van Cleve Morris.

What accounts for successful communication? Howard Gardner, after examining the lives of great leaders, concluded the prime ingredient is the ability to tell a story that resonates with the deepest ideals and aspirations of followers. For example, Martin Luther King, Jr., told a story of ordinary people vanquishing oppression through steadfast, courageous actions. Leaders who tell such stories—and embody them in their lives—forge a deep bond with their followers.

William Foster offers another perspective by arguing that a chief function of the leader is to clear away the distortions that enter language through some people's desire to maintain domination and power. For example, student failure may be casually explained by "unmotivated students" or "poor home environment," thus blaming the student rather than examining the school's failure to meet that student's needs.

Some labels are accurate, but others are not: leadership is telling the difference. Leadership involves the penetration of labels and communicative structures, of taking freely constituted democratic participation seriously, of assisting the growth of individuals caught in the cycle of domination through language. Foster, then, would have us reexamine what we mean by communication and leadership.

More prosaically, successful communication depends on finding the appropriate words, words that will convey the essential meaning and provide just the right tone. More than one promising leadership initiative has been smothered beneath a sea of verbal sludge; jargon, clichés, and dry statistics rarely inspire enthusiasm.

What does work? Bass found evidence that employees tend to remember brief messages that neatly summarize organizational values (for example, "If you're not helping, you're hindering"). Coleen Armstrong urges principals to communicate through stories that highlight the work and achievements of teachers, students, and parents. "People stories make dry concepts vivid and personal. They convey your affection for students, your respect and admiration for teachers, and even your passion for learning itself."

But communication is more than a matter of finding the right words—the message has to be delivered in a timely and appropriate way. Peter Wright and David Taylor argue that effective communication requires leaders to understand the situation (What are the issues?), be able to read people, and tailor the message accordingly. They identify a number of basic communication patterns, such as "tell," "tell and sell," and "problem-solving." Knowing which of these is appropriate is a key skill.

In addition, Bass notes a number of other factors that may be critical: timing, style (formal vs. informal), linguistic form (directive vs. request), nonverbal language, concern for individual differences, and the amount of time spent on communication.

Listening

Most researchers comment on the good listening skills of effective principals. Gorton and McIntyre found that effective principals listen to students, community, and staff. Blumberg says, "Every time I asked an administrator what was most important for him or her to be able to do well, the response was, 'Listening'."

Good listening goes beyond hearing the words. Rather, it demands complete attentiveness to the other person. A high school principal interviewed by Blumberg explained his approach this way:

> So a stranger, a parent, comes into your office. There are lots of things I pay attention to, 'cause I have to make a judgment about what to do. First, I try to remember if I've seen them in other places, in other settings. I watch how they approach me. I listen to the kinds of things they say, the adjectives they use, their tone of voice. I try to get a sense of whether or not they seem inclined to be even-handed or whether they seem to be exaggerating. And all those things put together helps me understand the kinds of things I may be able to do in the situation. Whether, for example, we can

hold a dialogue with each other or I just have to use my authority to shut them off.

This kind of attentive listening has two advantages. First, it communicates care and consideration, qualities usually associated with employee satisfaction, according to Bass. The principal's "personal touch," said one teacher in a restructuring school, "helps build my sense of empowerment because it establishes a foundation for mutual respect. It helps make you feel comfortable about discussing classroom problems because you feel that she values your feelings and opinions" (Joseph Blase and Jo Roberts Blase).

Second, careful listening may keep the administrator from making snap decisions based on false assumptions. Principal B. J. Meadows found that it allowed her to find common ground with parents who complained about misbehavior at bus stops. "In the past, I had sometimes proposed a solution before I understood a problem completely. I then became invested in my way of solving the problem and unconsciously set up a power struggle."

Personality

Some people assume leadership is an offshoot of "personality," a rather ill-defined term that usually refers to the distinctive ways people handle tasks, interact with others, and structure their lives. The problem for researchers is the overwhelming number of traits that can be considered a part of personality: enthusiasm, aggressiveness, sociability, self-confidence, emotional balance, sense of humor, emotional expressiveness, empathy, flexibility, and many, many others. (Jaques claims to have identified 2,500 adjectives describing different dimensions of personality.)

Although researchers have found correlations between leadership and many of these dimensions, they have never found anything that could be called a "leadership personality." Leaders come in all flavors, an insight that has been partly responsible for the enthusiasm about "styles." However, certain traits are worth a closer look.

Sociability

In their national study of the principalship, Gorton and McIntyre found that effective principals have as their strongest asset "an ability to work with different kinds of people having various needs, interests, and expectations." The researchers added:

> They seem to understand people, know how to motivate them, and how to deal effectively with their problems. It is primarily this factor, rather than a technical expertise, that caused the "significant others" to perceive these principals as accessible and effective administrators.

The same seems to be true for successful superintendents. Even sitting in the central office, seemingly far removed from students, teachers, and parents, they appear to profit from good social skills and abilities. Robert Wilson, in a study of successful Ohio superintendents, found that the successful superintendent "is a very personable and friendly individual who believes in the importance of human relations skills and demonstrates them daily."

These outstanding Ohio superintendents also participate widely in the community—in church, PTA, civic, social, and hobby clubs—because they depend heavily on face-to-face contact for building rapport with citizens. One of the superintendents interviewed by Crowson and Morris had this to say about the job: "But the really critical thing is dealing with people. If you do this well, you can learn all the rest."

This kind of interest in people also surfaces in studies of other types of leaders. Bass cites research showing strong correlations between leadership and extroversion—and a negative correlation with shyness. While this is unsurprising, we should be careful about equating "sociability" with gregarious, back-slapping camaraderie. Mary McCaulley, reporting on a number of investigations using the Myers-Briggs Type Indicator, found sizeable numbers of introverts among leaders in a variety of fields. She concluded that "it is wise for leadership research to allow for successful leaders with both the extraverted and introverted orientations." Apparently, one may like and be able to work with people without necessarily wanting to party with them.

In fact, it may be better to think of sociability as the recognition that people are at the heart of things, and the desire to work effectively with them. According to one high school principal interviewed by Blumberg:

> I want to know whom I'm working with, what touches them, what motivates them, why they are in education. I want to know what's going on in their lives because so often things that are affecting their lives outside of school affect their performance in school. I spend a great deal of time trying to figure out my subjects as if they were models on a tapestry. Like each one is a small part of that tapestry, but yet everyone of them has to fit together for the total tapestry to be complete.

Psychological Health

Psychological studies of great leaders often show them to be driven by forces that border on the pathological. For example, biographers have suggested that Lyndon Johnson's extraordinary will to dominate others was the result of deep-rooted insecurity, and that Woodrow Wilson's career was a lifelong attempt to escape his father's shadow. Collectively, accounts like this may create the impression that pathology is a leadership asset.

But Bass argues that psychoanalysis tends to focus excessively on personal flaws and neuroses, and that leaders, while subject to the normal human frailties, also have many healthy and creative impulses. He cites the views of Erik Erikson and Abraham Maslow that leadership results from a drive to be happy and healthy.

One problem (for researchers as well as leaders) is that with some traits, more is not always better. Robert Kaplan, for instance, has found that executives' "expansiveness" (highly focused energy and drive) is a valuable leadership trait, but only up to a point. Excessive levels of expansiveness turn the leader into a rigid, domineering tyrant with little sensitivity to others' feelings. Recognizing the dividing line can be difficult, says Kaplan. "Some excess is virtually unavoidable. It is too much to expect high-powered individuals to be finely calibrated at all times." Yet he notes that some executives consistently go over the line while others are able to "throttle back" and keep their drive in balance.

The importance of balance is echoed by Gough, whose work with The California Psychological Inventory has led him to develop a scale for measuring "integration." According to Gough, those who have integrated their traits into a balanced whole are more likely to be seen as leaders—no matter what their basic predilections.

Closer to home is the testimony of a number of Blumberg's principals. Like Kaplan's expansive executives, they had great energy and a strong determination to get things done. Yet they repeatedly mentioned the importance of not pushing too far, too fast. They talked of "planting seeds" and "dangling bait," and freely told stories of how overeagerness had gotten them into trouble. For these leaders, patience was not a natural condition, but they had learned its value from experience, and their psychological balance allowed them to make the adjustment.

Charisma

Sometimes the leader's personality is so striking it earns the name "charisma." Originally the term was coined to describe leaders whose authority was based on personal characteristics rather than official position. In recent decades, it has come to mean something akin to a magnetic personality.

Bass finds that leaders described as charismatic do have some common personal traits. They are emotionally expressive, self-confident, free from inner conflict, independent, insightful, eloquent, and energetic. They present a clear vision for the future and the conviction that it can be fulfilled.

However, he also notes that personality alone does not explain charismatic leadership; followers must be receptive to forming a strong identification with the leader. This identification may occur for psychological reasons (for example, low self-esteem) or for social reasons (a national state of crisis). To cite a classic example, Adolf Hitler had the necessary personal traits, but he also needed a crisis in German society (economic trauma and political instability) to become fully charismatic.

A leader who has charismatic traits but whose followers are not receptive to that kind of relationship may become what Bass calls an "inspirational" leader. Inspirational leaders create excitement and enthusiasm about social or organizational goals, but their followers invest loyalty in the ideas, remaining free to criticize the leaders.

While some scholars are leery of using the word *charisma* (fearing it has been overused and distorted), the concept plays an important role in the recent interest in transformational leadership (see chapter 2).

Character

Before social scientists talked about "traits," most people judged leaders by their "character," a word that implies humans are not just bundles of skills but embody a particular outlook on life, a certain integrity of belief and action. Some research studies have suggested that effective school leaders have particular character qualities that make them different from less effective leaders.

Beliefs

We've seen that the research linking intelligence with leadership indicates success depends on how—and how well—leaders think. But what leaders think may be equally important.

Samuel Krug, in arguing for a "constructivist" perspective on leadership, points out that surface behaviors may disguise deep differences in outlook that lead administrators to respond to the same event in very different ways. He gives an example of two principals required to personally supervise the cafeteria. One principal saw the duty as a time drain that interfered with "important" tasks; the other saw it as an opportunity for publicly recognizing student achievements, thereby reinforcing the school's academic mission and building school-parent relationships. In each case, the duty was the same, but one principal's beliefs turned it into something much more meaningful.

Are there particular beliefs that lead to success? The early effective-schools literature identified one: The best schools had principals who sincerely believed students could and would succeed. More recently, researchers interested in restructuring have suggested that school change requires leaders with a specific set of beliefs. Sylvia Mendez-Morse says effective change agents share a number of common beliefs and values. They have a distinctive vision, a mental image of what the school is capable of becoming. They believe the contributions of staff members are vital. They believe schools are for learning and students come first.

Leaders also have certain beliefs about themselves. Bass notes successful leaders have a high degree of "self-efficacy"—they believe they can make a difference and they have confidence in their actions. Not surprisingly, most studies show leaders to have high self-esteem (though there may be some cases in which leadership is an attempt to overcome low self-esteem).

Security

A related finding by Blumberg and Greenfield is that effective educational leaders are secure; that is, they are not threatened by new ideas or confrontations with others. "Their sense of themselves as people and what it is they are about seems rather highly developed." The authors believe this feeling of security and sureness about themselves fosters a high tolerance for ambiguity. They can survive in a confusing situation where rules are ill-defined, and they can live with uncertainty.

Similarly, Edward Wynne and R. Bruce McPherson argue that one of the categories or traits of an effective principal is "courage," by which they mean not so much physical daring (though that may not be irrelevant), but rather the willingness to consciously expose oneself to circumstances that may generate serious harmful consequences—economic, emotional, or physical. The research suggests that the leaders who follow rules to the letter, who never make waves, and who never challenge authority are probably less effective than leaders who stretch the rules a little or fight to accomplish goals important to them.

None of this means that leaders are free of self-doubts and anxiety. James Autry, a successful consultant and publishing executive, tells of a lunch conversation with a fellow executive:

> At this lunch, he stopped eating abruptly, put down his knife and fork and asked, "Do you ever get the feeling that one day they are going to come into your office and say, 'Okay, Autry, we found out about you'?" "Yes, yes," I said, almost shouting, "I frequently get that feeling. You, too?" He nodded, and we both began to laugh.

Autry concludes that even the highest leaders are never as self-assured as they seem, because they are always contending with the expectations of others. He suggests that effective leaders define success by their own standards of importance, realizing that "if you can achieve satisfaction and fulfillment in the very effort of trying, rather than in the accomplishment of *everything* you set out to do, you will have achieved 99 percent of the value of what success really means."

Goals

The beliefs of effective leaders are not limited to the here-and-now. Blumberg and Greenfield found that excellent principals seem to be "highly goal-oriented and to have a keen sense of goal clarity." These effective principals "were continually alert for opportunities to make things happen, and if the opportunities didn't present themselves, they created them."

Kenneth Tye, studying a curriculum innovation at eleven schools, found that principals had three ways of dealing with goals. "Focused" principals had a few strong goals that were clearly articulated to staff and community. "Diffuse" principals were quick to adopt goals but ended up with overlapping and conflicting initiatives. "Coping" principals responded to whatever goals were thrust upon them but showed more interest in keeping things running smoothly. Tye discovered that the curriculum change was most successful in schools led by focused principals.

In recent years, goal-orientation has evolved into "vision," a word that emphasizes the imaginative thinking required in a turbulent age. It has become virtually axiomatic that principals and superintendents interested in restructuring must generate and share a dynamic vision of the new direction.

Indeed, virtually every current study of leadership makes this point. And when you think about it, it makes perfect sense. To lead means to take somebody someplace. If you don't know where you're going, you can't really be leading someone "there"—and you won't know when you've arrived. Hence, the ability to visualize goals is a prerequisite for leadership. "Leadership," says Sylvia Mendez-Morse, "requires vision. It is a force that provides meaning and purpose to the work of an organization. Leaders of change are visionary leaders, and vision is the basis of their work."

Moral Strength

What do people value most in their leaders? Is it competence? Warmth? Flexibility? No, the word that shows up most often is "honesty" (James Kouzes and Barry Posner; Michael Richardson and others).

For a long time, twentieth-century images of high-powered leadership didn't leave much room for this traditional virtue. It was either taken for granted or ignored by social-science researchers who preferred to deal with more objective and measurable traits. But the 1990s have seen a surge of interest in values and morality. Words like "covenant," "stewardship," and even "spiritual" have been popping up regularly in discussions of leadership.

Empirical research in this area is still limited, but a growing school of thought says the leader's job is inherently moral: it is not just a matter of doing things right, but of doing the right things. Thomas Sergiovanni argues that this responsibility extends beyond personal ethics, and that the principal must be dedicated to creating a "moral community" and "virtuous school." Leaders who see themselves as stewards will be able to create school communities that are both collegial and responsive to the needs of community members.

The Genesis of Leadership

If leaders do have traits and characteristics that separate them from followers, these traits must be acquired somewhere. Some, like intelligence, come from a poorly understood combination of genetic endowment and early nurturing. Others, like cooperativeness and ease in groups, are believed to spring chiefly from parental influences. Many specific leadership skills are obviously learned through experience.

Heredity

One of the oldest debates in psychology is how much human behavior can be attributed to heredity. After decades of trying to untangle the threads of nature and nurture, the issue is still unresolved—and probably unresolvable.

In general, most modern researchers stress nurture over nature. For example, in their study of effective leaders, Warren Bennis and Burt Nanus say it is a myth that "leaders are born, not made":

> Biographies of great leaders sometimes read as if they had entered the world with an extraordinary genetic endowment, that somehow their future leadership role was preordained. Don't believe it. The truth is that major capacities and competencies of leadership can be learned, and we are all educable, at least if the basic desire to learn is there and we do not suffer from serious learning disorders. Furthermore, whatever natural endowments we bring to the role of leadership, they can be enhanced; nurture is far more important than nature in determining who becomes a successful leader.

It may well be people are born with certain genetic predispositions to behave in one way or another, but these tendencies are modified and shaped by experience.

Birth Order

Any child with siblings can tell you about the trials and tribulations of being the first-born or last-born or in-betweener. In recent years, popular psychology has made much of the "birth-order factor," but its relation to leadership is ambiguous. Some studies show the oldest child to be more socially maladjusted, more conservative, less aggressive, less self-confident, more introverted, and less inclined toward leadership than other children, perhaps because parents of firstborns are inexperienced and less secure in their marriage and finances, or because older children must adjust to decreased attention when siblings arrive (Bass).

At the same time, in some families (especially in stable, one-parent households or two-parent households where both work) the firstborn may be encouraged to take on leadership roles and thus may well acquire more leadership abilities than the younger siblings. Moreover, in extended families, where other adults are present to provide support for the new parents, the oldest child may not suffer from the lack of security and parental inexperience that hampers the parents of "nuclear" families.

Bass concludes: "In all, taken by itself, it would seem that birth order may or may not make a difference, depending on other aspects of family life."

Family and Community

Whenever people are asked to name the greatest influences on their lives, parents are at the top of the list. So it seems reasonable to ask how childrearing might affect the development of leadership.

Bass reviewed a number of studies that linked childrearing practices to traits believed to be valuable in leadership. In one study, children allowed to participate in family decision-making were more resourceful, self-reliant, cooperative, and at ease in groups. Another concluded "sociability and cooperativeness were greater when parents were clear and consistent, explained decisions to their children, offered opportunities for decision-making, had rapport with their children, and better understood their children's problems."

Studies of successful leaders also show that their parents instilled high standards, especially a strong work ethic, and provided opportunities to act independently. Leaders often report having at least one strong parent who provided a positive role model.

Going beyond the immediate family and into the community, Wynne and McPherson point to "an important preliminary hypothesis" that has emerged from their research: "Good principals may tend to come from family and community environments which socialize them to the skills and values associated with fostering community and comfortably exercising strong authority." Similarly, Crowson and Morris note that the suburban superintendents they interviewed seemed especially attuned to community values; they suggest this quality may be related to the rural and small-town roots of most of their subjects.

Socioeconomic Variables

Many studies over the years have found that leadership positions tend to be filled by those from higher socioeconomic groups. In spite of the myth that great presidents are born in log cabins, Bass says few have come from lower socioeconomic groups. He also mentions a study that found that town leaders tend to be children of town leaders and that 70 percent of the fathers of businessmen are businessmen.

As it happens, determining parental socioeconomic status is notoriously difficult because the different elements of status (occupation, income, education, and prestige) are not perfectly correlated. We need to be especially cautious about drawing conclusions about school leaders. Dan Lortie, in his landmark study of teachers, observed that teaching (the starting point for most administrators) has long had a reputation as a convenient path for the upwardly mobile. Using figures from the 1960s, he estimated almost a third of the teaching force had parents who were blue-collar workers. Emily Feistritzer, examining data from the mid-1980s, found that 20 percent of teachers' fathers had unskilled or semiskilled occupations, while another 15 percent were farmers.

On the other hand, those who go on to become administrators may differ from those who remain in the classroom. John Hemphill and colleagues, in comparing 232 elementary school principals to the population as a whole, found that disproportionately more were children of business or professional men and appreciably fewer were from laboring or farming families.

Hemphill's study applies to a previous generation, so we should be cautious in drawing conclusions about today's administrators. In any case, it's important to remember socioeconomic status is only associated with reaching a leadership position—not necessarily with distinguished performance. Class and wealth can smooth the way to the top but are less helpful in solving the problems that come with that territory.

Education and Training

If you ask superintendents and principals where they learned to do their job, the universal answer is "on the job." Blumberg agrees. His conversations with principals have convinced him school administration is a craft, learned inductively in hundreds of little episodes. School leaders don't operate from scientific principles or rigid rules, but from informal "rules of thumb" that have been tested in the fires of real life.

This is not to suggest it is easy to learn to be a leader. There is no simple formula, no rigorous science, no cookbook that leads inexorably to successful leadership. Instead it is a deeply human process, full of trial and error, victories and defeats, timing and happenstance, intuition and insight. Learning to lead is somewhat like learning to be a parent or a lover: your childhood and adolescence provide you with basic values and role models, books can deepen your understanding, but you can become proficient only by doing it.

Of course, not everybody survives this plunge into the deep end of the pool. Those who do, says Blumberg, are the ones who learn from mistakes, develop and trust their "sixth sense," and encounter both positive and negative role models.

And what of formal preparation programs? Blumberg suggests they play a modest (but useful) role by providing future administrators with a perspective—a way of thinking about their craft. Unlike dentists, who learn and hone their core skills in courses, school leaders get a more philosophical orientation. While some are frustrated by the lack of explicit skill training, Blumberg believes learning *what* to do may be more important at the initial stage than learning how to do it.

What We Don't Know About Leadership

We've learned a lot about leadership in the twentieth century. Compared to the simplistic beliefs of earlier times, current views seem diverse and sophisticated.

But simple fairness compels that we also ask what *isn't* known about the traits of leaders. Are there major gaps in our understanding? The answer seems to be "yes."

No Magic Bullet

The most obvious disappointment with the research is the lack of simple answers. Kenneth and Miriam Clark, summing up extensive research, say, "Our studies have found no single comprehensive list of leadership qualities. Every investigator who studies dimensions of leader and manager behavior comes up with a slightly different, or substantially different, list." They add, "Our studies have found no best measure to differentiate leaders from managers, or leaders from followers, or to identify those who will some day be leaders."

So there is no leadership gene, no ideal incubator for nurturing the kind of leaders we need and want. Who gets to be a leader, remains a leader, and thrives as a leader results from a complex process that eludes easy description.

New Faces, New Approaches

We noted earlier that current descriptions of leadership are built on a largely white, male population. Will the infusion of women and minorities into leadership positions force us to rethink our conceptions of leadership?

The answer thus far is "possibly." Charol Shakeshaft, reviewing a large number of studies, found evidence that female administrators interact more often with teachers and students, communicate in a more personal style, and use a more participatory approach to decision-making. Catherine Marshall reports that "atypical" administrators (mostly minority and/or female) use persuasion rather than top-down directives, are strongly sensitive to the needs of children and teachers, and willingly take risks when human needs collide with bureaucratic demands.

Other studies suggest gender differences do not apply to all administrative tasks. For example, Lee Bolman and Terry Deal reported relatively little difference between male and female administrators in the ways they conceptualized leadership dilemmas.

Because women and minorities come to leadership with a different set of experiences, there is reason to think these experiences may give them a unique perspective on the leadership role—a valuable asset at a time when the whole educational enterprise is being rethought. However, the enthusiasm for new models should be tempered by the need for more research; the ultimate irony would be creating new stereotypes just after getting rid of the old ones.

The Person Behind the Mask

Traditional social-science research gives us a fairly detailed picture of the leader as leader, operating professionally and authoritatively to get the job done. In recent years, a growing number of less formal studies have allowed us to hear the unfiltered voices of principals and superintendents. These voices remind us that every leader remains a human being, bringing to the job an individual history and a full range of passions, frailties, and idiosyncracies.

We don't know nearly as much as we should about how personhood affects leadership. For example, does parenthood affect leadership? Psychologist Abraham Maslow once said that a few months of watching his infant son convinced him behaviorism could never explain human behavior—thereby changing his philosophy, and the course of American psychology. Do school leaders rethink their craft for similar reasons?

More generally, we know little about how a person's life journey affects leadership. Charles Palus, William Nasby, and Randolph Easton contend every life is a story that seeks to reconcile "who I was, who I am, and who I might become." Working out that story—finding love, making one's place in the world, coming to terms with parental ghosts—is bound to affect the way people lead, but how?

The answers to these questions may lie more in biography than in correlational studies, but without them our portrait of the leader will always seem just a little bit hollow.

Implications for Administrator Selection

We return now to the advertisement that began this chapter. What can we say to the school in search of leadership? As members of the search committee wade through the stacks of applications and grill the sweaty-palmed applicants, what clues should they be looking for? Can we offer them a formula for success?

The short answer is "no." As we've seen, there is no sure-fire litmus test. The longer answer is more complex, but more hopeful. The portrait we have drawn does suggest some starting points for search committees.

1. *Good leaders are good thinkers, whether this is expressed as intelligence, technical knowledge, or basic beliefs.* Interviewers will want to engage applicants in a vigorous exchange of ideas on a variety of issues. The best candidates will not only *have* many ideas, they will be able to articulate them clearly.

2. *Good leaders are people-oriented.* Measuring such skills is tricky, though a number of instruments can provide a rough-and-ready estimate. The personal interview can be especially helpful in gauging how well job candidates or current administrators communicate and listen, especially if the questions are posed by a variety of people and stakeholders.

3. *Character is a crucial element in leadership.* Selectors must ask themselves some basic questions about the person before them. Is this someone who can be relied on? Someone who can stand up to the buffeting that every leader must take? Someone who is the kind of human being they'd be proud to know?

4. *Since so much of school leadership seems to be self-taught, selectors might want to discover how candidates view their craft.* What mistakes have they made and what have they learned from them? What are the most important things they know now that they didn't when they started? Who was the best (or worst) role model they had? The goal here is to decide whether this is a person who will continue to learn from experience. (Or, to borrow a well-known witticism, is this someone who has had ten years of experience or one year of experience ten times?)

The literature also offers a few insights into the training of administrators. School leaders often criticize their preparation programs as "impractical" or "too theoretical," and it's now easy to see why. So many of the characteristics of leaders—social orientation, initiative, psychological balance—are not easily taught (nor would most universities feel comfortable in using these traits to select candidates). Just as important, leadership is highly dependent on context. Effective principals don't just know schools, they know *their* schools—the history, the personalities, the sights, sounds, and smells. (Blumberg gives the example of a principal who detected something on the floor above that didn't quite sound right. She couldn't specify just what she was reacting to, and an observer hadn't heard anything unusual, but a quick investigation revealed several students who didn't belong in the school.)

So while training programs might do a better job of teaching specific skills (perhaps through simulations or case studies), whatever is learned will not have quite the flavor of the real thing. Any generalized skills will eventually have to be adapted to a highly specific environment.

Current training programs may not be that far off the mark when they provide candidates with an intellectual and philosophical perspective on the school system. As we've seen, leaders are good thinkers, with a particular set of beliefs and a strong sense of purpose. There may be no better time to confront future administrators with difficult questions. What is the purpose of the educational enterprise? Who are schools meant to serve, and how well are they doing it? And what are they, the future leaders, doing here? What can they accomplish as administrators that they can't do as teachers? While there is always a danger such speculations may become sterile, abstract exercises, it should take no great effort to connect them with the very practical problems school leaders wrestle with every day. Certainly, once administrators get caught up in the maelstrom of a working school, there will be precious little time for leisurely reflection.

Conclusion

A small part of our leadership portrait has been revealed by each of the research studies and reviews mentioned here. Now, like the pieces of a jigsaw puzzle, all the fragments can be assembled to reveal a more coherent (though by no means complete) portrait of an effective educational leader.

This portrait shows leaders are competent, both intellectually and socially. They have a high degree of energy and initiative, but have also learned the value of patience. They get along well with people and are skillful communicators. They are psychologically well-balanced, integrating their diverse traits into a smoothly functioning whole. They have a distinctive set of beliefs and values that they communicate clearly.

As children they were probably challenged by high standards and the opportunity to exercise responsibility. Much of what they know about leadership has been learned on their own, through practical experience.

As portraits go, this one is rather impressionistic, displaying nebulous shadings of color rather than sharp edges. There is much we don't know, and much of what we think we know will eventually prove to be misleading or just plain wrong.

Moreover, the sketch itself is not of a real leader but only of an imaginary one. The leader whose characteristics are set down here is a pure "form," who in actuality does not exist. Like the "typical voter" or the "typical consumer," the "typical leader" is only a composite of common characteristics. No real flesh and blood counterpart exists.

And even if we could find someone with all the traits we've listed, there is no guarantee he or she would be a leader. As Daniel Duke has said,

> It is conceivable that there are individuals who manifest all the behaviors associated with leadership, yet fail to embody leadership. Those who attempt to "train" leaders long have recognized this problem. Some master all the necessary operations—from planning to decision making—but they do not convey the impression of leadership.

Leadership seems to be a gestalt phenomenon, greater than the sum of its behavioral parts.

So what then is the point of this incomplete portrait of a nonexistent leader? Simply this: Becoming a leader is ultimately a do-it-yourself project. Examining views of leadership can teach us much about ourselves and our culture, our conceptions and preconceptions. The hope is that leaders, or future leaders, can find in these pages themes that resonate in their own lives and that can help them reflect more deeply on their own journey to leadership.

When things get rough and they are tempted to lock themselves in their offices, such a vision can remind them that human-relations and communication skills are important. When they are coasting along, day-by-day, not going anywhere in particular, it can remind them that being goal-oriented does make a difference. When they are criticized by superiors for breaking unnecessary rules and cautioned not to make waves, it can give them the courage to continue doing things their own way—as long as that way has been successful in accomplishing their highest priorities.

In short, the most important use for this portrait is the function performed by any ideal. It can caution us while at the same time offering us something to strive for.

CHAPTER

2

Leadership Styles and Strategies

Larry Lashway

Simple observation reveals that different leaders work in different ways. Some are visible and voluble, whirlwinds of loud activity who dominate a room just by walking into it; others glide quietly through the corridors, observing more than talking, pausing occasionally for brief conferences—a compliment here, a gentle nudge there. Some are dreamers, painting the future in broad, confident brushstrokes; others are mechanics, endlessly tinkering with organizational nuts and bolts. Some rush in where angels fear to tread; others wait for research showing which way the angels are headed.

When researchers after World War II turned their attention from leadership traits to leadership behaviors, they soon found distinctive patterns. For example, some leaders were task-driven, focused on the technical challenges of reaching organizational goals. Others, by contrast, were more concerned with the human dimensions of the job, concentrating on motivation and communication.

Eventually these findings led to the notion of style: the characteristic way in which a leader uses power, makes decisions, and interacts with others. Style was quickly accepted as an important element in leadership, partly because it provided an understandable explanation of everyday experience.

However, researchers are still far from a consensus on its significance. What are the critical elements of style? Can it be reliably measured? What style works best? The jury is still out on these questions.

This chapter explores the ways leaders behave. The first part looks at some of the major style theories and their implications for school leaders. The second part explores the idea that effective leadership is not just a matter of style, but of consciously chosen strategies.

Styles

Over the years, researchers have described style in a variety of ways—not all of them compatible. With some oversimplification, we can identify several broad themes in the literature.

Does the Leader Focus on People or Work?

One of the oldest and best-known themes in style research is the contrast between "task-orientation" and "relationship-orientation." Some leaders are fascinated by the technical challenges of getting things done: setting goals, organizing meetings, and monitoring activities. Other leaders seem more attuned to the people around them, displaying great skill at communicating and motivating.

Researchers have identified these as critical dimensions of leader behavior, but they disagree on a number of points. Perhaps the most divisive question is whether the two characteristics are independent (like intelligence and height) or opposite ends of a continuum (like thin and fat). Fred Fiedler, one leading style theorist, believes that leaders are able to focus on either one or the other but not both. Robert Blake and Jane Mouton, on the other hand, believe that leaders can be high on one dimension, both dimensions, or neither dimension. They devised a "managerial grid" that allows for four basic styles as well as a "middle road." One combination (high task and high relationship) is seen as especially powerful, while another (low task and low relationship) is considered to be "impoverished."

Despite these disagreements, the task/relationship distinction has had a long and vigorous history, and it appears to capture a fundamental difference in the way that different leaders approach their work.

Who Makes Decisions?

Another approach to style focuses on decision-making. Some leaders ("autocratic" or "directive") make decisions by themselves, without asking for input or participation from subordinates. Others ("democratic" or "participative") involve subordinates, trusting their ability to make good choices.

Unlike the task/relationship distinction, there is little doubt that decision-making is a single continuum—leaders cannot simultaneously be directive and participative. Robert Tannenbaum and Warren Schmidt, who developed one of the earliest descriptions, saw the range extending from "boss-centered" to "subordinate-centered." At the boss-centered end, leaders make the decision themselves and announce it (sometimes with an explanation). At the other end, leaders give subordinates great freedom within very flexible limits.

Tannenbaum and Schmidt believed that subordinate-centered approaches were good for both the employee and the organization, but they cautioned that subordinates should not be given more freedom than they were ready to handle. Foreshadowing a major theme in style theories, they argued that effective managers accurately analyze each situation and then adopt the appropriate style.

Do Males and Females Lead Differently?

As more women have taken leadership roles, researchers have asked whether gender makes a difference. Some advocates of diversity have argued that women, because of different temperaments or experiences, bring a more open, participative, relationship-oriented style to the job. Sally Helgesen, after studying a number of top women executives, characterized the difference metaphorically by saying women are more attuned to voice than vision; speaking and hearing imply dialogue, whereas seeing is a one-way process.

Does research show a difference? Alice Eagly and her colleagues did a careful meta-analysis of 117 studies on gender and style among school principals and found mixed results. Overall, female principals did not appear to be more relationship-oriented than their male counterparts, but they were judged to be more task-oriented (recall that task-orientation and relationship-orientation can be viewed as independent attributes). In addition, the female principals used a more democratic style.

Eagly's team also found evidence that gender differences were greater in more recent studies, as well as in cases where female principals had many female peers. This suggests that as female principals become more numerous, they feel more at liberty to be themselves, rather than imitating the dominant male style. Most significantly, the authors found no evidence that gender has any bearing on the ability to become an effective principal.

How Do Leaders Interact with the Environment?

Might each leader's style be a reflection of deeply rooted personal characteristics that show up in every part of life, from making dinner to choosing a career? Yes, according to one popular method for sorting people according to their personalities.

The Myers-Briggs Type Inventory (MBTI) was developed by Isabel Briggs Myers, based on a personality theory of Carl Jung, and has been widely used in a variety of settings. In essence, the theory says that human personality is structured along four dimensions, each containing two contrasting possibilities (Isabel Briggs Myers and Peter Myers).

Introversion-Extraversion. This dimension has to do with the way people relate to the world around them. Extraverts are outwardly oriented; they tend to get their psychic energy from interacting with large numbers of people in a spontaneous way. Introverts are inwardly oriented; they aren't necessarily shy, but find it uncomfortable to share their thoughts spontaneously with large numbers of people. When extraverts have to make a decision, they talk about it to anybody who walks into their office; introverts first figure out what they believe before opening it up to a wider audience.

Sensing-Intuition. This dimension focuses on how people gather information. Some, the sensers, need concrete, down-to-earth data; they need to see, hear, and touch things in the real world. Intuitives use a global approach, seeing large, abstract patterns and possibilities; they love dealing with hypotheticals and what-ifs.

Thinking-Feeling. This dimension has to do with the kind of data people use to make decisions. Thinkers tend to approach things rationally and objectively, basing decisions more on abstract principles than on specific situations. Feelers tend to use a more personal and subjective approach, paying special attention to how the decision will affect others.

Judging-Perceiving. This dimension has to do with the way people structure their lives. Judgers are methodical and well organized. They like to know what will happen when, and they enjoy checking things off lists. Perceivers prefer to keep their options open; they like to gather as much data as possible before making decisions, and they're quite comfortable with uncertainty and surprises.

In the Myers-Briggs system, everyone tends to favor one alternative or the other in each of the four dimensions. This results in a total of sixteen basic personality "types," each with a distinctive flavor and a unique way of approaching life. For example, Myers and Myers describe the ESTJ (extraverted / sensing / thinking / judging) types as practical, detail-oriented, analytical, and impersonal, with a strong desire to organize the world around them. (Not surprisingly, this is the most common type among executives, including school leaders.)

Unanswered Questions

Style theories have been highly influential, leading to uncounted workshops, seminars, and articles aimed at improving leadership through style. At this point, however, there is still little agreement on how to describe styles, much less how they affect leadership. (Table 1 presents a summary of competing views, including several that have not been discussed here.) We are left with a number of challenging questions.

Can Style Be Changed?

Just what are we looking at here? Are styles a reflection of deeply rooted personality factors—dispositions that are either innate or acquired through early family experiences? Or are they merely behaviors that can be changed at will? Answers vary.

The Myers-Briggs approach seems to give the most fatalistic answer, since it assumes that style is a reflection of personality, something so much a part of us that it is transparent—that is, the behaviors seem so natural that we don't even notice them.

Most Myers-Briggs specialists respond that whatever the psychological roots, styles eventually take the form of behaviors, which can be modified. However, significant change is unlikely to come quickly or permanently. It's a bit like writing with your opposite hand—you can do it, after a fashion, but it takes a major effort to become fluent. Leaders who become aware of their preferences can behave differently, but there will probably always be a tendency to drift back to the old way, especially in times of stress.

Opinion about the other style theories is more variable. Fiedler is one theorist who believes that leaders can alter their styles very little, if at all. He sees task-motivation and relationship-orientation as a part of personality and thus difficult to change, especially through short-term training. At best it takes several years of intensive psychotherapy to create lasting changes in personality structure.

A similar view comes from Gene Hall and colleagues, based on their work with principals. They believe that style is so closely tied to personality and history that changes will seldom be permanent.

On the other hand, Paul Hersey and Kenneth Blanchard, who have developed a popular model based on the task/relationship distinction, insist that successful leaders can and should adapt their style to meet the needs of the group. But even they hesitate to claim that every leader can become proficient in every style.

Can Style Be Reliably Identified?

The first step for leaders wanting to improve their use of style is to become aware of what their style is. Yet this seemingly simple task turns out to be complicated.

TABLE 1

Comparison of Leadership Style Theories

Dimensions	*Author*	*How Many Styles?*	*What Kinds of Style?*
Decision-Making	Tannenbaum and Schmidt	2	*Decision-Making* "Subordinate-centered vs. boss-centered" (Democratic vs. autocratic) (former most effective)
	Bonoma and Slevin	4	*Decision-Making* Four possible styles: autocrat, consultative manager, consultative autocrat, shareholder (all but the last are effective)
Perception of Employees	McGregor	2	*Views of Employees* Theory X (need extrinsic motivators) vs. Theory Y (self-motivated) (Latter view most effective)
Tasks and Human Relations	Halpin	2	*Task and Human Relations* Concern for initiating structure or consideration
	Fiedler	2	*Task and Human Relations* Task-oriented vs. Human relationship oriented (either can be effective)
	Reddin	4	*Task and Human Relations* Four combinations of human-relations orientation and task orientation. Four possible styles: integrated, separated, related, dedicated (each can be effective)
	Hersey and Blanchard	4	*Task and Human Relations* (both can be effective)
	Blanchard, Zigarmi,and Zigarmi	4	*Task and Human Relations* Four combinations of directive and supportive behaviors: directing, coaching, supporting, delegating (each can be effective)
Innovation and Risk-Taking	Hall and others, Hord and Hall	3	*Change Facilitator Styles* Initiator (most effective at implementing change), manager, responder
	Miskel		Several, including risk-taking propensity of leaders
Myers-Briggs	Myers and Myers	16	*Psychological Types* (Four bipolar dimensions: extraversion/introversion, sensing/intuitive, thinking/feeling, judging/perceiving (can be combined in 16 possible styles)

TABLE 1 *cont.*

Are Styles Mutually Exclusive?	*Do Styles Vary with Situations?*	*What Are the Components of the Situation?*	*Is the Leader's Style Flexible?*
Yes (leader cannot use both at the same time)	Yes	Forces in the manager, forces in the subordinates, and forces in the situation	Yes (leader chooses the style appropriate at the time)
No (all possible combinations of the styles are possible)	Yes	Where authority is placed and where information comes from	Yes
Yes	No	Not applicable	Not applicable
No (effective leaders have both concerns)	Not applicable	Not applicable	Not applicable
Yes	Yes	Most important component is leader situational control, made up of position power, leader-member relations, task structure	No
No	Yes	Organizational philosophy, technology, superior, coworker, subordinates	Some leaders are flexible and some are not
Yes (although leader can change from one to the other, does not use both simultaneously)	Yes	Follower maturity	Yes (must change with time)
No	Yes	Follower developmental level—competence and commitment	Yes (leader varies style with each follower and each task)
No	No	Not applicable	No
Not applicable	Yes	Leader years of experience and innovative management techniques	Not applicable
Yes	No	Not applicable	With effort (flexible behavior can be learned, but *preferred* style remains the same)

The Myers-Briggs system reminds us how hard it can be to perceive our own style. Traits like introversion, extraversion, thinking, and feeling go to the core of our identities. "The way we are" seems so natural that we fail to recognize it in ourselves, or to realize that others see the world differently.

This is especially true for leaders immersed in the rapid-fire pressures of organizational life. Hersey and Blanchard point out that awareness of perceived style depends on regular, accurate feedback, which is hard to come by. Employees are often reluctant to be honest with their superiors.

For this reason, many of the style systems use written assessments. The Myers-Briggs inventory, for instance, asks participants a number of forced-choice questions spanning the four major dimensions. Similarly, Fiedler and colleagues developed a teaching guide that helps leaders identify whether they are task-oriented or relationship-oriented. The guide asks leaders to rate themselves on a number of specific indicators, rather than asking them to make guesses about overall styles.

Such assessments should be used with caution, however, since any personal assessment has room for error. In looking at the MBTI, for example, David Pittenger raises concerns about the validity and reliability of the instrument. His review found a "conspicuous absence of evidence that 16 different types represent distinct and unique affective, behavioral, and cognitive propensities."

And while a well-written instrument can be more objective, any self-assessment will reflect the subject's blind spots. For this reason, Hersey and Blanchard provide two instruments, one to be completed by the leader and the other by subordinates.

In any case, leaders should not be too quick to embrace the judgment of any instrument. In particular, they should not make casual judgments about themselves and others, especially when making major decisions such as hiring.

Is There an Ideal Style?

One of the first questions that leaders ask about style is "Which approach is best? Which way will get the results I'm looking for?" Researchers have asked the same questions, but have reached a variety of conflicting conclusions.

Bernard Bass (1990), summing up a variety of studies, says that participative styles are generally associated with worker satisfaction and cooperation. However, he also cites studies showing that some workers may prefer autocratic styles, and even a few studies in which participation was not satisfying. More significantly, the available research provides no clear evidence that style affects productivity.

Blake and Mouton argue that the ideal leader combines high task-orientation with high relationship-orientation, and Bass agrees there is considerable theoretical and empirical evidence for this position. However, he also notes mixed or negative results in a substantial number of studies.

For their part, most Myers-Briggs enthusiasts, such as Robert Benfari, decline to promote one style over another, saying that each has its special contributions to make. Instead, they urge leaders to use their knowledge of style to improve mutual understanding and work relationships.

Does this mean that style makes no difference? Most theorists decline to draw that pessimistic conclusion. Rather, they argue that the effectiveness of different styles depends on the situation.

How Does Situation Affect Style?

Sometimes one style will work best; under other circumstances another style will be more appropriate. To use a highly publicized example, when principal Joe Clark took over a chaotic, drug-ridden high school in Paterson, New Jersey, he used an extremely directive style (dramatized by carrying around a bullhorn and baseball bat). He was highly effective in restoring order to the school, but then, in the new, calmer situation, people began to regard his tough style as unnecessary and even abusive.

What parts of a situation influence the leader's choice of style? Answers come from a number of researchers, including Hersey and Blanchard, Bass (1990), and Victor Vroom and Arthur Jago.

1. *The nature of the task.* A minor task that is simple and unambiguous may benefit from a directive approach. A major issue that is complex and ambiguous will often benefit from a more participative approach.

2. *The experience, expertise, and motivation of employees.* Employees with little training or expertise will often benefit from clear, detailed directions or emotional support; highly capable employees may resent micromanagement from above.

3. *Time.* When circumstances dictate a quick decision, participation may have to be sacrificed for efficiency.

4. *Organizational culture.* Culture has been characterized as "the way we do things around here," and these ingrained patterns of behavior may crimp leadership style. Pressure may come from superiors (for example, a superintendent who demands quick results); it may come from peers who are not eager to have their own comfortable styles challenged by new

ways of doing things; or it may come from subordinates who have gotten used to a particular administrative approach.

5. *The likelihood that subordinates will accept the leader's decision.* A participative approach may soften resistance to new ideas.

6. *The external environment.* Events in the surrounding community or the larger society may affect style. Ten years ago principals were being urged to use strong top-down leadership; today they are being encouraged to use participative approaches.

With so many influences on style, how can leaders make the appropriate choices? Hersey and Blanchard argue that it is impossible to consciously consider all factors. Instead, they advocate that leaders focus on what they call "follower readiness" in making style choices.

The Importance of Style

So where does all this leave school leaders? Should they rush out to take the first style assessment they can lay their hands on? Should they make a point of consciously altering their style for each new situation? Or is style one of those fads that will eventually find its way to the consulting attic?

After a period of enthusiasm, some researchers, like Lee Bolman and Terry Deal (1991), are becoming more critical. Part of their concern is the superficial approach sometimes used to teach style—what they call "thin books with thin advice." In particular, they argue that most style systems don't cover the full range of leader behavior. They also point out the lack of research validating the different style approaches. Speaking of the Hersey/Blanchard model, they conclude that there is "considerable reason to believe that the model is wrong and little evidence to suggest that it is right."

Balanced against these concerns is the fact that many leaders have found style to be a helpful concept that offers them a little more insight into their work.

Indeed, self-awareness may be the greatest benefit of considering styles. When we encounter people using other styles, their behavior may seem mystifying, deviant, or simply obtuse. When "judgers" run a meeting, they move through the agenda briskly, making a clean-cut decision and moving on to the next item. The "perceivers" in the group are likely to feel that the decisions have been made superficially. When perceivers run the meeting, they are likely to linger over each item, looking at all the options and worrying that some key information has been overlooked; they happily entertain motions to table, leaving the judgers in the group to mutter, "Why can't we ever get anything decided?"

Knowledge of styles thus helps leaders recognize how they operate and how others are affected; in turn, they learn that the other person's contrariness is really just a different style. Leaders may or may not be able to flex their style at will, but recognizing it will at least allow them to soften its impact on those around them. One of the effective principals interviewed by Arthur Blumberg said this:

> I really do like to control things, but I know that I have to keep that part of me under wraps. In the back of my mind, I frequently keep reminding myself, "Don't appear to be overly in control." Because if they feel everything is set before they even talk about it, then, in fact, it will backfire.

That principal understood his natural style and how it affected others. He couldn't change his personality, but he kept it from dominating his life, using it as a scalpel, not a sword.

Strategies

Some style theorists suggest that leaders can at least temporarily modify their natural tendencies to fit the situation. When they do this, are they just responding to each situation as it arises, or are they guided by some broader set of principles? Do they, in other words, use a strategy?

A leadership *strategy* is a consciously chosen pattern of behavior designed to gain the cooperation of followers in accomplishing organizational goals. Over time, some leaders consistently use a particular approach that seems to be more than a reflection of their psychological makeup. Despite the pushes and pulls of daily events that require them to be flexible and pragmatic, they have an image of the kind of leader they want to be, an image they can describe and justify—a philosophy, not just a style.

School leaders can choose from at least three basic strategies: hierarchical, transformational, and facilitative.

The Foundations of Strategy

Strategies originate in the minds of leaders as they confront the complexities of running a school. Two kinds of perceptions are especially important: the way leaders view power, and the way they size up the situation.

Power

Everyone agrees that leadership and power are closely related, but concepts like "power," "influence," and "authority" have been defined in many ways (Bass 1990). We'll use a definition offered by Hersey and Blanchard: *power* is "influence potential—the resource that enables a leader to gain compliance or commitment from others."

Some discussions of power recognize four or five types, but most can be sorted into two broad categories. One is coercive; the leader has the ability to control the environment in a way that will harm or benefit the follower. Coercive power may be based on raw physical force (as in many dictatorships), on legal penalties, or on the ability to offer material rewards for good performance. The leader-follower relationship is thus built on a straightforward contract: give me compliance, or bad things will happen; give me commitment, and good things will come your way.

The second type of power goes under various names but can be capsulized as moral power; the leader's influence comes from followers' respect for his or her personal qualities, expertise, or position. American presidents, for example, might be respected because of their honesty, their ability to handle foreign policy, or the simple fact that have been democratically elected. With moral power, leaders can have significant influence even when they have no coercive power.

In recent years, the difference between coercive and moral power has been characterized as "power-over" vs. "power-through" (Diane Dunlap and Paul Goldman). In power-over, followers are seen as instruments of the leader: the leader decides, the followers execute. By contrast, power-through recognizes the autonomy of the followers, allowing them wide discretion in pursuing organizational goals.

Every organization relies on some degree of coercive power (for example, if workers don't show up they won't get paid), but organizational excellence is frequently associated with moral power. Coercion may gain outward compliance, but moral power leads to performance above and beyond the call of duty.

No leader can avoid the issue of power. The choice is not whether to use it, but how. The way leaders answer that question will have a lot to do with the strategies they choose.

Strategic Thinking

Leadership strategy is also determined by the leader's analysis of the situation. What am I trying to do here—what's the goal? What are the barriers? What will help us? Who do I have to convince?

Bolman and Deal (1991) have offered a useful way of thinking about these issues, arguing that effective strategic thinking requires proficiency in four domains (or "frames").

The structural frame. Like other organizations, schools have a formal structure that gives everyone an officially assigned role defined by rules, policies, and contracts. Through this structure, the school formulates goals, makes plans to achieve them, and evaluates progress. Leaders using the structural frame focus on planning, supervising, communicating, and allocating resources. The ultimate goal is coordination and control through rational analysis.

The human-resource frame. Whatever their organizational roles, people never stop being people, and the leader must be able to recognize and respond to the human needs of employees. Leaders using the human-resource frame pay close attention to relationships, feelings, and motivation; the goal is to make the workplace congenial and rewarding.

The political frame. All employees have personal agendas—something they want to get from their relationship with the institution (security, salary, autonomy, job satisfaction). Since these agendas often clash, people continually jockey for power and resources to protect what is important to them. The result is a nonstop process of coalition-building, lobbying, bargaining, and compromise (much of it behind the scenes). Leaders using the political frame recognize and accept these tactics as natural; the goal is to resolve the conflicts peacefully and informally.

The symbolic frame. Schools are cultures, not just organizational structures. They have myths, heroes, and sacred rituals designed to symbolize and reaffirm the underlying meaning of events. Thinking in the symbolic frame is sensitive to these cultural factors. The leader is able to recognize, for example, that the year-ending faculty get-together, with its satirical slide-show, is not just a raucous party but a way of renewing emotional bonds, atoning for the year's sins, and celebrating one more revolution of the wheel. Leaders using the symbolic frame seek to create organizations with rich cultures that are shared and appreciated by everyone in the organization.

Bolman and Deal (1992) believe that effective leadership requires the use of multiple frames, but they report that only a quarter of the educational leaders they studied used more than two frames and that only one leader in a hundred regularly employed all of them. Each of the strategies examined next relies heavily on one or more of these frames.

The Hierarchical Strategy

In 1958, Robert McMurry, reacting to the growing interest in participative approaches, came to the defense of nondemocratic leadership, describing it this way:

> The benevolent autocrat structures his subordinates' activities for them; he makes the policy decisions which affect them; he keeps them in line and enforces discipline. He is like a good quarterback, who does not ask the line to decide what plays to attempt or what formation to use, but tells them—and woe betide the hapless player who refuses to follow his orders.

Four decades later, McMurry's portrait is still instantly recognizable; despite recurrent interest in democratic approaches, most organizations continue to rely heavily on leadership that is hierarchical (also called "top-down," "directive," or "autocratic").

While hierarchies have been around for thousands of years (mostly in the military and the church), it was only in the nineteenth century, when commercial and governmental organizations became bureaucratic, that the hierarchical approach blossomed into the standard way of doing business. One of the first scholars to recognize this change was the German sociologist Max Weber, whose study of bureaucracy is still useful in understanding today's organizations (H. H. Gerth and C. Wright Mills).

In Weber's view, hierarchy develops when organizations grow large and complex. Needing people with a variety of knowledge and skills, they divide themselves into departments, each having a specific responsibility that allows workers to concentrate on their area of expertise.

Unfortunately, specialization always threatens to fragment the organization, with different departments working at cross-purposes. To avoid this, clear lines of accountability are established, designating who is responsible for what decisions and to whom they report, resulting in the familiar pyramidal organization chart.

The leader's power is thus based on the position he or she occupies in the hierarchy, not on any unique personal traits. This power is usually spelled out by policies governing who can make what decisions at what time and in what manner. For the most part, the leader's power is coercive; failure to follow orders subverts the whole enterprise and will usually lead to discipline or dismissal. (However, Weber argued that because leaders are chosen for their expertise, at least some of their power will be moral.)

Hierarchy rests on logic and rationality; it assumes that there is one best way of doing things that can be identified through careful analysis by experts. Once the decision has been made, the organization's job is to carry it out as efficiently as possible, each worker doing his or her assigned part.

Hierarchy in Schools

Nineteenth-century schools were mostly small and rural, seemingly poor candidates to become bureaucracies. But as Raymond Callahan documented in his landmark study *Education and the Cult of Efficiency*, the rapid growth of schools, combined with the desire of school leaders to be seen as hard-headed businessmen, led many to argue that well-run schools are no different than well-run factories. As one leading advocate put it, school administrators should "keep the workers supplied with detailed instructions as to how the work is to be done, the standards to be reached, the methods to be employed, and the materials and appliances to be used." Metaphorically, management was the head, responsible for making decisions; labor provided the hands to do the actual labor.

In later decades, the extreme versions of this idea were softened by attempts to make schools more democratic, but many of the underlying practices remained the same. As recently as the 1980s, many school-reform plans contained strongly hierarchical assumptions. Even the "instructional leadership" model often portrayed the principal as a highly directive leader.

Advantages of Hierarchy

The impressive durability of hierarchical approaches implies that they meet some important needs. The most obvious advantage is efficiency. The emphasis on logical decision-making and worker accountability offers a clear formula for getting things done. Weber was convinced that bureaucratic approaches were technically superior, doing for organizations what machines did for manual labor. Anyone who has worked in the pressure cooker of public education understands the allure of a system that promises quick and decisive action. Every day brings a thousand details that require mastery by an expert, not drawn-out debate.

In addition, the emphasis on rules and accountability increases the likelihood of fair and impartial decisions, which is especially important in publicly accountable systems. Both workers and clients are more likely to accept decisions that have been made logically and even-handedly.

Another benefit was noted by McMurry in his tribute to benevolent autocracy: not all employees have pure motives and cooperative attitudes. Every organization has its share of slackers, gold-bricks, and subversives who just don't respond to democratic trust. For reasons of both fairness and efficiency, someone has to have the coercive power to deal with these individuals.

Finally, hierarchical approaches often work because people have what Weber called the "habit of obedience." Most recognize the value of having someone be in charge and are willing to accept leadership from whoever is in that position. Indeed, followers often don't want to be bothered with the responsibility of making decisions.

Limitations of Hierarchy

Despite their widespread use, hierarchical approaches have certain limitations. First, the same hierarchy that gives power to a leader also hems it in with rules that carefully prescribe what can or cannot be done—board policies, union contracts, and state laws. Principals who expect to operate in a purely top-down manner may find themselves sharing the fate that Harry Truman predicted for the newly elected President Eisenhower. "He'll sit right here and he'll say do this, do that! And nothing will happen. Poor Ike—it won't be a bit like the Army."

But even if school leaders had unlimited powers, they might not be able to use them effectively; teaching is an activity that doesn't march to administrative drums. Joseph Shedd and Samuel Bacharach note that teachers' roles are extraordinarily complex, involving instruction, counseling, and supervision of students who are highly variable in their needs and capacities. There is a high degree of unpredictability and little consensus on the best steps to be taken in any given situation. Detailed directives from the top simply don't make sense; teachers are in the classroom, and principals are not.

Another problem is the school's stubborn refusal to behave in logical ways. Jerry Patterson and colleagues have pointed out that the "if A, then B" assumption doesn't always work out in practice. People may fail to communicate through the prescribed channels; organizational goals may be ignored or tacked on as an afterthought to justify longstanding routines; decisions may reflect political clout rather than rational analysis. No organization chart can accurately capture the rich, varied, and occasionally quirky behaviors of human beings.

Another limitation of hierarchical power is its affinity for the status quo. It assumes that organizational goals are clear (or easily clarified), and concentrates on the how-to. If changes are needed, they are likely to be small-scale and incremental; major restructuring threatens the rules that define everyone's job. Teachers may find the annual evaluation irksome, useless, or mildly threatening, but the contract at least ensures that it will be predictable, staying within parameters they can cope with. Why risk leaving that for something uncertain, even if it sounds rather intriguing?

Finally, as even Weber recognized, the strengths of bureaucracies can turn into weaknesses. Impartiality based on rules can become insensitivity to individual circumstances. Bureaucratic expertise can lead to arrogance and manipulation. Emphasis on order can stifle the creativity and imagination.

The Exemplary Hierarchical Leader

For all its limitations, the hierarchical approach remains dominant in American schools; indeed, even critics generally concede that it is an essential part of the leader's toolkit. What's the secret to using it well?

One obvious skill is keeping the organizational machine well-oiled. Teachers can't teach if the books aren't ordered on time or the chalk runs low or the buses don't arrive when they should. In most schools, this is the primary expectation for principals; failing to do it well will undermine anything else they hope to accomplish. Clearly, effective hierarchical leadership requires looking at the school through a "structural" frame, seeing the rules, relationships, and resources that will get things from point A to point B on schedule.

Doing so requires a delicate touch, however. Teachers expect a smoothly running school, but they want it done painlessly. As Dan Lortie noted years ago, "Teachers want to teach." They are irritated by anything that takes attention away from teaching: stacks of paperwork, long announcements over the P.A., lengthy meetings on business that could be handled in a one-page memo.

Coordination is another essential hierarchical function. Teachers are specialists, preoccupied with doing their own work in their own classrooms, and having little time for learning what others are doing, much less coordinating their mutual efforts. Thus school leaders must continually pose questions that no one else has time to ask. Does the fifth-grade science curriculum prepare students for the sixth-grade science curriculum? Do teachers in different classrooms send mixed messages by using different discipline standards? Does early dismissal for athletic events create havoc with afternoon classes?

An especially important part of this coordination is establishing and maintaining organizational goals. Schools are subject to a multitude of cultural and political pressures that can easily deflect them from their path. No sooner has one set of goals been adopted than some new social crisis shoves them into the background. The leader's role is to act as the institution's conscience on goals, keeping it on target.

Effective coordination requires the leader to be fully aware of what's happening in the building. Hierarchies are notorious for filtering out bad news as it works its way up the chain of command, and leaders need to be aggressive about staying in touch. Blumberg calls this "having a nose for things," and says it doesn't come just from randomly walking around the school but from making a conscious effort to identify problems. One central-office administrator put it in terms of picking up subtle cues:

> For example, there's a teacher whom I know very well. One day he said, "Our high school principal, he's probably the best you can get." Interpretation: There are some things he screws up on. And my knowing this teacher and him knowing me, he's telling me that there's some communications lag taking place in the school, and there was.

Leaders must be ready to use the coercive power at their disposal. This is never particularly pleasant, especially in an institution that tends to be filled with tender-hearted idealists, and a heavy-handed approach can be counterproductive. However, every organization has people who aren't good at following the rules, and fairness requires that these situations be dealt with. Edwin Bridges, in his study of incompetent teachers, notes that much of the administrative anguish over nonperforming teachers is self-inflicted. Rather than dealing forthrightly with a problem, many administrators deny it, look the other way, or try to pass it on to someone else. When leaders fail to use their power to solve an obvious problem, it ends up diminishing their power.

While coercive power must be used, it must also be used sensitively, with recognition of the corrosive effects it can have on relationships and motivation. When acting hierarchically, leaders can ease tension by viewing events through a human-relations frame, something that seems especially important in schools.

Lortie found that teachers were most motivated by the psychic reward of reaching their students, and what they most wanted from their principals was support, appreciation, and fairness. While teachers will never quite forget that principals have coercive power, they respond warmly to simple friendliness. Joseph Blase and Jo Roberts Blase record one teacher's assessment of her principal: "She has a cheery attitude, almost always smiling, and always considerate and pleasant. This gives me encouragement to ask for help with my problems. She is not forbidding."

Listening is an important part of relationship-orientation. Even where leaders will make unilateral decisions, informal consultation with followers is possible and often desirable.

The flip side of listening is marketing. Teachers are a well-educated, critical group. Even when a decision will be made hierarchically, school leaders can't afford to neglect the need to enlist support by explaining the benefits and responding to concerns.

Transformational Leadership

Marcus Foster was principal and superintendent in some of the nation's most beleaguered urban districts during the volatile 1960s and 1970s. Against overwhelming odds, he revitalized the schools he was responsible for, reducing truancy, enriching the curriculum, and building bridges to a suspicious community. He had a zestful and highly personal approach, greeting everyone he passed in the hallways with smiles, handshakes, and compliments. After one contentious meeting with a community group that ran late into the night, one of the participants pulled up next to Foster at a stoplight: "I looked over and there he was with a smile upon his face, singing at the top of his voice. I can't begin to tell you the impression made upon me, because to me it typified the ebullience, the magnificent joy of life—the joy he took in working with the community" (David Tyack and Elizabeth Hansot).

Leaders like Foster leave an indelible impression on everyone they touch. Max Weber described them as "charismatic," having authority based on "gifts of body and spirit" that inspire excitement and loyalty. In 1978, James McGregor Burns picked up this theme and described a form of leadership he called "transformational." Transformational leaders were those who got results through persuasion, idealism, and intellectual excitement. They motivated their followers not by offering material ("transactional") rewards, but by convincing them that their deepest interests and values could be fulfilled through the organization's agenda.

What Burns had in mind was not just glib manipulation, but a genuine elevation of people to higher levels of motivation and morality. Effective leadership, in his view, was never just a matter of technical efficiency—it had to meet the genuine needs of followers. Thus, John Kennedy's inaugural address and Martin Luther King's "I Have a Dream" speech were examples of transformational leadership; Adolf Hitler's equally powerful speeches were not.

Burns's work touched off a whole new line of research, which has given us a rich portrait of leaders who generate deep commitment among followers. Bernard Bass (1985) describes them as self-confident and self-determined, with few self-doubts—they know what they want and are convinced they can get it. They have good insight into the needs of followers, making them skillful motivators. They are great actors, able to provide drama and flair to the rites of leadership. And, perhaps most important, they can influence the way their followers view the world.

Jay Conger, describing "charismatic" leaders, emphasizes the importance of a vision that creates a sense of tremendous challenge. The vision—no matter how brilliant—cannot be arbitrarily imposed on the organization; it has to reflect the deepest values and aspirations of the followers. This means that leaders must be closely attuned to the organization, recognizing its special characteristics. To use the language of Bolman and Deal, they must be adept in using the symbolic frame.

Nancy Roberts sums up many of these points by saying:

> This type of leadership offers a vision of what could be and gives a sense of purpose and meaning to those who would share that vision. It builds commitment, enthusiasm, and excitement. It creates a hope in the future and a belief that the world is knowable, understandable, and manageable. The collective action that transforming leadership generates, empowers those who participate in the process. There is hope, there is optimism, there is energy. In essence, transforming leadership is a leadership that facilitates the redefinition of a people's mission and vision, a renewal of their commitment, and the restructuring of their systems for goal accomplishment.

While Roberts' description captures the spirit of transformational leadership, researchers have not yet settled on a precise behavioral definition. Kenneth Leithwood notes that some definitions are based on the concepts identified by Burns and Bass, while others are based on the generic meaning of the word (that is, anything that leads to change is considered *transformational*).

Transformational School Leaders

Unlike hierarchical leadership, which is documented by written policies and regulations, transformational leadership is much harder to track. However, there is little reason to doubt that it has been present in schools for a long time (in fact, Roberts' summary is an apt description of Horace Mann's accomplishment in establishing a public educational system).

The number of transformational leaders does not seem to be large. One rough indicator comes from Peggy Kirby and colleagues, who asked fifty-eight educators to describe some "extraordinary educational leader" they knew. Their descriptions included many of the characteristics associated with transformational leaders, but only nine said they could easily identify such a person. Another indicator comes from Bolman and Deal (1992), who report that only 5 percent of the leaders they've studied use the symbolic frame in devising strategies.

Advantages of Transformational Leadership

The most obvious advantage of transformational leadership is its ability to motivate and inspire followers. Leithwood notes that this ability may be especially important in schools, because teachers are oriented to intrinsic rewards. Much has been written about the isolation and "loneliness" of classroom teachers; some of those barriers can be overcome by making staff feel part of a collective effort in a worthy cause.

Much of the motivating power comes from the leader's enthusiasm and self-confidence. Teachers, Lortie found, are always confronted with uncertainty, never being completely sure how much good they are doing their students. A leader with confidence and energy can dissipate those doubts and convince teachers of the "rightness" of their work.

The vision that comes with transformational leadership may be critical for schools trying to restructure. Facing the inherent risks of change, having seen many reforms come and go, teachers are unlikely to be moved by the usual incentives. Only when the leader helps them articulate their deepest hopes for the future does that future start to look achievable.

Limitations of Transformational Leadership

Given the apparent rarity of transformational leadership, we might wonder whether it offers a realistic path for all leaders. According to Leithwood, it requires highly developed intellectual skills—not the kind of thing that can be reduced to a two-day workshop. Moreover, transformational leaders seem to have forceful, outgoing personalities, qualities that are not evenly distributed through the leadership pool. It may take more than an act of will to become the kind of exceptional leader who becomes enshrined in memory. There are many talented basketball players; there are only a few Michael Jordans.

On the other hand, some strong transformational leaders have so much charisma that they become complacent. Conger notes a "dark side" to charisma: leaders become infatuated with their success, and confidence becomes arrogance. They then fail to exercise care in developing a vision, or use their excellent communication skills to manipulate others, or simply become sloppy about everyday management practices.

Another problem is that transformational leadership may create high expectations that cannot be easily satisfied. Max Weber (1958) explained it this way:

> The charismatic leader gains and maintains authority solely by proving his strength in life. If he wants to be a prophet, he must perform miracles; if he wants to be a war lord, he must perform heroic deeds. Above all, however, his divine mission must "prove"

itself in that those who faithfully surrender to him must fare well. If they do not fare well, he is obviously not the master sent by the gods.

Thus, Martin Luther King, Jr., was criticized and even abandoned by some of his followers who felt he was being too timid or too accommodating with the white power structure. Being an inspirational leader can be exciting and fulfilling, but controlling one's disciples is a constant problem—especially for school leaders, who are expected to show loyalty to the system even as they are trying to transform it.

Finally, transformational leadership is associated with change and restructuring. Once a school has achieved a new structure, what happens? Can intellectual excitement be maintained over a long period, or do people reach a plateau where they need to slow down and assimilate the changes? Do transformational leaders then move on to new jobs? Does incremental change again become important? So far we don't have answers to those questions.

The Exemplary Transformational Leader

Leaders interested in transformational strategies may initially be a bit intimidated by the prospect. How many of us can expect to be "extraordinary" leaders, especially when the usual role models are people like John Kennedy, Martin Luther King, Jr., and Winston Churchill? Although there may be a personal charismatic quality involved, when transformational approaches are analyzed as behaviors, most of them appear to be within the reach of mere mortals.

Leithwood has summed up much of the research by identifying six basic characteristics of transformational school leaders.

1. Transformational leaders take the leading role in identifying and articulating an *organizational vision*. This is not just a matter of formulating goals, as hierarchical leaders do, but something much deeper. Terry Deal and Kent Peterson say that symbolically aware principals "listen carefully for the deeper dreams that the school community holds for the future. Every school is a repository of unconscious sentiments, expectations, and hopes that carry the code of the collective dream—the high ground to which they collectively aspire."

Thus, while transformational leaders have strong personal values, the real source of the vision is in the group. The leader is the voice of conscience that keeps whispering, "We aren't yet all that we can be."

2. Transformational leaders foster the acceptance of *group goals*. That is, they promote cooperation and persuade employees to rally around the

common cause. Whereas hierarchical relationships are built on contracts, transformational relationships are built on covenants. Says executive Max De Pree: "A covenantal relationship rests on shared commitment to ideas, to issues, to values, to goals, and to management processes." A contract has nothing to do with reaching our potential, he argues; covenants fill deep needs and allow work to be meaningful.

Thomas Sergiovanni (1992) says that covenants are developed through continual dialogue that invites everyone—leaders and followers—to consider explicitly the values, beliefs, and behaviors that unite the school community. Often the results of these conversations are given visible form in a written statement of beliefs, but covenants are always more than abstract principles. Members of the community must be willing to examine their practices in the light of the covenant and hold themselves accountable to it.

3. Transformational leaders convey high *performance expectations.* As they communicate the organization's core values, they also make it clear that these values are nonnegotiable. Sergiovanni (1992) stresses the importance of "leadership by outrage"—visibly taking offense when basic standards are violated. The outrage can be directed at threats from outside the school or within the school. He tells how Principal Madeline Cartwright solved a problem with teacher attendance by personally answering the phone, rather than having a secretary take the sick calls. She told teachers, "You either talk to me or you come to school, simple as that."

4. Transformational leaders provide *appropriate models.* When administrators stand up and point to an exciting future, battle-scarred teachers are likely to say, "After you." As the most carefully watched people in the school, principals are expected to live out the visions they promote. Deal and Peterson argue that even routine activities can hold important symbolic weight, especially when used to affirm core values. Principals send important messages by how they use their time, how they arrange and decorate their office, whom they reward, and how they relate to teachers, students, and parents. In the end, vision is as vision does.

5. Transformational leaders provide *intellectual stimulation.* This initially sounds intimidating, but it often consists of small, low-key actions. One of Blumberg's principals gives an example:

> Here's the incoming mail pile here. I'll look through that tonight and there will be a zillion notes to people tomorrow, like "Will you stop in and see me about this or that?" Sometimes it's just that I want them to be aware of new things for the kids that they may want to check out. And I want them to know that I'm aware of what is going on and I want them to stop in and talk about it.

Another administrator described it as just being a matter of dangling a large enough variety of bait on a large enough number of hooks; eventually, someone will bite.

6. Transformational leaders develop a *strong school culture*, in particular reinforcing values that emphasize service to students, continuous professional learning, and collaborative problem-solving. As described by Deal and Peterson, they must be "anthropological detectives," constantly using the symbolic frame and always looking beneath surface events to understand how others interpret school life. Again it may be small acts that have the biggest long-term effect: giving recognition to those who support the school's core values; telling stories that connect the school's past, present, and future; and finding room for the idiosyncratic little rituals and celebrations that bind people together.

Facilitative Leadership

> The principal always felt we could handle problems and solve them! We, in turn, felt we could solve problems of the school. We felt in control, part of the school. We were always thinking of improving our school. We acted on problems and solved them without concerning the principal. (Blase and Blase)

This teacher had experienced a form of leadership that turns hierarchy on its head: facilitation. While researchers have long asked whether democratic approaches can be used in the workplace, schools have been slow to explore the possibilities. Indeed, facilitative leadership is so new that it doesn't yet have a clear identity of its own. The concept has evolved from the work on transformational leadership, and the two terms often seem to be used interchangeably. Both approaches are change-oriented, but there is a distinct, if subtle, shift in emphasis. Whereas the transformational leader remains center stage, a dynamic and inescapable presence, the facilitative leader works in the background.

David Conley and Paul Goldman define *facilitative leadership* as "the behaviors that enhance the collective ability of a school to adapt, solve problems, and improve performance." The key word here is *collective*; organizations are believed to work best when employees at all levels are actively engaged in solving problems. The leader's role is to get that involvement.

That much is similar to transformational leadership. The key difference is the view of decision-making. Transformational leaders ask followers to freely commit effort and psychic energy to the common cause, but "common cause" does not necessarily imply democratic decision-making.

Some transformational leaders operate in a top-down manner, and followers can become energized and excited without expecting formal involvement in decisions.

Facilitative leadership, by contrast, is explicitly based on mutuality and synergy, with power flowing in multiple directions. Whereas the transformational leader offers followers a vision that reflects their highest values, the facilitative leader offers a daily partnership in bringing the vision to life. There are still formal leaders, but they use their authority to support a process of professional give-and-take. Facilitative power is power through, not power over.

This kind of power is especially appropriate in schools, according to Dunlap and Goldman, because teaching requires autonomy and discretion, not standardized formulas. Teachers can't produce learning just by subjecting students to certain methods; rather, they have to work indirectly, creating conditions under which students will learn. Principals control learning even less directly; they have to create environments in which teachers can work effectively.

Despite the emphasis on mutuality, facilitative power does not rely on voting or other formal mechanisms. Dunlap and Goldman emphasize that facilitation occurs within the existing structure, meaning that whoever normally has legal authority to ratify decisions continues to do so. Similarly, facilitation is not delegation, where the administrator unilaterally assigns tasks to subordinates. In a facilitative environment, anyone can initiate a task and recruit anyone else to participate. The process thrives on informal negotiation and communication.

Conley and Goldman list half a dozen key strategies used by facilitative leaders: overcoming resource constraints; building teams; providing feedback, coordination, and conflict management; creating communication networks; practicing collaborative politics; and modeling the school's vision. Facilitative leaders inevitably make heavy use of the political frame, seeking to identify the key players, what they are looking for, and how their needs can be reconciled.

However, successful facilitation may depend less on any particular set of behaviors than on the underlying belief system. Conley and Goldman emphasize the importance of trust, "a letting go of control and an increasing belief that others can and will function independently and successfully within a common framework of expectations and accountability."

Advantages of Facilitative Leadership

As noted above, facilitative leadership seems especially suitable for schools, since teachers are already considered semi-autonomous professionals, at least within their own classrooms. Facilitative leadership extends this professionalism to the next level: collaborating on schoolwide issues. The results can be exciting:

> Trust just opened teachers up to their fullest potential. They began to get ideas and be creative. They figure, "Okay, we were allowed to do this little-bitty thing, maybe we can do something else." The first thing you know, you have teachers talking with each other, not about what they did last weekend or about the latest little piece of gossip. They're talking about instructional things—workshops they've been to, professional books they've read, ideas that they have. (Joseph Blase and others)

That kind of interaction helps teachers make the transition from the friendliness of congeniality to the shared values and commitment of collegiality (Sergiovanni 1992). Collaborative work is often difficult and frustrating, but that very difficulty provides a crucible for forging the bonds of community. Schools end up not only with a more cohesive program, but with relationships that are strengthened and enriched.

Facilitative approaches also provide the satisfaction of working in an institution whose practices are consistent with the deepest values of society. More than one critic has noted the irony of preparing children for life in a democracy by educating them in a strongly hierarchical system.

The issue is more than symbolic, however. According to Linda McNeil, there is a strong link between administrative leadership strategies and classroom teaching strategies. She found that in high schools where the principal was highly directive and controlling, teachers were more likely to use a constrained lecture-and-quiz approach, declining to use more dynamic but less predictable methods. Lynn Liontos also noted a direct relationship between a principal's collaborative approach and what was happening in his school's classrooms:

> Students have to learn to use their own minds and be creative and do problem-solving on their own. So what teachers really need to be doing is to show kids how to become learners themselves, so that they can then chart their own paths. And I think essentially what Bob is doing is modeling that approach to teachers, who may then pick up on it and use it with students.

Limitations of Facilitative Leadership

The radically different assumptions of facilitative leadership are likely to create ambiguity and discomfort. New roles can be difficult for both administrators and teachers. Nona Prestine observes that active participation by the principal is crucial, yet it must be a kind of participation that does not dominate. "Sometimes I have ideas," said one principal, "but I have to wait for the right time. I can't just go in and tell them what I think."

Even when principals try to sit back quietly, teachers may still see them as in charge, not quite trusting that the new roles can be taken seriously. In other cases, teachers may shy away from responsibilities that may plunge them into schoolwide controversies from which they are normally buffered, or may resent the frequent committee meetings that pull them away from their top priority—teaching.

Another serious issue is the blurring of accountability. Facilitative leadership creates a landscape of constantly shifting responsibilities and relationships, yet the formal system continues to turn to one person for results. Leaders may wonder about the wisdom of entrusting so much to those who will not share the accountability (Conley and Goldman, Prestine).

Administrators also face a juggling act in accommodating the unpredictable pace of facilitation with the inflexible demands of the hierarchical system. While trying to create schoolwide involvement, the principal is continually being pressured to act on a host of issues. For example, a proposal to replace basal readers with a whole-language approach is likely to generate a wide-ranging debate that deserves a full airing, yet looming over the process is an arbitrary requisition deadline. Some days, the principal must allow the issues to play themselves out; other days, he or she needs to say, "It's time to move on."

Like transformational leadership, facilitation may create great excitement and high expectations, unleashing multiple initiatives that stretch resources, drain energy, and fragment the collective vision. Somehow the principal must keep a hand on the reins without discouraging the innovators. At the same time, the risky business of change will intensify teachers' traditional demands for emotional support and protection from bureaucratic demands. The facilitative leader must know when to provide this support and when to challenge the comfortable status quo (Conley and Goldman).

The Exemplary Facilitative Leader

Although facilitative leadership is still in its infancy, we have enough accounts to piece together a picture of the facilitative leader at work (Hord, Conley and Goldman, Blase and Blase, Blase and colleagues).

Facilitative leaders create an atmosphere and a culture for change. This covers a lot of ground, but includes such things as supporting risk-taking activities even while acknowledging that mistakes are inevitable; cutting through red tape; ceaselessly talking, debating, and negotiating with teachers; facing conflict openly; selecting staff who are in tune with the vision; and nurturing rituals and traditions that express the school's values.

In carrying out these diverse activities, leaders must take on many roles: mediator, ambassador, knowledgeable resource, negotiator, cheerleader, skillful manager, and supportive colleague. Above all, they must strike just the right balance between aggressive action and watchful waiting. All the evidence so far suggests that facilitation is not a laissez-faire approach; a principal who simply delegates a task and walks away will be perceived as unsupportive or uninterested. At the same time, facilitators must communicate in word and deed that their involvement is not intended to dominate but to support collegial decision-making.

Like transformational leaders, they are keepers of the vision. But where transformational approaches credit the leader with an almost mystical ability to articulate the needs of the organization, facilitation explicitly sees vision as a creation of the entire school community, something evolved through dozens of daily encounters. Leaders contribute their values to this discussion, but may have to swallow their preferred images of the future. Their main role is to keep the conversation alive.

They provide resources. Facilitative leaders put money behind the rhetoric. They understand the importance of tangible support for change and use resource allocation as a way of communicating priorities and affirming values. In particular, they free up time for faculty members to do what needs to be done.

Because they understand that change and collaboration require deep personal changes for teachers, they make training and development a major priority. This goes far beyond hiring an occasional consultant; effective facilitators seek out qualified people in their own schools to serve as ongoing role models.

They monitor and check progress. Hord notes that nothing goes exactly as planned, requiring leaders to shift gears, adapt, redeploy, and change direction. The need to keep in touch requires them to be out and about on a daily basis; facilitative leaders will seldom be found sitting in their office.

They take the long view. They know that real change doesn't come overnight, and they don't let their attention flit to new plans with every shift of the winds. They recognize that there are ups and downs in any change process and help staff members get through the low spots; they encourage teachers to recognize the progress that is being made and celebrate major achievements.

Most of all, they know that "change is a process, not an event." Individuals must change before the institution can, and they do so in different ways and at different rates. Facilitators must adapt their strategies to these individual variations.

Is There a Best Strategy?

Clearly, leaders have broad strategic options that will lead them down very different paths. Is there a best strategy? This is an obvious question with a fuzzy answer. In the first place, the question itself may be unfair, since no one seems to be arguing that leaders should use one strategy all the time. Rather, it is a question of emphasis.

Much of the current literature seems to favor transformational and facilitative approaches, but wise administrators will try to distinguish enthusiastic advocacy from objective evidence. Lynn Beck and Joseph Murphy point out that metaphors for school leadership come and go; just since 1960, principals have been asked to be efficient bureaucrats, scientific managers, humanistic educators, instructional leaders, and now transformational/facilitative leaders. Beck and Murphy observe that prevailing images may say more about the preoccupations of society than the inherent needs of schools.

Although it's too early to expect conclusive evidence from empirical studies, advocates of transformational and facilitative approaches can cite research support (Blase and others, Leithwood). In particular, a number of qualitative studies have provided rich, compelling accounts of schools that are reinventing themselves and of teachers who see themselves, their schools, and their students in a dramatically new light. Clearly, the promises of transformational and facilitative leadership are not just idle fantasies.

However, a reality check is in order. Most recent studies of transformational and facilitative leaders have been carried out in schools that were consciously trying to restructure themselves. Undoubtedly, many of these schools had a predisposition for change, an itch that could only be scratched with major reform. Would the effects be the same in a complacent school? If the hallways are quiet, and teachers are competently teaching as they've always taught, and parents believe all the children are above average, will a school have the heart to take on the aggravation of reform? In other words, are transformational and facilitative approaches a realistic option for all school leaders? So far we don't know.

In addition, we should look carefully at what the research is actually saying. For instance, many studies measure perceptions rather than actual behavior; principals and/or teachers are asked to agree or disagree with statements about the principal's leadership strategies. While there is reason to respect these judgments, they have seldom been checked for possible biases. (It's worth noting that an earlier generation of research showed that teacher satisfaction was correlated with more hierarchical leader behaviors. Perhaps there is a kind of halo effect in which satisfied teachers rate principals higher on whatever scale is being used.)

Most of all, we should keep in mind that it is far too early for research to show that transformational and facilitative leadership are improving student learning. We can predict that definitive conclusions about effects on learning will be elusive, for as teachers and administrators rethink what it means to teach and learn effectively, their definitions of success will also change. The kind of easy correlations with standardized test scores that drove the instructional-leadership movement are unlikely to satisfy educators who work in transformational and facilitative environments.

The bottom line? As always, it rests in the hearts and minds of school leaders. The strategic choices they make will reflect their deepest values and their assessment of the school's needs. (To help the reader evaluate the hierarchical, transformational, and facilitative strategies, table 2 compares them on such dimensions as their views of power, teaching, and change.)

Choosing a Strategy

In talking of "transformational leaders" or "hierarchical leaders," we don't mean to imply that these are all-or-nothing choices. On any given day, leaders may shift gears from one hour to the next, at 1:00 cautioning an employee about excessive absences; at 2:00 chatting with a teacher about the feature article in this month's *Learning* magazine; at 3:00 sitting quietly in a technology committee meeting as teachers decide how to spend next year's state grant. Although leaders may differ in the emphasis they give to each approach, nothing requires using any one exclusively.

If so, how do leaders make their strategic choices? We have little direct evidence so far, but we can suspect that style plays a role. A principal who is a "judger" on the Myers-Briggs inventory will probably gravitate toward hierarchical strategies; the ambiguous nature of facilitation will always be somewhat stressful for this leader.

Certain strategic choices are unavoidable. Every leader with a formal position—principal, superintendent, curriculum coordinator—must use some hierarchical methods. The position is part of the hierarchy, and the job description calls for making certain judgments. Even if officeholders

TABLE 2

Comparison of Three Leadership Strategies

Dimensions	HIERARCHICAL	TRANSFORMATIONAL	FACILITATIVE
Task/relationship	Primarily task, but may be supplemented by relationship	Relationship	Relationship
Autocratic/ democratic	Autocratic	Ambiguous; leader invites *emotional* participation but may or may not share decisions	Democratic
Myers-Briggs	Thinking, judging, sensing will be especially useful	Intuitive will be especially important	Perceiving will be especially useful
Bolman and Deal's Four Frames	Primarily structural; may be supplemented by human resource (often with emphasis on material needs)	Symbolic; human resource (with focus on psychological needs)	Political and symbolic
View of power	Mainly coercive, with elements of moral	Moral; leader's authority rests on shared core values with followers	Moral
View of teaching	A technical activity, capable of being standardized	Diverse and individualized activity, but bound together by common ethos	Professional activity; dynamic and unpredictable; autonomy required
View of change	Rationally planned and incremental; future is predictable and controllable	Aims at wholesale transformation and paradigm shift; driven by common vision	Continuous and unpredictable; evolves toward shared vision through dialogue
Advantages	Technically efficient; clear accountability; emphasis on rational policies, not individual whims	Inspires and motivates followers; provides affirmation of core values and vision for the future	Affirms autonomy of teachers; creates collegiality and community; sets positive tone for school climate
Limitations	Oriented to status quo; emphasis on rules may reduce leaders's flexibility; fails to recognize nonrational behavior; may lead to bureaucratic insensitivity	May require exceptional traits; difficult to sustain over time; may create unrealistic expectations and overreliance on leader	Requires participants to learn new roles; unclear accountability; time-consuming

want to be completely democratic, no one else will forget that they hold coercive power.

Some choices will undoubtedly be made as a matter of philosophy. Many of the advocates of transformational and facilitative leadership simply believe that institutions in a democracy should be run democratically, and that every organization has a responsibility to nurture the talents and aspirations of its employees (Blase and colleagues).

But for most administrators, the choices will probably be more pragmatic. Just as styles can be chosen to fit the situation, so can strategies. Four principles guide the matching of situation and strategy.

1. Sergiovanni (1994) has suggested that organizations, like people, exist at different developmental levels. A school that has traditionally operated with strong top-down administrators may not be ready to jump into a full-blown facilitative environment. One principal reflected on her first year:

> I don't know that it was a real good idea to come in as a democratic leader the very first year before I got a reading of the staff. There was a perception that I didn't want to make decisions, that I couldn't make decisions, that I didn't want to accept the responsibility for decisions. (Blase and colleagues)

Other schools may have a strong tradition of faculty involvement so that even seemingly routine decisions should involve subordinates.

2. Not all decisions are equal. Many involve issues that are trivial or that don't directly affect classroom teaching. These can often be disposed of in a hierarchical way with the full approval of the staff. Others have direct consequences for the work that is most important to teachers; these usually call for more participative approaches.

More importantly, there are different kinds of problems. Ronald Heifetz notes that some problems are well defined and the solution is clear; the decision is technical in nature and can be made by anyone with appropriate expertise. In other cases, the problem may be well understood, but there is no obvious solution. Here Heifetz would suggest a more participative approach, if only because the leader doesn't have the answer. In still other cases, the problem itself may be poorly understood—for example, a faculty becomes concerned over an increasingly negative tone in student attitudes. In such cases, says Heifetz, organizations will have to collectively "learn their way forward."

3. Strategic choices also have to strike the proper balance between product and process. Leaders have a dual obligation: to achieve the goals of the organization and to nurture the people responsible for fulfilling them. At times, those obligations clash. No matter how much principals

may want to empower their teachers, there are times when school goals take precedence. According to one principal:

> My responsibility as a principal really is to the children, and if I see areas that are ineffective, I've got to say that we're not effective here and that we have got to change. I think it's my responsibility to be an instructional leader by helping teachers make informed decisions within particular guidelines of good education. (Blase and colleagues).

At times, the choice between process and product will reflect philosophical positions. For example, Blase and colleagues take the position that it is inherently good for schools to be run democratically. On the other hand, Conley and Goldman argue that the goal is not workplace democracy, but enhancing student learning.

4. Leaders should be alert to the possibility that the same action can serve more than one strategy. Deal and Peterson, who believe that a balanced strategy is essential, urge principals to develop the kind of "bifocal vision" that makes the most of any opportunity. Supervising bus arrivals, for example, serves an obvious hierarchical function, but it also presents an opportunity for greeting students, establishing visibility, assessing the social climate, and reinforcing key school values.

Conclusion

To be a leader is to act, and this chapter has reminded us of the enormous differences in the ways leaders act, differences that are in part due to their psychological makeup, in part to the conscious choices they make in pursuit of organizational goals. It's a delicate balancing act at times, trying to take the pushes in one direction and the pulls from the opposite direction, and hope that the result isn't a stalemate.

What gives it all coherence is the leader's sense of purpose. Blumberg tells the story of the sculptor who explains that the statue is already somewhere in the block of stone; his job is to chip away the parts that don't belong. Blumberg says the same applies to education. "It's as though for every school building, there's a beautiful school in there somewhere and, if you keep on chipping away, you'll find it. But you have to know what you're looking for."

CHAPTER

3

Developing School Leaders

Larry Lashway and Mark Anderson

Dip into almost any chapter in this book, and you'll discover that school leadership calls for a special kind of person. Everyone may have some leadership potential, but relatively few people can step into the role of a principal and carry it out with energy, vision, and finesse.

How to find, nurture, and keep those special people is a major priority for any school district, particularly as large numbers of veteran administrators continue to retire. Adding to the urgency is a dramatic rethinking of the entire educational enterprise that promises "new paradigms" and "revolutions" and raises the question of whether even the best traditional practices will produce leaders who are up to the job. And, whether one is looking at traditional programs or twenty-first century possibilities, there is the knowledge that school leadership still does not fully represent the diversity of the population.

This chapter looks at the school's responsibility for developing leaders, with a particular emphasis on the principalship. It takes the position that school districts have a broad responsibility for developing leaders that goes beyond simply hiring the best candidate. School districts also have a role to play in attracting the best people to the profession, giving them state-of-the-art training, and providing continuing support for their professional growth and development.

Attracting the Best: The Pipeline Problem

For most schools, thinking about leadership begins when the vacancy occurs. That may well be too late, since the choices will be limited to whatever candidates happen to be available.

Consider the dilemma of the district that sincerely and actively seeks to add diversity to its administrative team: No matter how aggressive the recruiting, it can't find the right people if they're not in the applicant pool. At best, recruitment is a zero-sum game; one school's gain is another school's loss. The only long-range solution is to increase the number of outstanding candidates, including women and minorities, who want to become administrators.

Although it's less obvious, the same problem exists with the entire pool. For all practical purposes, principal candidates are self-selected. A teacher who wakes up one morning and says "I want to become a principal" needs little more than tuition and a decent academic record to get into a preparation program. If it's a good program, the future principal may emerge with the values and skills to be an effective leader—but he or she will emerge, regardless.

The metaphor often used is that of a pipeline. Somewhere up the line, administrative aspirants make the decisions that get them into the system; at the other end, schools turn on the tap and wait to see what comes out. In recent years, however, some proactive districts have tried to intervene much earlier in the process.

Early Recruitment

One critical opportunity comes long before college, when students first begin to think seriously about careers.

Admittedly, as Catherine Marshall and Katherine Kasten note, "Few 6-year-olds say, 'When I grow up, I want to be a principal'." But many of them do want to be teachers. Since almost all principals come from the ranks of teachers, recruiting talented people for teaching will ultimately benefit administration.

Schools have an enviable advantage when it comes to career recruitment: a captive audience that sees the job being modeled every day, that knows firsthand the impact teachers can have, and that leans toward idealism. Yet most schools fail to seize the opportunity and may even send messages that discourage young people from thinking about teaching. One exceptional elementary teacher recalls how her counselors kept pushing her toward business because, in their words, "You have too much talent to be a teacher."

James Delisle laments, "In both my university and in many K-12 schools, a career in education is considered the lowest of the low in terms of professions that matter. And the people one would assume to be most enthusiastic about what they do—educators themselves—are often the field's most vocal opponents." Fortunately, many teachers counteract these messages by encouraging young people's interest in teaching.

Many schools have found that they can go beyond serendipitous messages by offering formal opportunities for students to explore their interest in teaching. Harriet Hunter-Boykin describes a number of programs that combine high school coursework, practicum experiences, career counseling, mentoring, job shadowing, and training in study skills for students who express an interest in teaching. Similarly, Anne Lewis tells of a highly successful statewide effort in South Carolina, where the Teacher Cadet program operates in more than half of the state's high schools.

Many of these programs are especially designed to attract minority students on the premise that early involvement will set them on a path to the classroom. In the first three years of the Teaching Professions Program in Washington, D.C., between 50 and 73 percent of participating students maintained their interest through graduation, with most entering teacher-education programs in college (Hunter-Boykin).

Making the Transition from Teaching

Schools can also influence the thinking of classroom teachers whose careers are still in the formative stage. Every staff has natural leaders, skilled teachers who are committed to students and who can work collaboratively to elevate the quality of teaching in the whole school. If these talented people can be persuaded to enter administration, the profession will gain.

To determine how, we have to ask what leads teachers to become administrators. This is actually a two-part question. First, we need to know what motivates teachers to dream of principalships. What do they hope to gain? The second, less obvious, part is How do they come to make the decision? What moves them at a particular time and place to head in such a different direction?

Leadership Motivation

Stephen Jacobson notes that administration has traditionally attracted teachers for several reasons. First, it promises an expanded working year with increased salary and benefits. Second, it offers an "escape" from the classroom for those who don't enjoy teaching. Third, it attracts the ambitious (those who enjoy power and status) by offering a hierarchy with a clearly marked upward path. However, for teachers whose professional life centers on teaching and learning, "school administration as presently conceived offers little in the way of inducement," says Jacobson.

This traditional perception may partially explain the low numbers of women in administration. In her interviews with female administrators, Sakre Edson found that most were motivated by a combination of wanting a challenge, believing in their own abilities, and wanting to help students. Charol Shakeshaft likewise argues that women are more likely to be committed to teaching as an activity, and Patricia Kleine found that even after entering administration, many women seek positions that will keep them closer to the classroom or involved with instructional issues (for example, the elementary principalship or curriculum coordinator).

Whether this is purely a gender distinction, or partly a generational difference, is not yet clear, since most recent research has focused on women. But it does seem likely that many teachers screen themselves out because they see administration as taking them too far from the classroom, something requiring them to become "paper-pushers" or to "play politics."

These dedicated teachers might be attracted to administration if they could see it as a different way of fulfilling their professional mission. One assistant principal told Edson: "After teaching for a few years, it dawned on me that the person in charge sets the tone for the curriculum, discipline or whatever. Instead of just affecting the lives of the children I saw each year, I could affect many, many more children if I were in charge. And things would go the way I wanted them to go."

Some teachers reach this conclusion on their own, but others would benefit from exposure to the right kind of role model: a principal who is willing to engage teachers in collaborative dialogue to find the best ways of meeting the needs of children. Teachers without such models are likely to conclude that administration is not for them.

(Ironically, role models that are blatantly negative can sometimes lead teachers to take the plunge. One of Edson's interviewees said, "I'm sorry, but most of these male administrators are just jocks! They don't know anything about public relations or faculties or curriculum. And kids? You never hear them mention kids! That's why I want to be an administrator." This is not generally recommended as a recruitment technique, however.)

One positive development in recent years has been the trend toward collaborative and facilitative strategies of leadership that put teachers in decision-making roles. As they start to see the relationship between organizational decisions and student learning, and also start to sense their own potential for bringing about change, they may be more inclined to consider formal leadership roles.

The Tap on the Shoulder

Recognizing administration as an attractive occupation is one thing; actually making the decision to become a principal is something else. Career decisions are never as logical or as inevitable as they may seem in retrospect; many moves are unplanned and spontaneous, and even people with well-defined goals don't know when the right opportunity will come along.

Edson found a variety of things that spurred her subjects to take action. Some, from the beginning aware that teaching wouldn't always be fulfilling, were actively looking for opportunities. Some were responding to life changes, such as divorce, and wanted a fresh start. Some were stimulated by taking graduate courses.

One especially important stimulus was being approached by someone in a leadership position and being encouraged to join the ranks:

> I had never thought about administration until my principal pointed out that as a specialist I was really managing a part of the school. He thought I should consider a principalship, because I had organizational skills and could handle money, resources and people well. I looked into it right away. But I would never have thought of a principalship if he hadn't shown confidence in me and my skills in the first place.

Marshall and Kasten say this "tap on the shoulder" can be a crucial moment in the development of a career. Being asked to join the ranks provides confidence that the goal is achievable, and it also holds out the exciting possibility of a mentor who will ease the way.

If nothing else, simply asking the question plants a seed that may blossom later. One high school teacher recalls sitting in the library as a college sophomore when his English instructor came up behind him, gave him a little shove, and said, "You! You ought to be a teacher!"—and walked off, leaving him nonplused. He had never considered teaching, and she never mentioned it again, but that single comment set off a chain of decisions that led him, a few years later, to his own English classroom.

Not every tap is that literal, but anecdotal evidence suggests this sort of personal invitation is a fairly common prelude to leadership. Unfortunately, the call is not evenly distributed. According to Marshall and Kasten, "sponsors are more likely to identify with and support protégé(e)s who are very much like themselves in values, gender, ethnicity, social and cultural backgrounds, and behaviors." Because there are fewer women and minorities in administration, fewer women and minorities are likely to get the call.

Whatever the reason, the usual informal networks do not seem effective in promoting leadership diversity. For example, Gloria Murray and colleagues surveyed twenty-six African-American teachers and found that while twenty-two of them expressed an interest in administration, only four said they had ever been approached by anyone, and twenty-three were not aware of any special preparation programs that might help them get to that goal.

However, the "tap" can be institutionalized, as in South Carolina's Minority Administrators Program (MAP), which has involved hundreds of minority educators since 1986. MAP candidates (who are usually within

a year of gaining certification) are accepted to the program after structured interviews and rated on communication skills, judgment, and administrative potential. Once in the program, they meet monthly for a combination of presentations, cases studies, panel discussions, and reflection. They receive career and professional counseling, develop individual growth plans, and benefit by having their names distributed to state school districts (Thomas Thompson).

Another effective approach was Arizona's "Castle Hot Springs" program, which trained 238 women for administrative positions over a five-year period. The workshop agenda was built primarily around activities that simulated a job search. It also taught skills such as interviewing for a job and writing a resumé. According to Christa Metzger, the program "changed the attitudes of potential and current women administrators about their own worth and their career opportunities." Significantly, by 1984 almost 50 percent of new (first- and second-year) Arizona principals were graduates of the workshop.

Yet another example, described by Mark Anderson, comes from the David Douglas School District in Portland, Oregon, which uses its STAR (Selecting and Training Administrative Recruits) program for identifying, recruiting, and training prospective principals from within the district's teacher corps.

The first phase involves a series of ten weekly afterwork classes about educational administration, specific to the district, focusing on both the frustrations and the joys of contending with a principal's role. Aspiring principals are oriented to the principal's role in coordinating programs, improving instruction, and managing buildings.

Phase 2 includes a week-long practicum experience, using mentor relationships. Interested candidates also attend an assessment center for evaluation and training. Finally, promising candidates are placed in formal internships.

Anderson notes the program has proved helpful for teachers who have already decided to become administrators, as well as those looking for advice. The program also tells employees the district values their competence and is interested in supporting their professional growth and career development.

Training Principals

If administrator-training programs were movies, the reviews would be unanimous: "two thumbs down." Over the years, critics have strained for adjectives to express their low opinion: "dismal," "dysfunctional," and "zombie" are typical epithets. Joseph Murphy has summarized the long list of specific complaints:

- little effort to weed out poor candidates
- an ill-defined knowledge base with few standards
- minimal academic rigor
- a fragmented curriculum
- lack of connection to the world of practice
- uninspired instructional methods
- poorly regarded faculty
- lack of diversity in students and faculty
- reliance on an academic rather than professional model
- a part-time student body that is tired, distracted, and pressed for time

Without a doubt, the most common complaint is the lack of relevance to real life in schools. Edwin Bridges explains why. Whereas principals' work is fast-paced and unpredictable, academic work is leisurely and ordered. Whereas principals' work depends on face-to-face communication, academic work is mostly solitary. Whereas principals' work is filled with emotional engagement, academic work is intellectual and neutral. The result, he argues, is "trained incapacity."

Not all the voices are negative, however. Arthur Blumberg takes a more benign view, agreeing with Bridges that programs don't directly teach job-related skills, but speculating that may be an unrealistic goal. Blumberg sees school leadership as a craft, something necessarily learned through experience; there is no way a graduate school can duplicate the "feel" of real work.

Rather, academic programs provide a perspective, a way of looking at and talking about the work of a principal. As one of Blumberg's subjects said, "I got handles for things and I was able to describe things for myself and, more importantly, I was able to describe events to others in that language and that helps me understand it better for myself." In other words, graduate school may provide a philosophical grounding that will influence many of the administrator's later decisions.

Calls for Reform

Calls for the reform of administrator training are old news. What's different about the current environment, says David Seeley, is an imminent paradigm shift in goals (toward adequate education for all children) as well as process (toward a collaborative rather than bureaucratic instructional system). Because of this change, "it will take extraordinary leadership, and leadership of a different kind from what we have had in the past, to ensure the transition of the American public school system from the lumbering dinosaur it has become to the effective mobilizer and developer of human capacities that [it] must become in the future." What makes this leadership doubly difficult is that the transition requires not only expertise in the new paradigm, but the simultaneous ability to run schools under the old paradigm.

Murphy agrees, citing a growing sense that education is on the brink of major shifts in philosophy and practices. One doesn't have to look far down the road to see new learning paradigms, new relations between the school and its clients, new forms of organization, and new metaphors for school leadership.

Responding to these new conditions, Murphy says, will require comprehensive reform of preparation programs. Programs must establish new goals, including a new emphasis on values, a focus on education rather than management, the development of critical-inquiry skills, and an understanding of the human condition. The curriculum should emphasize depth over breadth, focus on authentic problems of practice, and develop the capacity to learn rather than accumulate information. Instructional methods should be student-centered, action-oriented, team-building, and outcome-based.

These are not small changes, and some observers have expressed skepticism that education schools can rise to the occasion. Lars Björk and Rick Ginsberg argue that previous reform efforts have accomplished little because universities have settled for minor changes rather than fundamental reform. True reform would require a paradigm shift: sharing control, redesigning institutional reward structures, and redefining educational administration as a field. They suggest such major changes are not likely to succeed in established departments with strongly entrenched interests but in new programs that can be built from the ground up.

A more hopeful view is supplied by the Danforth Foundation, which in 1987 launched a five-year project with twenty-two carefully selected universities aimed at developing innovative programs in cooperation with local school districts. Participants reported a variety of successful changes, including expanded internships, mentoring programs, cohort groups, and collaboration with local practitioners who served as mentors, advisors, instructors, and curriculum developers. They also listed advantages such as better integrated coursework, enriched content, and better instruction.

In addition, they were successful in recruiting a diverse group of students, including 22 percent African-American and 8 percent Hispanic-American, as well as 74 percent female (Paula Cordeiro and colleagues).

Reviewing these programs, Kenneth Leithwood found positive results. Graduates found the programs to be valuable (ranking 3.46 on a 4-point scale, about halfway between "somewhat" and "extremely valuable"). In addition, colleagues of the graduates (peers and teachers) rated them as effective leaders (3.47 on a 4-point scale). More importantly, Leithwood found a significant statistical relationship between effectiveness and the specific features of these innovative programs. He concluded that formal preparation makes a noticeable difference when built around robust, relevant theories and instructional methods that lead to practical skills.

As usual with externally funded programs, it is uncertain how long they will survive beyond the funding period, or whether they are feasible without such funding. But the results offer hope that new approaches can work.

What Do Good Preparation Programs Look Like?

No single model stands out as clearly superior. But effective programs are likely to have many of the elements described below.

Bridging the Gap Between Theory and Practice

Good programs will use instructional strategies that simultaneously provide students with a solid theoretical framework and a practical understanding of real-world problems. For example, in problem-based learning (Edwin Bridges and Philip Hallinger), students are presented with a detailed description of a realistic leadership problem and a set of related readings. They are then divided into teams and given nine to fifteen hours in which they must frame the problem (which is usually messy and ill-defined), decide how to use the knowledge gained from the readings, and arrive at a solution. During this process, the instructor plays a limited role ("a guide on the side" rather than "a sage on the stage").

Bridges and Hallinger maintain that students are more likely to learn when they are encouraged to relate new ideas to their current knowledge; when they are given many opportunities to apply the new information; and when they learn the new knowledge in contexts similar to those in which it will be used.

Anderson describes other "bridging" strategies. In performance simulations, students must respond to life-like situations (inbasket exercises, group activities, stress exercises, and supervisory simulations). Organizational, institutional, and business games ask trainees to make sequential decisions and then live with them. The common element in these approaches is the use of appropriate theoretical constructs without losing the flavor of real-life challenges.

New Delivery Systems

It's a familiar scenario for anyone who has taken certification courses: At 7:00 p.m. every Wednesday, a group of would-be administrators gathers in a university classroom to hear a lecture or participate in a rambling discussion. Tired after a long day of teaching, preoccupied with tomorrow's lesson, still digesting a hastily gulped dinner, the participants take notes, make a few comments, and keep wondering if something is wrong with the clock.

Administrative education typically takes place in the margins of the day, when both students and professors are at low ebb. But schools such as the University of Oregon are experimenting with new patterns of instruction. In Oregon's program, a cohort of two dozen students spends the first year in a series of weekend seminars devoted to discussion, reflection, team-building, and presentations on subjects such as organizational culture, change, and conflict. The summer is spent in a series of courses focusing on legal issues, budgeting, and other practical concerns. The final year, each student is teamed with a practitioner mentor and offered internship experiences, along with five twenty-hour seminars. In evaluating the program, Richard Schmuck notes graduates are better able to articulate their philosophy than traditional graduates; have more favorable attitudes toward the program; have double the normal success rate in finding administrative jobs; and perform well during their first year.

Field-Based Experience

Another way of bridging the gap between theory and practice is field-based experience, such as interviewing administrators, designing a staff inservice plan, conducting a teacher evaluation, attending regional or state conferences, or shadowing principals for a day or two.

More extended field experiences may involve indepth projects that require the aspirant to conduct a real-world project, such as initiating a new inservice procedure, improving a school's discipline or attendance procedure, developing a volunteer-recognition program, or improving curriculum articulation within a school.

Field-based activities work best when scheduled throughout a candidate's program (not just at the end), and they require close collaboration between universities and school districts. The best activities are those that enable students to see how theoretical or technical aspects of school administration can be put into practice. Ideally, the assignment should ask students to bring about some change. For maximum value, experiences should be accompanied by the opportunity for discussion and reflection (Anderson).

Internships

The capstone of a good preparation program is a carefully designed and supervised internship in which aspiring principals are placed in a school and asked to function as a principal. Getting certified without an internship is akin to getting a driver's license without behind-the-wheel experience. Hands-on involvement captures the job as no classroom presentation can.

However, internships in principal preparation have had a rocky history. The primary problem is financial. Aspiring principals are usually full-time teachers; a true internship normally means they must take an unpaid leave of at least a semester. Some schools agree to finance such leaves, but this option has become increasingly rare in the face of reduced education budgets. As a result, many candidates end up with minimal internships (a few weeks, grabbed at opportune moments) or scattered experiences that are only a pale imitation of the real thing.

In addition, internships have often been conducted on the premise that experience alone is sufficient, a point disputed by John Daresh (October 1987). On the basis of his study of beginning principals, he believes aspiring administrators need to spend a great deal of time reflecting on and analyzing the skills they learn in the field and the activities in which they are engaged. "Practice without reflection," he notes, "is not of great value to learning anything." Mike Milstein, summarizing results of the Danforth experience, agrees, saying "the more students can explore meaning through reflection with peers and others, the more that they can make sense of their experiences." He recommends weekly or biweekly reflection sessions.

One exemplary program is run by Brigham Young University in collaboration with five Utah school districts and the National Association of Secondary School Principals. Candidates are carefully screened (including formal recommendation from the school district) and placed in a 1,400-hour internship divided into three phases at different schools and grade levels. The interns spend four days a week in the field, under the direction of a mentor principal, and one day a week at Brigham Young, participating in classes and seminars. NASSP contributes several problem-oriented workshops emphasizing decision-making and communication. In addition, interns develop a portfolio used for reflection and evaluation (Ivan Muse and E. Vance Randall).

The Brigham Young model, financially supported by the Danforth Foundation and the school districts, may be beyond the reach of most programs; even among Danforth schools, the average internship is only 600-700 hours. However, the key ingredients can be applied even to scaled-down versions of the program: sufficient time-on-task in challenging situations; multiple experiences at different sites and levels; well-trained mentors and supervisors; and time for reflection (Milstein).

Getting Involved

Over the years, school districts have been somewhat passive partners in training programs, but the climate is changing. School districts can become actively involved in a number of ways. First, they can seek input into the development and implementation of university training programs. Practitioners can provide a critical source of guidance as graduate schools seek to integrate theory and practice. Some states, such as Wisconsin and Washington, now require training programs to establish advisory committees of practitioners; even in states where this isn't the case, school leaders can offer advice informally.

Second, K-12 practitioners are often recruited to teach courses or serve as mentors. Administrators can have a satisfying and significant influence on the next generation of principals this way. Florida State University, for example, has established a successful "visiting clinical professor" program, in which outstanding school leaders spend a week on campus, giving presentations, leading discussions, and answering questions (Joseph Beckham).

Third, districts can offer internships and other field-based opportunities for aspiring administrators. According to Deanna Gordon and Margaret Moles, an intern brings new ideas and perspectives into the school and puts the mentor in touch with the latest educational thinking. Because interns are viewing the school as outsiders, their questions and opinions can provide a fresh look at "business as usual," as mentors are forced to reflect on their practice and explain the assumptions that guide their decisions.

Finally, districts may offer release time for internships to promising administrative candidates. Because of the financial implications, this is a difficult proposition, and smaller districts with few openings may wonder about the wisdom of supporting a candidate who is likely to end up in another district. However, support can be provided in a variety of ways:

sabbatical leaves, personal leaves, tuition stipends, and reduced-duty assignments. If nothing else, a sincere willingness to work through the logistics with prospective administrators will send a positive message about a critical part of leadership training.

Finding the Right Person

Vacant principalships confront school districts with a serious decision that will have far-reaching implications. The person selected will have a major impact on the quality of school life for teachers, students, and parents, and may end up influencing policy and practice in the district for decades to come. Yet, faced with this prospect, many districts seem content to follow one simple rule: "Post it, and they will come."

In a study of hiring practices, D. Catherine Baltzell and Robert Dentler found that "educational leadership is not a well specified or widely applied criterion for selecting principals." Instead, selectors in many districts seem to rely on vaguely stated notions of "good fit," which often turn out to be characteristics such as physical size, grooming, and values compatible with community expectations. In essence, "most districts operate essentially closed selection procedures for principalships," resulting in applicant pools that are relatively small and not too different from current school leaders. While these methods "do succeed in fending off or weeding out grossly unqualified candidates," the selection of highly meritorious applicants is often the result of "chance."

Baltzell and Dentler argue that these restricted procedures are not the result of laziness or ineptitude, but instead come from superintendents' efforts to juggle a multitude of conflicting pressures and priorities. Superintendents manage their systems through the work of principals; critical areas such as parent relationships, student discipline, and union negotiations can easily erupt into crisis if principals fail to act judiciously and in synch with district priorities. District leaders thus have a vested interest in ensuring that the applicant pool consists of people who will work comfortably within the system. Consequently, leadership competency becomes only one element among many calculations.

Shakeshaft sees selectors as applying a progressive series of "filters" to the candidate pool, gradually shaping it to match their preconceived notions of what an administrator should look like. Such filters are not necessarily conscious, nor are they inherently illegitimate, since some kind of filtering is needed to find the best candidate. Rather, the challenge is to use the right kind of filters at the right time. The remainder of this section examines ways that districts can do this.

Vacancy Notices

The first filter is the declaration of a vacancy, which involves much more than a simple announcement. Every notice should reflect a conscious, informed judgment about the kind of person needed. Not every district will be looking for the same qualities; not every school has the same characteristics and culture.

Daniel Duke and Edward Iwanicki say the success of principals depends not just on competence, but on "fit." That is, when the principal's role expectations match the expectations of significant stakeholders, success is more likely. The more clearly a district identifies the expectations it holds, the better able it is to choose the right person; in turn, candidates are better able to decide whether the position is right for them.

Thus, if the district wants a principal with special expertise in teacher evaluation, it should clearly say so; if it wants an administrator who can operate in a facilitative manner, it should say that. Generic announcements draw generic candidates.

Of course, vacancies don't always occur in a predictable or timely way, as Baltzell and Dentler note, and many superintendents find ways to subvert official posting requirements to give themselves as much flexibility as possible. The authors urge districts to develop formal apprenticeship and training programs (such as the ones described earlier in this chapter) so well-qualified candidates are always at hand. However, they agree that identifying specific criteria for selection is crucial.

Recruitment

For many districts, publishing job announcements is simple and routine: an internal posting, a letter to the nearest university placement center, perhaps a small ad in the local paper. Aggressive school districts know that at this point in the process they should cast as wide a net as possible. The U.S. Department of Education's *Principal Selection Guide* recommends making announcements in large city newspapers within a 500-mile radius. In addition, search committees should advertise in education newsletters and journals, and through professional associations. "The most important thing," says the guide, "is to avoid a narrow search that ends too soon."

Networking can also add strength to the applicant pool. Sharing information informally with contacts in other districts, universities, and state associations will help get word out to people who may not be actively seeking a new position but would respond positively to the right opportunity.

This kind of informal recruitment runs the risk of perpetuating unconscious images of "the right kind of person." Recruiters should actively seek out new networks, not just the comfortable channels that have been used in the past. This is particularly true when districts wish to add diversity to their leadership team.

Screening

No district has time to interview all the applicants for a position, which means someone must sift the applications to find those worthy of an interview. This is a critical part of the process, since the screeners must make complex judgments based on a rather skimpy collection of documents. There is always the danger of prematurely eliminating good candidates or, conversely, letting subpar candidates slip through the screen.

The first filter in this phase is rather routine and can be performed by the personnel office: eliminating any applicants who do not meet the minimum specified standards. If the announcement calls for five years of experience, then those with only three or four will be eliminated; if the position demands a particular license, those lacking it can be set aside.

While this is a straightforward process, it shows why the initial list of specifications is so important. If an announcement asks for previous building-level experience (simply because it has always done so), it may automatically eliminate some otherwise highly capable candidates.

The second part of the process is more difficult; there is no science of resumé reading and no list of rules. Instead, it requires mature human judgment, a deep knowledge of school environments, and the ability to read between the lines. We know relatively little about how screeners make their decisions, though anecdotal evidence suggests a process of elimination in which they look for "red flags" that may signal problems: a lukewarm letter of recommendation, a pattern of job-hopping, a sloppily packaged application.

Because screening is inherently subjective, districts should consider several approaches that can provide a more balanced view. Baltzell and Dentler believe school districts should involve staff members, students, community members, and administrators in the selection process. When decisions are made by a small, tightly knit group, they often suffer from "groupthink"—the tendency to develop shared assumptions, mutual reinforcement, and collective blind spots. Broad-based involvement can combat the "groupthink" syndrome, as well as create trust in the process.

When a group does the screening, members can use a standardized ranking system to judge each applicant's file systematically. Exemplary districts have screeners conduct blind ratings of each candidate, assigning a numerical score to each candidate's lengthy application and reference documentation.

Alternative Sources of Information

Some districts, not satisfied with the usual resumé/transcript/recommendations package, seek to generate other information on candidates.

Written Assessments

A number of districts require some type of written communication as part of the selection process. Writing assignments serve a dual purpose. Most obviously, they provide good evidence about a candidate's written communication skills, which are especially important in someone who will represent the district as the model of an educated person.

In addition, asking for short written essays may give insights into candidates' philosophies or their views on bringing about change. While these questions can also be asked during interviews, a written exercise makes it more difficult for applicants to shape their answers by reading body language and playing to the audience.

Assessment Centers

The standard application paperwork doesn't really address the critical question: How will this person perform? Applicants who are shrewd or verbally adept can often raise an impressive smoke screen that obscures the important issues.

One screening alternative is the use of NASSP skill-assessment centers, initially established in the 1970s and since shown to be an effective, powerful tool for making judgments about administrative expertise.

By putting candidates through a variety of simulations, the assessment center helps districts pinpoint potential principals' specific strengths and weaknesses in a dozen job-related areas: problem analysis, judgment, organizational ability, decisiveness, leadership, sensitivity, stress tolerance, oral communication, written communication, range of interests, personal motivation, and educational values. The result is a twelve-dimensional profile of each candidate, which can be used for professional development as well as screening.

M. Claradine Johnson and Rex Douglas point out that assessment centers are especially valuable for female and minority administrators; they report that "several of the women who received promotions as a result of the center experience indicated that data provided by the center represented the only evidence of administrative skills in their credentials." Such experience not only offers the participants useful job preparation, but also gives them a chance to measure their real desire for the job in light of the actual responsibilities and pressures involved.

Interviews

The final filter in almost every case is a personal interview. Despite evidence that interviews are often poorly conducted and overly influential (Anderson), they can play a crucial role as long as selectors approach them systematically, seeking evidence that the desired criteria are present and not forgetting evidence that has been obtained in other parts of the process. A more detailed description of exemplary practices can be found in chapter 11.

The Key

In the second phase of their study, Baltzell and Dentler located a number of districts that had developed exemplary practices by using clear criteria and systematic processes. The result? Less cronyism, more diversity, and greater credibility. "Furthermore," they add, "those changes appear to ramify widely across other features of local school systems, raising levels of staff morale, improving the quality and efficiency of service, and upgrading the learning opportunities for students."

In every case, the exemplary districts had made a conscious commitment to improve the selection of school leaders, a commitment that was backed by the school board and executed in good faith by the superintendent. The changes took years to assimilate and required expenditures of money and time, but the long-term results were tangible.

Inducting Principals

When it comes to developing administrative skill, school leaders are apt to fall back on the cliché "There's no substitute for experience." Most can tell war stories about the first year on the job, when they felt overwhelmed and underprepared, and wondered if they had made a horrible mistake. Only gradually, through trial and error, did they develop a sense of direction and a feeling of confidence.

Some of these tribulations are inevitable, but many result from a laissez-faire approach to leadership development. Too often, schools hire a promising candidate and assume that experience alone will provide the seasoning. All too rarely is there an effort to monitor how administrators are responding to the experience or to provide opportunities to shape that experience.

The Trials of the First Year

No matter how good a leader's preparation, the first year is qualitatively different from anything previously experienced. The activities and issues may be the same as those experienced during the internship, but they come faster and harder, and they are intensified by the knowledge that the training wheels are off the bike: any mistakes will result in real scrapes and bruises. Several features of the first year seem to be especially troublesome.

Isolation

For many beginners, the extreme isolation of the principalship comes as a shock. Aside from some brief orientations, many districts simply give newly hired principals the keys to the building, in effect saying, "Have a nice year." Without guidance, newcomers often make serious mistakes.

Robert Nelson, in a study of beginning administrators in Northwest districts, noted the newcomers were isolated and had "little opportunity to collaborate in their new position." Daresh (April 1987) documented similar feelings of isolation and lack of collegial support among principals he studied in the Midwest.

Technical Problems

Technical skills are another hurdle. Each day is filled with mundane tasks that require learning a whole new language. New principals must grapple with such concerns as how to fill out state-required reports, how to set up for assemblies and lunch, how to address various legal issues, and how to operate the bells, clocks, and firebells. One principal remembers:

> When it came time to do budgeting, I opened that sucker up [the budget printout] and looked at all that stuff. It was like Greek. I didn't have a clue, not a clue, as to where to start. You talk about codes. It is written in code, and I had to take a great deal of time just to learn how to decipher it. (Anderson)

Getting To Know the School System

A third area of concern for new principals is understanding the particular culture of their new school system. Both Daresh and Nelson found beginners had difficulty learning the unstated role expectations connected with their position. For example, one principal told Daresh he felt rather foolish after following the procedures for requesting new equipment. Going by the book, he asked the assistant superintendent in charge of administrative services. Only after getting no response did he discover that the real procedure was to deal directly with the director of buildings and grounds. The assistant superintendent was too busy dealing with other matters that were not listed as his responsibility in the policy manual.

Many new principals realize there may be discrepancies between the policy manual and actual practice, but their isolation from peers makes it difficult to get good advice. Newcomers may also feel embarrassed to ask what may seem to be obvious or simple questions.

Lack of Feedback

Beginning principals also report lack of feedback on how they are doing. Performance evaluations by superiors can provide useful guidance, but many beginners report such performance feedback is infrequent and, when done, not specific or helpful. Daresh says of the beginning principals with whom he spoke, "They never knew if they were really doing what was considered to be a good job, and no one in their schools or districts appeared inclined to provide much feedback or direction to help them understand how they were doing."

According to Shakeshaft, lack of honest feedback is a particular problem for women. When women fail to perform well, male superiors may be reluctant to give them the same kind of candid response they would give to other men. As a result, women don't get a fair chance to improve their performance. Because of continuing self-consciousness and awkwardness about race relations, the same analysis likely applies to ethnic minorities.

The Atypical Principal

While American schools continue to make progress in building a more inclusive leadership cadre, most people still visualize the typical administrator as a white male. Consequently, minorities and females continue to find themselves in the role of pioneer—a status that can add to the loneliness felt by every newcomer.

Betty Jones, describing the dilemma of "the only one," says such pioneers suffer from "a surplus of visibility." They are invariably seen not just as individuals but as representatives of a group. Thus they find themselves automatically drafted by committees that want "the woman's view" or "the African-American perspective," and, at the same time, members of their own group may expect them to carry the flag in a very public way. Combined with professional isolation and continuing (if subtle) discrimination, this visibility can create enormous pressure.

Even experienced leaders who have made it to the top are not immune from feeling some ambivalence about their atypical status. Susan Chase, in her study of twenty-seven female superintendents, found most of them were very aware of discrimination, could talk with feeling about it, and had developed different ways of dealing with it, ranging from gentle enlightenment to hard-nosed lawsuits. But they weren't able to treat it as just another problem. For example, while a female superintendent might walk into a meeting of mostly male peers and freely talk about a problem she is having with a recalcitrant board member, she would not feel comfortable sharing a problem about sex discrimination. Chase concluded there was a real "disjuncture" between purely professional issues and the issues arising from gender and ethnicity.

The Socialization Process

As a result of these pressures, the growth of newcomers is highly variable, and very likely dependent on whatever level of readiness they bring with them. Forrest Parkay and colleagues, observing a dozen new high school principals for three years, were able to identify five stages, stretching from "survival" to "professional actualization." The survival-oriented principal is in shock, feels besieged, and is trying desperately to sort everything out. The turmoil lessens somewhat in stage 2 ("control"), as the principal looks for ways to assert control and establish priorities. In this stage, he or she is more likely to rely on coercive power than on persuasion.

In the third stage ("stability"), effective routines have been established, and the principal is beginning to feel comfortable in the role. Leadership in this stage still tends to be "custodial"—aimed at keeping things running smoothly rather than bringing about major changes. However, in the fourth stage ("educational leadership") the principal is beginning to focus on curriculum and instruction, relying more on personal authority than coercive power. The final stage is "professional actualization," in which the principal is working toward a long-range vision through empowerment of teachers.

Not all principals progressed through all five stages in an orderly way. At the end of three years, only one had progressed from stage 1 through stage 5, and one was still mired in the first stage; one principal, though, had consistently operated in stages 4 and 5 from the beginning. Significantly, the authors note that progress by the end of the first year accurately foreshadowed development over the next two years.

One lesson, then, is that experience alone was not enough for all the new principals. Some had (or developed) the necessary inner resources;

others bogged down. Moreover, the newcomers had to suspend their ambitious plans for change while they struggled to assert control over daily routines. As they moved into stage 4, however, they began to put those dreams into operation. Clearly, a district that wants successful, change-oriented leaders should be ready to provide help.

Promising Induction Programs

A growing number of schools are no longer willing to settle for the sink-or-swim approach. Instead, they provide a structured, systematic process for on-the-job learning. The best of these programs are designed to ease some of the problems cited earlier. In particular, they seek to:

- Reduce isolation by providing regular contact with experienced peers
- Provide a "space" in the hectic work week in which the newcomer can consciously reflect on what is happening and why
- Provide systematic orientation on policies and procedures (official and unofficial)
- Provide regular feedback on the novice's performance

In short, effective induction programs structure the work environment in a way that allows the new principal to have a coherent experience, not just a chaotic barrage of experiences. They accomplish these aims in a number of ways.

Mentoring

One of the most common approaches is to use mentoring, a strategy that pairs veteran principals with rookies in a sort of "buddy system" that can take many forms. David Parks describes the possible roles of mentors this way:

> For principals, it means teaching leadership and management skills, nurturing the development of educational values, guiding the acquisition of political savvy, counseling in times of trouble, nourishing creativity, assisting with securing the first job, and advising on career, job, and personal decisions.

All this is done, he adds, "in an atmosphere of genuine caring for the learner."

Mentoring takes many forms. Sometimes it is spontaneous, as a new principal seeks out an esteemed college professor for advice, or a veteran takes the newcomer aside and explains the facts of organizational life. At other times, school districts initiate the relationship by formally pairing off veterans and novices, charging the senior partner with providing information, advice, and performance feedback.

Whether spontaneous or formal, such relationships can be critical, especially for women and minorities, who may face special pressures that make encouragement vital. Edson notes that mentors play a special role in providing the kind of experiences that develop skills and build confidence. One assistant principal said, "My principal has given me a wide variety of experiences. I've done curriculum, budgeting, discipline, attendance and end-of-the-year reports. I've had the run of the store several times; he just leaves it in my hands."

Anderson cautions schools to choose and train mentor principals carefully. Mentoring requires a delicate balance between giving advice and encouraging initiative:

> Untrained mentors may simply pass on ineffective practices to new principals, perpetuating traditional processes and norms that may need to change. Effective mentors, therefore, must not tell beginning principals what they should do, but instead guide newcomers so that they are able to make their own decisions, based on a thorough understanding of the potential consequences of their choices.

Finding effective mentors may be difficult, especially for small districts. Some form of interdistrict cooperation may be helpful, perhaps through the agency of educational service districts and professional associations.

Orienting Beginning Principals

A simple but meaningful induction strategy is to provide a comprehensive orientation program rather than simply handing out the keys. Scheduled presentations can give the newcomer a working understanding of the business office, transportation, maintenance, public relations, personnel, and other important offices. At the building level, principals should be informed about existing schedules, procedures, staff characteristics, and community expectations.

Orientations should not overwhelm the new principal with information, Anderson says, but must at least explain who or what to consult when information is needed. Barbara Von Villas urges outgoing administrators to leave a written handbook for their successors, covering such issues as budget information, record keeping, state reporting data, attendance procedures, and scheduling.

Structuring Beginners' Workload

Beginning principals have a lot to learn; they should spend most of their time in their buildings, learning to work with staff, students, and parents, and mastering the everyday routines. Thus, senior administrators should deflect committee assignments and special projects away from the newcomer until a basic comfort level has been established. Even veteran principals find these outside meetings distracting; new principals may find them overwhelming.

Providing Feedback

Beginning principals should be given detailed, constructive feedback on their performance, preferably beyond the formal evaluation done for accountability purposes. According to Anderson, feedback should focus on clear performance expectations embodying key organizational values. For example, if the school has a strong commitment to communicate with parents, the leader's performance in this area should be evaluated. To maintain trust, Anderson recommends a collegial supervisory process that emphasizes peer sharing, reflection, and goal-setting.

Encouraging Professional Growth

To help sort out the multitude of demands they face, newcomers should be encouraged to develop a plan for growth that includes specific learning objectives, activities to help in the development process, an implementation time line, and an evaluation plan.

Districts should also bring together beginning principals in reflective seminars to discuss their experiences and to offer suggestions for handling specific problems. Because most districts do not have enough beginning principals to create such peer interaction, cooperative arrangements between districts may be necessary. State professional associations, educational service districts, and even universities can assist in coordinating seminars that bring beginning principals together for supportive and reflective discussions.

Professional Growth and Career Development

For most districts, leadership development ends with the induction program. With a leader who is now well acclimated to the job and performing ably, they see little reason to do more.

Unfortunately, the conditions that create an ideal match between principal and school won't last forever. Says Daniel Duke (1993): "A profession is never mastered. Professionals grow older and face different life circumstance. Clients change. New research and technology appear. Social and political priorities are reordered."

Typically, districts leave it to principals to work their way through these changes and to direct their own continuing training and development. In the long run this laissez-faire approach may be costly, since not all leaders are effective self-developers (almost every superintendent can tell a story of a once-effective principal who "lost it" somewhere along the way). Underperforming principals present districts with the painful dilemma of what to do about loyal, aging employees who are on a glide path to mediocrity. On the other hand, principals who outgrow their jobs often resolve the dilemma by moving to other districts, taking their hard-earned expertise with them.

Districts that want to get the most from their administrators may need to become more involved by providing both challenge and support. To understand the possibilities, we must first examine two concepts: "the administrative career" and "professional growth."

The Administrative Career

Most people have come to expect that when they enter an occupation, they will not just find a position and stay there, but instead will move through a series of positions, steadily growing in knowledge, skills, and wisdom, while advancing in responsibility, salary, and prestige. The concept of career is a way of providing coherence to one's professional life, tying together experiences and events that might otherwise seem random and directionless.

The most common metaphor for careers is "climbing the ladder," a steady upward progression to the top ranks. This pattern is best known in the corporate world, but it also exists in school leadership. For reasons that range from money to altruism to sheer exuberance, some administrators enter the field with the intention of shooting to the top. One of Edson's interviewees confided, "Someday I would really like to be superintendent of public instruction for the state. I like to be in charge and would welcome the challenge. I need something bigger to do all the time."

Flora Ortiz has described the most typical progression: from teacher to assistant principal to high school principal to superintendent (in larger districts, a central-office position may come between the principalship and superintendency). Interestingly, the elementary principalship is not as common a route to the top.

But this pyramidal ladder does not completely define the administrative career. For one thing, there isn't enough room at the top for everyone; some administrators with ambitious goals will have to reconcile themselves to a career that plateaus at a lower level. Second, the ladder is based on male conceptions of careers that focus on a single-minded dash to the top. As Sari Biklen has noted, ambition is typically judged by the willingness to immerse oneself in the job, to the exclusion of all else. Women still carry a disproportionate share of child-rearing duties, often interrupting their careers for a few years of at-home child-rearing, or continually juggling job and home.

Duke (1988) interviewed an outstanding principal who expressed her ambivalence about administrative meetings that ran close to 6 p.m., which was the time her day-care center started charging a late pickup fee of a dollar a minute. She noted that the male administrators in the group never seemed to face that same pressure, and she added:

> I keep on my desk a note that my daughter typed in a school typewriter one weekend when I went in to work to get caught up. "Dear Mommy, I love you very much, Please find ways to spend more time with me." That note makes me go home.

Perhaps most importantly, not everyone wants to become a superintendent. One of Edson's interviewees put it this way: "Personally, a principalship is as far as I want to go. I'm not very interested at all in the county office level, because I don't want to be that far away from kids."

Thus, for some administrators, career development will be more horizontal than vertical, a matter of moving to progressively more challenging jobs at the same level or seeking to develop ever-greater expertise in the same position. Viewed from the outside, this sort of career may appear to have a "flat trajectory," but it has an internal dimension that represents significant change and growth.

Challenging Leaders To Grow

Because professional-growth needs have so often been ignored by schools, we have few well-defined or thoroughly tested models that can be consulted. However, the literature does offer a few clues to districts wishing to improve their practices.

Evaluation

One motivation for growth is the desire to live up to a standard; having a specific target permits energies to be focused and resources to be marshaled. By implication, one way districts can encourage administrators to grow is by embedding worthy achievable goals in their evaluation process.

Unfortunately, according to Anderson, many districts use evaluation primarily for accountability purposes; that is, evaluation is an attempt to determine minimal competence or eligibility for compensation and promotion. While these are essential functions, they do not usually encourage growth. In part, this is because they are poorly done. They use summative judgments rather than offering suggestions for improvement, and they are often carried out in a perfunctory way. In part, as any high school student could tell us, the goal on a test is to look good, not necessarily to be good. (This may help explain Jerry Valentine's discovery that evaluation goals set by principals "frequently reflected activities already completed or nearly completed.")

Nonetheless, evaluation can be oriented around professional growth by observing several key principles.

First, all participants should understand the purpose of the evaluation: to encourage growth, not to measure competence. Growth-oriented evaluation assumes basic competence in routine administrative tasks and instead seeks to encourage the development of new capacities. Worthy goals for professional growth are not achieved overnight; in some cases, a principal who falls a little short of an ambitious goal will have accomplished more than one who opts for a safe, simplistic objective. Administrators who know the evaluation is aimed at growth rather than summative judgment are more likely to take risks.

Second, goals should be clearly articulated, allowing all participants to make reasonable judgments about the progress being made. This isn't always easy, especially for ambitious goals, but failure to clarify the objective may derail the whole process. For instance, if the chosen goal is "improving school climate," the principal and the evaluator should answer a number of questions. Why is this an important goal? What are the signs that current climate needs to be improved? What are some possible ways of reaching the goal? What will be used as tangible indicators that the climate has improved? Going through this process will both affirm the importance of the goal and provide a clearly focused target.

Third, principals should be involved in the goal-setting process. Districts may appropriately establish basic growth priorities for the system, but every school and every school leader is different. A district undertaking an ambitious restructuring program may wish all its principals to develop skill in shared decision-making, but each principal will begin the year with different capabilities, and each school will present a different challenge based on its unique characteristics. Meaningful goals will reflect those individual differences.

Finally, principals should be able to track performance indicators on a continual basis. Anderson says, "The formative phase of collecting information is the most important phase in an evaluation process designed to promote personal growth and organizational development," but he notes that many principals are unclear on what evaluation information is being gathered and how it is being used. Reviewing data only at the end of the year will eliminate many opportunities for timely corrective action.

Staff Development

Some districts attempt to encourage growth through organized staff-development activities. However, Duke (1990) makes a distinction between professional growth and staff development. Staff development emphasizes skills and concepts, focuses on the school's agenda, and aims at collective growth in a common direction. While there is a need for staff development, it is not always responsive to individual needs, and it also has a history of being executed in a lethargic, uninspiring way. Duke (1993) characterizes it as "little more than an institutionalized insult."

Supporting Professional Growth

Well-organized evaluation and staff development activities can help school leaders develop skills in key areas but will only indirectly help them as they grapple with the larger meaning of their work. A sense of professional vitality is the product of an intensely personal quest that weaves professional activities into the fabric of a whole life. Here the district cannot say, "This is where you should be headed." It can only ask, "How can we help you answer those questions?"

Understandably, the literature offers few concrete models for districts to follow. It may, however, offer a few morsels for reflection.

Respecting Adult Learning Styles

First, many critics argue that professional development will succeed only if based on the recognition that effective adult learning requires a particular set of conditions. M. D. Richardson and R. L. Prickett identify five key principles:

- Adult motivation comes from the belief that learning will satisfy individual needs and interests.
- Adult learning should be organized and arranged around life situations, not academic subjects.
- The core methodology for adult learning should be the analysis of experience.

- Adult learning should involve a process of mutual inquiry, not the transmission of knowledge.
- Because individual differences increase with age, adult learning should be flexible in style, timing, and pacing of learning.

Most of these principles can be reduced to the insight that adults have their own learning agenda. Activities that allow them to pursue their goals in a meaningful way will result in growth; activities that impose somebody else's agenda will be ignored, subverted, or grudgingly gotten out of the way.

The Invitation To Grow

Many of the most important growth issues are the most personal—not the kind of thing to be casually mentioned in a formal meeting. Is it possible to establish settings in which those questions can be addressed?

One possible model comes from the Maine Academy for School Leaders, a federally funded leadership-development program that worked with experienced principals and teacher leaders. The academy was based on the assumption that leadership growth requires not only changes in thinking, but changes in behaviors with others, which in turn requires self-examination and reflection (Gordon Donaldson and George Marnik).

Over a sixteen-month period, participants set goals for professional growth, tried out new behaviors in their workplace, and evaluated the results. The key element in the program was the creation of colleague-critic teams that provided emotional support, honest feedback, and challenging questions. By the end of the sixteen months, almost all participants reported significant growth in leadership style, confidence, and relationships with others.

Portfolios

One promising tool for professional growth is the professional portfolio. Analogous to the portfolios now frequently used in classrooms, professional portfolios serve as both a marker of development and a tool for reflection. John Daresh and Marsha Playko suggest that portfolios may include such things as a current resumé, a statement of educational beliefs, references, transcripts, credentials, goal statements and assessment, and personal reflective statements. Daresh and Playko say such portfolios can be used for career development, evaluation, or professional development.

When used as part of a comprehensive program of professional growth, portfolios may be valuable as a stimulus to reexamine the direction of one's career, and they may provide a tangible representation of themes and issues that are normally elusive.

Conclusion

This chapter has suggested five ways schools may find and nurture the special kind of people needed to be leaders:

- Encourage talented people to become leaders.
- Participate in the training of future leaders.
- Carefully locate and select the best candidates available.
- Provide organized induction programs for newcomers.
- Provide opportunities for the professional growth of leaders.

Each school district must find the particular ways in which it can best make a meaningful contribution, but there is no escaping the responsibility.

PART 2

The Values

CHAPTER

4

Ethical Leadership

Larry Lashway

A principal on the verge of initiating dismissal proceedings against an incompetent teacher is delighted to learn that the teacher is seeking jobs elsewhere. A few days later, he receives a call from an administrator in a neighboring district, asking for a recommendation on the teacher. An honest answer will probably result in the teacher not being hired.

After grappling with severe budget restrictions, a district's administrative team reluctantly decides that its plan to provide each elementary classroom with a multimedia computer is out of reach. Instead, they decide to encourage the PTA at each school to take it on as a fund-raising effort.

A parent complains to a high school principal about the longtime football coach, saying that his high-pressure, verbally abusive approach damages the self-esteem of adolescents, especially those who are not stars. The principal shares the concerns, but the coach is a popular, almost legendary figure in the community and his teams are always in contention.

To be a school leader is to live with ethical dilemmas. Not just a few times a year, not just weekly, but every day. The dilemmas come in various forms. Sometimes they announce themselves like flashing neon signs; sometimes they try to slip past disguised as mere technical problems; and sometimes they just lurk in the background, throbbing like a toothache that won't quite go away.

How do administrators meet these ethical challenges? How *should* they? Unfortunately, at this point we know less than we'd like. Most research on school leadership has been conducted within the social-science tradition, which prefers to deal with objective facts or cause-and-effect relationships rather than the more subjective questions of what *should* be done. The result, according to Lynn Beck and Joseph Murphy, is that for a long time "value issues remained largely overlooked in the profession in general and were regularly ignored in preparation programs in particular."

Recently, however, some educational thinkers, taking a new look at school leadership, have concluded that it is unmistakably "a moral art." Christopher Hodgkinson, for example, asserts that education connects with the whole range of human values and that administrators must be aware of "the deep roots of purpose" that underlie their schools. William Greenfield (1991a) argues that school leaders face "a unique set of ethical demands." Not only are schools devoted to promoting social norms, students are compelled to attend and have little say in what happens there. For these reasons, the leader's conduct "must be *deliberately* moral," Greenfield says.

This chapter explores a number of perspectives that illuminate the leader's ethical responsibilities. Unlike other topics in this book, ethical thinking relies less on the objective research of social science than on the reflective deliberation of the humanities. Dialogue in the humanities aims at persuasion rather than proof; it concedes that while truth may never be known with absolute certainty, striving for it will sharpen our awareness and improve our practice.

An Aristocracy of Character

Contemporary school leaders are wary about explaining their work in moral terms. This would have surprised nineteenth-century educators, who regarded themselves as constituting an "aristocracy of character" that had a profoundly moral mission. Much of their energy and self-assurance came from an unshakable conviction that what they were doing was simply *right* (David Tyack and Elizabeth Hansot).

In turn, the institution they served gained status as a moral authority, "a fixed article of faith in the American creed," according to R. Freeman Butts. American schools have often exuded a sense of moral purpose, ranging from the early support of religion to the modern desire to create a more democratic society. For many early educators, teaching was God's work, both in the religious sense and in the sense that there was no more worthy human endeavor.

But by the middle of the twentieth century, according to Tyack and Hansot, school leaders were basing their authority on science rather than morality. Instead of relying on character, leaders now sought expertise; instead of fighting evils, they now solved problems. What happened?

First, public education in the early twentieth century became infatuated with the efficiency movement, which sought to reduce costs by stripping human labor to the bare essentials needed for a job. As documented by Raymond Callahan, the movement originated in industry, where efficiency experts prowled offices with tape measures and notepads, calculating the shortest distance between desk and file cabinet and insisting that employees follow that route. School leaders, searching for ways to increase public confidence in their institutions, were quick to hop on the bandwagon.

Frank Spaulding, a turn-of-the-century superintendent, exemplified the new attitude in his assessment of his school's curriculum. After computing the relative cost of different subjects, Spaulding concluded:

> I am convinced... by very concrete and quite local considerations, that when the obligations of the present year expire, we ought to purchase no more Greek instruction at the rate of 5.9 pupil recitations for a dollar. The price must go down, or we shall invest in something else. (Callahan).

Bolstered by the newborn field of educational psychology, which promised precise, scientific measurement of learning, educational leaders saw efficiency as a convenient, defensible, and culturally approved standard for running their schools. Administrators became increasingly preoccupied with questions of fire insurance, plumbing, and janitor service, while learning was equated to industrial output.

Second, after World War II the training of administrators was dominated by the belief that administration was a science (Beck and Murphy). That is, one could understand administration objectively, accurately analyzing cause-effect relationships and determining how things worked. Determining how things *should* work was another issue; value questions were considered beyond the reach of science. Thus, two generations of school leaders received training that minimized ethical issues.

A third influence has been the apparent splintering of moral consensus. Since World War II, disagreements within American culture have become louder and more public. Lingering traces of the school's religious heritage have been gradually eliminated by court decisions, creating widespread resentment; the emergence of ethnic consciousness has challenged the school's traditional "melting-pot" rhetoric; and a rapidly changing moral climate undermined trust in the school's ability to defend traditional values. The result is a seemingly unmanageable pluralism, leading some to suggest that the only solution is a free marketplace where clients can pick and choose the options they wanted.

This fragmentation has alarmed many observers. Social critics such as Alasdair MacIntyre and Amitai Etzioni have lamented our inability to find common moral ground. Educators themselves have begun to ask whether they have evaded the issue too long. David Purpel and Svi Shapiro, after criticizing the shallow public discourse on education, blame educators for sticking to a narrow strategy that glorifies technical expertise and evades the underlying moral issues. What we need, they claim, is a "moral and spiritual language that addresses questions of meaning and purpose and that recognizes the importance of community."

Midway through the 1990s, American education lacks such a common language, yet there are signs of an emerging dialogue, a public conversation, that takes seriously the school leader's ethical responsibilities. In the following sections we explore some of the directions that this dialogue is taking.

The Ethical Behavior of School Leaders

If Beck and Murphy are right, most school administrators have been thrust into the hurly-burly of leadership without much formal preparation for the ethical issues they will be facing. This implies that their behavior will depend either on whatever ethical sensitivities they bring to the job or on the way they are socialized by colleagues or superiors. William Greenfield (1985) argues that informal socialization is a strong conservative force in the development of school leaders, pushing them to uphold the status quo.

But how do school leaders view ethical issues? Few systematic studies have been done, so the question can be answered only very tentatively. To begin with, school leaders often see their job in moral terms. Arthur Blumberg and William Greenfield found that the exceptional principals they studied operated with "the unwritten law of the principalship...'Thou shalt be an advocate for children'." In another study, Greenfield (1991b) found that one elementary principal's influence was based on her appeal to a common moral vision. "The ideal of service to children in desperate need is the moral standard against which daily practices are judged. Teachers and principal alike are held to this standard by one another; nobody is allowed off the hook!"

There is also ample anecdotal evidence that school leaders are keenly aware of moral dilemmas. For example, Blumberg and Greenfield recorded one principal's doubts about punishing a student who may have been innocent:

> He ended up serving detention last night. It was a real conflict. I really don't think he threw it. So here I am penalizing him for something I really don't think he did. But I believe in the concept

> that I have to support my staff, whether it's a teacher, a custodian, a cafeteria worker who's involved. I don't feel good about it. I wrestle with it.

The dilemma that this principal faced was very typical in one respect: A moral belief collided with an institutional reality. School leaders constantly face the need to keep the school moving forward while fending off a host of disruptive forces. In this case, the principal decided that the disruptive potential of not backing a teacher outweighed the possible injustice to one student.

Work by Peggy Kirby and colleagues suggests that this kind of tradeoff may be common. They asked principals to respond to several hypothetical ethical dilemmas and also to estimate how "a typical colleague" would respond. The principals consistently reported that colleagues would be more likely to take "the path of least resistance" by deferring to superiors or taking refuge in official policies. Kirby and her colleagues speculate that these hypothetical colleagues actually reflect the norm.

Similarly, Katherine Kasten and Carl Ashbaugh asked administrators to indicate what would be most important when considering a difficult personnel decision. The most commonly cited issues were concerned with prudence (How will the organization be affected?) and precedent (Is the decision consistent with past practice?). At the same time, administrators did not completely ignore transcendent principles such as fairness, honesty, and human worth, presumably setting up some difficult conflicts. Kasten and Ashbaugh, noting the inherent limitations of studying hypothetical dilemmas, were reluctant to draw major conclusions but did observe that "administrators are a cautious group."

Thus, the research tends to reveal school leaders who are sensitive to moral issues, but who often have to balance those concerns with their responsibility to maintain a smoothly functioning school.

Making Ethical Decisions

Ethical beliefs belong to the category of "normative statements"; that is, they claim to tell us how we *should* behave. Greenfield (1991a) points out that not all normative statements are ethical; to say that tulip bulbs should be planted in fall is normative, but of little ethical consequence. Ethical issues arise when our behavior affects other people.

Rushworth Kidder notes that such issues occupy the domain between freedom and law. That is, there are certain decisions we can make without restraint, based purely on our own preferences; other decisions are regulated by society through a system of laws. Choosing between roast turkey and prime rib is a matter of freedom; leaving the restaurant without paying is not.

Ethical questions arise when people believe a certain behavior is highly desirable but the law is silent. (For example, no law requires us to notify a neighbor that he has left his headlights on, but most people would agree that this is something that we should do. Similarly, an administrator may be able to resolve a problem by lying or blaming an innocent party, but most people would agree that this is *not* desirable behavior.) Kidder cites Lord Moulton's comment that ethics is "obedience to the unenforceable."

Ambiguity and Uncertainty

Ethical issues are inherently ambiguous; the absence of formal laws forces us to consult beliefs, which are seldom unanimous. Even where there is consensus (for example, that lying is wrong), the beliefs are stated so abstractly that we still have to determine how (or if) they apply to a particular situation. (Is it wrong to lie in order to spare someone's feelings?)

This ambiguity means that before we can do the right thing, we have to *determine* the right thing. This may be especially difficult for school leaders, who work in a complex public arena where an increasingly diverse society generates conflicting moral standards. Greenfield (1991a) says, "It often is not clear what is right or wrong, or what one ought to do, or which perspective is right in moral terms. Or, it may be clear what one ought to do, in moral terms, but circumstances may not permit that course of action."

This sort of uncertainty constitutes an ethical *dilemma*. A decision must be made; there are at least two possible choices, each of which will affect other people for better or for worse; and each choice can be plausibly supported by citing various moral principles.

Kidder argues that a true dilemma forces us to choose between two competing goods (or between the lesser of two evils). If we hesitate over a choice between right and wrong, we are facing a *moral temptation*, not an ethical dilemma. Thus, the thought of lying to cover up a mistake constitutes a temptation; the thought of lying to evade a harmful bureaucratic regulation is a dilemma.

School leaders experience ethical dilemmas on a daily basis. Some of their dilemmas are universal in nature; that is, they involve the fundamental moral rules that all humans grapple with—telling the truth, respecting others, being fair. The principal who agonized over punishing an innocent student was dealing with a dilemma of this type.

Other dilemmas arise from the special challenges of the education profession. Should schools distribute condoms? Should parents be informed if a counselor learns that their daughter is considering an abortion? Should corporal punishment ever be used? Educators are often divided on what is in the best interests of the child.

A third major type of dilemma comes from the principal's status as middle manager. School leaders have a responsibility to higher authority, but they have a simultaneous obligation to the teachers and students in their school. When the bureaucratic demands clash with student needs, principals must make a choice.

In summary, then, it is clear that school leaders cannot avoid ethical uncertainty. The only question is whether they can find a way to resolve the dilemmas.

Ethical Codes

When ethical questions are raised at work, many people instinctively look for some set of rules to follow. Professions (such as law and medicine) typically provide guidelines in the form of ethical codes.

C. J. B. Macmillan says that a professional code has several essential characteristics:

- It is formulated and enforced by autonomous practitioners.
- It goes beyond the general moral code of society to articulate the special responsibilities of those who belong to the profession.
- It provides a mechanism for clients or members of the public to seek redress when the code has been violated, with meaningful sanctions for violators.

School administrators formulated a code in the 1970s as a cooperative effort of the National Association of Secondary School Principals, the American Association of School Administrators, and several other administrator associations (Arthur Smith and colleagues). According to this code, the school administrator:

1. Makes the well-being of students the fundamental value in all decision-making and actions.
2. Fulfills professional responsibilities with honesty and integrity.
3. Supports the principle of due process and protects the civil and human rights of all individuals.
4. Obeys local, state, and national laws and does not knowingly join or support organizations that advocate, directly or indirectly, the overthrow of the government.

5. Implements the governing board of education's policies and administrative rules and regulations.
6. Pursues appropriate measures to correct those laws, policies, and regulations that are not consistent with sound educational goals.
7. Avoids using positions for personal gain through political, social, religious, economic, or other influence.
8. Accepts academic degrees or professional certification only from duly accredited institutions.
9. Maintains the standards and seeks to improve the effectiveness of the profession through research and continuing professional development.
10. Honors all contracts until fulfillment or release.

This code has provisions for enforcement but is seldom invoked. Nor is it easy to tell when a violation has occurred; "the well-being of students" and "sound educational goals" are broad abstractions that could mean almost anything.

In addition, despite the claim that student well-being is the ultimate guiding principle, points 4 and 5 remind us that administrators are accountable to rightful authorities. School leaders are likely to hit the ethical wall when the governing powers ask them to do something that might hurt the well-being of particular students (such as identifying and reporting illegal immigrants).

On the whole, there is little evidence that national codes (the National Education Association has a similar one) have had a significant impact on educational practice, leading some critics to suggest the development of *local* codes. Hugh Sockett, for example, argues that moral accountability must be based on trust, which is best gained through repeated face-to-face encounters; therefore, small interactive communities offer the best chance of providing the conditions for meaningful accountability.

Socket offers a number of guidelines for developing such a local code.

1. The code should be in the form of guidelines rather than specific prohibited acts. The principles should be broad enough to cover many situations, but specific enough to provide real guidance.

2. Public and parental input is essential so educators can understand the perspectives of other stakeholders. To avoid role-blindness, professionals should adopt the "what-if-it-were-my-kid" test.

3. The code should be publicly promoted "until it becomes a living thing in the minds of the public to whom it is owed." Parents must know what to do when they believe an educator to be violating the code.

4. The code should contain meaningful sanctions. Sockett notes that sanctions threaten the usual norms of collegiality and may be especially offensive to those educators who would behave appropriately anyway. Coercion is never pleasant, Sockett notes, but rules without sanctions do not inspire trust among the public.

As an alternative to codes, Betty Sichel recommends that schools form ethics committees similar to those found in many hospitals. Such committees would raise awareness of ethical issues, formulate ethical codes, and advise educators grappling with ethical dilemmas. Sichel emphasizes that the committee would not make rulings in any specific case; the goal is not to make decisions for educators but to create a climate in which they can make more responsible decisions.

It is not hard to imagine specific issues that might benefit from this approach. Should schools accept money or equipment from private companies if it means exposing students to commercial advertising? Should a mainstreamed student be graded on the same standards as other students? Should an entire group of students be punished for the misbehavior of a few? Too often teachers and administrators are left to agonize over these dilemmas in isolation from a supportive community of peers.

Ethical Reasoning

No matter how thoughtful and comprehensive the ethical code, it will never eliminate the need to deliberate on moral issues. A code provides a guideline, a reminder of core principles; each practitioner must examine the case at hand to determine how the principles apply.

Moreover, reliance on a code may not fulfill a leader's ethical responsibility. Barry Bull and Martha McCarthy dispute the common assumption that behavior can be separated into distinct zones of "ethical" and "unethical." In this view, once a person has determined which behaviors are impermissible, everything else is a matter of personal and professional discretion. In reality, Bull and McCarthy argue, ethical principles touch almost everything administrators do.

Thus, professionals must be capable of skillful ethical decision-making; confronted with a decision, they must be able to recognize its ethical dimensions and determine their responsibility. Given the painful choices that are often involved, how do they choose what is fair, ethical, and wise? (Or, more modestly, how do they make a choice that will permit an undisturbed night of sleep?)

Moral Intuition

One school of thought says that moral reasoning is not a matter of deep abstract thinking, but simply the willingness to respect the moral impulses that we all have. Scholars such as James Q. Wilson and Robert Solomon argue that humans by nature have an intuitive moral understanding. Solomon says:

> Justice is to be found, if it is to be found anywhere, in us, in our sense that there are wrongs in the world to be righted. You don't need an all-embracing sense of justice to recognize the presence of injustice, often right in front of your nose. Justice is not an ideal state or theory, but a matter of personal sensibility, a set of emotions that engage us with the world and make us care—as reason alone with all of its brilliant arguments... cannot.

Similarly, Anne Colby and William Damon, studying exemplary moral lives, found that their subjects had a strong, self-assured grasp of what was right. "Among our exemplars, we saw no 'eking out' of moral acts through intricate, tortuous cognitive processing. Instead, we saw an unhesitating will to act, a disavowal of fear and doubt, and a simplicity of moral response. Risks were ignored and consequences went unweighed."

Is moral decision-making then just a matter of listening to our hearts? Kenneth Strike and colleagues disagree, saying that not all moral intuitions are equally useful; not all stand up against further examination. (A common moral intuition of nineteenth-century Americans, for example, was that "inferior" peoples were not entitled to the same consideration as were "civilized" nations—a belief that is rejected today.) Rather, intuitions are just the initial raw material for the decision-making process. We must also consider factual evidence and reflect on the principles behind our intuitions.

The Facts of the Case

Ethical decisions are not made in a vacuum; like legal decisions, they involve particular people in particular circumstances. Change the circumstances and the decision may change, even though our guiding beliefs remain the same.

Thus, faced with an apparently ineffective teacher, a principal must first ask some basic questions about the case. What is the evidence of ineffectiveness? Has the teacher tried to improve his performance? In what ways are students being put at risk? Is the teacher demonstrably less effective than colleagues? How long has the teacher been with the district?

What will be the financial and psychological costs of dismissing the teacher? What impact would a dismissal have on the morale of other teachers? What will happen to the dismissed teacher? The answers to these questions will strongly influence the decision simply because they help shape our view of what is at stake ethically.

Moral Reasoning

Strike and colleagues note that even with sensitivity to our moral intuitions and a clear knowledge of the facts, we may be left in doubt because basic beliefs are in conflict. The case of the ineffective teacher may lead us to a brutal conclusion: we can impair the education of a large number of students or ruin a teacher's life. Two evils—how do we choose the lesser?

Weighing the Scales of Justice

One of the best known frameworks for moral reasoning is Lawrence Kohlberg's. Building on the work of Jean Piaget, Kohlberg saw moral reasoning as a developmental progression from amoral egocentric thinking to abstract principled thinking. At one end is the young child, defining "right" by immediate personal consequences; at the other end is the thoughtful adult, reasoning from universal principles with full awareness of obligations to others (Dawn Schrader).

At the pinnacle of moral reasoning, people make decisions consciously, give reasons for them, and justify those reasons. Moral maturity is defined by careful reflection and logical thinking, not by the content of beliefs. Thus, in one well-known example, subjects are presented with a description of Heinz, whose dying wife can be saved by a miracle drug that costs more than he can afford. Should he steal the drug? A person who says "yes" (because human life outweighs other considerations) may be given high marks for using an abstract principle. However, so would a person who answers "no" (because taking the law into one's own hands subverts the notions of community that make life worth living).

Kohlberg's system, while frequently used as a way of sharpening moral reasoning, has been widely criticized, primarily because it seems to reduce complex life situations to either/or choices between abstract principles. Critics like Carol Gilligan have objected that such cold-blooded logic leads to treating subtle dilemmas as "math problems with humans." In reality, she argues, every moral decision is embedded in a rich context of facts, perceptions, and intentions.

Consider some hypothetical possibilities. The drug company is seeking extortionary profits; Heinz and his wife have seven children; the odds are 50-50 that he would be caught; Heinz's wife has frequently been unfaithful. None of these considerations dictates a decision, but each is likely to awaken certain moral intuitions that don't fit neatly into logical categories. Gilligan argues that these intuitions should be respected; the goal is a wise decision, not impeccable abstract reasoning.

Moral Principles

The Kohlberg system is process-oriented, seemingly more concerned with the quality of reasoning than with the decision reached. In real life, however, we are more likely to be preoccupied by the particular standards that allow us to tell right from wrong.

Some standards, of course, are the same ones we were told to follow in childhood: always tell the truth; share with others; keep your word; be fair; and do unto others as you would have them do unto you.

Other principles are more abstract. Strike and colleagues list several that are likely to be important for school leaders:

- *Intellectual liberty*: People have the right to hold and freely express their views.
- *Personal liberty*: People have the right to conduct their lives as they see fit, except as their behavior infringes on the rights of others.
- *Equality*: Each person should be treated the same, or at least be provided equal opportunities.
- *Due process*: People in apparent violation of rules and laws should be given a fair chance to defend themselves before any penalty is applied.
- *Democracy*: Members of a community should have an equal opportunity to participate and have an influence in making decisions that will affect them.

Most of these principles are rooted in the American democratic tradition, and they have an inherent "rightness" to anyone raised in that tradition. They are also rather abstract, leading some critics to look for principles that reflect the rich emotional interactions that characterize classroom life.

The most frequent nominee is "caring." Beck says that caring is best defined by its goals (promoting human development and responding to human needs) and by the behaviors it implies: appreciating the perspective of another person, responding appropriately to this understanding, and remaining in the caring relationship for as long as required. Whereas many moral principles seem intellectual in origin, caring has emotional roots and is personal in nature; we don't just care in general, we care about particular people.

The Difficulty of Deciding

Even armed with these principles, school leaders will not find it easy to resolve many ethical dilemmas. For example, Strike and colleagues present a hypothetical situation in which a superintendent must choose between two new programs, one to benefit children of migrant workers, the other to benefit gifted and talented students (there is not enough money for both programs). The relevant principle here is equality, but what exactly does that mean? Does equality require treating everyone the same, or does it mean making sure that all parties get what they need? Is it important to look at who has the greater need? Should we consider what would benefit society the most?

In this predicament, as in most worthy dilemmas, a clearcut answer does not leap to the forefront; we can easily imagine different leaders (of equal good will and moral sensitivity) making different decisions. Does moral reasoning eventually reach a dead end? Must we ultimately take refuge in relativism, declaring that moral claims are irreconcilable and making decisions purely on practical grounds?

Strike and colleagues strongly disagree, noting that befuddlement is not necessarily permanent. If nothing else, we can make progress: "If the process of moral deliberation is not always decisive or clear, or completely objective, it is also rarely fruitless. Moral reasoning and debate always gets us somewhere, and as moral agents we are obligated to participate in it."

Although there are no easy recipes for moral reasoning, we can find guidelines.

1. *Seeing what is important in a situation.* Moral reasoning is not just a matter of abstract ideals; it occurs in specific cases that come attached with names and facts. Some of those facts have a legitimate bearing on our decisions; others are irrelevant. For example, in the case of the two competing programs, does it matter that most of the migrant students will probably move out of the district by next year? That the school is in a region attracting numerous high-tech industries? That the gifted students will probably be able to make satisfactory progress even without the program?

David Bricker argues that we recognize what is important not through objective reasoning, but through an act of perception that resembles artistic appreciation. This perception can be developed by having our attention repeatedly called to the moral dimensions of problems. Culture plays a large role, giving us an appreciation of certain issues but a blindness to others. For instance, contemporary American culture is oriented toward individual freedom while Japanese culture tends to emphasize responsibility to the group.

How can we learn to recognize what is important? The best strategy may be opening ourselves up to the perspectives of others, particularly those whose experiences and backgrounds differ from our own. Colby and Damon found that their moral exemplars showed a lifelong pattern of engaging in dialogue with others, attentively considering alternative views, and gradually assimilating other perspectives into their own moral framework. A similar approach may be especially helpful to school leaders, who serve an increasingly diverse constituency.

2. *Reflecting*. Strike and colleagues say that moral intuitions are never sufficient, if only because they tend to be unexamined. In a school community that brings together so many different viewpoints, leaders have the responsibility of subjecting their intuitions to conscious reflection and evaluation. Failing to reflect on how one lives "is to refuse to be responsible for one's self. In a fundamental way, it is to refuse to be a person."

Reflection is often thought of as a solitary activity. Rabindra Kanungo and Manuel Mendonca claim that it is only in silence that leaders can hear the "inner whisperings" that will point them to the right path. They seem to be suggesting that ethical problem-solving is very different from the kind of hard-driving, action-oriented posture that leaders need to get through their day.

Moral decision-making can also be effective when carried out in communities of like-minded individuals who can raise provocative questions, challenge each other's assumptions, and provide emotional and intellectual support. Such communities need not be large (half a dozen may be sufficient) as long as they share intellectual honesty and a commitment to search for moral truth. Karen Osterman and Robert Kottkamp have provided a detailed description of one such community, in which a number of administrators in the same district periodically met for unstructured discussion of the issues they confronted. Over time, the meetings evolved into a trusting, supportive, sometimes moving experience that allowed participants to voice ideas that had no other forum.

3. *Searching for alternatives*. Moral dilemmas are agonizing because either choice is painful. Kidder says we can sometimes avoid that pain by challenging the assumption that there are only two choices. Some dilemmas are actually "trilemmas," offering a third path that avoids the negative

consequences of the first two. For example, faced with a parent who objects to a particular homework assignment on religious grounds, many principals have been able to negotiate an alternative assignment, thereby preserving academic integrity without trampling on parental rights.

4. *Weighing the choices.* School leaders are not philosophers, but they can benefit from using standards that philosophers have employed for centuries. Kidder suggests three.

First, we can examine the *consequences* of each choice and attempt to identify which will lead to the most positive outcome. This requires determining who will be affected, and in what ways. Historically, this principle has been characterized as "the greatest good for the greatest number."

The idea of maximizing happiness has great appeal, but Kidder notes that it requires more than counting heads. Sometimes a small benefit to many people will be outweighed by a great harm to only one person. Moreover, it isn't always easy to determine how people will be affected by an action.

Second, we can invoke *moral rules.* Rules are based on the belief that the world would be a better place if people always behaved in a certain way (for example, telling the truth). Rules ask us not to make exceptions to allow for individual circumstances, because every exception nibbles away at an important value. (One Northwest school district illustrated this belief when it suspended a junior high school student whose mother accidentally packed a beer instead of a soda in her lunchbox. Despite criticism for punishing an apparently innocent student, the district reasoned that making an exception would erode its "zero tolerance" alcohol policy.)

Rule-based approaches can make people uncomfortable because they seem impossibly strict, sometimes snaring the innocent. Moreover, rules often conflict, leaving us in doubt about which one should have priority.

Third, we can examine a dilemma from a perspective of *caring.* Kidder sums up this principle with the Golden Rule: How would *we* like to be treated under similar circumstances? He argues, "Ethics is not a blind impartiality, doling out right and wrong according to some stone-cold canon of ancient and immutable law. It is a warm and supremely human activity that cares enough for others to want right to prevail."

Caring is an appealing stance because of its apparent compassion, but it has important limitations. For one thing, decisions affect different people in different ways; who should we care for the most? There is also the practical reality that people would often like to be treated in ways that benefit their self-interest rather than the greater good.

Kidder suggests that each of these perspectives throws a different light on a dilemma, highlighting certain features and obscuring others. Using all three as "filters" will provide a much firmer foundation for making an informed decision.

The Virtuous Leader

Students of ethics are unanimous on one point: moral leadership begins with moral leaders. In that respect, morality is unlike technical expertise. One can effectively lead a high school without being able to teach all subjects; one can coach a sport without having the refined skill of an athlete; but no one can create an ethical institution without being ethical.

Howard Gardner says of great leaders that they embody the message they advocate; they teach, not just through words but through actions. James Kouzes and Barry Posner (1995) over the course of a decade have surveyed 20,000 business people to find out what they value in leaders. The results have been clear: "Credibility is the foundation of leadership." They boil it down to one simple slogan: DWYSYWD (Do What You Say You Will Do).

While modern philosophers have tended to emphasize "rule ethics" (searching for the appropriate moral principle to cover a case), a much older tradition is concerned with the art of being the kind of person one should be. In this tradition, dating back to the Greeks, character is more important than cognition; the key question is not "How do I solve this particular dilemma?" but "How do I live a worthy life?" (David Norton).

This section explores the different ways school leaders can answer this universal question. The points of interest in this exploration are, first, basic human virtues, and then the character of school leaders.

Seven Classic Virtues

Leaders are people first; within every moral leader is a moral human being. As we will use the term here, *virtue* comes from consciously trying to live one's life in a certain kind of way, striving to do the right thing, even when tempted to do otherwise. As Aristotle observed long ago, virtue is less an act of reason than it is a disposition to live well, cultivated in a hundred daily acts, not just in those dramatic moments when a full-blown crisis descends on us.

Any list of "cardinal virtues" is arbitrary, since it is difficult to imagine any virtue that wouldn't help leaders. But the following seven are likely to be essential.

Honesty

Honesty may be the fundamental virtue; as Sockett observes, it would be impossible to carry on a meaningful social life without being able to assume that most people are telling the truth most of the time. This is why Kouzes and Posner (1995) have found that subordinates consistently list honesty as the most desirable leadership trait.

In both personal and professional life, temptations to be dishonest are legion. To avoid confrontations, soothe feelings, or simply get through the day with sanity intact, it seems so easy to lie, shade the truth, omit crucial information, or just let people believe what one knows to be untrue. Lying, in fact, may be the least common offense, if only because it is so easy to get caught. But anything that keeps us from saying what needs saying is deceitful:

- employing euphemisms that whitewash an ugly reality with soothing words
- managing meeting agendas to choke off important but painful topics
- ignoring a difficult situation in the hope that it will go away on its own
- failing to challenge others who are spreading misinformation
- answering questions like an attorney, dealing in technicalities rather than responding to the human need behind the questions

The worst thing about these evasions is that they seldom fool anyone for very long. Instead, they just put the institutional stamp of approval on denial as a way of life. In the end, the leader's peace of mind will last only until some previously avoidable problem erupts into crisis.

Loyalty

Whenever we commit ourselves to work with others in a common enterprise, we are called upon to maintain that commitment over time, even in the face of obstacles, disappointments, and distractions. "Placing our loyalty somewhere is an important act of identity," says Ira Chaleff. "We can place it in ourselves and often this is important to help us stay a difficult course. But if we place no loyalty outside ourselves we become a kind of brigand, justifying any action regardless of its cost to others."

The challenge of loyalty is determining precisely what we owe to whom. School leaders can be especially torn because they are responsible to so many people. They are expected to support and protect subordinates, especially teachers; at the same time, they owe loyalty to superiors and the governing board. Most importantly, according to Chaleff, they also have a commitment to the mission of the institution they serve.

These conflicts can pose painful choices, but Chaleff argues that loyalty to institutional purpose is the priority. When others threaten to undermine the common goal toward which we are working, the time has come to challenge, or even to disobey. When life or health are at risk; when common decency is violated; when laws are violated; or when the interests of many are sacrificed to serve the interests of the privileged few—these are times when blind loyalty is a vice rather than a virtue.

The most obvious threat to loyalty is self-interest, often in the form of careerism. While few districts expect a lifetime commitment from administrators, they do ask that promises be fulfilled. Many can tell stories of dynamic new leaders who won the community's heart with eloquently stated visions and who stirred teachers and parents to accept the risks of wholesale change, only to jump ship when the first attractive job offer came their way, leaving behind a wounded and disheartened community.

Courage

It isn't difficult to see that school leadership requires courage. In the course of a typical year, a principal may have to:

- publicly take the blame for someone else's mistake
- make a decision for the greater good that is hurtful to an individual
- approve a highly visible innovation that has no guarantee of success
- disappoint esteemed friends and allies by compromising on an emotional issue
- trust subordinates to make good decisions on sensitive issues
- tackle a messy, complicated issue that might be ignored for a while longer

M. Donald Thomas defines *courage* as "congruence between one's actions and one's principles," adding that it is "the ability to practice what one preaches, to stand on principle if the need arises, and to accept the consequences of one's actions without excuse or attempt to circumvent them."

Chaleff notes that courage requires an unnatural act—embracing risk rather than reducing it or running from it. However, the fear itself may generate the emotional energy to rise above it, especially if we can see clearly what inspires us to take the risky course. For some, the source of courage is religious values or personal philosophy; some draw inspiration from personal heroes; some are deeply conscious of their commitment to others; and some act in response to previous experiences that have affected them deeply.

A perverted form of courage is martyrdom. Some leaders say (justifiably) that leadership is not a popularity contest but then use that as a rationalization for acting arbitrarily or refusing to consider the views of others. These leaders collect criticisms and complaints as trophies that prove their courage. In reality, their goal is to dominate others.

Respect

Strike and colleagues equate the principle of equal respect with the Golden Rule, saying "it requires that we regard human beings as having intrinsic worth and treat them accordingly." This means that we cannot treat them as objects or as means to advance our own ends, and that we must respect their freedom of choice.

This is a paradoxical virtue in a society that values individualism. On the one hand, respect seems easy to practice because everyone demands it: when dialogue breaks down or grievances arise, people automatically take refuge in their rights. But recognizing the autonomy of others sometimes becomes an excuse for avoiding debate. True respect implies that we hear people out and engage them in dialogue.

Respect must be shown concretely—by soliciting feedback, being accessible, promoting constructive debate, and listening carefully (Kouzes and Posner 1993). Experience in school settings suggests that similar behaviors are crucial in empowering teachers to accept the risks of significant change (Joseph Blase and colleagues).

All this requires time, which may be the biggest barrier to showing respect. But another danger is professional arrogance; because of their special expertise, educators may be too quick to discount the views of lay people. One newspaper columnist who complained about educational fads reported numerous responses from educators asking the same indignant questions: "'Who are you? What is your expertise? What is your advanced college degree in and where did you get it?'" (Maggie Gallagher).

Respect is also easy to forget when working with children. Educators find it all too easy to treat students as objects or as tactical problems to be solved. But immature or not, children have a deep sense of dignity. As one sixth-grader confided, "You know, kids really like to learn; we just don't like being pushed around" (John Holt).

Caring

Caring—in the classical literature, *love*—is frequently mentioned by contemporary educators, with a sense of urgency. "Without caring," writes

Joan Lipsitz, "individual human beings cannot thrive, communities become violent battlegrounds, the American democratic experiment must ultimately fail, and the planet will not be able to support life."

Nel Noddings emphasizes that caring is not just an abstract concern for the welfare of children. It is a highly personal commitment to particular individuals at a particular time:

> When I care, I really hear, see, or feel what the other tries to convey.... When we watch a small child trying to tie her shoes, we often feel our fingers moving in sympathetic reaction. This is motivational displacement, the sense that our motive energy is flowing toward others and their projects. I receive what the other conveys, and I want to respond in a way that furthers the other's purpose or project.

This kind of caring requires full attention to the other person; the caregiver must "empty the soul of its own contents," momentarily putting aside his or her own preoccupations. For that reason, it can be difficult to achieve, especially when one is expected to care for many people.

Sockett notes that caring has its limits, easily mutating into overprotectiveness or sentimentality, and causing us to lose our professional objectivity. He also suggests that it isn't always appropriate to accept the others' goals; sometimes we can care best by neglecting what they most want.

Justice

Justice asks this fundamental moral question: What do we owe to whom? In a world with scarce resources, how do we allocate goods in an equitable way? In a world where every life is unique, how do we determine what is fair?

Philosophers have debated such questions for millennia. Thomas Sergiovanni, drawing on a variety of philosophical traditions, offers three standards. First, he suggests using Kant's "categorical imperative" of always treating others as ends first and never just as means to an end. When we need to enlist people to our cause, they should be persuaded, not manipulated.

Second, he discusses John Rawls' "veil of ignorance," which asks that we make decisions as if we didn't know our personal interests in the case. For example, in handling a parental complaint about a teacher, we should act as though we were somehow prevented from knowing whether we were the parent, the teacher, the student, or the principal. Under those conditions, we would have much more incentive to be fair-minded and consider the interests of everyone.

Finally, Sergiovanni mentions Habermas's "moment of empathy," which asks us simply to place ourselves in the other person's shoes.

These three principles imply that one threat to justice is self-interest: when the decider will be affected by the outcome, there is always reason to raise questions of fairness. In the case of the principal who punished a possibly innocent student, the discomfort came from a feeling that his own need to maintain good faculty relations might be overwhelming his fairness. In general, school leaders will always be vulnerable to this temptation because almost everything that happens in a school affects their interests.

But there are other difficulties as well. Most standards of fairness involve some notion of "treating everyone the same"; yet people are so different that the same treatment may have very different effects. For example, a $500 fine is far more burdensome for a poor person than a rich person. So one danger is administering justice too abstractly, forgetting the individuals involved and how they will be affected. The other danger is being so swayed by individual circumstances that we lose sight of the larger principles involved.

Grace

Unlike the other virtues on this list, grace is not instantly familiar (perhaps because it is much less common than it used to be). Kenn Rishel and Suzanne Tingley define the term to include elements of "elegance, dignity, stature, bearing, and ease of movement." As they describe it, it involves forbearance—not giving in to displays of temper and pettiness that might be fully justified. They give the example of a superintendent who was arbitrarily nonrenewed but refrained from arguing with the board or complaining to the press; instead, she served out her term with unflagging dedication. In another case, a superintendent had been continually badgered by a woman who came to every board meeting with a highly critical attitude. When the woman's failing eyesight made it impossible to continue driving, the superintendent made a point of personally driving her to each board meeting. He explained that her opposition was just honest disagreement, and he refused to take it personally.

Grace is difficult to achieve because no one would blame us for not showing it. Everyone would understand anger at an unjust dismissal or a sigh of relief when an annoying adversary disappears. Yet it is precisely the refusal to indulge themselves that allows some leaders to gain the enduring confidence of their followers.

Living a Virtuous Life

Where do these virtues come from? How can they be nurtured? Although some preparation programs are now adding courses in ethics, Robert Starratt (1994) says that a leader's moral force comes from something much deeper:

> It will be found in the narrative of that person's life—in the influences of parents, role models, and heroes; in the lessons learned from a multitude of positive as well as painful experiences; from reflection on the commentaries of historians, poets, and novelists. Such moral force comes from a life of trying to make sense out of experience, of asking how life should be lived, of exploring utopias and infernos. In short, the moral force of leadership comes from a lifetime's search for meaning and purpose in human existence.

As Starratt hints, it would be a mistake to see this search as a solitary quest. MacIntyre suggests that virtues are nurtured in communities having shared traditions and shared standards of excellence. As members of such communities, we learn virtues from the words and actions of others, and we discipline ourselves to behave virtuously through our sense of social obligation.

Communities of virtue vary in size, makeup, and location, and people may belong to more than one. Families are one type of moral community; churches are another. Sometimes people in a certain geographic area share common standards; sometimes professional colleagues do the same. The key, according to MacIntyre, is that there be a sense of commitment to the community and to its standards.

Finally, we can add some 2,000-year-old advice from Aristotle: virtue is a habit. Just as musicians develop musical ability by playing an instrument, people become virtuous by practicing virtue. As Chaleff notes, "Our 'courage muscle' will develop to the degree we exercise it. If we exercise it when the risks are small, it will be strong enough to meet the challenge when the risks are large."

School Leadership as a Calling

While basic human virtues provide an essential foundation, every profession faces unique challenges that call for special character traits. These special qualities are sometimes reflected in the concept of "vocation" (in the older religious sense of "calling"). "A vocation," says Dwayne Huebner, "is living life intentionally and openly, not routinely." It represents consistency between the inner self and the outer person. Those who have a calling are called by something outside them; it is a feeling of having been born to be something.

But if school leadership is a calling, exactly what are leaders called to be? The question is not often discussed in that form, but the literature provides a few clues to the special obligations of leadership.

It's easy to overlook the moral dimensions of everyday leadership. So much of it seems to involve mundane, straightforward, technical tasks such as budgeting, scheduling, and monitoring bus duty. Yet, as Thomas Green has pointed out, "budgeting is the principal means of making values concrete." A district that talks boldly of visions and empowerment and schools for the twenty-first century, but then slashes its inservice budget, sends a message that teachers have no trouble deciphering.

Thus, leaders must maintain a dual perspective, focusing not only on their day-to-day interactions with others, but on the ethical impact of the school's policies, practices, and structures. Starratt (1991) suggests that individual ethical excellence is futile in an institution that fails to serve moral purposes. Simply to assume that schools embody desirable standards is "ethically naive, if not culpable."

The Ethical School

Green observes, "Educational leaders may have moral problems in their practice, not because they are unethical or because they lack a sense of honor, but because they lack an understanding, a clear vision, of what their practice is centrally about, namely what it means to educate."

Sergiovanni agrees, saying that moral leadership revolves around a *covenant*—a shared sense of purpose that forms the basis for all actions and decisions. In schools with covenants, educators share beliefs about what students need, how students learn, and how schools work. Furthermore, they hold one another accountable to those shared standards.

Schools do not develop deeply held covenants by accident. It takes conscious, determined effort in which leaders play a key role, not only by modeling their own strong convictions, but by raising fundamental questions about purpose and practice. Who are we serving? How well do we serve them? Do we treat all students equitably, or are there hidden biases in the way we operate? What does it mean to be well educated? What kind of human beings are we growing? Is that what we want?

These are difficult questions, both in the sense that the answers are not immediately obvious, and in the sense that many people are afraid of what the answers will be. It takes strong leadership to puncture the comfortable illusions and evasions that sometimes sustain us.

Power and Restraint

Power may be the fundamental ethical issue for leaders. Every one of the leader's daily unglamorous tasks has moral weight simply because it carries with it the power to affect the lives of others. For students and teachers, the school is a place where they spend almost half their waking hours, a place that can be a source of productive enterprise and deep satisfaction or, in Arthur Wirth's phrase, a place that makes them crazy. The necessary regulations of school life, if not leavened with a recognition of their effects on people, can quickly become oppressive, belittling, and demoralizing.

The leader's power is legitimate, and everyone expects that it will be used. Yet power is a poor substitute for virtues such as caring, respect, and justice. Karl Hostetler uses the example of agenda control, in which a principal structures an upcoming faculty meeting in a way that leaves no time for teacher complaints about the new duty roster. This fails to treat teachers as thinking beings, trying instead to manipulate them.

The antidote to overreliance on power is *stewardship*, which Peter Block defines as "the willingness to be accountable for the well-being of the larger organization by operating in service, rather than in control, of those around us." It means accepting responsibility for outcomes without trying to impose control on others.

Kanungo and Mendonca speak of a similar outlook that they call *altruism*. "Our thesis is that organizational leaders are truly effective only when they are motivated by a concern for others, when their actions are invariably guided primarily by the criteria of the benefit to others even if it results in some cost to self."

Robert Greenleaf calls it *servant leadership*. The servant leader is a servant first and only gradually chooses to lead. The true servant leader puts others first: "Do those served grow as persons? Do they, while being served, become healthier, wiser, freer, more autonomous, more likely themselves to become servants?"

The notions of stewardship, altruism, and servant leadership present leaders with a formidable challenge, since they clash with conventional images of leadership. Here we have a leader, vested with power and status and expected to act with authority, who is contrarily asked to adopt the demeanor of the humblest member of the organization. Can it be done?

Greenleaf says the secret is developing the disposition to listen first, so others will recognize us as servants. Block says we must be scrupulous about our own accountability before worrying about that of others. And, if those aspirations seem too lofty, we might just remember the words of the political satirist: "No matter how high or great the throne, What sits on it is the same as your own."

Applying Ethical Principles: A Case

Discussions about ethics tends to gravitate toward ideals and abstractions. Busy administrators may be excused for wondering how these concepts would actually work in the rather messy realm of everyday practice. For that reason, this chapter ends with an extended example of a hypothetical case involving a principal who must deal with a poorly performing teacher.

The Case

Paula Kellner faces a difficult decision. Over the last two years, she has received a growing number of complaints about Ed Halley, a veteran English teacher. The complaints are always the same: poor discipline, uninspired lessons, and a failure to challenge students.

Although Kellner is only in her third year as principal, she knows that Halley was once considered a competent, dedicated teacher. Indeed, his dedication has never been in doubt; he often arrives at school early, is seldom absent, and has often been a moderating voice among more militant teachers.

Her observations of Halley's classroom have confirmed many of the complaints. Halley often seems to be going through the motions; his lessons are flat and lifeless, consisting mostly of teacher monologue. While student behavior is not extreme, there is far too much restlessness, inattention, and chatter to permit much learning. Halley seems to ignore the lack of student attention; when he does admonish students, they feel free to ignore him. On at least two occasions, she has seen students talk him into canceling a homework assignment.

Kellner has raised these issues in postevaluation conferences, but Halley denies there is a serious problem. He concedes that students are not wholly attentive, but blames it on television and lack of discipline at home. "I don't like it either," he says, "but you can't fight a whole society." At fifty-five, he admits he "may have lost a step or two," but pointedly adds, "Aging isn't a crime."

At this point, Kellner agonizes over her options. It's clear to her that if Halley were a second-year teacher, she would be preparing for a nonrenewal. Too many students are losing learning opportunities in this classroom, and the instructor is not improving. If Halley were a year from retirement, she might be tempted to wait it out, but he has told other teachers that for financial reasons he plans to teach until he is sixty-five. Ten years is just too long.

On the other hand, Halley has thirty years of experience. While Kellner is convinced she could meet the greater legal hurdles in nonrenewing a tenured teacher, she worries about the impact on him. Early retirement would apparently leave him in a financial bind, and at fifty-five his job prospects are dismal. Moreover, she is bothered by the thought of humiliating a man who has given three decades of loyal service to the school. Halley has deep roots in the community (he plans to remain here after retirement), and Kellner can imagine the pain of facing family and friends after being fired for incompetence. And, she reminds herself, the man is not a cynical burnout, merely tired; he still cares about students.

Applying the Principles

Using the ideas presented earlier in the chapter, how could Kellner start to resolve her dilemma?

1. *Deciding what is important.* This is the type of dilemma that Kidder describes as "justice vs. mercy." The conflicting demands on the principal are clear. Justice demands that students get the good education they are entitled to, and that a teacher who cannot deliver on his obligations should be dismissed. Yet mercy urges us to recognize the impact of the decision on a man who has given long and loyal service to several generations of students.

2. *Reflection.* As she mulls over the dilemma, Kellner's first instinct is to search for alternatives. One attractive alternative may in fact be demanded by the contract: working with the teacher to improve his performance. Although the problem appears to involve more than a lack of know-how, exploring this option seems preferable to arbitrarily closing the door on three decades of experience.

Another possibility is to look at Halley's work assignment. Sometimes working with a different age group will lessen the problem; indeed, a new assignment sometimes shakes up comfortable routines enough that something of a renaissance occurs. Conceivably, there may be nonclassroom positions that the teacher could fill.

A third possibility is to encourage Halley to consider early retirement. His current intention to keep teaching is apparently based on financial need; if he has reached this conclusion without the aid of expert financial counseling, the school might arrange to have a knowledgeable retirement planner work with him.

Practical alternatives are not always within reach, of course, and Kellner may be stuck with an either-or choice. Here Kidder's ethical "filters" may be helpful.

1. *Consequences.* If the principal decides in favor of nonrenewal, the most obvious consequence is to Halley, who not only loses his job but sees

three decades of service come to a bitter end. If Kellner decides *not* to take action, students will pay a price in lost learning opportunities and negative attitudes that may carry over to other classes.

The decision may also have an impact on other teachers. Nonrenewals can threaten morale and increase tension throughout the staff, especially when a veteran teacher is involved; aside from the obvious political fallout, productivity throughout the school may be affected. At the same time, the decision will send an important signal about standards and expectations.

2. *Moral rules.* Kellner seems to be grappling with two implicit rules. First: Do not knowingly expose students to inadequate teaching. Schools exist to educate students; accepting poor teaching undermines that mission. Second: Do not cause pain for others. There is no way to pretend that Halley would not be deeply hurt (financially and psychologically) by a nonrenewal. These rules are clearly in conflict, with no obvious way to reconcile them; Kellner must decide which one has priority.

3. *Caring.* As someone whose whole career has been in education, Kellner can readily put herself in Halley's place: too young to leave, too old to start over. If she is honest, she will admit that she would not want to be cut loose by an institution to which she had devoted her life, even if her performance was not all that it had once been.

On the other hand, Kellner must also care for the students whose education is suffering from Halley's poor teaching. Were she a student, compelled to come to this classroom each day, she would want those in authority to provide a worthy teacher.

Does all this reflection lead to a clearcut solution? Not really—at least not in a hypothetical scenario. The discussion has clarified what is at stake, but at this point Kellner must turn to her own conscience. Her decision will ultimately rest on the relative priority she puts on the conflicting values, as well as her indepth knowledge of the people, institution, and community around her. (For example, if her school has developed a covenant that puts excellent teaching at the heart of the mission, she will find it almost impossible not to act.)

In the end, the decision may rest less on logic than on the kind of person she is, and on the strength of the virtues she possesses. Lacking courage, she would almost certainly take the less controversial course of retaining Halley. Possessing grace, she would be more confident about managing the painful process of nonrenewal. Living a life of honesty, she would be less likely to pretend the problem doesn't exist. In this way, living virtuously is the foundation for ethical decisions.

Conclusion

To be an ethical school leader, then, is not a matter of following a few simple rules. The leader's responsibility is complex and multi-dimensional, rooted less in technical expertise than in simple human integrity.

Leadership stretches that integrity, pitting it against a host of pressures and demands that threaten to deflect us from our purpose. Negotiating the turbulence requires a leader who thinks carefully and reflectively yet acts decisively; who cares about others but has the courage to confront them; who has a sense of history but also sees the world as it might be. Most of all it requires leaders who are fully aware of their own humanity, with all its faults and virtues.

It sounds overwhelming, but William Bridges provides some career advice that may help. "Most of what has been worth doing since the beginning of time has been accomplished by people who were (like you and me, most of the time), tired, self-doubting, ambivalent, and more than a little discouraged." He urges us to concentrate on one essential task: becoming the kind of person we are capable of being. In the words of Rabbi Zusya, "In the world to come, I shall not be asked, 'Why were you not Moses?' I shall be asked, 'Why were you not Zusya?'"

CHAPTER

5

Visionary Leadership

Larry Lashway

> When [the common school] shall be fully developed, when it shall be trained to wield its mighty energies for the protection of society against the giant vices which now invade and torment it;—against intemperance, avarice, war, slavery, bigotry, the woes of want and the wickedness of waste,—then, there will not be a height to which these enemies of the race can escape. (Horace Mann, 1848)

At a time when school leaders are being urged to create new paradigms for the twenty-first century, it is worth remembering that the present school system grew out of one of the most successful visions in American history.

Although no one would claim that public schools have accomplished everything Mann envisioned, most Americans still accept the mission that he and his generation laid out. However, many have lost faith in the vehicle used to implement it. Schools today are routinely described as "nineteenth-century bureaucratic dinosaurs," said to be "beyond repair" or "dysfunctional." Some critics urge dismantling the entire system and turning it over to private enterprise.

For their part, school leaders don't need outside critics to tell them that business as usual is a feeble response to expanded expectations, declining resources, a rapidly changing society, and a cynical, distrustful public.

The irony is that Mann's original vision has been so successful for so long that it takes a determined act of imagination to visualize other possibilities. Virtually everyone has attended school and has absorbed the same unspoken assumptions about what school is supposed to be like. Those with alternative visions have struggled to make a lasting dent in the existing system. Reform efforts have typically been local, incremental, and short-lived (David Tyack and Larry Cuban).

Thus, school leaders in the 1990s find themselves enticed by the talk of visions for the twenty-first century but also skeptical and unsure of where to begin. Advice is plentiful but often vague; leaders are urged to "have vision" without being told what a good vision looks like or where it comes from.

As David Conley and colleagues note, vision in school settings simply hasn't been studied much. We don't yet have an extensive literature on how school leaders establish a vision, or what current educational visions look like, much less the best way to establish one. Vision-building is still more of an art than an applied technical skill.

At the same time, it would be a mistake to consider vision a mystical process reserved for a few high-powered leaders. Increasingly, it is regarded as a core leadership task that can and must be mastered by *all* leaders. This chapter provides school leaders with a practical guide for developing and implementing a vision in their own institutions.

The Nature of Vision

Burt Nanus defines *vision* "a realistic, credible, attractive future for your organization. It is your articulation of a destination toward which your organization should aim, a future that in important ways is better, more successful, or more desirable for your organization than is the present."

James Kouzes and Barry Posner say that vision is a kind of "seeing"; that is, it creates *images* of what the future might hold. A principal interviewed by Linda Sheive and Marian Schoenheit exhibited this ability when he said:

> I believe you need to carry around dreams. You begin to see scenarios in your head. We're going to combine our two high schools some day, and I can already see the first assembly when all the kids come together. I can already see the parade through town when we celebrate it. When you're in a place long enough, you actually attend one of those scenarios [that you dreamed], that really is exciting.

Arthur Blumberg and William Greenfield identify vision with "moral imagination," a quality of character that gives someone "the ability to see that the world need not remain as it is—that it is possible for it to be otherwise, and to be better." In their view, vision is thus more than a technical task—it reflects the leader's values and is the source of his or her moral authority.

Some extend the definition of vision to cover not only the ultimate goal but the process of getting there. A. Lorri Manasse argues that leaders must have the organizational insight to see what structural changes are required to actualize the vision, as well as the strategic insight to map out a route from present reality to future dream.

What Vision Is Not

Definitions of vision are still loose and unsettled, and many educators associate the concept with "mission" and "strategic planning." However, some argue that there are important distinctions among these ideas.

Nanus, for example, asserts that mission is *purpose*, a statement of core principles; it answers the question "Why are we here?" Vision imagines how that mission will be fulfilled in the future.

Thus, a typical mission statement might look like this: "Asimov Elementary School exists to provide a positive environment in which all children can actualize their potential." For Nanus, this would not be a vision because it does not spell out a future state that is noticeably different from the present.

The mission is linked to the vision, since it points to the kinds of changes that are needed. If teachers at Asimov Elementary come to the conclusion that not all students are actualizing their potential, or that societal changes will make current methods inadequate, they must visualize a future in which the mission is fulfilled: "Asimov students will become skillful, self-directed learners by participating in a linguistically enriched, integrated curriculum, with portfolio-based assessment and a strong emphasis on self-evaluation." (Another school with the same mission might arrive at a very different vision; as Kouzes and Posner note, each organization is unique, and there are many ways to achieve the same results.)

Another related term is *strategic planning*, which has received considerable attention in the past decade. Like visions, strategic plans imagine a future state that is different; unlike visions, plans offer a systematic, sequential strategy for getting to the future. The entire plan is mapped out at the beginning with specific, quantifiable objectives, in enough detail that the entire process can be captured on flow charts (Roger Kaufman).

Visions likewise are goal-directed, but they don't always map out a clear pathway, especially if the goal is something that has never been done. Most descriptions of vision seem to suggest a looser, more improvisational approach. For example, Conley and colleagues note that in some of the schools they studied, the vision emerged only after several years of experimenting with alternative strategies. Apparently, teachers and administrators had to see some ideas in action before they were ready to articulate a vision they could commit to. Karen Louis and Matthew Miles found the same thing in urban high schools they studied.

In theory, the tools of strategic planning could be used for implementing visions; indeed, Kaufman portrays planning as a means of achieving a school's "ideal vision." However, the two approaches seem to have very different "flavors." Plans are roadmaps, offering a predictable itinerary; visions are more like compasses, pointing out the right direction, but leaving a lot to interpretation.

What Vision Does

The right vision, says Nanus, has powerful, positive effects on the organization:

- It attracts commitment and energizes people.
- It creates meaning in workers' lives.
- It establishes a standard of excellence.
- It bridges the present and the future.

Warren Bennis and colleagues add that when organizations have a widely shared vision, employees better understand their own roles and "are transformed from robots blindly following instructions to human beings engaged in a creative and purposeful venture." Believing they can make a difference, workers are more likely to bring vigor and enthusiasm to their tasks, aligning human energies toward a common end.

A clear vision offers a core of meaning that unambiguously expresses what it means to work in a particular school and provides a shared standard by which teachers can gauge their own efforts. According to one teacher in a school that had recently developed a vision, "People are speaking the same language, they have the same kinds of informal expectations for one another, more common ground" (Conley and colleagues).

The Leader's Role

In the last decade, scholars of leadership have been almost unanimous in declaring vision to be one of the essential attributes of the leader. Bennis and colleagues write:

> If there is a spark of genius in the extraordinary manager at all, it must lie in this transcending ability, a kind of magic, to assemble—out of all the variety of images, signals, forecasts and alternatives—a clearly articulated vision of the future that is at once simple,

easily understood, clearly desirable, and energizing.

Howard Gardner describes this genius as the ability to relate a story that provides meaning to the lives of followers, a story in which the leader and followers are principal characters. "Together, they have embarked on a journey in pursuit of certain goals, and along the way and into the future, they can expect to encounter certain obstacles or resistances that can be overcome."

But is a vision the single-handed creation of a charismatic leader who bowls people over with passion, eloquence, and sheer force of personality? Robert Kelley is skeptical of this notion.

> Many leadership books tout the "visionary" role of leaders. Like Moses descending from the mountaintop, the leader unveils the new order. For their part in this scenario, dependent followers are supposed to stop wandering about aimlessly. Instead, they dutifully applaud, thank the leader profusely, and line up behind the leader's vision.

A more recent view sees the leader's role as facilitative, aimed at helping the entire school community to develop a *collective* vision. Rather than creating the vision and selling it to others, the leader negotiates a shared vision with the school community by challenging, communicating, and empowering. The facilitative leader, though having a personal vision that influences others, is not automatically considered the chief author of the school's vision. Indeed, leaders may have to let go of some parts of their own vision for the common good (David Conley and Paul Goldman).

Whether the leader uses heroic individual effort or shared decision-making, building a vision goes far beyond stating it in words. Robert Starratt points out that the vision must be translated into organizational reality. Leaders must allocate resources, formulate workable policies, and negotiate permission with higher authorities. Thus, leaders must not only be comfortable with discussing the purpose of school but must also be technically adept in providing the administrative structure that will sustain that purpose.

Marshall Sashkin argues that successful visionary leaders have a repertoire of behaviors that work together to push the vision along. By focusing attention on key issues, communicating effectively, being consistent, displaying respect for self and others, and taking calculated risks, leaders can create an environment in which visions are made real.

Perhaps most important, the leader embodies the vision in thought, word, and deed. Visionaries do not just communicate their dreams in so many words, says Gardner; "they convey their stories by the kinds of lives they themselves lead and, through example, seek to inspire in their followers." Clearly, leaders remain the key people in the process even if they are not the sole authors of the vision.

The Sources of Vision

Where do visions come from? Despite widespread agreement that vision is essential, there are few detailed descriptions of how it develops in school settings, nor has anyone reduced it to a convenient formula. At times the process seems straightforward and logical; at other times it seems intuitive and mysterious. Sometimes it is elevating and exhilarating, reawakening dormant idealism and recharging low batteries; sometimes it is frustrating and baffling, seemingly an act of creating something out of nothing.

Despite these contradictions and uncertainties, we can identify some of the key issues that school leaders must confront in developing a vision. First, it is important to distinguish between having *vision* and having *a* vision. Vision is the human capacity to see the implications of one's values and beliefs, not only today but projected into the future. Having *a* vision is what happens when this ability is applied to the needs of a particular institution. This section discusses vision as a human capacity; the next section explores how a vision can be developed for a particular school.

The Challenges of Vision

For beleaguered principals, sitting in the shadow of inbaskets stacked with mundane tasks, vision can seem abstract and nebulous. Administrators tend to see themselves as doers, not dreamers, taking pride in managing real-world complexities rather than speculating on hypothetical possibilities. Is it realistic to expect them to engage in what seems to be a very creative process? The answer is clearly "yes."

We can take a cue from fiction writers, who are often exasperated by fans who ask, "Where do you get your ideas?" Writers find the question difficult to answer. On the one hand, they certainly don't pull down an Idea Encyclopedia and pick a plot; on the other hand, they don't sit around in a trance-like state waiting for inspiration to strike. Rather, it appears that the best writers are engaged with life, keeping their eyes open for the dramas, characters, and oddities that make up human existence. At some point, inspiration bubbles to the surface, but it would be wrong to say it comes out of nowhere.

Kouzes and Posner, arguing that intuition is "the wellspring of vision," claim there is nothing mystical about it. It is simply an accelerated mental process that reflects considerable experience and great expertise in a domain. An idea may seem to come out of nowhere, they say, but "it's the years of direct contact with a variety of problems and situations that equip the leader with unique insight. Listening, reading, smelling, feeling, and tasting the business—these tasks improve our vision." Thus the foundations of vision lie in everyday experience.

Small Beginnings

Kouzes and Posner point out that in the beginning the grandest vision is only a glimmer of an idea, "a vague desire to do something that would challenge yourself and others." At this stage, the operative word is "possibility," not "probability." What counts is that it *could* happen, not that it is probable.

They cite the example of teacher Nolan Dishongh, who begins each year believing that each of his at-risk students wants to be a responsible, informed human being. At the beginning of the year, an objective observer might not see this as a likely outcome, but the fact that Dishongh sees the possibility increases the probability.

Roland Barth concedes that practitioners' visions are usually "deeply submerged, sometimes fragmentary, and seldom articulated.... But I am convinced the vision is there." Too often, he suggests, people begin their educational careers with a strong sense of idealism and "a 20/20 personal vision," only to have it collide with bureaucratic procedures and mandates. Most people learn to keep their visions in the closet to avoid the painful discrepancy between real and ideal.

Barth suggests that the vision begins to reemerge when leaders allow themselves to complete open-ended statements like:

- "When I leave this school I would like to be remembered for..."
- "The kind of school I would like my children to attend..."
- "The kind of school I would like to teach in..."
- "I want my place to be a school where..."

Edward Chance and Marilyn Grady similarly suggest that vision may originate in the principal's answer to these questions:

- "What are my five greatest strengths?"
- "What are my five greatest weaknesses?"
- "What are three things I value most in my professional life?"
- "With which leadership style am I most comfortable?"
- "What do I want to prove as a leader?"

All these authors seem to be suggesting that the seed of vision is in everyone; it merely needs to be cultivated.

Vision and Values

Sheive and Schoenheit found that the administrators they studied invariably linked their visions with their sense of values. At some point in their careers, those values collided with organizational realities, bringing the vision to the surface. One superintendent put it this way:

> It happens when you are deeply committed and it appears that outside forces constrict you. It is an irritant. Just like with an oyster, you create a pearl around the grain of irritation.

Starratt notes that vision is always based on "assumptions and beliefs about the nature of learning, about the essence of being human, about the nature of human society, about the purpose of schooling. The leader dwells inside these beliefs and meanings, and calls attention to them through a vision statement."

Resting at the heart of this belief system are myths—the fundamental meanings by which people make sense out of their lives. Starratt says that myths are so basic and taken for granted that they are almost inaccessible at an everyday level.

Leaders with vision are the ones who struggle to bring these buried beliefs and assumptions to the surface, where they can be critically examined and either reaffirmed or abandoned. This kind of searching is at the heart of vision. Gardner says leaders are distinguished by how well, or to what extent, they do it. Ordinary leaders tell the culture's traditional stories; innovative leaders take neglected stories and give them a fresh twist; and visionary leaders actually create new stories.

Developing vision, then, is an act with fundamentally moral implications, which makes it all the more important for school leaders. Schools, invested with a "public trust," carry the hopes and aspirations of an entire community. But Neal Postman observes that schools don't just serve a public, they create a public—for good or for evil.

Cultivating vision thus requires posing some thorny questions:

- What gives life meaning?
- Is there hope for the future?
- Under what conditions do children learn best?
- What are the greatest needs that children bring to school?
- Under what conditions do teachers teach best?
- What would best help children prepare for their future?

These are not small issues, nor is it easy to articulate answers. But those with vision make an effort, however fumbling, to do so.

An Eye to the Future

One obstacle to developing worthwhile visions is the natural tendency to assume that the near future (five to ten years) will be much like the present. But the environment is always changing, and a vision that fails to anticipate change is a vision that won't have much impact. (Imagine a buggy-whip company in 1905 that sets a ten-year vision of making the world's best buggy-whip.)

John Hoyle points out that the future is not something that simply shows up unannounced a few years down the road; instead, it is something that is *created* by the actions we take today.

> We must assume that we can change our course as a captain would steer a boat to the harbor or down a rapidly moving river. Change must occur early if the boat is to arrive safely at the mouth of the river. We are often tied to a successful past, and when trouble strikes, we are unprepared to make changes in time to avoid running aground.

"Future sight" seems especially important now, at a time of unprecedented social change. Business analyst Peter Drucker puts it bluntly, saying that work, society, and government in developed economies are "qualitatively and quantitatively different not only from what they were in the first years of this century but also from what has existed at any other time in history: in their configurations, in their processes, in their problems, in their structures." He believes the changes will not have peaked by the year 2000.

So a reasonable person would anticipate that schools in ten years will find themselves in an environment that differs noticeably from today's world. But what will the changes be? Does vision require predicting the future?

Peter Schwartz, an expert in long-range planning, says prediction is not the point. No one can know the future with certainty; instead, the goal is to increase awareness of possibilities. Having considered what *might* happen, a leader is better prepared for what *does* happen.

Imagine, for a moment, the following scenarios:

- High-quality self-contained educational programs become available on the Internet, easily downloaded for a small fee.
- The emergence of voucher systems places schools in a highly competitive market.

- The number of high-risk students grows dramatically.
- New technology permits students to participate in "virtual classes" anywhere in the world while sitting at home.
- Parents become insistent on using a back-to-the-basics approach, with a heavy emphasis on test scores.
- The town's major employer closes down.
- A major high-tech company establishes an office that will attract thousands of well-educated workers to the community.
- Increased demand for adult education leads schools to remain open fifteen hours a day for all kinds of courses.

Obviously, no one knows which (if any) of these scenarios will actually unfold, yet any of them *could.* Exploring the possibilities serves several purposes. First, some important trends may become obvious once we take the trouble to look for them. The enrollment decline of the 1970s and 1980s was perfectly predictable, yet many schools were caught unaware, forcing them to lay off teachers and close schools in a crisis atmosphere. In the 1990s, demographic projections show a continuing increase in student diversity, especially in populations that schools have been least successful with. The impact may not affect all schools equally, but educators ignore the trend at their own risk.

Second, even those possibilities that never come to pass may stimulate useful thinking. For example, the prospect of a high-tech boom is wishful thinking for most communities, but simply asking the question generates some interesting thoughts. Aside from the obvious issue of facilities, the influx of well-educated workers into the community might raise some curricular questions. Would the newcomers demand more academically challenging classes and a stronger college-prep program? Where *is* our curriculum? Whose needs are we meeting? Even if the high-tech company never comes here, our children will be growing up in a high-tech world—will they be ready for it?

Looking to the future takes us out of the here-and-now, reminding us that our best efforts today may fall far short tomorrow.

Reflective Practice

What's clear from the above discussion is that visionary leaders are reflective; they not only act, they think about the significance of their actions, now and in the future. This does not imply abstract, disembodied theorizing. Starratt says that leaders' thinking "is not something that they are consciously aware of; it is something habitually beneath the surface of their decisions and responses." He adds, however, that at times this stream of thought needs to be brought to the surface, preferably through dialogue with members of the school community.

What sort of reflection? Starratt gives three examples.

1. *Problem-naming* is a conscious effort to diagnose a problem rather than just categorizing it by its most obvious features. Thus, a high rate of teacher absenteeism might quickly be blamed on "lack of responsibility," whereas a closer look would show it to be the result of low morale or a sense of futility. How the problem is defined determines how we will act.

2. *An educational platform* is one's philosophy of education—the basic beliefs and assumptions that provide the foundation for vision. Starratt notes that the platforms of leaders tend to be visible more in their actions than in any formal statement. Nevertheless, brief written exercises can be helpful. For example, leaders can complete short open-ended statements such as "Students learn best when...." or "Classroom learning ought to emphasize...." Leaders can use such statements to assess their own leadership (Does my school live up to these beliefs?), as well as generate dialogue with others.

3. *Double-loop learning.* Citing the work of management expert Chris Argyris, Starratt says that much administrative thinking involves *single-loop learning*; that is, problems are treated as separate entities. Leaders assess the situation, pick a strategy, evaluate the results, and move on (or try again). By contrast, *double-loop learning* deals with the immediate problem while simultaneously seeing it as part of the larger context of institutional dynamics. For example, a poorly performing teacher presents not only the surface problem of finding a way to improve instruction, but also affects relations with the union, the teacher's career, the reputation of the principal, and the learning of the students. Double-loop learning leads to a better understanding of the institution as a whole.

Creative Thinking

Perhaps the greatest challenge in reflection is escaping the bonds of the "mental models" that direct our thinking along well-worn paths. Margaret Wheatley cites Albert Einstein's belief that "no problem can be solved from the same consciousness that created it. We must learn to see the world anew." W. Patrick Dolan adds that when a system is dysfunctional, early attempts at improvement "will generally be a magnification of its pathology."

Bennis and colleagues suggest that less analytical kinds of thinking may be helpful. Logical reflection tends to keep us in a mental world that is realistic, constrained by our experience with things as they are. The most exciting visions imagine things that have never been.

The authors urge leaders to cultivate intuitive thinking that breaks conventional mind sets. They suggest that such thinking is best done in relaxed, receptive states of mind, and that it relies more on visual images than abstract language. For example, principals could take a mental walk through their ideal school. Strolling through the corridors, what will they see? What are students working on? How are they working? What's on the walls?

Vision *sees*, and in the seeing it becomes real. Reflective thinking may lead us to what we think works best; intuitive thinking leads us to what we most desire. Together, they form a powerful visionary tool.

Blocks to Vision

Sometimes, of course, the ideas don't come. Bennis and colleagues suggest a number of causes:

- Being too focused on daily routines. (The concreteness of the daily routine tempts one away from the more ambiguous challenge of developing a vision.)
- Wanting to be just one of the crowd. (A bold vision is risky; it calls attention to oneself and creates new expectations.)
- Flitting from one thing to the other. (Some people are overwhelmed by possibilities; in trying to cover everything, they end up without a clear focus on anything.)
- Reckless risk-taking. (Some leaders enjoy a high-wire act in which they are the stars.)
- Clinging to established principles to avoid ambiguity. (Creating a new future is filled with uncertainty; some leaders just tinker around the margins.)
- Being too open-minded. (Some leaders find it difficult to choose.)
- Believing you have all the answers. (In their hearts, some leaders simply don't believe that major change is needed.)

Charting an Organization's Vision

Through sensitivity to values, attention to the future, and careful thinking, principals can expand their own capacity for vision. But that ability will mean little unless it can be applied to the needs of a particular school. This section explores how school leaders can get from vision to *a* vision.

Preparing the Way

Before any action is taken, the leader must resolve several critical issues. Developing a vision is not something to be done lightly; barging ahead recklessly is likely to result in failure (thereby increasing cynicism and diminishing confidence in the school) or a "paper success" (with the vision statement plastered on every piece of paper in sight but otherwise cheerfully ignored). The vision process can unleash powerful forces, threatening the existing order and making people aware of uncomfortable facts or philosophical disagreements. Unwary leaders may find themselves with a boiling pot and no way to turn down the flames.

Knowing the Limits

The first issue is the question of limits. Every school is a part of a larger system, subject to rules and regulations that may limit the school's freedom to innovate. The leader must thus determine: How free are we to reinvent ourselves? Are certain changes off limits? (Could we, for example, decide to operate our school from 10 a.m. until 5 p.m. or is the district's bus schedule sacred?) Will resources be available to put our ideas into effect? Is the union receptive to changes in teachers' work roles? Leaders who can't answer these questions would be well advised to do more research.

Dolan argues that vision development is unlikely to succeed without "deep buy-in" from the board, superintendent, union, and anyone with effective veto power over the school's vision. Getting public, formal approval from these groups diminishes skepticism that "the system" won't permit real change.

Such explicit approval is not always available, of course. Those responsible for managing a whole system are not always eager to encourage mavericks who may disrupt the bureaucratic machinery by seeking special treatment. In this case, the principal may have to quietly negotiate informal "understandings" that will provide a sense of the political and economic limits.

Involving Others

Another major issue is deciding how to involve others in the process. As noted earlier, recent thinking has tended to downplay the idea of a heroic, charismatic leader singlehandedly articulating a vision and then persuading everyone to accept it. However, it is by no means clear how, when, and to what extent others should become involved. The instinctive response is to start establishing committees, but they can be unwieldy tools, especially if their purpose is vague or their members are not deeply committed to the process.

There is no recognized formula here, but several principles may be helpful.

First, it is important to recognize that not everyone has to vote on every decision. Members of the school community may play different roles at different times. In any decision, some need to vote, some need to be consulted, and some just need to be informed.

Second, deciding what is needed in any given case requires a leader who is fully in touch with the views of key stakeholders. Communication must be incessant, not just in committee meetings, but in the multitude of daily interactions that make up any administrator's day. Brief, spontaneous corridor discussions can be more productive than lengthy committee meetings.

Finally, despite the limitations of committees, establishing a well-informed monitoring group can be healthy. Dolan recommends a site council representing all constituencies; its primary role would not be to make decisions, but to evaluate the process and keep things on track. The group should receive training in group problem-solving and consensual decision-making and should address the inevitable difficulties and misunderstandings that will arise. Does the principal have an accurate perception of teachers' attitudes toward the vision? Do some people feel left out of the process? Do other people feel overburdened or confused? The steering council must be a place where such questions can be discussed honestly.

Taking Stock

Just as leaders must know their beliefs and values, they must know their schools—the strengths, the weaknesses, the climate and "personality." Nanus recommends a series of questions that can point the way.

1. *What values and beliefs guide decision-making in this organization?* Prevailing norms often determine attitudes toward the vision. For example, a faculty might be guided by these values (often unstated):

- Academic proficiency is the highest goal.
- Teachers never criticize other teachers' methods.
- Go along to get along.
- Above all, students should learn to believe in themselves.
- Parents should be an integral part of the school.
- Some students just can't learn.

Leaders need not be fatalistic about accepting norms; indeed, part of the vision process is designed to get people to bring these assumptions to the surface and examine them. But the leader must recognize them.

2. *What are the organization's strengths and weaknesses?* Visions are easier to fulfill if they can build on the school's strengths or avoid its weaknesses. For example, an analysis may show that the school has:

- strong relationships with parents and community
- a diminished tax base that threatens finances
- a rapidly changing population bringing more students who need individual attention, remedial work, and access to social services
- a capable, veteran staff that works hard to meet students' needs
- a capable, veteran staff that is comfortable with the status quo
- aging buildings
- a cohesive written curriculum for all grade levels

All these factors will affect the vision.

3. *What strategy is currently being followed to fulfill the current mission? Is it working?* Unlike the private sector, where competition forces companies to think strategically, schools may see themselves as steady-state service providers whose main responsibility is to provide a protective, supportive environment for teaching and learning. A true strategy explicitly links activities and programs to the mission. For example, recently added programs (such as drug education) often represent a conscious strategy; the role of more traditional offerings (such as science) may be taken for granted.

4. *Does the organization currently have a clearly stated vision? If so, what is it?* If a vision already exists, the leader's task changes; reviewing and renewing a vision requires a somewhat different approach than creating a vision for the first time.

5. *If the organization stays on the current path, where will it be heading in the next decade? Is that good?* Here is where leaders must apply their future vision, trying to determine how the environment may change in coming years, and how the changes will affect the school.

6. *Do key people in the organization know where it is headed and agree on that direction?* This is an important reality check; the mere existence of a formal vision statement does not guarantee it a significant role in the school's culture. Do people accept the official plan? Is it part of their everyday professional vocabulary? Do they judge their actions by their effect on the vision? Or do they give only lip service to the statement?

7. *Does the system—structures, processes, resources—support the current direction?* For example, if the vision calls for "technological literacy," does the budget provide sufficient technological resources? If the vision calls for a significant shift of direction, are teachers being provided with appropriate training or the time to collaborate on necessary changes?

Energizing the School

At this point, the leader faces what may be the most crucial part of the process: enlisting members of the school community in the search for a common vision.

Schools differ in their readiness to undertake this process. Ironically, as David Hurst points out, organizations in crisis may be the ripest for change. When employees are bombarded with daily evidence that things just aren't working, when they can see the organization's failure in their own experience, they are more likely to listen to someone who says there is a better way. (Indeed, Hurst goes as far as to say that if no crisis is on the immediate horizon, the leader should create one by shaking up normal organizational routines and expectations.)

Leaders who are new to their school may also have certain temporary advantages. New principals don't carry the weight of long-established routines and relationships; teachers recognize this blank slate and are usually anxious to know what the new agenda will be. Often there is a honeymoon period in which the staff, recognizing the principal's need to make a mark, will good-naturedly accept some new initiatives. At this stage, even small actions by a leader can have a major impact on the school's future direction.

The biggest challenge may be faced by an established principal in a good school where teachers are competent and committed, resources are adequate, and the community is satisfied. People who are content with the present have little motivation to go looking for the future. How can the leader deal with this?

One perfectly logical response is to accept the judgment of the staff and leave well enough alone. The problem, of course, is that today's "well enough" may become tomorrow's "totally inadequate." A school without a tradition of self-examination and forward thinking will be ill-prepared when a crisis hits.

Instead, a visionary leader can gently challenge the staff in a number of ways. One starting point is to initiate some low-key discussions focusing on the school's mission. Why are we here? Who are we serving? How well are we succeeding? How could we do better? The answers can serve as a reminder of basic priorities as well as a springboard to thinking about the future.

Tony Wagner describes how fourteen school districts around the country have used this approach by forming teams of parents, educators, community members, and older students to conduct focus groups and interviews with constituent groups in the community. The result was a thoughtful dialogue that helped each group see how their concerns connected with others, and that provided a solid foundation for developing a vision for change.

Hoyle suggests structured exercises in which participants are asked to design their ideal school or imagine what it would take to be a world-class school in 2010. He also recommends "scenario-building," activities that speculate on alternative futures that the school may face.

Providing Inspiration

The initial discussions are likely to be tentative and meandering, with participants looking nervously at one another and wondering how honest they can afford to be. At the end, if all goes well, the school will see the birth of a vibrant, motivating vision. In between is an ambiguous period in which participants move from skepticism to hope, from the attitude of "just another meeting" to genuine excitement. How that happens often seems mysterious, even to the participants, but a number of observers have pointed to some very concrete leadership behaviors that will help.

1. *Empowering People To Voice Their Dreams.* Many teachers learn to keep their ideals to themselves. They have seen too many clashes between vision and bureaucracy or too many grand schemes that went nowhere, and have reached the cynical conclusion that educational bandwagons are usually drawn by a team of white elephants.

Yet Michael Rose, visiting classrooms across the country, found that most of the teachers he observed had a strong belief in the worth and potential of all their students and were willing to "push on the existing order of things" to help realize that potential. Perhaps, as Barth suggests, the vision has not died but is merely kept from view, a private possession rather than a public commitment.

The leadership challenge is to make conversation about ideals a regular, valued part of professional interaction. Principals can do this primarily by the power of their own example. If they set aside time at faculty meetings for such questions, it sends an important message; if in their daily interactions they give ideals equal standing with budgets, schedules, and reports, it empowers teachers to bring their own visions out of hiding.

2. *Encouraging Innovation.* Talking about vision is one thing; following through is another. Long before the creation of a formal school vision, the principal can send the signal, through innumerable small actions, that acting on personal vision is not only permitted but encouraged. Teachers get the message:

> The principal is very receptive to new ideas and ways of doing things. She values the opinions of all her staff members.

> She realizes that our school and our students are unique and welcomes suggestions and ideas for improving instruction. We have an instructional task force that continually teaches new methods of instruction and we are encouraged to try new techniques. (Joseph Blase and Jo Roberts Blase)

Blase and Blase emphasize that it is important for teachers to be able to carry out this experimentation in a nonthreatening environment, without fear of criticism when ideas don't work.

3. *Inspiring Others.* Kouzes and Posner note that most people, even though they don't consider themselves inspiring, can have inspirational effects by being emotionally expressive:

> Expressiveness comes naturally to people talking about deep desires for the future. They lean forward in their chairs, they move their arms about, their eyes light up, their voices sing with emotion, and a smile appears on their faces. In these circumstances, people are enthusiastic, articulate, optimistic, and uplifting.

In part, then, inspiration is a matter of expressive style; words and gestures that convey enthusiasm and excitement are likely to be contagious. Kouzes and Posner add, however, that this is not something that can be simulated; the leader's convictions must be genuine.

4. *Finding the Common Ground.* Personal dreams take tangible shape when we realize they are shared by others. As leaders talk with teachers, they should be listening for the common ground, looking for the signs that say, "This is what this school is about!" Kouzes and Posner say:

> Leaders find the common thread that weaves the fabric of human needs into a colorful tapestry. They develop a deep understanding of the collective yearnings; they seek out the brewing consensus among those they would lead. They listen carefully for quiet whisperings in dark corners and attend to subtle cues. They get a sense of what people want, what they value, what they dream about.

Those signs are out there, in words, stories, body language, and most of all in actions. Leaders can find them if they look, if they devote enough time to roaming the hallways and talking to teachers, students, and parents.

As leaders begin to sense the areas of consensus, they can feed their impressions back to the faculty, helping them confirm vague impressions and sparking further reflection and discussion.

5. *Keeping a Positive, Uplifting Focus.* The power of a vision is its ability to help people feel they are part of something special, part of an effort that is not just going to make improvements but transform their work. William Cunningham and Donn Gresso argue that developing a vision should not be looked on as merely a matter of solving problems:

> Problem-solving creates a group dynamic of defensiveness, protectionism, power struggle, mistrust, and an ultimately adversarial relationship. Applied to the improvement of schooling, the model usually results in feelings of failure, incompetence, and depression.... A sense of inadequacy develops within the culture.

A visionary approach, they say, puts aside the need to justify failures and instead asks, "Where do we go from here?" Bennis and colleagues characterize it as the difference between saying, "I am cutting stone" and saying, "I am building a cathedral."

Even simple language habits may make a difference. Kouzes and Posner urge leaders to say "will" rather than "try." They say this does not require being naive or unrealistic about the difficulties, which should be openly recognized. It is more a matter of projecting an attitude that says, "I'm confident we'll work through all the difficulties and reach the goal."

Starratt also points to the importance of language, noting that vision statements often employ vivid imagery that hits home. Metaphors that liken school to "gardening," "family," "symphonies," and "journeys" will touch the heart as well as the mind.

6. *Dramatizing Core Beliefs.* As the vision begins to emerge, it will initially seem tentative and shaky; the leader's role is to dramatize it. As abstract statements of principles, visions may seem distant and unreachable; connected to the drama of human life, they take on deep meaning.

Terry Deal argues that organizational improvement takes on life when portrayed through metaphor, poetry, drama, stories, and rituals. For example, one of the things that lets teachers talk about visions at all is the occasional classroom encounter that makes a better future seem possible. Encouraging teachers to tell stories about these exciting moments is a good way to spread the excitement and make the vision seem reachable.

Something as simple as meeting offcampus can lend drama and significance to the effort. One experienced teacher, veteran of many a reform, observed that just once it would be nice to launch a change with a nice meal at a carpeted conference center instead of with stale doughnuts in a drafty cafeteria.

Stating the Vision

All these activities may lead a school closer to its vision, generating excitement and enthusiasm. Yet at some point the vision must be articulated and publicly disseminated.

Having created enthusiasm and a stimulating atmosphere in which teachers feel free to experiment, principals may be tempted to let things ride. After all, isn't our vision truly in what we do rather than in what we say?

And surely there are risks in the seemingly innocent act of committing words to paper. Part of the early excitement in vision formation is the sense of unlimited possibilities, the implicit belief that we can do it all. Stating the vision forces us to choose between equally attractive futures; teachers who believed that the vision would incorporate their own philosophy may be dismayed to find their colleagues leaning in another direction. Moreover, stating the vision produces accountability. Having said it, we are now expected to do it.

Yet a vision that is not clearly articulated is a vision that is likely to wither. The initial excitement may carry people for a while, but eventually the usual mundane concerns (which never seem to go away) begin to crowd out the experimentation; the inevitable missteps may discourage some, causing them to put their ideas on hold. Through all that, the existence of a written statement helps keep the vision real.

However, there is no need to produce the statement according to any particular schedule. Nanus suggests allowing time for ideas to simmer. Slowly start to sketch out possibilities; at some point, begin to draw up alternative visions, write them out, and share them with others.

How does one know the statement is ready? Here again there is no textbook answer, just a need for finely tuned professional judgment. Nanus suggests some possible criteria, saying the vision should be:

- future oriented
- utopian (leading to a better future)
- appropriate for the organization
- reflective of high ideals and excellence
- indicative of the organization's direction
- capable of inspiring enthusiasm
- reflective of the organization's uniqueness
- ambitious

The best sign of a ripe vision may be in the emotions it arouses. Bennis and colleagues quote Kevin Kingsland:

> When you have found your vision you do not ask yourself whether you have one. You inform the world about it. If you're wondering whether you have a vision, then you haven't got one.
>
> When you've discovered your vision you abound with inspiration. Your eyes sparkle. You can see it in the atmosphere. It is pulsing with life.

Living the Vision

Having formulated a written statement, there is, at least psychologically, a pause for breath. The statement is a considerable achievement that should be recognized and celebrated before moving on to the next step.

And there is a next step. One of the major errors in vision-building is confusing the statement with the vision. In their work with businesses, Michael Hammer and Steven Stanton have found that the official statement is usually given a major publicity blitz, in memos, posters, and wallet-sized laminated cards (not to mention key rings, buttons, and notebook covers). Unfortunately, they say, this effort is often wasted on empty slogans or feel-good words like "excellence," "integrity," or "teamwork." The problem is not that the visions are somehow wrong, but that they never become more than glittering generalities trapped under the plastic.

Likewise, Nanus observes, "A vision is little more than an empty dream until it is widely shared and accepted. Only then does it acquire the force necessary to change an organization and move it in the intended direction." A complete discussion of change processes is beyond the scope of this chapter, but several issues are especially pertinent to vision.

Gaining Acceptance

If the vision has been developed through a collaborative process and is truly responsive to the beliefs of the staff, acceptance is likely. Yet there is no such thing as 100 percent acceptance. There will always be those who lack enthusiasm and commitment to the vision. Dolan estimates that for most major changes, 10 percent of the teachers will be flatly opposed, 20-25 percent will be in favor, and the rest will be skeptical but willing to be convinced.

Resistance

Resistance occurs for a variety of reasons. Some objections may come from an unwillingness to change comfortable routines and lesson plans that have taken years to develop. But other resistance is political, rooted in the challenge to existing patterns of influence and status. For example, a high school department chair may fear that collaborative decision-making will diminish his or her influence on curriculum decisions.

Sometimes resistance is a matter of honest philosophical disagreement. There are those on every staff who gravitate toward child-centered, open-ended environments, while others believe in highly structured, academically oriented approaches. Ironically, those who care the most about what they do may be the strongest opponents of the new vision.

Finally, some resistance is simply good sense. As Andrew Gitlin and Frank Margonis point out, when a proposed change imposes extra burdens on teachers without providing additional resources, resistance is just a way of saying, "This is unrealistic."

It is also worth noting that what we call "resistance" is often just a normal human response to change, one that everyone (including the leader) is likely to experience. Management consultant William Bridges points out that any major change requires a significant psychological transition. He outlines three stages.

- First, every new beginning is actually an *ending* that requires letting go of the old order, sometimes even inducing a grieving process.
- Second is a *neutral zone* that represents a kind of limbo in which the old way is gone and the new isn't yet comfortable.
- Finally comes the actual new *beginning,* in which the new way begins to seem natural and normal.

Bridges argues that all three stages are necessary and ultimately healthful; they need to be properly managed, not avoided.

Whatever the cause of resistance, Hammer and Stanton caution leaders against looking for logical reasons. "Ultimately, it is how people feel about a new situation that determines how they will respond to it. If they feel frightened, or threatened, or uncomfortable, or uncertain, then their reaction is likely to be a negative one."

Responding to Resistance

Hammer and Stanton point out that resistance is actually a positive sign, an indicator that something significant is happening. It is a natural human response, not a sign that the vision is somehow deficient.

Yet resistance presents leaders with a sensitive human-relations dilemma. On the one hand, the vision embodies the core values of the school and demands allegiance from everyone who chooses to work there. While the vision should allow teachers reasonable autonomy and flexibility, it also makes certain nonnegotiable demands. Thomas Sergiovanni says, "It is the leader's responsibility to be outraged when empowerment is abused and when purposes are ignored."

When teachers conspicuously fail to honor those purposes, or continually disparage and demean the vision, or even settle for passive resistance, they can spread a contagious dampening cloud over the whole project.

On the other hand, directly confronting the resisters doesn't always work. For one thing, direct confrontations sometimes escalate into dramatic showdowns that tenured teachers seldom lose. Moreover, such drastic action may, in the long run, be counterproductive; even teachers who support the vision may be unnerved by the idea that there is a "politically correct" view that affects job security.

Bridges does not attribute resistance to animosity or stubbornness, but to normal human psychology (even among those who support the change). He suggests a number of approaches that may be helpful to people in the midst of a transition.

1. *Identify what the resisters may have lost.* It may be a position of influence or status; it may be a philosophical allegiance (for example, a teacher who has long prided herself on teaching the basics may feel that effort is being abandoned as the school moves toward a whole-language approach).

2. *Honor what is being lost.* The old ways may no longer be appropriate for the new century, but in their day they may have served many children well. The need for new directions does not mean that those using the old ways have wasted their lives.

3. *Mark the endings.* People often cope with change through ceremonies (funerals, birthdays, graduations) that dramatically and publicly announce the new order.

4. *Emphasize the continuity in the new vision.* As noted earlier, a good vision will build on the organization's past. The vision may be a shift in course, but it's still the same ship.

5. *Publicly recognize the inner turmoil that everyone is experiencing.* People are often reluctant to talk about confusion and negative feelings, thereby denying themselves the comfort and counsel of others. Leaders must set the tone by being open and honest about their own confusions and uncertainties, as well as being sensitive to the uncertainties of others.

6. *Make sure that everyone has a part to play.* This means that they not only understand what changes the vision requires of them but have an opportunity to take part in the vision process. As people invest time and effort in a goal, they begin to acquire a psychological stake in its success.

7. *Be consistent.* The vision calls for certain new behaviors and attitudes, which should be implemented and rewarded. Principals can be sure

that teachers will be watching closely; failing to act with the vision may be taken as a sign of wavering or even hypocrisy.

8. *Strive for early successes, even small ones.* In the early stages of implementation, when not everyone is fully convinced, results are often magnified out of proportion to their actual importance. By highlighting certain low-risk tasks, or arranging for some long-sought concession or resource from higher authorities, leaders can score important points when it matters most. Bridges says, "Quick successes reassure the believers, convince the doubters, and confound the critics."

Institutionalizing the Vision

As the previous section suggests, the leader must continue to be chief cheerleader and communicator for the vision, working to make it real in the hearts and minds of the school community and to weave it into the fabric of the school's culture. Beyond this kind of transformational leadership, leaders must turn their attention to the more familiar territory of hierarchical leadership, using their administrative skills to create the policies, resources, and structures needed to implement the vision.

Starratt visualizes the school as an onion. At the core are the beliefs, assumptions, goals, and myths that are the source of vision. The outer layers are composed of policies (the basic rules governing organizational behavior), programs (the division of the school's work into departments, grade levels, and offices), organization (the distribution of resources through budgets, schedules, and staffing), and operations (the visible work of classroom teaching and learning).

Unless the outer layers are infused with the spirit and implications of the core values, and aligned with the goals, the vision is unlikely to last or have an impact on student learning. For example, if a middle school seeks to develop a team approach, it must adjust the schedule so teachers on the same team have common planning time. Likewise, a commitment to technological literacy will require acquisition of considerable hardware, and the desire to move to a whole-language program will be undermined if the school continues to emphasize achievement tests closely linked to basal readers. In short, the vision must be institutionalized if it is to survive.

As Starratt describes it, integrating the vision and the organization seems to require ambidextrous principals. With one hand, they *administer*, managing materials and resources to get the job done; with the other, they *lead*, nurturing the organization's soul.

At times, implementing the vision will seem prosaic and technical, as in the vision action-plan recommended by Jerry Herman:

Step #1: Identify all tasks that must be accomplished without regard to the order in which they are to be completed.

Step #2: Place a sequential number beside each task that has been identified.

Step #3: Identify the person or persons who are responsible for completing each task.

Step #4: Identify the resources necessary to accomplish the objective.

Step #5: State the measurement that will be used to determine whether or not the objective has been achieved.

At other times, the way will be unclear and the vision will appear nebulous or even unrealistic. At those moments, the principal must turn again to the leadership skills that nurtured the vision in the first place.

Often this means turning to teachers. If the vision is shared, so is the implementation. Conley and colleagues found that vision-building was "iterative," requiring repeated attempts to find the right way and modifying plans as appropriate. The classroom, rather than the principal's office, is the natural location for these efforts.

One high school principal found that pursuing the vision had broadened the leadership base:

> We now have a great number of people and a wide variety of people who really see the organization differently, who see the whole picture rather than just what goes on in class. That's the way to move an organization. (Ron Renchler)

Beyond Vision: The Learning Organization

James Collins and Jerry Porras, in their study of visionary companies, found that "a charismatic visionary leader is absolutely not required for a visionary company and, in fact, can be detrimental to a company's long-term prospects." Rather, effective leaders concentrated on building an *organization* that was visionary. As the authors put it, "They sought to be clock builders, not time tellers."

They compare George Westinghouse, the visionary leader who created the alternating-current power system, with Charles Coffin, the first president of General Electric. While Coffin never invented anything, he did create the General Electric Research Lab, which came up with a multitude of inventions and improvements.

According to Collins and Porras, visionary companies share several characteristics:

- They have strong organizational ideologies ("cult-like cultures").
- They have towering ambitions ("big hairy audacious goals").
- They ceaselessly experiment ("try a lot of stuff and keep what works").
- They develop their own leaders ("home grown management").
- They keep trying to top themselves ("good enough never is").

In short, visionary companies are *learning* organizations that see change not as a threat but as a spur to become even better.

The traditional view of organizational change has been described as "unfreeze, change, freeze." That is, change was seen as a temporary process to get you from one status quo to the next. Organizational excellence was a matter of developing the best system possible and maintaining it as long as you could.

Today, change is regarded as a permanent process, and the best organizations are those that have found a way not only to cope with change but to use it as a driving force for excellence. Learning organizations are a lot like surfers: they can't control the wave they're riding but they can continually adapt to it, using its energies to get them where they want to go.

In this process, vision is crucial, not because it marks a beginning or an ending, but simply because it reminds us where we want to go. We may never arrive quite where we think we're headed, but visioning assures us that the journey will be worthwhile. Along the way, it provides an uplifting and ennobling spirit in a job that threatens to swamp practitioners in trivia and daily crises. As Peter Senge quotes George Bernard Shaw:

> This is the true joy in life, the being used for a purpose recognized by yourself as a mighty one.... being a force of nature instead of a feverish, selfish little clod of ailments and grievances complaining that the world will not devote itself to making you happy.

CHAPTER

6

Cultural Leadership

Stephen Stolp and Stuart C. Smith

Ask any student, teacher, or administrator; indeed, ask anyone who has spent even a short amount of time in different schools: Each has its own distinct "feel" or "personality" that can be recognized soon after entering its doors. At lunch, during class, or in the privacy of the front office, one senses the mood and tenor of a school. Get to know several schools well and you will discover they are as different as the people walking their hallways; at the same time each is as familiar as an old friend.

Some schools are perceived as "good" schools—desirable and perhaps even exciting places to work and learn. Others are perceived as just the opposite—places where one would probably not spend much time were it not for legal or financial compulsions to do so. Still other schools are considered "ordinary" by most observers—not particularly exciting, but not particularly threatening either.

For decades, school researchers and practitioners attempted to capture the "subtle spirit" of a school with the term school *morale*. In the past thirty years or so, this "spirit" has generally been called *school climate*. Both terms have a confusing past, and few educators seem to agree on exactly what the two terms mean.

In recent years, the term *school culture* has entered the vocabulary of educators, having drawn its meaning from the concept of organizational culture in the corporate workplace (Terrence Deal and Allan Kennedy). Principles learned from the observation of effectively managed businesses, it has been assumed, can be applied with benefit to the operation of schools.

This chapter is about recognizing and, if need be, changing a school's culture. Every school has its own unique culture. It is either an ineffective culture, characterized by the absence of vision and cohesiveness, or an effective culture, where staff and students exhibit such qualities as confidence, trust, cooperation, and commitment to do their best. Our goal is to help educators trade in their tired, worn-out, ineffective culture for one that will be a positive force for excellence in their school.

We begin with a discussion of what *culture* is and how it relates to *climate*. Next, we establish the importance of culture by reviewing some of the research evidence.

We probe deeper into the meaning of culture by examining three levels of organizational culture outlined by Edgar H. Schein (1984): tangible artifacts, values and beliefs, and underlying assumptions. Then we describe several instruments and qualitative procedures that a leader can use to identify and measure school culture at each of Schein's three levels. The final section offers ideas and strategies for transforming a school's culture.

What Is School Culture?

The term *culture* has a long history. The meaning of the word has been discussed for many years in a number of different fields, including anthropology, sociology, history, English, and rhetoric. From humanities to the hard sciences, the meaning of the term has inspired conversations and stirred controversy.

Noted anthropologist Clifford Geertz may have contributed the most to our current understanding of the term. For Geertz, culture represents a "historically transmitted pattern of meaning embodied in symbols." Those symbols include both the written (explicit) and hidden (implicit) messages encoded in language. A school's mission statement may identify some goals in the written text that focus on student achievement. But perhaps not written into the text is the implicit value the school places, or does not place, on academic success. Both the goal (better student achievement) and the underlying value (academic success) are part of school culture.

Some important elements of culture, according to Geertz, are the norms, values, beliefs, traditions, rituals, ceremonies, and myths upheld by a particular group of people. Thus, the values expressed in lesson plans and classroom teaching, the way the principal runs staff meetings, and the decorations displayed in hallways are all integral parts of school culture.

Indeed, Geertz's definition encompasses all human symbolic behavior, everything from nonverbal communication (Does a teacher nod and smile when passing a student in the hallway?) to the walls of the school cafeteria (Are they painted in institutional green or decorated with a mural?). The most important aspects of culture are those whose meaning is shared by members of the social system.

Much of the literature on school culture reflects Geertz's interpretation. Terrence Deal and Kent Peterson refer to culture as "deep patterns of values, beliefs, and traditions that have been formed over the course of [the school's] history." Paul E. Heckman describes school culture as "the commonly held beliefs of teachers, students, and principals" that guide their actions. Others, like T. W. Maxwell and A. Ross Thomas, suggest that culture is concerned with "those aspects of life that give it meaning."

In summary, we define school *culture* as historically transmitted patterns of meaning that include the norms, values, beliefs, traditions, and myths understood, maybe in varying degrees, by members of the school community.

In practical terms, educators speak of their school's culture when they explain to newcomers "the way we do things around here." Some aspects of culture, however, are not necessarily apparent even to those who work in the school. These are the assumptions that, as Schein (1984) points out, come to be taken for granted and eventually drop out of awareness. But those hidden assumptions continue to shape how people think about their work, relate to their colleagues, define their mission, and derive their sense of identity.

Strong Culture a Prerequisite for Reform

The meaning and importance of culture become clearer when we contrast it with some other phenomena on the education landscape that typically get more attention. Site-based management, multiage grouping, inclusive education, and authentic assessment are some of the most popular reforms in the structure, organization, and process of education that are being instituted in schools today. Educators and policy-makers have also sought, at various times, to improve the performance of schools through merit pay, performance-based budgeting, differentiated staffing, better testing and accountability systems, and a host of other programs and structures that have been implemented in classrooms, schools, districts, and even entire states.

"What we have learned from a long history of structural change is that it does not work!" exclaim William G. Cunningham and Donn W. Gresso. Educators have been tinkering with the structure and organization of schools for decades with the assumption that an appropriate structure will produce an effective work culture. Cunningham and Gresso say the truth is just the opposite: "Structure should not be used to change organizational performance and effectiveness. It should be vice versa—focus on the culture of excellence and the structures will evolve to support that culture."

In a recent study of factors that contribute to the development of professional community in schools, Karen Seashore Louis, Helen M. Marks, and Sharon Kruse found evidence in support of the argument that the structural elements of "restructuring" have received excessive emphasis in many reform proposals, while the need to improve the culture, climate, and interpersonal relationships in schools have received too little attention. While it may be easier to imagine how to restructure schools rather than to change their culture, the latter is the key to successful reform.

Why does culture exert such a powerful influence on a school's effectiveness? Because the culture tells people in the school what is truly important and how they are to act. As Bruce A. Lane says, "The power of the school culture model lies in its recognition that movement of schools toward greater effectiveness must begin with attention to the subtle, habitual regularities of behavior that comprise the culture of the school."

Leaders who are cognizant of the cultural realm know that there is yet another crucial way in which culture determines effectiveness. People commit their energy only to what they believe in, what captures their enthusiasm and imagination. Tragically, in schools lacking a culture of excellence, people labor without inspiration. As Cunningham and Gresso state, "There is a lack of excitement in the symbols, traditions, stories and sagas of the institutions. The culture serves as a self-perpetuating counterforce to effectiveness."

Some of the structural innovations referred to above have a lot of potential to improve schools, but only when supported by an effective culture. The challenge for leaders is to develop a consensus around values that constitute an effective culture, such as high expectations, commitment, mutual respect, confidence, continuous improvement, experimentation and risk-taking, and an insistence that students will learn. If individuals buy in to these beliefs, values, and behaviors, the school will grow into an effective learning community. Later we look at some steps leaders can take to build such a culture.

Relationship Between Culture and Climate

If culture plays such a pervasive and vital role in the life of the school, how does the concept of climate fit in? We regard climate as a narrower concept than culture. *Climate* is the term typically used to describe people's shared perceptions of the organization or work unit, whereas *culture*, as we have seen, embraces not only how people feel about their organization, but the assumptions, values, and beliefs that give the organization its identity and specify its standards for behavior. When discussing climate, the focus is on the impressions, feelings, and expectations held by members of the school organization. These perceptions are aroused by the organization's structure and setting, as well as by the social interactions among those who work and learn there.

James Keefe notes that climate may in practice be understood as one measure of culture. He further differentiates between *climate* (perceptions of culture that are shared by members of an organization) and *satisfaction* (the view of aspects of the organization's culture held by each individual).

A teacher once suggested, "It's easier to feel a part of culture than climate. Climate is something that we are told surrounds us, not necessarily something that is an integral part of us. Culture we take with us wherever we go." These words illuminate the more inclusive framework of culture, which embraces not only the immediate environment but also what people believe and value.

Culture: An Expanded Vision

Culture includes climate, but climate does not encompass all aspects of culture. This is one reason that understanding culture is so critical for the practitioner. Examples of how two imaginary high school principals sought to improve their faculty's effectiveness illustrate the expanded vision culture offers the practitioner.

At Claremont High School, Principal Jennifer Brown wanted to build a collaborative work environment for teachers. To lay groundwork for the collaborative process, Principal Brown offered a retreat for faculty members in which they shared their previous experiences of working with colleagues, discussed the benefits and costs of collaboration, and wrote a statement of the values and beliefs that would guide them as a learning community. She then had the teachers form work teams to plan the instructional activities on which they would collaborate during the coming school year.

Across town at Jackson High School, Principal Jerome Thomas also wanted to foster faculty collaboration. As a first step, he polled the faculty to find out its concerns about collaboration. When the teachers overwhelmingly said there was no time in their workday for meeting with their colleagues, Principal Thomas decided the best strategy was to free teachers from class time one hour each week so they would have more time to meet together for collegial planning and decision-making.

These two principals used different strategies to achieve a common goal. Principal Thomas changed the immediate environment by giving teachers more time to plan. Principal Brown chose a broader cultural approach by focusing on the values and beliefs of teachers. She wasn't content to elicit the opinions of teachers and, in response, implement a structural change; rather, she stimulated teachers to think about their philosophy of what a faculty ought to be. Each principal's strategy can be effective, but only the framework of culture includes both principals' strategies. Because the cultural perspective allows for more indepth analysis over time, it expands an administrator's framework of understanding and ability to effect change.

Evidence from the Research

Does it really matter whether a school has a "healthy" culture? Is it worth taking the trouble to try to improve culture? What would be the rewards of such an undertaking?

Certainly the satisfaction and morale of students and staff are higher in schools with healthy cultures than in schools with unhealthy ones. Indeed, many instruments designed to measure school culture and climate do so indirectly by measuring satisfaction with the school. But is there any hard evidence that culture influences the final outcomes of education—how much and how well children learn?

Researchers have accumulated some compelling evidence in support of the proposition that deliberate changes in a school's culture and climate can make the school a place in which teachers feel positive about their work and students are motivated to learn. A positive school culture is associated with higher student motivation and achievement, increased teacher collaboration, and improved attitudes among teachers toward their jobs. In this section, we review a representative selection of studies that emphasize the importance of culture in areas such as teachers' commitment to change, student motivation, and student academic achievement.

Culture and School Reform

Successful school reform requires commitment from all who participate in the process of education. Teachers are especially critical to the process of reform, because they control the quality, mood, and tempo of daily instruction. Less-than-cooperative teachers make systemic change nearly impossible.

A research project by Kenneth Leithwood, Doris Jantzi, and Alicia Fernandez addressed some of the important variables that influence the success of school reform. Specifically their research evaluated the relationship between school culture and teacher commitment to change.

For their study, the researchers surveyed staff members in nine secondary schools about "perceptions of conditions affecting their school improvement efforts." The nine schools were located in an urban school district consisting of more than 140 schools. The total school population included 26,000 students and 1,700 teachers. District-level personnel nominated the nine schools chosen for the study based on significant engagement in school-improvement efforts. A total of 168 teachers in the nine schools responded to the questionnaire, and virtually all respondents (91 percent) were involved in school-improvement efforts.

Teacher perceptions about conditions for school improvement were measured in three areas: personal goals, belief in the school's commitment to change efforts, and belief in the ability or capacity of the school to meet those change efforts.

The first level of results reported by the researchers focused on the importance of certain leadership qualities. Leadership practices that had the greatest influence on teacher commitment to change were creating vision and building consensus around goals. These practices had a significant influence on teachers' motivation for change. In addition, teachers' belief in the school's commitment to change and capacity for change increased dramatically when leaders had a strong vision and willingness to work toward change together with teachers and staff.

The second level of results related to school restructuring and culture building. According to Leithwood, Jantzi, and Fernandez, "Conditions in the school, as teachers interpret them, have the strongest direct effects on teachers' commitment to change." "This suggests," the researchers say, "the need for school leaders, first of all, to attend consciously to the content, strength, and form of their school's culture." School culture in this study was the most significant factor in determining the success of school restructuring. The authors conclude that strategies for building school culture are crucial for any successful school reform and restructuring effort.

Student Motivation

School culture plays an important role in determining student motivation and achievement, say Leslie J. Fyans, Jr. and Martin L. Maehr. The results of their research are particularly applicable for a variety of different ethnic groups.

Fyans and Maehr distributed 16,310 questionnaires to fourth-, sixth-, eighth-, and tenth-grade students from 820 schools in the Illinois public school system. The students represented a diverse ethnic population from both rural and urban areas.

These two researchers assessed five dimensions of school culture: emphasis on excellence and pursuit of academic challenges; emphasis on interpersonal competition and socially comparative achievement; emphasis on social recognition for achievement; perceived sense of community; and perception that the school stresses certain purposes and goals. These five areas were measured against a scale designed to assess student motivation.

Students in the study were given the questionnaire and asked to compare varying degrees of motivation in relation to the five dimensions of school culture. The students answered questions such as "How important is it for you to do well on a test?", "When I perform well on an assignment in school, it is because...", and "Does this school give recognition for good performance?" Students' answers to these questions helped the researchers to characterize the relationship between school culture and student motivation.

Fyans and Maehr concluded, "Clearly, these studies present strong preliminary evidence that the perceived culture of the school relates to motivation and ultimately school achievement." Although "psychological environments" play different roles, school culture was found to be "important for the motivation of children of different ethnic backgrounds." These results were consistent with those of earlier studies by Fyans and Maehr that also identified a relationship between school culture and academic achievement.

Leadership and Organizational Culture

The research of Marshall and Molly G. Sashkin supports an interrelationship between leadership and organizational culture. To assess leadership and culture in twelve schools in one district, they collected data from principals, vocational education supervisors, teachers, and students.

Using three instruments, the Leader Behavior Questionnaire (LBQ), the School Culture Assessment Questionnaire (SCAQ), and "Frames of Reference," Sashkin and Sashkin measured leadership characteristics such as self-efficacy and the leader's impact on organizational culture in relation to group factors like attaining goals, working together as a team, and sharing values and beliefs. They first measured leadership behaviors with the LBQ and then correlated the findings with the SCAQ and "Frames of Reference."

The results point to "a strong web of relationships . . . among leadership variables and organizational culture." The variables with the highest correlation included "a relationship between visionary leadership behavior and teamwork, between time-span and use of symbols, between culture building and adaptation, and between culture building and strength of shared values and beliefs." According to the Sashkins, all these relationships were statistically significant.

Strong versus Weak Cultures

Yin Cheong Cheng profiled effective and ineffective organizational cultures in thirty-two schools, sixteen with "strong culture" and the other half with "weak culture." The distinction between strong and weak was decided on the basis of a variety of organizational characteristics. Strength of organizational ideology, participation, intimacy, charismatic leadership style, and authority hierarchy represent just a few of the limiting variables.

After determining the variables that correlate with weak and strong cultures, Cheng compared the schools in the areas of organizational structure, teacher job attitude, and school effectiveness. "Strong culture," Cheng concluded, "is associated with positive organizational characteristics, teachers' job attitudes, and students' academic outcomes." That is, teachers who enjoy their jobs and students who do well academically are more likely to be found in strong school cultures than in weak ones.

These and other studies offer a variety of perspectives for understanding the complex nature of school culture. They tell us why school culture is important—for student and teacher motivation, teacher collaboration, school reform, community building, and student achievement.

Three Levels of Culture

School culture is expressed in different levels of abstraction. Schein (1984) suggests organizational culture exists at three levels: "the artifacts level, the values and beliefs level, and the underlying assumptions level." Schein's model offers insight into the complicated meaning of culture by uncovering different levels of abstraction.

Tangible Artifacts

The "artifacts level," the most visible of the three, is perhaps the level most closely associated with what we think of as school climate—how people perceive the school. A school's artifacts are those daily rituals, ceremonies, and icons that are most conspicuous to the casual observer. Students' math papers, roll call in class, the bell for first period, and the smell of a long hallway represent elements of the artifacts level of culture.

The initial "feel" of the school emanates from this tangible level of experience. Thus, people who appear at the school for the first time are most likely to recognize this level of culture. They may experience it as a mood or feeling, a certain style, or a physical presence.

If we want to trace the complex pattern of school culture, we should begin at the artifacts level, but identification of culture at this level only scratches the surface of understanding, offering but a glimpse of the complete picture. The second level of culture provides deeper analysis into the ideas that guide the school's sense of its mission.

Values and Beliefs

The "values and beliefs level," according to Schein, defines the basic organizational character of the school. As the National LEADership Network Study Group on Restructuring Schools suggests, "Through shared values and beliefs, members of the organization develop a sense of direction that guides their day-to-day behavior" (Joan Burnham and Shirley Hord). Values are enacted as part of the daily school routine. If the school has designated respect as an important value, people are expected to treat others with consideration and concern.

Likewise, teachers, principals, and other staff members express certain beliefs about the value of education. Practitioners bring with them a particular set of principles that reflect the nature of education at the school. For example, a teacher's belief in the value of experiential learning becomes an expression of culture as reflected in her actions.

Values and beliefs are not always explicit, however. The third level of Schein's model recognizes the hidden aspects of culture, those cultural patterns that become taken for granted over time.

Underlying Assumptions

At the deepest, least tangible level of organizational culture are "underlying assumptions"—the symbols, values, and beliefs that are not clearly recognizable but continue to shape the behavior of the organization's members.

In fact, we may not recognize this level at all. Some values are hidden in the unconscious dimensions of school life and taken for granted by those who work there. As C. A. Bowers and David J. Flinders note, cultural patterns "are experienced by the individual as part of a worldview that is transparent or taken for granted."

A principal tells parents that "buses and front gates are monitored by teachers before and immediately after school." The explicit message assures the parents that their children will be safe before and after school. The implicit or underlying message evokes safety as a high priority and value of the school, principal, and staff.

Schein's three-level representation of culture is not static. Daily routines, rituals, even school architecture become part of the taken-for-granted realm of culture as time passes. Put in a new schedule for classes, remodel classrooms, or write and implement a new mission statement for the school. Teachers, students, and staff will immediately notice the changes, but as time passes what was once new becomes part of a taken-for-granted attitude. The conspicuous artifacts, values, and beliefs slip into the realm of the unconscious. The explicit becomes the implicit, and what were once easily recognizable artifacts, values, and beliefs move into the underlying-assumptions level of culture.

This fluctuation among the three levels can make cultural change difficult to recognize. The need for a barometer to identify and measure culture is the subject of the next section.

Identifying and Measuring Culture

The leader who seeks to reshape a school's culture should, as a first step, try to better understand the existing culture. With this imperative in mind, we offer some ways to identify and measure school culture at each of the three levels introduced in the previous section: artifacts, values and beliefs, and underlying assumptions. Then, attention turns to several instruments designed to measure school climate and culture.

Artifacts and Change in School Culture

Teachers and administrators who are looking for a practical way of understanding school culture might first ask themselves what makes their own school unique. One distinguishing mark is the language and symbols used in the school. For example, to boost his student's morale, one elementary principal passes out "Dolphin" slips, which can be redeemed for prizes. In another school, a principal teams up at-risk students with "Breakfast Buddies."

List the artifacts that are significant in shaping school culture. Begin with the language people use in offices, classrooms, and hallways. The list doesn't have to be exhaustive but should include language heard in everyday conversation. "Take a slip to the pass room," "Use the time off as an X day," or "Cover my midterm conferences" represent just a few examples.

In addition to dialogue, pay attention to the school's symbols, routines, rituals, and traditions. These might include the smell of the hallway, buzzers instead of bells, Snoopy Slips, rubberized asphalt playgrounds, Friday assemblies, pep rallies, parent visitation night, spring picnics, or

Wednesday staff meetings. The list will never be complete and may reflect certain individual biases, but it does begin to paint a picture of school culture as expressed by the immediate effects of the climate.

The list is useful as a tool for comparison. Other schools may share some similarities or highlight differences. Talking with teachers, students, and administrators from other schools or visiting their facilities helps put into focus those elements that are unique to the culture of one's own school.

Another strategy for collecting artifacts is to have students and staff members write brief descriptions of the school culture. This process could be initiated by having participants describe their day or write down their feelings about school. An accumulation of written descriptions offers some insight into the school's cultural ecology.

History and Change in School Culture

An original list of tangible school artifacts becomes particularly useful as one evaluates the historical changes of the institution. How artifacts change over time provides a barometer for variations in school culture. This also may be the best way to begin to understand how values and beliefs are expressed in a school setting. As the culture changes, it leaves behind a host of subtle clues.

At first these clues might appear insignificant, but even short-term observations can be important. One might consider how a list of artifacts changes over the course of a year. How do the language and symbols used at the beginning of a school year differ from those at the end? This is an important question for the practitioner, because the differences reflect pieces of a changing culture. What values and beliefs do the routines, rituals, ceremonies, and symbols communicate?

The school exists as a collection of experiences and shared meanings that shape its present condition. Schools have a life. Exploring past relationships and the important symbols of school culture, one begins to understand the values and beliefs embedded in a school's life history. By looking at those variations and differences and observing how artifacts change, the principal can better comprehend the nature of school culture.

But remember: Not all elements of the school culture are visible. To better understand this dimension, we need to be aware of what is left out of our analysis.

Underlying Assumptions: Defining 'What Isn't'

The distinction between levels 2 and 3 of Schein's model is very subtle. We may recognize the values and beliefs expressed in the mission statement of a school, but the assumptions implicit in how the mission statement guides education aren't as visible.

The underlying-assumptions level of culture prompts us to ask, "What is being left out?" In part, those beliefs and values that are left out help us identify the assumptions that implicitly define what the school considers important. A mission statement that focuses on academic achievement may leave out social needs, cooperative learning, or a liberal education. The hidden assumption of this mission statement is that academic success has a higher priority than these other values.

A school leader who aspires to be a culture builder should be concerned with "what isn't." That is, she should be concerned as much about the values and beliefs that are not highlighted as those that explicitly guide the institution. This kind of concern addresses the underlying assumptions implicit in each administrative decision.

Instruments for Measuring Climate and Culture

Instruments for assessing school culture and climate come in a bewildering array of formats, reporting procedures, and often untested psychometric properties. Most of the instruments that have been used to measure school climate focus on measuring levels of satisfaction and how people perceive the patterns of interaction and communication among the school's staff members (particularly between teachers and administrators). A few instruments, however, particularly those developed in recent years, do attempt to measure values and beliefs. Educators may even find some instruments helpful in identifying the assumptions underlying their beliefs and actions.

Nevertheless, because the terms *climate* and *culture* are often used interchangeably, and the instruments vary greatly in the phenomena they purport to measure, we have not sought to differentiate among them by our own definitions of these terms. Nor have we made an effort to classify the instruments according to Schein's three levels of culture.

NASSP's Comprehensive Assessment of School Environments

From 1982 to 1992 the National Association of Secondary School Principals conducted a longitudinal study of school environments that suggested some important directions for school restructuring. According to James W. Keefe, the study identified the creation and maintenance of a positive school climate as an essential characteristic of effective schooling.

In an effort to create and assess better school environments, the NASSP developed the School Climate Survey and Student, Teacher, and Parent Satisfaction Surveys to measure student, teacher, and parent perceptions of school climate and satisfaction. These surveys are part of the Comprehensive Assessment of School Environments—Information Management

System (CASE—IMS), a program that takes a systems approach to the diagnosis of school status and restructuring. As Keefe notes, "Its eight steps define the gestalt of school improvement":

1. Forming the school-improvement management team
2. Raising awareness
3. Collecting baseline data
4. Comprehensive assessment
5. Interpreting data and formulating a school-design statement
6. Priority setting and planning
7. Task force organization and coordination
8. Summative evaluation and reporting

These eight steps express the overarching evaluative purpose of CASE—IMS, which includes the NASSP School Climate Survey as part of this systemic approach to school restructuring.

The survey has ten scales: teacher-student relationships, security and maintenance, administration, student academic orientation, student behavioral values, guidance, student-peer relationships, parent and community-school relationships, instructional management, and student activities. James W. Keefe and Edgar A. Kelley point out that when the survey is used correctly, it identifies areas in which school climate can be improved. They offer the following example of how just two of the ten survey scales provide the practitioner with some different approaches to changing school climate:

Teacher-Student Relationships
1. Initiate or upgrade a teacher adviser program.
2. Establish teacher-student teams for the development of needed social activities, academic programs, or peer-coaching arrangements.
3. Initiate an academic-recognition program for students.
4. Identify teachers skilled in instruction or working with students and develop peer-coaching activities for teachers.
5. Help teachers select or develop classroom feedback forms to collect information from students about their perceptions and needs.

Student-Peer Relationships
1. Develop or extend the school's orientation program for new students; e.g., develop a "buddy system."

2. Schedule staff development workshops to assist teachers in planning student cooperative-learning activities.
3. Establish or improve student-recognition programs that reward cooperative and collaborative efforts by students, especially those that are cross-age, cross-SES, or cross-ethnic in nature.

These few examples, offered by Keefe and Kelley, "represent the many types of interventions that can be formulated and implemented from a review of CASE data." The CASE—IMS Climate Survey provides the practitioner with an evaluative vision for changing school climate systemically.

School Culture Assessment Questionnaire

A recently developed instrument that can be used to identify elements of school life at the values and beliefs level is the School Culture Assessment Questionnaire (SCAQ). Designed by Marshall Sashkin and Molly G. Sashkin, the questionnaire assesses the effectiveness with which an organization performs four functions: adapting to change, attaining goals, working together as a team, and sharing values and beliefs ("cultural strength").

The SCAQ can be used in conjunction with "Frames of Reference," an instrument that characterizes human behavior in an organization in terms of four perspectives: structural, political, human resources, and symbolic. According to the Sashkins, these instruments are effective in defining the "web of relationships" that exist between leaders and organizational cultures.

Other Assessment Instruments

To help school leaders choose an instrument that will provide the kind of information they want and yield the most reliable and valid data, several guides review and rate the instruments. Three of the best guides were written by Judith Arter, Denise C. Gottfredson and colleagues, and Ann E. Witcher.

No one model or instrument will accurately characterize all elements of a school's culture or climate. Most models illuminate the more tangible artifacts but fail to capture the entire value or belief system. Therefore, we must look to historical changes in artifacts as clues for understanding Schein's second level of culture, as explained earlier.

The next section offers some suggestions for changing a school's culture. Change is possible if the leader commits to a course of action that involves all members of the school community in defining a vision for the school.

Transforming School Culture

According to Edgar Schein (1985), "Leadership is intertwined with culture formation." Developing an organizational culture and shaping the creative process of its evolution is the "unique and essential function" of leadership. Nevertheless, the principal alone cannot bring about change in the norms of a school because, by definition, cultural transformation is a collaborative activity. The principal must engage others both inside and outside the school if he or she is to effect any meaningful changes in the school's culture.

Facilitating a Shared Vision

No one should fault a principal for arriving at a school with a preconceived vision of what that school ought to become. After all, the principal's strongly held convictions about educational goals and outcomes probably figured heavily in the superintendent's decision to assign the principal to that school. The question for the principal now becomes How much should I push my own vision?

We suggest that principals who are in this situation listen to the advice of one of their colleagues. Nancy Wilson, a principal of fifteen years, at the time of this writing assigned to Boekman Creek Elementary School in Wilsonville, Oregon, suggests that the best way to approach changes in school culture initially is to "do nothing." Her advice is to "talk to teachers, talk to staff, and learn something about the culture you're in first." Take time to thoroughly understand the organization. Then and only then, a principal can begin to approach change by empowering staff and negotiating a shared vision.

If a leader starts with a preconceived vision, he or she should proceed with extreme caution. As a person in a position of power, the principal may place students and staff members in the uncomfortable position of feeling obligated to conform to the principal's wishes.

For any vision, no matter who proposes it, to make a difference, all members of the work group must support it. A principal who appreciates the need for vision to drive a strong work culture knows that the power of a vision comes not just from the soundness of its ideas but from the unity of purpose that is achieved when all members believe in, claim as their own, and act on that vision.

There are many paths to excellence; what is indispensable is teamwork once a particular path has been chosen. Viewed in this light, the principal's role is best seen not as originator of the vision but as facilitator of the vision.

Another way to put it is that the principal's personal vision ought simply to be that everyone in the school *agree* on a vision. Rather than control the specifics of the vision, the principal facilitates the process by which all teachers, aides, office staff, custodians, parents, and students decide on their common vision. The leader's role is to smooth the way and garner the support and resources for such a consensus to be realized.

Perhaps the best way to begin is to encourage an atmosphere where staff and students feel comfortable offering visionary ideas. Bob Anderson, principal of a high school in Eugene, Oregon, does that by creating a safe environment where staff feel inclined to participate. According to Lynn Balster Liontos, he does this through:

> (1) his strong sense of caring, (2) his openness and approachability, (3) his ability to let people know that it's okay to disagree with him, (4) his encouragement of risk-taking and trying new ideas, (5) his ability to allow people to feel it's okay to make mistakes or fail, and (6) his strong support for staff.

Many times students and staff remain outside the creative process. Bob Anderson demonstrates that by paying attention to the values and interests of all members of the organization, the principal can better facilitate a shared vision.

Using Narrative

Storytelling is one way for a principal to influence cultural change. As Deal and Peterson note, "It can show the listeners, the school community, what the principal values without direct moralizing."

The values implicit in the story often go unrecognized by the listener. Many times, the storyteller must facilitate the process by interpreting what values and beliefs are integral to the story. Consider the following example, a story told about a teacher, Phil MacCullum, who was giving a lecture on the Boston Tea Party to his class of fifth graders:

> Phil, a large boisterous man with a silvery mustache, captivates his students with an exciting tale. So much so, they seem to genuinely lose themselves in the description of the Colonists' rebellious act. "In the dead of night, dressed as Native American warriors with tomahawks and face paint, they dumped the crates of tea into the Boston Harbor," he tells his students in a low and intense voice. He pauses and the classroom steeps in silence. The students' eyes are wide. From the back of the room a small uncertain hand rises for a question. "Yes, Eric, what is it?," Phil in-

> quires, commanding the attention of the entire class. A genuinely concerned Eric asks, "Have they been caught yet?"

This story could be used in a number of different ways. The interpretation might focus on the power of a good teacher to captivate students and excite them about learning. The story could facilitate a discussion of the differences between teacher intent and student comprehension. Or the storyteller might expand on the value of protest for a worthy cause. There are many possibilities.

The principal can use the power of a story to germinate and spread the important values of the institution. Principal Joan Andrews uses a story about Marty Matthews to relieve first-year teachers of their anxiety about teaching.

> No one in your room this year is like Marty. Marty was a bit of a hyperactive kid. I think his parents even had him on Ritalin to control his behavior. Anyway, I was a young first-year teacher when I had Marty, and I was quite nervous about doing everything just right. I did my lesson plans two weeks in advance and my bulletin boards three weeks before school started. I was very careful that year about setting a consistent example. At the first sign of trouble, I sent kids down to the vice principal's office.
>
> Marty was making clucking sounds all through silent reading and had adamantly protested when I asked him to be quiet. True to my word, I sent Marty to the vice principal for the rest of the day. Well, the next day in class, Marty had drafted a petition that he was having every student sign. The petition read, "Sign Here If You Hate Mrs. Andrews." You can imagine how I felt, but these are just the lessons of a first-year teacher. (Betty Seigrist, personal communication, January 14, 1994)

Andrews uses this story to relate a number of different values—expressing support for teachers, finding humor in difficult situations, setting consistent examples in the classroom, and emphasizing the importance of experience.

Two critical elements of the story-telling process are (1) to use stories with an associative quality, having content that fits the audience and the occasion; and (2) to facilitate or direct the interpretive process. Effective use of narrative can help principals build stronger institutional cultures.

William A. Firestone and Bruce L. Wilson suggest making use of "old-timers" to communicate the values of the institution. Past employees and older graduates can recite narratives of the school's history, thus serving as role models to the uninitiated. "They establish a positive link with the newcomers that builds ownership and pride in the school." These old-timers may also play a key role in establishing or reestablishing important rituals and ceremonies.

Organizing the School Day

Scheduling may seem like a small factor in determining school culture, but in practice it may be one of the biggest. Consider that the scheduling of the school day affects almost all school activities. It determines how students are grouped, how they use their free time, and what choices they make. The same conditions apply to teachers. Scheduling affects how teachers plan lessons, what they do with their free time, and where they see themselves in the organization. In fact, say Martin L. Maehr and Rachel M. Buck, "Action in these areas is critical to determining and transforming the culture of the school and is an important way in which the learning and motivation of students is influenced."

Maehr and Buck use the forty- to fifty-minute class period as an example. They suggest that this type of class is well suited for more rigid didactic instruction. Schools interested in project-centered instruction would probably want to consider a longer class period. This would allow for instruction beyond the school walls and would help students and teachers develop and understand projects more fully.

We are not suggesting that one form of scheduling is better than another. Rather, the illustration emphasizes the importance of coordinating schedules with the values important to the institution. More flexible institutions would want to choose more flexible schedules. Likewise, a more traditional emphasis in the classroom would function better with a more traditional schedule. But these are choices that must be addressed by the principal and staff.

Setting a Consistent Example

Actions speak loudest. The most effective and efficient way to change cultures is to model the behaviors, beliefs, and values important to the institution. A principal who acts with care and concern for all will most likely encourage similar behavior. Likewise, a principal who has little time for staff or students will participate in creating a selfish culture.

Modeling sets an example. People see and feel the behaviors of others. The principal who leads by action makes beliefs and values of the institution highly visible and inspires others to follow his or her example.

Selecting Compatible Staff

Perhaps one of the principal's toughest yet most vital tasks is selecting staff members who share his or her values and beliefs about education. There is nothing more counterproductive to creating a healthy school culture than for the faculty and principal to hold incompatible convictions about what schooling should be. A principal who is mindful of culture-building seeks faculty members who are not only technically qualified but whose values are consistent with the school's vision of excellence.

Effective school leaders go to great lengths to build a cohesive faculty, using the processes of recruitment, selection, and induction to shape their schools' culture. They not only carefully recruit and select new faculty, but they help teachers who do not share their values to find positions at other schools. They use the selection interview as an opportunity to clearly communicate the school's culture to each candidate. And after they hire a teacher, they socialize the new faculty member into the core values of the school.

Five principals profiled by Deal and Peterson agreed that "getting the right staff" is an essential component in the creation of a healthy school culture. Frank Boyden of Massachusetts' Deerfield Academy went so far as to say he was "delighted when a teacher turned down a more highly paid job" to remain at his school. This was a signal to him that the values of the institution were more important than money or status, and he often used instances of teachers' declining better paying job offers as examples in stories.

Recognizing Staff Members

Daily life in an organization has peaks and valleys. Teachers know the highs and lows of classroom instruction. One day can be a celebration of high test scores and student cooperation. The next day can be a futile struggle to maintain order and teach basic skills. The competent teacher takes both days in stride.

An insightful leader recognizes the importance of these peaks and valleys. Peaks provide an opportunity to celebrate accomplishments, and valleys call for some timely encouragement.

Recognition of faculty members must be both significant and genuine. Its aim is both to improve staff morale and to draw attention to an important value, such as high expectations for student achievement.

Informal and formal recognition of staff members can be expressed in a number of ways: remarks in staff meetings, email messages, hand-written or typed notes, and breakfast or dinner events to recognize teachers with humorous and/or serious awards.

A method of formal recognition is to recommend teachers for district, state, and national awards. Principals can talk to district officials about establishing new awards or nominate teachers for those already available. Local papers and school publications can also be used to celebrate the hard work of teachers.

Lessons for the Principal

Jane Arkes of George Middle School in Portland, Oregon, says, "The toughest lesson for any principal is learning to be patient." In her career, she has seen many good school leaders come and go. "The reason is often the same: Principals try to do too much, too fast." Her suggestions for bringing about changes in school culture are simple and practical:

1. Work on team-building.
2. Get acquainted with staff; know where your support is.
3. Focus on doing less rather than more.
4. Facilitate new ideas from groups and individuals.
5. Identify the most important and salient problems.
6. Put your agenda second.
7. Get people excited about the work at hand.
8. Remember that some things just come with time and experience.
9. Learn from students and staff.
10. Accept the fact that it's not all going to get done.
11. Put people before paper.
12. Know that you don't have all the answers; everyone has limitations.
13. Consider the values of staff and students in relation to your own.
14. Ask others' opinions.
15. Get some distance when evaluating changes.

(Personal communication, September 13, 1993)

These words of wisdom emphasize the importance of people and relationships. The role of the principal should be to facilitate reforms while at the same time reflecting on how changes affect staff and students. The principal can make a difference only by putting people first.

Conclusion

The challenge for principals, whose busy workdays pull them in a hundred directions at once, is to make each day a positive learning experience for students. An understanding of school culture is an important tool in maintaining this focus on student learning. The lens of culture allows school leaders to shape learning experiences with an eye toward the health of the school community, which inevitably determines the direction and effectiveness of education.

The most important lesson to be learned by administrators is that they, too, are part of the school culture. A school leader does not make decisions from outside the institution. Change comes as part of the daily routines that affect all participants, including the principal.

Principals who can identify the strengths and weaknesses of their school's culture and see their place in the organization will be more effective school leaders. This simple lesson can be learned if administrators are willing to approach the process of cultural change with patience, reflection, and humility.

PART 3

The Structure

CHAPTER

7

School-Based Management

Lori Jo Oswald

School-based management (SBM) is a widely instituted governance reform—a means of decentralizing the authority to make decisions. It is a system of administration in which the school, rather than the school district, is the primary unit of educational decision-making over budget, curriculum, and personnel matters. Decentralizing authority in these three key areas, it is argued, empowers those people who are in the best position to make decisions—principals, teachers, parents, community members, and students.

Early proponents of SBM seemed to assume that if decisions were made closer to the students, the students themselves would benefit. School personnel, released from constraints, would devise strategies to improve curriculum and instruction, and student achievement would rise. Yet the body of research on SBM offers little support for this assumption or for the ability of SBM to generate other supposed benefits such as higher employee morale and strengthened schoolwide planning (B. Malen, R. Ogawa, and J. Kranz; R. Ogawa and P. White).

Since it is not likely that a change in the structure of school governance alone will improve the performance of schools, experts now advise educators to bundle SBM's structural changes with other elements to make sure emphasis properly focuses on student learning. Thomas R. Guskey and Kent D. Peterson, for example, say that if SBM is to have any impact on day-to-day classroom practices, the following steps are crucial:

1. Begin with a clear mission that focuses on student teaching and learning.
2. Set clear and explicit goals for the decision-making process.
3. Ensure that school-based decision-making is seen as a process for bringing about a broad set of reforms, not as a goal in itself.

4. Alter governance structures to give administrators, teachers, and parents real power and authority.
5. Be responsive to parents' concerns, and involve them in the school community.
6. Redesign schedules to give teachers time to participate in decision-making.
7. Invest in high-quality professional development, and make significant changes in the way these activities are planned, organized, and carried out.
8. Obtain the necessary expertise on which to base decisions.
9. Ensure active support from all levels of the organization.
10. Reward accomplishments, large and small.
11. Work to establish a collaborative school culture focused on improvement.

These imperatives foreshadow the advice and insights of other researchers, consultants, and educators themselves on the pages that follow. This chapter clarifies the changed roles and responsibilities of personnel involved in SBM, describes the operation of the school council, sets forth guidelines for implementing SBM, and comments on the ingredients necessary for SBM to succeed.

New Roles and Responsibilities

Both the district and schools have distinctive roles to perform in an SBM system, and only when they work collaboratively can SBM be truly successful. Decision-making authority must be proportionately distributed among the stakeholders: school board members, superintendents and other district officials, principals, teachers, parents, and community members. Some also feel student participation is essential, particularly in high schools.

Unless stakeholders are empowered with authority, SBM is merely a theory, not a practice. Therefore, the distribution of authority is crucial, but how that power is distributed is for each school district to decide. As this section makes clear, there are at least as many opinions about stakeholders' roles and responsibilities as there are types of SBM systems.

The School Board

The school board's role does not change significantly in an SBM system. The board gives general direction to the district by providing goals and policy statements, keeps informed about the district's progress toward new goals, and acts as a decision-maker of last resort. Only the boards that have direct involvement in school operations, such as specifying the types of equipment allocated to each school, will have to change dramatically.

The board will need to issue new policy statements to reflect the distribution of responsibilities and accountability. For example, the National School Boards Association (NSBA) suggests that the school board provide school-site councils with a specific policy that requires them to "work within the laws, policies, and contractual obligations that are binding on the board. Otherwise, the board is inviting decisions the board itself could not legally make." In fact, advises the NSBA, "written procedures to guide most aspects of a team's work will reduce confusion as people who are unfamiliar with one another begin to work together."

Roles

Researchers and educators highlight the elements of "trust" and "patience" as key ingredients of successful leadership by the school board. In SBM, board members function as visionary leaders, guides, supervisors, and arbitrators.

In a study of Edmonton Public Schools in Alberta and of Langley School District in British Columbia, Daniel J. Brown found that when SBM was instituted, the role of the school board changed from "providing exact solutions for specific school problems" to that of "policy making." The board "now moves directionally as opposed to exactly.... [Its] concern is not with schools doing things right but with schools doing the right things ... [and] is no longer making rules for schools," Brown observes. The board has the following roles:

- setting and revising policies to promote and support SBM
- handling negotiations
- allocating overall funds
- establishing a climate supportive of SBM
- determining district priorities
- monitoring the SBM program's success
- interfacing with senior governments
- serving as public advocates for SBM

(Brown)

Boards could also conduct strategic planning, "convene community forums on major educational issues," formulate citizen or consultant specialty groups, and review how individual schools are meeting district and site goals (Linda Chion-Kenney).

The board's challenge in SBM is to "find ways to assist schools and guarantee uniformly high quality in a school system whose basic premise is variety, not uniformity" (Paul T. Hill and others). Along these lines, the Oregon School Boards Association advises board members to give unconditional support to superintendents, provide startup resources, receive training in shared decision-making, set clear expectations through policy, move resources (people and money) to schools, clearly define parameters, participate in and teach shared decision-making, show visible support to risk takers, and recognize and reward collaboration.

Control

Since shared decision-making promotes diversity instead of standardized conformity, John Prasch contends that the board must work as a coordinator and monitor results rather than processes. "The board must also accept a public relations role in celebrating the diversity among its schools and in championing the right of school sites to be different."

By making a clear commitment to SBM, the board will assure the public that it is not always the board's role to fix problems, say Hill and colleagues:

> Concerns about lunch menus, school dismissal schedules, a teacher's competence, and methods of teaching bilingual education all arose during our study—and school board members were strongly tempted to resolve all of them. Refusing to do so on the basis of the board's commitment to decentralization takes political courage, but it is easier to do if the board and superintendent have thoroughly informed the public about their reform strategy.

Relationship with School Councils

Responsibility for decisions about individual school activities rests in the school council (a team of SBM decision-makers, including teachers, parents, and other community members). Questions have been raised about whether the SBM council's function as a mini school board to the individual school may decrease the school board's power and authority. However, in their study of districts across the U.S., William Clune and Paula White found that "the respondents did not feel that SBM councils presented a threat to school board authority"; instead the board "developed a new openness to listening to the needs of the individual schools."

Some Constraints

"Full and continuing support for SBM from members of the board of education may be one of the more difficult hurdles," writes Prasch. Board members may lose patience with SBM for any of a number of reasons. They may feel more comfortable with conventional management models and more knowledgeable about bureaucratic arrangements. They were elected to control, so they must prevent their constituents from perceiving schools as chaotic or permissive. The public, they may reason, prefers simple, easy-to-understand organization. Tight organizational models therefore are preferable to loose ones. Moreover, overestimating the extent to which their decisions affect classroom behavior, board members may feel their intervention is in the best interest of students (Prasch).

Another constraint to successful SBM implementation is the fluctuation of board membership, with new office seekers often promising to bring about change. "Given the long timespan necessary from successful installation and implementation to noticeable results," Prasch says, "continuity of leadership is a critical factor."

The National School Boards Association (NSBA) contends that the board must oversee decisions because board members are held accountable through elections: "Anyone exercising decision-making authority within a school district must recognize that the school board will ultimately be held responsible for the results of the decisions regardless of who made them." SBM does not change the fact that legal authority for the school district continues to reside in the school board:

> School board members and their successors may be under significant pressure to recapture the delegated authority when the public is dissatisfied with decisions. Thus, all parties must recognize that shared decision-making arrangements, even when created by board policy, do not replace school boards. Groups to which decision-making has been delegated do not have independent authority created by statute. They are accountable to the general public through the school board.

Unless the state legislature "gives authority directly to school site teams," the school board must regularly review and evaluate "the performance of those with decision authority," the NSBA states.

A possible solution is mentioned by Chion-Kenney: States can rewrite statutes to change school boards into "local educational policy boards" that "concentrate less on administration and more on policy."

The Superintendent and the District Office

Although school-site autonomy is basic to SBM, this does not preclude some form of central control (or uniformity). The central office can still specify basic curriculum guidelines and insist that schools follow budget-allocation procedures. Concern about widening the disparities among schools through the practice of SBM can be tempered by developing effective instructional leadership in schools so that resources are successfully matched with the students' needs.

Traditionally, the district's chief business official has been responsible for three main functions: (1) maintaining tight fiscal control over school budgets, (2) providing technical assistance to the schools, and (3) monitoring district expenditures. In an SBM system, the principal and/or the site council takes over the first function, while the district continues to handle the other two. Prasch explains how this works in practice: Schools receive an annual budget from the school district based on the number of students and program needs. Then, the principal becomes "responsible for the requisition, management, distribution, and utilization of supplies within the building." The district's business officer is "responsible for the actual purchasing, warehousing, and distribution of supplies to buildings and for providing the necessary forms and establishing efficient procedures to facilitate the process."

The key word that describes the administration's role in SBM, then, is *facilitate*. Having delegated control over expenditures, curriculum, and personnel, district administrators now facilitate schools' actions by formulating and defining the district's general polices and educational objectives.

The superintendent and the district office also have a managerial function in providing support services and objective evaluations instead of "mandatory directives." In other words, they facilitate instead of dictate. Thus, their role changes from telling schools what to do to "helping schools accomplish what schools, themselves, decide to do" (Priscilla Wohlstetter and Kerri L. Briggs).

The Superintendent's Role

In SBM, the role of the superintendent has been much less publicized than that of the principal. Yet, the transference of decision-making power cannot be effective without the willingness of the superintendent to share power. In fact, according to Clune and White, "because the superintendent is frequently instrumental in introducing SBM to a district, the manner in which he or she chooses to do this may influence both the organizational structure and the attitudes of the school community towards SBM." The superintendent will always be the chief administrator of the district and the one person responsible to the school board for administrative decisions.

If the above descriptions of the superintendent's role seem vague, it is because, as Jackie Kowalski and Arnold Oates explain, "The superintendent's role in school-based management is not operationalized by one definition or with a specific set of steps because school-based management is unique to each school and unique to each individual school district." What is certain, they say, is that under SBM, superintendents must have the following leadership skills:

1. *Instructional Leadership:* The instructional leader has the qualities of fairness, communication, visibility, high expectations, and a sense of priorities.

2. *Transformational Leadership:* Superintendents are people-oriented rather than task-oriented. They facilitate; foster teacher development and a collaborative, professional school culture; help staff members solve problems together; delegate power to school campuses; actively communicate the district's cultural norms; and emphasize group discussion and decision-making.

3. *Visionary Leadership:* "Superintendents should learn to anticipate and envision a totally new system of education" and seek collaboration in the formation and implementation of the vision.

In addition, the superintendent must have the following characteristics, say Kowalski and Oates: good listening skills, trust-building skills, conflict-management skills, risk-taking skills, and the ability to be a change agent.

The District Office's Roles

In an SBM system, the district office still has important duties. The central office develops student and staff performance standards, offers technical assistance to schools, and acts as the comptroller of district expenditures. Prasch lists the following as "essential functions" of the district office: purchasing of equipment as per school requisitions, warehousing and distribution of supplies to buildings, and establishing the forms and procedures to facilitate the distribution of supplies.

Clarifying the distinct functions of the district office and the school is essential. Any decision that applies externally, is centrally mandated, and is an extension of the building, such as support services, should pertain to the district office. Depending on the type of SBM implemented, central-office personnel may handle any of the following functions:

- developing districtwide priorities
- developing educational objectives for students at each grade level
- developing curriculum to meet those educational objectives
- determining the district's educational budget
- supervising capital expenditures such as new construction and major repairs
- selecting textbooks
- selecting principals
- screening applicants for jobs, with the actual selection made at the building level
- translating board policy and priority goals into short- and long-range district plans for implementation
- providing data related to the district's major problems and goal areas identified by the board
- approving and monitoring school instructional programs
- providing staff development to accomplish the goals and objectives of approved school-improvement plans
- modeling the behaviors expected of principals and site councils
- developing staff performance standards
- offering technical assistance to schools
- carrying out systemwide planning, monitoring, and evaluations
- establishing attendance zones and otherwise determining the composition of the student body
- defining the criteria for student success or failure with promotion standards, attendance requirements, and local graduation requirements
- setting the tone for the district and shaping the expectations and work norms of the staff
- conducting collective bargaining and contract enforcement
- establishing the length of the school day
- providing research data to the schools and the school board
- making recommendations regarding personnel employment, promotion, and dismissal
- raising and allocating revenue
- overseeing compliance with state and federal mandates
- coordinating busing and equipment purchase
- reporting to state and federal authorities

- providing districtwide programs, including special education
- providing the political support needed for schools to make their own decisions (and mistakes)
- monitoring quality control to ensure that schools are meeting district goals

(Sources: Barbara Hansen and Carl Marburger 1988, Kowalski and Oates)

The Principal

At the building level, the principal, by virtue of his or her role in fostering shared governance within the school, is the key figure in SBM. As a member of an SBM task force said, "If principals didn't exist before school-based management, they'd have to be created to carry out the system" (AASA and others). In SBM, principals not only have increased responsibility but also increased accountability.

According to Clune and White, the principal in an SBM system has more authority and responsibility in three areas: school programs, shared governance, and district decision-making. Wohlstetter and Briggs list the principal's "emerging roles" under SBM:

> designer/champion of involvement structures (by developing and empowering decision-making teams), motivator/manager of change (by encouraging staff development), and liaison to the outside world (by bringing to the school new ideas and research about teaching and learning, for example).

The school's role (as opposed to the district's role), under the guidance of the principal, is to establish goals based on schoolwide assessments of need, develop or choose curricula, determine instructional methods, provide training for parents, work in consort with other district schools to align curricula, allocate school funds based on goals and needs, determine the numbers of staff and positions needed, and hire staff (Hansen and Marburger 1988).

Principals as Managers

Management issues are an essential part of the principal's role under SBM. Principals are assuming greater responsibility in determining budget priorities, establishing staffing patterns, and developing educational program objectives. The principal's managerial functions expand in the areas of personnel management, business management, facilities maintenance, property management, security, counseling, communication, and community relations.

The principal acts as manager, coordinator, facilitator, and delegator. To be a successful leader in an SBM program, the principal must have a vision to integrate all the activities into a meaningful whole.

Human-relations skills are vital. The principal must be able to facilitate group processes, excel in interpersonal communication, and build team spirit, while affirming the efforts of all participants.

Also vital is the ability to discern the aptitudes, areas of expertise, and interests of teachers and community members so as to delegate appropriate responsibilities to them. Above all, the principal should have enough influence to help everyone work together to attain goals.

In short, says Prasch, "the principal's new role is to find ways to empower all staff members to maximize their contributions in successfully attaining the school's goals." Undoubtedly this requires trust, patience, and a firm belief in the positive outcomes of group involvement.

Some Constraints

Principals are perhaps more concerned about the potential downside of SBM than any other individuals or groups. For example, William R. Drury warns, "In the various SBM models now in place around the nation, the role of the building principal ranges from chairing the local council to being—for all practical purposes—a mere employee." Drury quotes from reports that predict teachers will one day take over curriculum, budgets, schedules, and staffing decisions. "Proceed with caution" he advises superintendents and school boards considering SBM, to avoid "losing principals as members of the management team, and having to face them in a more adversarial role typical of collective bargaining."

Others say that principals have the opposite concern: too much authority and therefore accountability under SBM. Related concerns have to do with how the principal delegates some of that authority.

Better training and dialogue between district officials and principals at the outset may ease mistrust. Effective training programs build on past experiences, including mistakes. James E. Mitchell recommends hiring an outside consultant to train staff in "consensus building, group-process skills, and shared decision-making." Principals should be taught collaborative management skills such as compromising and reaching consensus, forming new relationships, and building teams to facilitate change. Educating principals about what SBM is and how the councils usually have stronger advisory roles, not outright control, can also help ease concerns (Del Stover).

Teachers

Teacher empowerment and accountability are major ingredients of SBM. Teachers influence decisions by participating in planning, developing, monitoring, and improving instructional programs within the school.

Teachers consistently have said they want a voice in decisions that affect them (Paula White, Gail Thierbach Schneider, and Linda H. Bair), particularly decisions about budget allocations, curriculum, student discipline, and community interaction, as well as many other matters that directly or indirectly affect them. Moreover, teachers do not want token participation, but they want to play an active role in the decision-making process.

"While SBM has not required major changes in the roles and responsibilities of teachers," say Clune and White, "SBM has provided teachers with greater flexibility and opportunity to make changes." Teacher empowerment should be limited to instructional matters, says Prasch: "Teachers must be empowered to do what they do best, which is to teach students."

In an SBM plan that focuses on instructional improvement, teachers may work collaboratively with other stakeholders to consider district and school priorities and to select goals, help identify programs and practices necessary to achieve school goals, participate in staff development to help them achieve their goals, provide inservice training for other teachers, collect and interpret data related to their goals, and assist the principal in managing the resources to attain the school's improvement plans.

A task force of administrators found that, under SBM, teachers "will participate in designing programs that meet the school's educational objectives" (AASA and others). Teachers' input will include decisions about the school climate, student attendance, discipline policies, selection of materials in accordance with district policy, teaching methods and strategies, staff development, and goal-setting.

To participate in an SBM system, teachers may need to expand their knowledge base in policy and procedural matters, group dynamics, large-scale issues affecting all schools, and research results regarding instructional improvement.

Among the claimed benefits of teacher involvement in SBM are the following:

- higher morale
- increased commitment to the school and lower levels of absenteeism and turnover

- improved management decisions
- greater acceptance of change
- enhanced cooperation and reduced conflict
- more effective enforcement of discipline
- better informed teachers
- improved teacher communication with and across schools
- improved student motivation
- increased incentives that serve to attract and retain quality teachers
- improved school climate
- increased commitment to shared decision-making
- improved relationships between teachers and administrators

(Hansen and Marburger 1989; White; Caldwell and Wood)

Some Constraints

Despite these reputed benefits, SBM still elicits among many teachers mixed feelings. Whereas some are enthusiastic about trying out new programs and innovations, others fear the uncertainty that accompanies changing roles, and still others question whether the time and effort is worthwhile. Mark A. Smylie says that "substantial evidence exists that participation in decision-making is related" not only to teacher job satisfaction, loyalty, and goal commitment, but also to "stress, militancy, role ambiguity and conflict, and work alienation."

Paradoxically, even if the purpose of SBM is to improve student learning, it places on both teachers and administrators additional administrative burdens that may divert them "away from the central issue of schooling—learning and teaching" (Joseph Murphy). Some teachers suggest hiring additional teachers' aides to assume some of their duties while they are busy in SBM activities. This type of proposal is not often carried out because of lack of funds, which may, in turn, dampen teacher interest in SBM programs.

Parents and Community Members

Involvement of parents is essential to successful implementation of SBM. The challenge is to determine how much decision-making authority parents should have. Too much authority leads to too much power with no accountability, and too little authority erects a barrier to true community input.

Community involvement enhances public support of schools, which, in turn, become more responsive to community and student needs. Parents derive a sense of ownership through active involvement in local schools. In addition, SBM "has the potential to give families and communities access to the resources needed to participate in the real improvement of school programs," say Ameetha Palanki and colleagues.

Ultimately, the argument for parent involvement rests on benefits to children. "Studies have shown that students get better grades, have better attitudes toward school and have higher aspirations if parents are aware of what's happening in school and encourage their children," says Leon Lynn.

Most principals and teachers in schools practicing SBM welcome parent involvement in decision-making, but the extent of that involvement is usually restricted. Although some school leaders believe that parents who serve on councils should have power equal to that of other members, in reality, parents' participation is often token. Palanki and colleagues write that only a few states give "priority to involving parents in important planning, policy making, or decision-making roles." Overall, says David Peterson-del Mar, "districts have not distributed substantial formal authority to parents or other community members."

Some principals believe parents and other community members can be effectively involved only in issues that are reasonably stable, such as policy matters. According to one principal, time is the main factor preventing total participation of parents in all school issues. Those issues requiring immediate resolution generally get settled without the involvement of parents.

Students

Students, generally the least consulted of all the public school constituencies, bring a special knowledge and perspective to that which they are experiencing. Most school councils at the middle and high school levels do include students. An occasional elementary school will even involve students. Students are selected from existing student councils or on the recommendation of staff.

Students who are included in the school's SBM process gain a greater sense of ownership of the school and a better understanding of the operations of the school and school decision-making. SBM has been found to improve relations between students and teachers and to produce programs and activities geared more specifically to students' needs since students helped to shape those activities.

Students serving on SBM councils are often articulate and confident. Nevertheless, say Clune and White, "it is difficult for parents and teachers to learn to listen to students and for students to realize that parents and teachers will listen to them."

Function of the School Council

Most schools implement SBM through a formal management structure called the SBM *council,* also known as the site council, school team, advisory committee, or management team. The purpose of the council is to ensure representation of constituent bodies in decision-making at the site. Teachers, parents, community members, and, in some cases, students are involved from the outset of the decision-making process, thereby enhancing the quality of decisions. Some school councils include the principal as a member; in others, the principal receives the council's recommendations or decisions.

The council, then, usually serves in one of two capacities. First, the council assists and advises the principal in the areas of budgeting, curriculum, and personnel, but the principal alone has the authority to make decisions. Or, second, the council is the primary decision-making unit in the school, with the principal serving as a facilitator. Under this option, councils have full power to formulate goals and allocate resources.

In some schools, authority is split along subject lines. For example, the principal may retain authority for personnel selection, but all other decisions concerning the school budget, curriculum, and new programs are made by the council through a consensus voting process. The principal serves as chairperson but cannot veto council decisions.

Wohlstetter said in an interview that even in "principal-based" SBM models, where the principal has final accountability and authority for school performance, the most effective principals "always set up structures, usually formal structures, whereby various stakeholders have input."

The selection and roles of council members vary in each district and school, based on district philosophy, school needs, and available resources. Most councils are composed of the principal, teachers, staff members, parents, and sometimes community members and students. Support staff—custodians, secretaries, aides, and crossing guards—also make valuable council members because they frequently hear from parents and are aware of informal school decision-making. In addition, some councils include professional support staff members, such as school psychologists and attendance officers.

The composition and roles of SBM councils range from a three-member leadership team to large committees that involve all the faculty members in the decision-making process. In some schools, several committees work concurrently, the scope of each committee determined by the nature of the issue. Council size should be between seven and fifteen, Hansen and Marburger (1989) advise, though the size may depend on whether the school's major constituencies are represented. It is essential that the members realize they represent not just themselves but constituencies who wish to be consulted before the council makes decisions.

Wohlstetter noted in the interview that in actively restructuring schools, "there is never one single council that is empowered to make decisions. There's always a web or network of organizations to make decisions. In some way, nearly the whole faculty is involved in these high-performance schools." In practice, "the site-based council is supported by a series of subcommittees that are basically the work horses of the council." The work of these subgroups lessens the burden on the council and has other benefits, she said: "More seems to get done, the council is more productive, there is less teacher burnout, and communication among the faculty improves because those subcommittees or working teams meet on a regular basis."

Implementation Guidelines

In an SBM system, principals and their staffs often gain decision-making authority in three areas: budgeting, curriculum, and personnel. In this section, information is provided on how SBM schools can make use of their new-found authority in these areas. Also included are steps to follow when shifting to an SBM system.

School-Based Budgeting

School-based budgeting refers to the delegation of the budgetary authority to the school. The distribution process at the building level is largely dependent on the administrative style of the principal. Generally, school-based budgeting can be done one of the following ways:

- The principal has complete authority and accountability for the building budget.
- The principal and a small group of other administrators and department heads can make the decisions.
- A special budget committee handles budget decisions.
- The site council controls the budget.

In most districts practicing SBM, the individual schools prefer to leave purchasing, warehousing, and acquisition of supplies to the district office, even though the schools are free to use the allocated budget for essential support services. For example, one California school district has established the departments of maintenance, data processing, printing, food services, transportation, and personnel as independent budgeting units. Schools buy the services out of their budgets each year and can carry over surpluses they have.

Budget control may be the heart of SBM because the curricular and personnel decisions are largely dependent upon budgetary decisions. It is common for districts to allocate a fixed "lump sum" to each school, usually based on the number of students and the special needs of the school. Each school is free to spend the money according to its priority plans and needs, while the district retains control over the budget expenditures to provide support services.

Richard G. Neal cites several advantages of school-based budgeting: First, the school district's resources are put more effectively where they are needed. Second, schools have a greater incentive to control spending in certain areas (such as utilities) in order to have more money available for other areas (such as supplies for students). And finally, budgeting decisions are more likely to be supported since there are "greater feelings of ownership" among stakeholders.

The Salem-Keizer, Oregon, school district allocates funds to schools on a per-pupil basis. Each principal in the district has total control over the allocated funds for redistribution within the building on the basis of priority needs. However, the reallocation of the budget within the school building is confined to expenditures for program development, general administration, and other instructional matters. The principal does not have the authority to hire extra personnel without central-office approval. Through its five Area Offices, Salem-Keizer allocates additional funds, similar to discretionary funds, to each school based on individual school needs.

How principals allocate funds varies from school to school. At Salem-Keizer's Hayesville Elementary School, the leadership team and the principal jointly decide budgetary matters, on the basis of input from the staff. At Richmond Elementary School, also in Salem-Keizer, the principal allocates funds to the respective teacher teams based on enrollment and team needs. At North Salem High School, the site-based committee and other groups give input on priority programs and needs, and the principal allocates funds accordingly to facilitate program implementation.

In her interviews with teachers from SBM schools, White found that teachers who were involved in budget decisions felt important, in charge, and knowledgeable about how much money was available. They also experienced a sense of community with other teachers and were better able to communicate school goals and teaching objectives to parents.

> Teachers... stated that they were more careful with allocations when they were in charge of balancing their own account. They set their own priorities and purchased materials and equipment that they needed the most. As teachers met and discussed budget priorities with other teachers and administrators, they became more informed about school needs and expenses. As teachers became engaged in setting budget priorities, they developed better understandings of which items were affordable and which were not.

School-Based Curriculum

Most SBM systems grant to schools the authority to design, develop, and focus the school curriculum within the framework provided by the school board. In some districts, schools are free to design their own curricula as long as they meet the state guidelines regarding content. In other words, the schools have control over the "hows" while the district or state guidelines determine the "whats" of the instructional program (Priscilla Wohlstetter and colleagues).

In some cases, the central office may maintain a selection of curricula from which district schools can develop their own, which are then reviewed by the superintendent. Schools in Martin County, Florida, design their curricula based on state guidelines, choosing among selected textbooks that are restricted to three or four standard series. Based on interviews with over 100 teachers and administrators, White found that "school-based curriculum development has enabled teachers to recommend new courses, to redesign report cards, to make scheduling changes, to select in-service workshops, and to participate in textbook selection."

In some large districts, school boards prescribe basal texts and delegate decisions regarding supplementary reading materials and teaching methods to the schools. Some districts also provide centralized preservice teacher training to establish content expectations for each subject.

Prasch mentions another type of school-based curriculum: The district provides a written curriculum in each subject area that includes goals, objectives, teaching methods, and recommended teaching materials. The schools are free to adopt the district curriculum or develop their own teaching materials and methods with written permission from the associate superintendent of instruction.

Clune and White cite examples of schools that have used surplus funds to meet several unmet needs. Some schools have developed new math textbooks and changed their language arts and science curricula. Others have developed peer-tutoring programs and added an emphasis on thinking skills. The Edmonds, Washington, school district added an eighth period to provide assistance to students who were behind in their work.

Personnel

In SBM, staff selection is often the responsibility of the principal. In some schools, council members and teachers assist the principal in selecting teachers from a pool of qualified applicants maintained by the central office. In others, applicants contact the principal after the district office provides information about vacancies. In both cases, the principal has the final authority over hiring and firing personnel. The district usually negotiates salaries, working conditions, benefits, and grievance procedures with the union.

White interviewed teachers who were involved in staff selection, often by serving on hiring committees, and found that these teachers had positive views about their experiences:

> Teachers reviewed applications, developed interview questions, interviewed applicants, and interacted with other teachers and administrators. They believed that their input was valued since their recommendations were often followed. Teachers believed that in contrast to previous job interviews conducted primarily by administrators, their interviews emphasized questions on teaching skills and philosophy....
>
> Teachers received positive feedback from administrators, who were willing to listen and accepted suggestions from them. Teachers felt more of a responsibility for the new teachers and were eager to support the new teachers if they had a role in hiring them.

However, White found that the teachers did not want to be involved in firing decisions. "Teachers' responses indicated that even in decentralized districts where teachers are highly involved in school decision-making, teachers desire strong leadership from the principal."

In many districts, schools determine the number and mix of paraprofessionals and teachers they hire. Wohlstetter and colleagues explain that having control over personnel frees the school to hire staff members who will conform to the culture of the school and to create a mix of staff positions that support "the teaching and learning strategies of the campus."

Most district offices retain some authority over personnel by providing schools with district-approved lists of applicants. For example, the Portland, Oregon, school district maintains a pool of qualified applicants who have passed an initial screening. Then, depending on their building policies, principals hire teachers on their own or after consulting with the entire staff or team leaders. The Salem-Keizer district also maintains an applicant pool. If suitable candidates cannot be found from within the pool and if the school identifies a qualified person who is not part of the district pool, the principal may hire the person with central-office assistance.

Steps To Take

The American Association of School Administrators, the National Association of Elementary School Principals, and the National Association of Secondary School Principals offer the following steps for schools planning to implement an SBM system:

1. Develop awareness throughout the system, from the school board through community members.
2. Determine whether your school or system is ready.
3. Establish a development committee composed of stakeholders.
4. Survey the community and assess educational strengths and unmet needs.
5. Set educational goals and objectives.
6. Decide on a timeline, allowing plenty of room for training, selecting committees, improving information access, and setting up new budgeting procedures.
7. Decide on an approach for implementation, such as pilot programs in a limited number of schools, during the first year.
8. Train committee members.
9. Implement the program.
10. Monitor, evaluate, and adjust as necessary throughout implementation.
11. Be prepared for and work to eliminate obstacles, such as unrealistically high expectations, inappropriate "downsizing," some collective-bargaining agreements, inaccurate beliefs about equity, state initiatives, and skepticism from staff members.

From the outset, the school board should ensure that a framework is in place to hold principals and school councils accountable for their actions. It may be wise to establish a districtwide committee to oversee the councils, say Peter A. Walker and Lawrence Roder. This committee could evaluate councils "on defined criteria, such as the performance of students, the degree of involvement of staff, parents and the community in school operations, financial performance and other appropriate measures."

The Cultural Context

The school's culture is the soil in which SBM, like any innovation, is planted. This system of norms, beliefs, and values that govern the way people think and behave can be hard as clay, causing SBM to wither on the vine, or fertile and tillable, allowing it to flourish.

As Guskey and Peterson point out, SBM "requires that traditional school roles be redefined so that teachers and parents can work collaboratively on schoolwide decisions." SBM thrives on norms of collegiality, open communication, sharing of knowledge and resources, and a willingness to learn. Conversely, people's inability to work as a group, their fear of reprisal if a decision backfires, their unwillingness to subordinate individual goals to those of the group, or leaders' attempts to create the illusion of reform without committing necessary resources are problems of the heart and mind that stunt SBM's growth in any setting.

Each school's culture can be assessed at the outset to identify both its strengths and its potential barriers to SBM. For instance, participants could be invited to share their goals, beliefs, and assumptions about schooling as one step in the process of defining a unified vision for the school. "Ceremonies, retreats, and joint recreational activities can cultivate a collegial spirit," say Guskey and Peterson. The strength of SBM is the freedom it gives each school to build its own unique culture in the pursuit of excellence. Wohlstetter spoke of the need for this culture-building in schools with SBM:

> A part of SBM that appeals to me is that successful SBM schools all have a unique culture or very strong community feeling that governs the school. SBM allows schools to become a community, to define their own personality. This is critical to a high-performing organization.
>
> The strong community feeling is facilitated by the ability of people at the school site to define their vision for the school and what makes them different from the school down the street. To tailor their programs, they need some budget and curriculum control, as well as some staffing control to be able to hire people

who fit in with that vision, with that school personality and community.

The Importance of Policies

Some state, district, and school policies may have to be revised for SBM to be implemented successfully. Flexibility is called for by policy-makers—as well as simplicity.

At the district level, policy-makers must avoid limiting the principal's authority too severely. School boards need to clarify district goals and spell out with precision the extent of principals' and site councils' authority over budget, personnel, and curriculum decisions. For example, boards can "establish overall objectives for curriculum but not be involved in curriculum development" (Committee for Economic Development). At the school site, the principal and site councils need to rewrite policies and goals collaboratively. Clear school policies enable teachers and students, for example, to understand what is expected of them.

Overall, the consensus of educators and researchers seems to be that, for SBM to work, policies should be clear, flexible, simple, and kept to an absolute minimum.

How Successful Is SBM?

Supporters of SBM claim the positive outcomes it brings about include gains in achievement, lower dropout rates, increased attendance, and reduced disciplinary problems. Some have argued that SBM can only be considered successful if it helps to make schools more effective in helping students achieve. Similarly, Prasch believes that "the most telling evaluation of SBM will, in the long run, rest on the question of improved student achievement." Carl D. Glickman concurs: "Site-based innovations mean nothing if a school cannot determine if the efforts have had an effect on students."

In Salem-Keizer, Oregon, Superintendent Homer Kearns says, "The entire focus of reorganization is based on the improvement of student learning. That is the key. The only reason for restructuring is so that we might do a better job of teaching kids, not to make the organization more comfortable."

Whether SBM will contribute to student performance is still unproved. Little or no evidence reported so far indicates any impact on student achievement (Malen and others). Peter J. Robertson and colleagues conclude that "a shift to school-based management does not guarantee subsequent school improvement." Anita A. Summers and Amy W. Johnson, who examined twenty studies on the effects of SBM, say, "The results of SBM appear to be some increased sense of empowerment and involvement of the stakeholders (though not uniformly so), and virtually no evidence that SBM translates into improved student performance."

"Improving school performance may be an unrealistic expectation for a *governance* reform that alters the balance of power within educational systems toward schools," Wohlstetter and colleagues explain. As Wohlstetter told this writer, SBM is not an end in itself but a tool for achieving higher performance by the organization.

High-performing SBM schools, she explained, have combined the governance reform of SBM with "a push toward innovating in the classroom."

> That combination is very important. Without it, SBM becomes a political reform whereby the council at the school site ends up spending its time deciding who is empowered and who isn't or issues such as who can use the copy machine instead of improving classroom practices.
>
> SBM must be combined with an overall push for curriculum and instructional reform. This gives some substance to the decisions the council is making. They can then focus on broader organizational issues such as how to structure your classrooms in ways that improve academic performance and make schools more interesting places to work.

Murphy likewise believes that "what is needed is a marriage between SBM and our most powerful conceptions of learning and teaching"; therefore, revisions in governance and organization must be "more tightly linked to revisions in curriculum and instruction."

SBM is a managerial technique that, if implemented correctly, gives those closest to the students the freedom to make decisions that lead to improved student achievement. The flexibility of SBM as a management system is the schools' greatest asset as they seek to achieve their particular educational goals. What must be remembered is that "because the children they serve are different, schools need to adopt different programs" (AASA and others). It is up to the stakeholders to evaluate student needs and find ways of matching resources to those needs. Carol Midgley and Stewart Wood conclude that SBM needs to be seen "as an *important process* for achieving substantive school reform" rather than an end in itself.

Robertson and colleagues argue that schools are more likely to implement curriculum and instructional reform if seven factors are present. School officials can refer to these factors as benchmarks when evaluating the success of their SBM systems.

1. *Power.* "The school has significant influence over key decision areas and a greater range of stakeholders are actively involved in the decision-making process."
2. *Knowledge.* "More individuals participate with greater frequency in a broad range of professional development activities oriented toward building schoolwide capacity for improvement."
3. *Information.* "A broad range of relevant information is disseminated both internally and externally and the school acquires information regarding stakeholder satisfaction."
4. *Rewards.* "Individual and school evaluation is based on performance in terms of goals or outcomes, and rewards and/or sanctions are tied to performance."
5. *Instructional Guidance.* "There is agreement among staff regarding the instructional direction of the school, which is guided by a state or district framework and/or a school vision or mission."
6. *Leadership.* "The principal insures widespread involvement, shares information broadly, and takes on more of a managerial role, and a broader range of leaders emerges at the school."
7. *Resources.* "The school increases its resource base through the acquisition of outside funding and/or partnerships with the community."

Conclusion

While not sufficient in itself to make schools more effective in educating students, school-based management gives school personnel who want to perform better an added means to do so. SBM gives site administrators and faculty members an opportunity to reexamine their goals and practices and to secure resources suitable for the improvement strategies they devise.

In addition to SBM's benefits as a management technique, the philosophical beliefs on which SBM is based—responsibility and accountability, shared decision-making, trust, and open communication—can help to stimulate school improvement.

In summary, the following conditions are essential for successful SBM implementation: ongoing district support, trust and support among staff members, a focus on student learning, training in leadership and management skills, education of stakeholders about SBM's rationale and practice, a commitment of time for startup and implementation from all stakeholders, access to information for decision-making, and communication among all stakeholders.

CHAPTER

8

Quality Work Teams

Lori Jo Oswald

Is the phrase "committee decisions" an oxymoron? That indeed was the claim of a headline in a recent college magazine. But many people in education believe team decision-making is the best thing to come out of two decades of school-reform efforts. Management teams, advisory committees, site councils, and other types of work groups are addressing topics that traditionally were the domain of one superintendent, principal, or teacher.

The premise of teamwork is that education "can be greatly improved by simply strengthening the connections among people who work at all levels within the organization," say William G. Cunningham and Donn W. Gresso. Ultimately, the argument for work teams in education is that students will benefit when more people with wider perspectives contribute their ideas and expertise.

By the early 1990s, many businesses and public-sector organizations had "changed their organizational design to revolve around self-managing work teams responsible for key processes within the organization" (Stephen Murgatroyd and Colin Morgan). Leaders in such organizations were realizing that "those closest to a process have a greater understanding of these processes and are therefore better able to improve performance."

But how did these executives come to view teams as key decision-making entities? In large part, it was due to the influence of an American businessman named W. Edwards Deming, whose ideas transformed how Japanese businesses were managed. Deming is considered the founder of total quality management (TQM).

Deming and School Work Teams

In his book *Out of the Crisis,* Deming listed fourteen points about management theory. One point taken to heart by educational theorists and administrators calls for breaking down barriers among departments. Charles A. Melvin III says that in schools the "challenge has been to get everyone involved and do so in such a way that each individual recognizes he or she has something to contribute and does so without fear."

In Deming's view, instead of being "bosses," managers should collaborate with workers; he contends that when people work together, the end result—the product—is of a higher quality. In other words, managers should cooperate, not coerce. When put into practice at schools, Deming's philosophy is said to reduce competition among individuals and departments and increase the energy available for creating environments more conducive to learning (Yvonne Siu-Runyan and Sally Joy Heart). In organizations that adopt Deming's philosophy, everyone must change perspectives. As Siu-Runyan and Heart explain, "Teachers and school executives must work together to rethink what they do, how they do it, and how they measure it."

Many education reformers are promoting Deming's views. Improving the *quality* of education, they contend, requires structural changes in the system. "According to these reformers, most school problems originate from the system itself, and management is responsible for the system," Siu-Runyan and Heart note. "So, the way to generate improvement in schools is to reform school management."

What Schools Can Learn from Businesses

In a business, work teams give employees "control over everything from work schedules to how to perform the work and from hiring to firing," says Gene Maeroff. Such teams are "vehicles for increasing efficiency, effectiveness, and motivation at the worksite." Maeroff lists the assumptions that underlie the formation of such teams in business:

• Those closest to the work know best how to perform and improve their jobs.

• Most employees want to feel they "own" their jobs and are making meaningful contributions to the effectiveness of their organizations.

• Teams provide possibilities for empowerment not available to individual employees. In the 1970s, corporations such as General Foods, Proctor and Gamble, and Digital Equipment Corporation shifted to the use of self-regulating work teams and experienced several positive results, including "greater innovation; improved employee attitudes; and reduced work stoppages, employee turnover, and absenteeism" (L. E. Scarr).

Karolyn J. Snyder and Robert H. Anderson say that the concept of teams can be applied to U.S. public schools much the way it is in successful Japanese companies. In Japan, teams are formed either to solve problems or to meet a continuous need. Team objectives take precedence over individual objectives. "No individual credit or blame is given. Collectivism emerges from group work, causing people to work well together and to encourage better efforts."

Japanese business teams are responsible for team-leader selection, "job assignments, peer evaluation and control, absenteeism, record keeping, scheduling, budget, and evaluation," says Maeroff, and "sharing work decisions with management lies at the heart of team success."

What can educators learn from Japanese businesses? According to Snyder and Anderson, organizations that foster collaboration are more likely to achieve their goals than those in which individuals perform isolated tasks.

How TQM Drives Effective Teams

The American Association of School Administrators stresses that work teams are integral to applying TQM principles at the school site: "One important tenet of systems thinking is to involve those closest to the 'action' in the decision-making process.... Decisions about a process are best made by cross-functional teams, which would include a representative of every step involved in that process."

Teams are given very specific goals and the freedom to attain those goals. As Murgatroyd and Morgan explain, "The team is empowered to determine how it will achieve the goals it has been given in a context of a shared vision and understanding—in a climate of trust." Team members reflect, plan, and take action to achieve vision-related goals.

Carol Davis, deputy superintendent of the Salem-Keizer School District, in Salem, Oregon, said administrators in her district are trained in TQM principles. "We are attempting to make ourselves more efficient but not exactly a business model. We use pieces that fit." Currently, the trainees are addressing the following questions: Should there be a process by which we all learn? How can we do things differently? Is it possible to make bureaucracies in schools and districts work quicker? How do the concepts of TQM apply to our district?

Work teams in Davis's district conduct research and ask other school district partners and business partners about their experiences applying business techniques such as TQM to schools. Davis believes the principles of TQM are successfully applied in her district's work teams, even though the process is a striking change from what's familiar:

> Most of us have come up through a system that has operated really traditionally, a hierarchy. We're now trying to put the decision-making at the level where people are most affected. To do that you have to involve your community. I believe it's more cumbersome, more time-consuming, but the results seem to be more positive, and it's important for school districts to have a community that's in synch with where the district is moving. Teams help that happen.

Making the transition to TQM is not a smooth process, Davis noted, "but it's worth it." Forming work teams based on the principles of TQM is a radical departure from how most educational institutions have traditionally been managed, but, as the next section suggests, the process has several advantages.

Rationale for Work Teams

There are many reasons group decision-making is preferable to individual decision-making in schools. Team members are accountable to others, which often increases the quality of their work. More and better information and actions emerge from a group of people with a range of backgrounds, experiences, and skills. Fresh ideas and outlooks are often presented in work teams, and members continually learn from one another. In addition, because more people are involved, there is a greater likelihood mistakes will be caught and corrected. And perhaps most important, there is strength in the collective power of a group that increases the acceptability and probability of risk-taking.

Why Teams?

Demands placed on schools today are increasing while funds are decreasing. This situation makes collaboration—especially through work teams—essential. Some areas requiring collaboration identified by Snyder and Anderson include managing and instructing staff members, developing materials, "researching influences on school achievement programs," and "creating models of schooling capable of launching schools well into the twenty-first century."

Work teams are effective because they broaden and integrate responsibilities, says L. E. "Bud" Scarr, superintendent of Lake Washington School District in Kirkland, Washington.

Whereas bureaucracies focus on inputs and processes, work teams emphasize outcomes. Whereas bureaucracies define the process for employees, work team members create their own process. Members of work groups possess numerous skills and have relative autonomy and adequate information to make decisions concerning various tasks or services. They focus on what needs to be done as well as how they will work together to get it done.

Simply put, teams are promoted as the best method to handle decision-making in schools and districts because those closest to the students are involved and empowered. Team members, who may include administrators, teachers, parents, community members, and students, understand the needs and goals of a particular school or district. In addition, when more people are involved in making a decision, the likelihood is greater that the decision will be implemented. Maeroff says team members do not have the "vulnerability" of being lone innovators and they are not "hampered by the unwieldiness that comes with trying to make change agents of a whole faculty at once."

Advantages of Team Decision-Making

Cunningham and Gresso list several advantages associated with team decision-making in education: connections are developed among subgroups; organizational cohesiveness grows; a sense of school or district culture is enhanced; participants "gain new perspectives, insights, commitments, and cooperative efforts"; and the information, knowledge, and decision-making base is broadened. The philosophy behind teams is summed up by Ernie R. Keller: "None of us is as smart as all of us."

Murgatroyd and Morgan cite additional benefits of teams:

1. They maximize the creative talent within an organization and promote learning.
2. They are learning units in that they encourage the transfer of knowledge and skills.
3. They promote problem ownership.
4. They encourage a wider range of problem-solving than can be tackled by a single individual, especially when the teams are cross-functional.
5. Working as a team is more satisfying (when managed well and associated with team development and training) than working alone.
6. Teamwork carries lobbying power in terms of support for proposals that will lead to change.

Some Reservations

Unlike some other school-reform topics, the concept of quality work teams has few opponents. Perhaps this is because teams are relatively new in many schools and districts, so insufficient time has passed for research to reveal their weaknesses and shortcomings. On the other hand, work teams may simply lead to more positive results than negative ones. Still, a few educators expressed reservations about teams that proponents should take into account.

Carmen Chan, principal of Robert Frost Elementary School in Kirkland, Washington, believes a major drawback to site councils is that the school board, the central office, or the principal is still ultimately accountable for problems. Also, Chan, who already puts in eighteen-hour days, recognizes that the existence of a council might place even more demands on her time. "If you have to go through a site council for decisions, it takes time to process through how to make decisions and to train people in group decision-making." Conceptually, work teams are a great idea, Chan said, but in practice, she wonders if they are all they are made out to be.

Finally, it is important to note that not all decisions in a school or a district need to be made by teams: Routine decisions should be made daily by individuals at all levels—from students to superintendents. The next section clarifies the missions and goals typical of most teams and gives examples of types of teams commonly used to fulfill specific missions.

Types of Teams

Teams vary in size, mission, and duration. Districtwide teams and school councils are permanent and have a general focus. A variety of smaller groups may address specific tasks during a defined period. This section begins by providing a brief overview of the types of teams used in schools and districts today. Attention then focuses on two major types of teams: vertical teams and multifunctional teams.

Snyder and Anderson list two major categories of school-based teams. *Permanent teams* specialize in a particular ongoing function such as curricular or age-level teaching. An example would be an instructional team comprised of the entire teaching staff of a school's English department. *Temporary teams* are "organized for a particular short-term purpose and are dissolved when the task is completed." Examples include a task force for K-6 math curriculum and a work team that oversees development of a gifted program for a high school.

At the district level, the most common type of team is the *management team*, which usually includes the superintendent and other central-office administrators, and possibly a board of education member and principals. Management teams have responsibility for districtwide policies, missions, or decision-making. Many subgroups may also be found at the district level.

Nancy Vollmer, of Linn-Benton-Lincoln Education Service District in Albany, Oregon, said districts in the five-county region she serves are using more work teams because "they build ownership and understanding by being a good communication tool." Many Oregon districts have districtwide teams with members from each school-site council. These districtwide teams have different purposes, but usually they act in a liaison role, helping to ensure districtwide consistency in policies.

A district subcommittee that Vollmer worked with, for example, was established to revise some curriculum for that district. Such subcommittees work with the schools and the district-office staff and present their findings to representatives of each group. Examples of district subcommittees are subject-area teams, such as humanities, science, or technology.

Management teams—sometimes called *administrative teams* or *leadership teams*—can also be found at the school level. Generally, management teams assist the principal in decision-making. Therefore, many site-based councils could be considered administrative teams. Leonard O. Pellicer and colleagues found that the "most effective schools had functioning administrative teams, and supplementary advisory bodies to assist in the problem-solving, planning, and decision-making processes. The team provided a focus for appropriate delegation of responsibility and authority."

Snyder and Anderson list some of the kinds of work teams that can be found at the school site: subject-area teams, leadership teams, instructional teams, vertical curriculum teams, task forces structured to produce a product, planning teams, schoolwide goal-setting teams, training teams, social-functions committees, outside-school-activities teams, evaluation task forces, human-relations committees, parent-advisory groups, and faculty-advisory groups.

In addition to the leadership team, broad specialty teams in a school can include:

- *Production teams*: Committees, work groups, or other units with assigned responsibilities, such as production of a video program for visitors to the school.
- *Curriculum-development teams*: Teams assigned to coordinate the school program (for example, K-6, K-12, 7-12), usually within specific content areas. A mathematics team in an elementary school, for example, might include one math-responsible delegate from each grade- or unit-level, and the team's job would be to make sure the K-6 math program has good pace, continuity, and validity.

• *Councils and study groups*: Teachers and parents or others from outside the school concerned with review and analysis of questions, topics, or concerns.

• *Task forces*: Groups on special assignments of schoolwide interest (for example, a task force to develop a schoolwide program for creatively gifted students) (Snyder and Anderson).

Vertical Teams

Most often when we think of work teams we have in mind people who come together from the same levels of an organization. Examples are teacher curriculum committees, parent advisory groups, and all elementary principals in a district.

In contrast to these horizontal teams, *vertical teams* are made up of individuals from different levels of an organization who join together to accomplish a task or engage in planning.

In a district, a vertical team might consist of administrators from high schools, middle schools, and elementary schools, while in a single school it might include a superintendent, principal, teachers, support staff, parents, and students. For example, Snyder and Anderson describe a vertical curriculum team that has representatives from each school level—preschool, primary, intermediate, middle school, and secondary—and that is responsible for ensuring a specific program (such as science or math) has "appropriate cohesion and continuity" from kindergarten through grade 12.

The general missions of vertical teams are consistency and trust-building. Establishing such teams facilitates "the important exchange of information among individuals who share a common purpose but operate on different levels and who thus have very different organizational perspectives," write Cunningham and Gresso. Such teams facilitate the development of a "shared culture that supports implementation efforts and creates long-term school effectiveness." Without this shared culture, "school effectiveness programs are either never implemented or disappear after implementation" (Cunningham and Gresso).

Members of vertical teams are able to communicate their ideas and needs to others at various levels in the organization, as well as to hear others' views and experiences. The result is better understanding. Cunningham and Gresso cite district personnel who claim the following benefits from vertical teams: improved communication, respect, and collegiality; increased awareness of other team members' problems and needs; more confidence and trust in other stakeholders' and their roles; awareness of each team member's roles and responsibilities, as well as a sense of how each member fits into the entire system; ability to see how a change in one level affects stakeholders at other levels; and wider points of view. Cunningham and Gresso conclude:

> One of the most common benefits expressed by those who participated in vertical teams was the increased insight that occurred from being exposed to a broad diversity of perspectives. Members saw themselves as part of an organization in which individual horizontal groups were able to achieve far less than what was possible by working together as an entire organization. They began to recognize, value, and actively seek members at all levels within the organization who might help them achieve improved organizational effectiveness. Most participants on vertical teams concurred that exposure to the expertise and viewpoints of others enabled them to function more effectively in their jobs.

Perhaps most important, the use of vertical teams in a district can help to build an effective districtwide culture. In horizontal teams, the valuable exchange of information among like-minded colleagues can actually prevent the creation of a districtwide culture and cohesiveness (Cunningham and Gresso). Therefore, the American Association of School Administrators and the Institute for Development of Education Activities, Inc. promote the "District Learning Leadership Team" as a means of ending the separation of teachers from administrators and school board members. Vertical teams facilitate the formation of bonds and cohesion, which are essential to a districtwide culture (Cunningham and Gresso).

Multifunctional Teams

A term commonly seen today in writings about work teams in the business arena is *multifunctional team* (also referred to as multidisciplinary team, cross-functional team, or cross-disciplinary team). This type of team seeks to encourage "cooperation between different functional areas of the larger organization to speed the cycles of product and process innovation and renewal" (Bernard M. Bass and Bruce J. Avolio). A districtwide vertical team, then, is an example of a multifunctional team, but so is a school-improvement team that includes representatives from each academic area or from administration, teaching, and nonteaching staff.

According to Bass and Avolio, multifunctional teams are designed by upper management (in the case of a school or district, by administrators or the school board). Management "helps to set the initial direction, shares the vision, and empowers" the multifunctional team members to carry out their responsibilities.

The following examples demonstrate the kinds of work teams that operate at district and school levels.

Bend-LaPine School District

Bend-LaPine is an example of an Oregon school district that uses vertical teams. Superintendent Scott Mutchie's management system includes four horizontal teams and three vertical teams, as well as school-site councils. Each vertical team consists of representatives from high schools, middle schools, and elementary schools in one of three regions within the district, as well as supervisory members. Vertical teams "make sure communication goes on between K-12 and we're on track as far as standards across the grades," said Mutchie. The vertical teams research problem areas, evaluate textbook materials and adoptions, determine ways to meet state requirements, and set timelines.

The composition of Bend-LaPine's four horizontal teams is as follows: one consists of all high school principals in the district; another, middle school principals; the third, elementary principals; and the fourth, central-office supervisors. Each team determines what goes on "horizontally" at its school level. In Bend-LaPine, decision-making is cyclical and communication flows back and forth between the horizontal and vertical teams.

Salem-Keizer School District

This district of fifty-three schools has a cabinet made up of district-level administrators. "We try to have representatives from all the different areas of the district," said Carol Davis, deputy superintendent. "The cabinet is the management, leadership, and problem-solving group. Each of us brings to it a different perspective." Topics discussed include staff issues, budget, policy, regulations, and organization.

Davis told how a unique team came into existence as the district sought to make progress on school-improvement initiatives:

> We diagrammed all the groups in the district. We had a strategic planning and advising committee and other committees. What was missing was a group of people who understood the district and how it operated and understood the community and were able to get things done, to take an idea either from our citizens group or board or superintendent or cabinet and make it functional. So we then developed the *core team*.

The core team's major purpose is to facilitate the strategy for meeting the state's school-reform requirements. Each person on the core team agrees that student learning and education goals are important to the district, Davis said. The members, who meet twice a month, are coordinators, not decision-makers.

Three additional teams were formed last year to focus on decision-making, organizational effectiveness, and goals for student learning. A member of the core team sits on each of these work teams.

Whereas the core team has eight to ten members, the size of the work teams ranges from twenty-four to over one-hundred members. The size of a team depends on the scope of the charge and how many people it takes to get the job done, Davis said. The largest team, the student learning-goals group, is divided into smaller subcommittees.

Each school in the Salem-Keizer district determines the structure of its site council, the method for selecting members, and the degree of participation the principal, teachers, classified staff, parents, and community members will have.

Schools often have other teams in place. For example, North Salem High School has an administrative team, made up of the principal, the assistant principals, and the office manager. This team makes decisions regarding management of the school, safety, personnel, and budget. It also manages the school calendar, student activities, athletic events, community events, and public relations.

The high school's leadership team, made up of administrators and department coordinators, works with the faculty to give input to the principal in the areas of management, staffing, budgeting, and building the master schedule. Other subcommittees, such as the technology committee, faculty advisory committee, discipline committee, and faculty welfare committee, provide feedback to the leadership team, department coordinators, and site council regarding needs, concerns, and priorities.

Lake Washington School District

In 1991, with 38 schools, 24,000 students, and 2,200 employees, Lake Washington School District in Kirkland, Washington, decided to reorganize its central-office staff, building administrators, and support personnel into four work teams. Superintendent L.E. Scarr describes how this arrangement works:

> The three regional teams each include one high school and the schools that feed into it. These teams focus on supporting the operations and restructuring efforts of schools in their area. A fourth team provides services to schools and teams including business, facilities, and personnel.
>
> Approximately 12 schools are assigned to each of the three regional teams. Each team is made up of approximately 75 people: principals, central office administrators, teachers, support staff,

students, parents, and businesspeople. Teams are divided into subgroups charged with specific responsibilities and tasks.

Scarr said Lake Washington formed work teams for two reasons. First, they transformed the focus "from a narrow, compartmentalized view to a broad and far-reaching perspective." And second, they created a structure for participation by people at all levels of the organization. The overriding mission of Lake Washington's teams is to increase students' "mastery of relevant skills, knowledge, and abilities."

Team Functions and Roles

Most teams adopt the same basic structure and define members' roles similarly. This section provides information on what these structures and roles are, as well as describes what every new work team needs to learn to function effectively.

Determining Team Tasks

Those writing about work teams agree on at least one point: the team's mission must be clear to all team members. The first task of a team should be to agree on what its mission is. After that, it is useful to determine what the responsibilities of the team are, who will be the facilitator and what his or her roles will be, what the roles of other members will be, and how decisions will be made. Other matters to be determined are planning and reporting systems, composition of the team (Will it include parents, teachers, students, the principal, community members?), expected outcomes and deadlines, and communications systems (Snyder and Anderson).

Generally, every team and every team meeting focuses on one or more of the following objectives: informing, planning, problem-solving, decision-making, training, evaluating, or increasing morale, cooperation, and communication (Margot Helphand). For guidelines on meeting management, see chapter 14, "Leading Meetings."

Members: Understanding Roles

A team's membership ought to be governed by its mission. To determine who should be on a team, consider the skills necessary to accomplish its purpose. Also consider the size of the team needed, the strengths and weaknesses of individual members, their talents and skills, the overall school mission, the number of task forces needed, the time required and time available from members, and the members' willingness to receive training in group problem-solving, planning, and group leadership (Snyder and Anderson).

Team members must be committed and motivated. "You have to have someone with the time and interest to work on this," said Keller, "not people who are lukewarm." Also, members need to have something to offer to the team—such as knowledge, ideas, or enthusiasm.

Teachers, in particular, may find teamwork especially challenging, says Maeroff, because "the measure of most teachers' success usually rests on how adept they are at working on their own." Training in teamwork is not intended to break down this "separateness." Rather, trainees "are meant to return to their buildings as a cadre of committed individuals eager to engage in educational discussions and available for mutual reinforcement," says Maeroff. "Together, they launch a crusade. The Holy Grail they seek is better education for students."

Davis believes teams are stronger when there is diversity among members. "Traditionally, you would have all special-education people sit down and discuss special-ed problems," she said, but now district teams incorporate people from many schools, grade levels, and programs; teams also include people of different ages and experiences. "This brings all of the perspectives together, and we usually end up with a solution that we don't have to 'sell' because every group has some input."

Team members—especially the leader, facilitator, recorder, and process observer—need to be aware of the roles and responsibilities they will be expected to assume.

The Leader's Role

Leaders' new role of empowering their staff by organizing them into teams is the most important aspect of leadership, say David D. Johnson and Roger T. Johnson.

The superintendent or principal does not—and should not—serve on every team in the district or the school, but as team leader may facilitate, administrate, or coordinate team functions.

Keeping communication channels open and delegating authority to team members are key responsibilities of the team leader. In addition, the leader reminds members how the team's work dovetails with the district's or school's mission, vision, and goals (Helphand).

A team leader will probably be more effective if he or she has some of the following qualities, say Bass and Avolio:

> knowledge of group process, ability to think and react decisively, ability to articulate a position clearly and succinctly, knowledge and competency in the subject area, sensitivity to group trends and needs, self-restraint and respect for others, ability to vocalize group sentiments, ability to clarify objectives again and again, and persistence in achieving difficult objectives.

The Facilitator's Role

The facilitator balances team members' emotions, as well as topics and time. Generally, the facilitator helps the group get organized, become more effective, and determine and accomplish goals, while also enjoying the group experience (Helphand). Specifically, the facilitator ensures group members understand the purpose and agenda of each meeting, delegates responsibilities, sees to it that meetings stay on track and start and end on time, and determines how much time to devote to each agenda item. After each meeting, the facilitator checks with team members regarding their progress on assigned tasks.

The American Association of School Administrators recommends that facilitators should have the superintendent's and board's confidence; credibility with other team members; a "non-controlling, others-centered ego"; an interest in trying new ideas and in lifelong learning; the ability to adjust to changing needs, conditions, and priorities; "a vision of what might be that is beyond current practice and conventional wisdom"; a goal-directed personality; the ability to bring out the best in colleagues; the ability to stick with a long-term project; and patience, encouragement, and flexibility.

Consultant Ernie Keller has been the facilitator on numerous grant-proposal teams. Central functions of the facilitator include suggesting the time and place for people to get together, building an agenda, facilitating the agenda during and after the meeting, taking the basic minutes of the meeting, doing the "pick-and-shovel" work between meetings, and developing a draft for people to examine.

Keller said facilitators should not be too thin-skinned. "They must be willing to listen when people say, 'This can be done a better way'." Yet facilitators should also feel free to disagree with other members of the team when it seems appropriate.

Communication skills needed by facilitators include the ability to ask open-ended questions and close-ended questions, to use requests, to use positive reinforcement, to ask for specifics, to redirect questions or defer to the group, to encourage under- and non-participators, to ask for different points of view, to paraphrase for clarity and understanding, and to use nonverbal reinforcement (Helphand).

The Recorder's Role

Before each meeting, the recorder reviews with the facilitator the proposed agenda for the current meeting and the minutes of the previous meeting. The recorder also gathers materials necessary to record what happens at the meeting (Nancy Vollmer). During each meeting, the recorder

- Describes the setting for the meeting (place, date, time, and so forth)
- Lists the participants
- Copies the agenda in the order agreed upon
- Records the major views expressed and information offered on each agenda item
- For each agenda item, writes a short summary of decisions made, understandings achieved, and action to be taken

Finally, after each meeting, the recorder collects any charts developed during the meeting and attaches a typed copy to the minutes; checks the clarity and completeness of the minutes with the facilitator; types, copies, and distributes the minutes to all members; posts the minutes for nonmembers' information; and adds a debriefing item to the agenda (Vollmer).

The Process Observer's Role

To some extent, each member of a team is a process observer, a role that Vollmer defines as "examining the effectiveness of interactive processes soon after every meeting." Vollmer recommends that every team spend the last fifteen minutes of each meeting engaged in "process observing" (also called "debriefing"), to be aware of the dynamics that were at work."

In addition to this informal monitoring of group processes by individual members, however, one member should be designated the "process observer" and have the following responsibilities:

- Learn what type of information the team wants you to seek.
- Pay particular attention to *process* rather than *content* during meetings.
- Record observations and impressions about meetings.
- Organize this information for dispersal to the group.
- Report observations to the other team members, making sure to "describe observed behavior to support your interpretations of what was happening in the group."
- When the team reaches an impasse, "ask members to stop and discuss what is preventing them from accomplishing their purposes."
- Finally, ask for feedback from other team members about how well you are fulfilling your role. (Vollmer)

Effective teams pay as much attention to how they structure their work as to how they actually do the work. Vollmer believes teams in today's schools are more conscious of processes such as the steps for problem-solving and different decision-making models.

Team Cohesiveness

For a high-quality team to exist, two factors must be present, say Cunningham and Gresso: bonding and cohesiveness. Both establish a sense of team culture. "The strength and potential of the team" develop "once people join together to form a single, united, and cohesive culture." A team with a strong culture is characterized by "purposefulness, pride, confidence, enthusiasm, empowerment, commitment, loyalty, and satisfaction."

Bonding ensures that team members will commit their time, knowledge, skills, and energy to the team and its goals, Cunningham and Gresso say. "Bonded" team members are not only more enthusiastic, but also are more loyal to the school and the team. Fortunately, bonding is a "natural process in all humans," the authors note. Team members bond because they like, trust, understand, or respect one another. Members can begin this bonding process during the very first meeting, as they evaluate their purpose, goals, roles, and individual and group responsibilities.

Cohesiveness is defined by Cunningham and Gresso as a "sense of togetherness, or community, within a group. A cohesive group is one in which there are incentives for remaining in the group and a feeling of belongingness and relatedness among the members." Cohesive teams are effective teams.

Training

Robert Kessler, superintendent of Reed Union School District in Tiburon, California, describes how hiring a trainer early on helped his district analyze its personal styles and develop effective group dynamics. This training enabled the new team to form team agreements: "to commit to operate by consensus, respect one another's styles, speak honestly, and advocate the team's decisions to our constituencies." Since everyone's goal is the same—consensus—members listen carefully to each other's concerns, and when members raise objections, they also provide suggestions to reach consensus.

"A day or two to do the training works every time," said Lake Washington Superintendent Scarr. "The team must be willing to make that kind of investment. Let's take the family unit, which is a team. Families that are successful work out the groundrules of how they're going to operate." Most teams need to work out the groundrules more than once. When someone quits, said Scarr, "what they don't understand is that the whole chemistry of the team is ruined. You have to start over." Training helps members of the "new" group to trust one another.

Scarr admits that training takes time, but he contends that "you have to spend some time to save some time." Devoting time to training is a good investment. Training work teams in group skills might take a day or two; retraining when a new member joins will probably take one to two hours, he said.

Vollmer advocates ongoing training, which can help team members to understand the structures, strategies, and philosophy of quality work teams and move to a higher level of "teamness." That is, training can enhance members' understanding of group dynamics and show them how to lead effective meetings, how to ask for help from a consultant or secure someone to intervene, and how to deal with conflict.

Maeroff advocates sending team members outside the institution for specialized training if possible. Team members "can be steeped in knowledge of the change process and transformed into a team by the experiences in an institute or academy designed specifically for building teams." During such training, team members learn group-process skills and "practice techniques that they can use to engage their colleagues in analyzing conditions in their school" (Maeroff).

Even when the mission is clear, team membership is diverse, and roles and responsibilities are outlined, every work team encounters some of the common barriers described in the next section. But if team members are well trained in group dynamics, they will understand that communication problems and personality conflicts are merely part of the team process.

Challenges and Action Steps

Every attempt by a team to improve a school is a tale of struggles to overcome obstacles. Maeroff warns, "Schools are not institutions that wait passively to be changed. When it comes to building teams, there are major barriers that must be breached."

When problems arise, the attitude of team members toward those problems is most important to the success of a team. If members know what to expect and recognize that several common barriers will almost certainly appear as well as understand how to respond, they will avoid panicking or getting off track.

Why Teams Fail

Larry Lezotte offers five reasons why teams fail to work together effectively: (1) members don't understand the function, purpose, or goals of the team effort; (2) members don't understand their roles or responsibilities; (3) members don't understand how to do their tasks or how to work as part of a team; (4) members fail to buy into the function, purpose, or goals of the team effort; or (5) members reject their roles or responsibilities (personal communication with Nancy Vollmer, no date).

Superintendent Scarr offers an additional factor that can interfere with team success. He has seen team members "become so attached to one another psychologically and emotionally that the very purpose of the team is defeated because you don't want to hurt someone's feelings." Teams sometimes assume such a congenial relationship that members "almost feel obligated not to ask questions and challenge ideas."

Maeroff identifies several other problems that can beset teams in schools:

- *Societal factors.* When issues such as safety in the school environment are a problem, team-building "can easily be seen as a frivolity, and the work of teams is certain to be more difficult."
- *Budgets.* Team building costs extra money; "anything that adds to school budgets these days begins at a disadvantage."
- *Unions.* Inflexible unions can constrain teams.
- *Teachers' knowledge.* Building teams will not fix problems such as a teacher's lack of knowledge in a subject area or lack of commitment.
- *School schedules.* Teachers are often so busy it is difficult if not impossible to add time for teamwork to their schedules; schools are often reluctant to redesign existing schedules so that teamwork and restructuring can take place.
- *Continuity of staffing.* When school personnel are transitory, moving from school to school, the time and money expended on building a solid team are wasted.

Problem Behaviors

The individual behaviors of members can prevent teams from obtaining their goals. A set of problems can arise when individuals seek to meet their own needs at the expense of group goals. Self-oriented behaviors are likely to occur, Vollmer notes, "when groups fail to recognize or deal with any of four underlying emotional issues of members": control, needs and goals, identity, and acceptance of intimacy. By learning to express themselves in a more helpful, constructive way, team members can avoid using these negative behaviors:

• *Blocking*: A member interferes with the progress of the team by going off on a tangent; cites personal experiences unrelated to the team's problem; continues arguing a point the rest of the team has resolved; rejects ideas without consideration; prevents a vote/consensus.

• *Attacking*: A member criticizes or blames others; shows hostility toward the team or some individual without relation to what has happened in the team; attacks the motives of others; deflates the ego or status of others.

• *Seeking recognition*: A member attempts to get attention by excessive talking, extreme ideas, boasting, boisterousness.

• *Pleading special interest*: A member introduces or supports ideas related to one's own pet concerns or philosophies beyond reason; attempts to speak for "the people on the shop floor," "management," or so forth.

• *Withdrawing*: A member acts indifferently or passively; resorts to excessive formality; doodles or reads; whispers to others.

• *Dominating*: A member tries to assert authority in manipulating the team or certain members of it by "pulling rank"; gives directions authoritatively; interrupts contributions of others; talks too much.

By using positive communication techniques—such as agreeing with at least part of an argument, asking for more specific objections, offering to give up one thing if the other person will do the same, postponing a discussion, disclosing feelings, communicating wants and needs, and listing options to choose from—team members can deal with all these barriers, Vollmer says.

Sometimes people use the threat of a legal problem as an excuse to avoid moving ahead. "You just don't do much around schools where legal issues don't arise," said Ernie Keller of the Wasco Education Service District. Keller believes laws and policies don't need to deter teams because "for every problem, there's a solution."

Focus on Student Achievement

Members are more likely to embrace group, rather than individual, goals if the group's mission captures their imagination and appeals to their professionalism. In schools, work teams should focus on student needs, as Maeroff states:

> Team building that seems not to be sufficiently focused on the most serious needs of students runs the risk of appearing peripheral to the show being performed in the main ring. Team building in such circumstances would be little more than another sideshow, and education already has more than enough of these.

Stephen N. Elliott and Susan M. Sheridan recommend the following problem-solving strategies for a multidisciplinary team concerned with a student issue such as improving student test scores:

Step 1. Define and clarify the presenting problem. The team "must state the presenting problem in concrete, explicit terms" to avoid vagueness and ambiguity.

Step 2. Analyze the context of the problem. Team members should look at assessment information such as test scores and evaluate it to understand the problem.

Step 3. Brainstorm alternative solutions. Four brainstorming techniques will be useful here: (1) Together, team members should list as many possible solutions as they can; (2) creative thinking should be encouraged; (3) during these first two steps, no judgments should be made on the listed alternatives; and (4) members should try combining and modifying the alternatives to find additional solutions.

Step 4. Choose among the alternatives. "After careful consideration of all alternatives, the team selects the solution or solutions that it believes will be most appropriate."

Step 5. Specify responsibilities and timelines. "High-quality solutions are sometimes not implemented because of a failure to specify clearly each individual team member's responsibilities. This step of the process addresses the who, what, when, and where aspects of agreed-on solutions."

Step 6. Obtain consensus of team. "At this point in the process, the team's leader should check with the members to ensure that there is a consensus regarding future actions to be initiated as a result of the meeting. If a lack of consensus exists, it may be necessary to go back to a prior step in the problem-solving process."

Step 7. Plan for future actions on unaddressed problems. If there are multiple problems or issues, and time constraints prevent them from being addressed, "the team should explicitly discuss the process of how other problems will be handled."

Step 8. Follow up. After the team meeting concludes, at least one team member should monitor progress. "Follow-up provides an opportunity for adjusting intervention plans and also provides team members with feedback about their decisions."

In summary, teams must be willing to seek help whenever something is bogging them down. Training is key to overcoming barriers and helping team members learn how to lead effective meetings, communicate with one another, and move from being a congenial team to a collaborative team.

Stages of Experience

One way to ensure that problems do not overwhelm a group is to understand that teams naturally go through changes and stages, and problems will arise at many points in time as the group matures. Bass and Avolio list four developmental stages that teams typically encounter.

Forming involves the "development of mutual acceptance, in which members learn to accept one another and develop mutual confidence and respect." *Storming* involves the "development of open discussion of conflicts instead of reserved politeness, as the group focuses on examining differences in ideas on problem solving and on developing ways in which it will reach decisions and agreements."

Norming involves cooperation and productiveness. When the group reaches this stage, it is considered to be mature enough to set standards for its members and itself." *Performing* is when "the group is fully matured and operates effectively in accordance with established norms, making the best uses of available human and material resources. In this stage, group membership is valued, and the group is interdependent, flexible, and able to effectively meet higher-order challenges."

An important thing to remember is that the group may have to go through these stages again and again as it takes on new members or new assignments. It is up to the team leader, in particular, to understand these stages and "how to effectively move the team from a lower to a higher level of development" (Bass and Avolio). For example, during the forming stage, the leader must work to ensure that a team culture is developed and nourished. This will strengthen the team and lead it to progress into the other stages, as well as to handle conflict.

The Value of Conflict

Conflict, perhaps the most misunderstood part of teamwork, is actually an essential element in successful teams, as well as successful organizations (see chapter 15). Effective teams "engage in controversy to ensure that all alternative solutions get a fair hearing" (Johnson and Johnson). And while negative personal attacks on others should be discouraged, "differing views about tasks, policies, procedures, allocation of resources, and other group issues can actually be helpful" (Helphand).

Keller agrees: "Conflict is a powerful engine. Sometimes the fact there's a conflict might be the very reason people show up for a meeting." And finally, conflict often eventually leads to consensus, the ultimate goal for team decision-making.

Facilitators can use several techniques for managing conflict, says Helphand. These include asking for other points of view—even asking someone to play "devil's advocate." The facilitator can raise questions or ask for clarification, being careful to dissociate the idea from its originator (instead of asking, "What do you think of Mary's idea?" ask "What do you think about the suggestion to move the office?"). Focus on the problem, not the people working on the problem, says Helphand.

Conclusion

Educators who have experimented with teams generally agree that districts and schools should make use of teams for decision-making, planning, and action. But each individual's qualities and contributions should be recognized and valued as well. Patricia McLagan says, "The team is not and will not be a total replacement for the individual as a unit of focus.... The team that subsumes individuals instead of enhancing them in some way will not excel." Successful organizations, she says, have both "high-performing teams and high-performing individuals within and outside of teams."

Quality work teams have members who "feel responsible for the team, the goals it has set, and the success of its activities" (Kansas State Board of Education). Also, all members are allowed to express their views before important decisions are made together. Meeting agendas and activities are specifically planned, but the team can change these if the need arises. In addition, when members try new skills, the team is supportive. Also, the team engages in an ongoing process of self-evaluation.

Effective work teams set clear goals, keep connections strong between the team and other stakeholders such as administrators and teachers, hire a professional trainer initially to teach group communication strategies, and ensure the roles of team members are clearly defined. And always, no matter what the purpose of the team, members are aware that improved student learning is the ultimate mission.

CHAPTER

9

Shared Decision-Making

Lynn Balster Liontos and Larry Lashway

Shared decision-making (SDM) remains a prominent issue in local school governance. Many educators are gaining experience with the process, though research on the effects of collective decision-making in an educational setting is still scanty. In districts where SDM has been mandated, school leaders may feel pressure to "jump on the bandwagon" without being fully aware of what SDM can and cannot do.

The purpose of this chapter is to clarify the intent of SDM and explore its benefits, drawbacks, and implementation. It also looks at how the principal's role changes, stresses the need for training, assesses SDM's track record, discusses the structure of SDM, and offers lessons learned from pioneers. Although there is no one "right" way to "do" SDM, this chapter provides recommendations from the literature and suggestions from those who practice SDM.

Defining SDM

Educators use a variety of terms to refer to SDM, which is confusing at best. Two often-used terms are *school-based decision-making* and *shared governance.* The term *shared decision-making* (SDM) will be used throughout this chapter, except when a quoted author uses an alternative term.

Two terms often incorrectly interchanged with SDM are *decentralization* and *site-based management.* Decentralization refers to the transfer of authority to local school units; whether decisions are shared at the school level is at the discretion of the principal. Thus decentralization may or may not include SDM. The same is true of site-based management (SBM), which can refer solely to the concept of decentralization—a shift in power from district offices to individual school buildings. Site-based management may also include SDM, but SDM is not a necessary component of SBM.

SDM is an elusive, complex concept. It involves fundamental changes in the way schools are managed, including changing the roles and relationships of all members of the school community. One key to successfully implementing SDM, states Scott Bauer, is building consensus about what the process is. School decision teams discover, "with alarming regularity," that they are unsure precisely what SDM is. Bauer provides a working definition:

> Shared decision making is a process designed to push education decisions to the school level, where those closest to children may apply their expertise in making decisions that will promote school effectiveness and ensure that the most appropriate services are provided to students and the school community.

Bauer emphasizes that SDM is content-free; that is, it does not deal with specific topics or programs. Rather it is an ongoing process of making decisions in a collaborative manner. SDM "cannot be done once and then forgotten," states B. J. Meadows.

SDM must be placed in the broader context of school district governance. Statutory authority to govern school districts resides in the school board. For this reason, the National School Boards Association (NSBA) defines SDM as "the planned delegation of decision-making authority to a group of people who are accountable to the public through the school board." Site councils or teams are not autonomous decision-makers but rather are accountable for their performance to the school board and ultimately the public.

The face of SDM looks different in different schools, depending on local factors.

Shared Beliefs and Premises

All SDM processes are built on four common premises or beliefs:

1. Those closest to the students and "where the action is" will make the best decisions about students' education.
2. Teachers, parents, and school staff should have more say about policies and programs affecting their schools and children.
3. Those responsible for carrying out decisions should have a voice in determining those decisions.
4. Change is most likely to be effective and lasting when those who implement it feel a sense of ownership and responsibility for the process.

The primary purpose of SDM is not to make teachers feel more satisfied with their work, though it may have this effect. As a result of SDM, teachers should have a greater impact on decisions, be better informed, and have greater commitment to making their decisions work. The purpose of SDM is to improve the quality of educational services and to ensure that schools are more responsive to the needs of students and the community.

Advantages of SDM

SDM has the potential to improve the quality of decisions, as well as bolster their acceptance and implementation, strengthen staff morale and teamwork, build trust, and increase school effectiveness.

In a fifteen-month study of six schools that adopted SDM, John Lange found that as autonomy was achieved, better decisions were made than would have been made under centralized school management. More ideas can be generated and analyzed when more people are involved.

Because more people have a voice, SDM also promotes varied and innovative approaches to issues. Some research indicates that more satisfying decisions are made in groups that generate and test ideas than are made by individuals or poorly functioning groups.

While not necessarily the aim of SDM, increased teacher satisfaction and a more positive school culture may be products of SDM. Lange found that when principals actively sought staff input prior to making decisions, teamwork and unity were fostered. Both principals and staff also developed new interpersonal skills, and trust increased. Staff gained a better understanding of the principal's role and the complexities of school management, and principals developed more trust in faculty judgment.

Teachers in Oregon's School Improvement and Professional Development Program also reported both a greater willingness to collaborate and more effective collaboration (Paul Goldman and others). The program, initiated by the Oregon Legislature in 1987, funds the development of school-improvement plans that were initiated and administered by teacher-led site committees. Some teachers have reported more motivation and excitement in their work as a result of their new role in decision-making.

In shared decision-making, the principal actually gains support for the implementation of decisions, according to Sue Mutchler and Patricia Duttweiler. They note, "Decision-making participants have a vested interest in the decision and all that is necessary to follow it through." The National Education Association, which has worked directly with more than five-hundred schools to develop SDM models, reports that involving more people *has* enhanced ownership (Sharon Robinson and Robert Barkley).

Collectively made decisions are usually easier to carry out, have more staying power, and gain greater acceptance.

Finally, school reform in Chicago illustrates how increasing public involvement through local school councils accompanied school-improvement efforts. Researchers found that schools with strong democratic climates were far more likely to be pursuing systemic change (Ann Bradley). Sixty-six percent of "strongly democratic" schools were making such improvements. Schools were characterized as "strongly democratic" if their school councils met regularly, if teachers were actively involved in planning, and if principals sparked discussions about educational issues.

In contrast, more than 80 percent of the schools with "adversarial politics" were judged to be "unfocused" in their approach to reform—adding on programs, engaging in limited discussion of educational issues, and showing little collaboration among teachers. Among schools where the principals "run the show," only 26 percent reported systemic change.

Disadvantages of SDM

The benefits of SDM should be weighed against its apparent inefficiency, an increased workload for participants, and the frustrations produced by a slower decision-making process. In implementing SDM, teachers and administrators are asked to significantly change their behavior; such change takes time and extra effort.

Those with firsthand SDM experiences frequently mention the demands on their time and the increased duties and responsibilities that accompany the process. Some also acknowledge mistakes they made, such as inadequately preparing and training participants, or trying to do too much too quickly, which resulted in setback and failure.

The time-intensive nature of SDM deters many schools from pursuing the process. "There's no way around it," states James Mitchell, "involving employees in administrative decisions is time-consuming, and that can be frustrating." Both administrators and teachers can become irritated by the length of time it takes to make decisions by committee or group, and teachers may feel pressured by the additional workload that SDM demands of them outside the classroom. Decisions are often slow and difficult, especially in the early stages, when staff members are learning new skills.

Fortunately, there is a learning curve with SDM. As teachers and administrators gain skill with the process, their communication tends to become more efficient (Fred Lifton). Henry Levin, a professor at Stanford University, found in his work with the Accelerated Learning Program that over time staff demonstrated "a rising sophistication and ability to make decisions over an ever-widening range of issues."

Doris Sanchez Alvarez characterizes the process as "cumbersome" and "time-consuming." But once SDM is in place, "most teachers will have a heightened sense of commitment to the organization and a new awareness of the role of the classroom teacher in the school organization."

Participant Concerns

Both administrators and teachers may have fears, concerns, or a sense of reluctance about initiating or implementing SDM. These concerns need to be recognized and addressed.

Administrator Concerns

When surveyed by the Southwest Educational Development Laboratory (SEDL), administrators expressed fear about relinquishing power to teachers or school councils as well as changing roles and responsibilities (Mutchler and Duttweiler). Some administrators view decision-making as a territorial issue. They may be more concerned with protecting their own turf than "seeing the big picture." Principals, noted one survey respondent, need to be convinced that teachers are "not going to take over the building, make all the decisions, and do away with principals."

Fear often clouds understanding of SDM, states Bauer. In addition to fear of loss of power, some principals also wonder whether the process will really lead to positive outcomes for students. Many also question whether they have adequate training, skills, and time to initiate and maintain the process.

Goldman and others asked administrators in schools in Oregon's School Improvement and Professional Development Program whether teachers see administrators as "more or less central" to decision-making. One principal replied, "I think they see me as central, but I think they see themselves as powerful, too." This suggests that as decision-making opportunities grow, "power itself expands."

Teacher Concerns

Alvarez, a principal, encountered teacher reluctance when she initiated SDM in her high school. Some teachers opted out because of lack of time to devote to the process. Others were only interested in making classroom-level decisions or were subject to pressure by colleagues to resist—perhaps because SDM was seen as just another fad. If principals decide to initiate change, Alvarez recommends that they be prepared to work with teachers over a long period, and seek to determine teachers' understanding of the meaning of the change.

In the SEDL survey, many respondents mentioned that teachers were unwilling to assume new responsibilities. In some cases, this may be due to teachers' lack of confidence in their decision-making ability. It may also be due to the extra time and workload involved. One respondent commented on the link between responsibility and accountability: "In the beginning, the newly empowered decision makers were, in many cases, frightened by the responsibility and the danger of being held responsible for mistakes" (Mutchler and Duttweiler).

Lack of trust is also an issue for teachers in some schools. Survey respondents noted that trivial matters stored up over the years from lack of input impeded progress at their site. "Complaining sessions" were needed before any movement was made.

In Oregon schools in which many teachers are involved in decision-making, some teachers are uncomfortable with the decline of the principal's role as the central authority figure and would prefer to have the principal make all the decisions (Goldman and colleagues). Strong norms exist against teacher involvement in administration and exercise of power. One team leader said that to some teachers "the very idea of power is a threat." These teachers typically left the school to work elsewhere.

Sequence of Participant Concerns

Gene Hall and Gary Galluzzo outline various types of concerns participants tend to focus on when a change or innovation is being introduced. When use of an innovation such as SDM becomes "real" for the participants, their concerns center on "self," or their own performance. For instance, they might ask, "How will using SDM affect me? Am I capable of doing it?" As the innovation begins to be used, "task" concerns take over. People's thoughts focus on the time and procedures involved in using the innovation: "I seem to be spending all my time getting material ready."

Only when "self" and "task" concerns are resolved do participants raise "impact" concerns. "Impact" concerns may be expressed through questions such as "How is the use of this affecting kids and the school as a whole?" or "I have some ideas about something that would work even better." For the change process to be completed successfully, these stages of concern need to be recognized, addressed, and resolved, say Hall and Galluzzo. This calls for ongoing support, training, staff development, and coaching.

The Principal's New Role

For SDM to work, principals and staff must establish a collaborative partnership. This role is very different from the one learned by most principals and involves different functions and a different kind of power. Although to some principals the idea of having their role altered may be threatening, other principals welcome the demise of their role as lone decision-maker: "No longer did I alone have to justify the budget discussions for we were making decisions together," states Cecil Daniels, principal at Myrtle Grove Elementary School in Opa-Locka, Florida.

Letting Go

Although the principal's role changes, the principal remains essential to the process and plays an important role in both establishing and maintaining SDM. "As a school executive, you are critical to the process," states Bauer. "But to make things work, you must truly let go of those decisions you decide to let the school council handle. There is no surer way to sabotage shared decision making and create an atmosphere of distrust than to override a decision you have delegated to a school council."

Principals in schools participating in Oregon's school-improvement program described changes they've made in terms of "stepping back," "keeping their mouths shut," and "getting things started and letting them run" (Goldman and others). One principal said that when someone would approach him with a question, he would direct the individual to the person or committee responsible for that area: "You have to be ready to let go and keep on letting go, so others know that they are really in charge of something and really take responsibility for it" (Goldman and others).

Becoming a Facilitator

Principals participating in the Oregon program speak of using "facilitative power" (see chapter 2) to help staff develop and implement goals. They see themselves as "human-resource managers," individuals who help acquire and organize resources. In addition to managing money, they also find space and time for staff to meet, rearrange scheduling, and help groups work together effectively. They find ways to involve staff and provide regular feedback and encouragement. They share useful information and data regularly with teachers.

An important part of facilitating also involves monitoring. According to Amie Watson and others, "Minimizing distractions and other obstacles so that decision-making groups can meet and keep on track becomes a key function."

David Stine describes the principal's new role as that of organizer, adviser, and consensus builder, someone who utilizes the power of the group's thinking. Bauer refers to principals who engage in SDM as "internal consultants" rather than "decision makers." He suggests that principals offer input and provide school decision-making bodies with current research.

Principals need to accept that they may not agree with all decisions SDM councils or teams make and that some decisions will fail to bring about the desired outcomes. If this happens, it is important for the principal not to come to the rescue, but to be especially supportive of staff in these instances (Judith Huddleston and others).

Establishing a Climate of Trust

SDM is fragile, especially in the early stages. Many teachers are skeptical that the school really means to give them this authority, and they will watch carefully for any signs of backsliding. As the person whose power is being shared, the principal will be a special focus of attention. Failure to project enthusiasm and wholehearted commitment will often lead teachers to the conclusion, "This, too, shall pass."

Commitment is shown not just by verbal affirmation, but by active participation; principals who take a hands-off approach undermine faith in the process (Nona Prestine).

The shift from "an autocratic to a democratic position," say Mutchler and Duttweiler, involves "supporting" and "enabling" behaviors, such as listening actively, creating opportunities for staff to express ideas, providing a supportive environment for collaborative planning, and establishing school goals and programs through staff participation.

The principal must create a noncompetitive, win-win school climate by promoting trust through modeling and teaching group skills (Meadows). Principals also need to model values and behaviors such as collaboration, equity, and professional development. These "set the direction and tone of the school in order for change to occur," state Goldman and colleagues. One teacher commented, "He [the principal] makes it easier for everything to happen, because he has always modeled listening and caring about people's input."

"It is as important for us to admit our mistakes publicly as it is to announce our successes," states Meadows, who suggests deemphasizing perfectionism by valuing the self-worth of staff members and by consistently recognizing things they do well. Principals must resist forcing their solutions on staff so that the faculty "owns" the decisions and group trust is not damaged.

Developing Readiness

Principals are intimately involved in preparing schools for SDM. Some of the ways principals can accomplish this are by believing in the process of SDM, conveying trust in staff decisions, and recognizing that behavioral changes are difficult and take time. Principals should not give up when teachers express a desire for a strong leader who makes all the decisions.

Principals should open up channels of communication for everyone. "All staff members must believe that they can influence the final decision," say Huddleston and colleagues. "For that to occur, procedures must be established for them to voice their opinions." In their new role, principals need to continually seek different ways to communicate with and involve staff.

Even though principals may have their own concerns about SDM, part of their role in establishing SDM involves addressing the concerns of faculty. "How well they address teacher concerns, work with those inside and outside the school, and develop a shared vision that guides day-to-day actions and decisions is a critical key to successful implementation of SDM," state Hall and Galluzzo.

Preparation: Training, Skills, Knowledge

Lack of skills was one of eight barriers to changing traditional behavior that Mutchler and Duttweiler found when they surveyed schools using SDM. Thirty percent of respondents in the Southwest Educational Development Laboratory (SEDL) survey indicated a critical lack of knowledge and skills in areas needed to implement SDM at their site. Staff need training to develop the knowledge, skills, and attitudes that will help them to accept and then participate in SDM.

The Need for Training

Frequently, teachers make classroom-related decisions and administrators make school-related decisions without conferring with others. Thus most teachers and administrators are not accustomed to exercising collaborative decision-making skills (Hall and Galluzzo). Parent and community representatives may also need assistance in learning how to perform new tasks, as well as becoming comfortable with new roles and responsibilities. If this is not done, caution Hall and Galluzzo, "we could arrive at a place where 'more people are happier with dumber decisions'." Investing time and energy in preparing participants for new roles is one way administrators can prepare their schools for SDM.

The areas most frequently targeted for training are not normally covered in teacher-education programs. For example, teacher education does not usually instruct students in management or group skills. Also, teachers traditionally do not assume management roles in their jobs, or work in groups to any great extent. Usually teachers are knowledgeable about their students, the subject matter they teach, and pedagogical techniques. "As they become more collaborative, they have to learn what their colleagues are doing and what they need," note Goldman and others.

The ability to exercise "productive power is dependent in part on one's access to resources and information," say Philip Hallinger and Don Richardson. Teachers have traditionally been disconnected from other classrooms, other schools, and the central office. "In order to address issues and problems with others in the larger system," teachers need opportunities to obtain information about instruction, the students, and the school's needs.

Areas in Which Training Is Needed

Respondents to the SEDL survey indicated that SDM participants require special skills to move from solitary thinking toward collective thinking and group decision-making. Nearly one-fourth of the respondents reported insufficient skills in consensus decision-making. Sixty-two percent of the respondents listed decision-making skills as an area in which training is needed, while 75 percent indicated collaborative skills should be a priority in training (Mutchler and Duttweiler).

Decision-making skills include problem-solving and critical thinking, priority-setting, resource utilization, and the design of accountability and evaluation plans. Collaborative skills include consensus-building, conflict resolution, team-building, and commitment skills. Staff must be trained, note Mutchler and Duttweiler, to deal with the substantive and technical aspects of the issues about which decisions are being made.

Survey respondents also indicated that participants need to be knowledgeable about SDM. One reason teachers in Kentucky were reluctant to participate in SDM was lack of sufficient information about school councils (Jay Goldman).

According to Marianne Strusinski, the most commonly requested area for additional training in Dade County, Florida, schools is "professional skills" such as problem-solving and time management. Also frequently cited is "interpersonal skills" ("group relations" or "team building" was mentioned by half the schools). Followup training and support are crucial for new staff members and for the refinement of SDM.

Methods of Acquiring Training and Information

SEDL respondents suggested several approaches to training, skill building, and establishing a knowledge base. Some recommended the use of professional consultants or experienced facilitators to guide participants as they make the transition to SDM. One respondent said her school had hired a shared-governance specialist who, in addition to conducting training, served as a consultant to help the school deal with problems.

Other survey respondents recommended a "train-the-trainer" approach, with selected staff undergoing training and in turn training their own faculty and community. Some suggested a "full staff approach," in which all staff participate in gathering information, gaining decision-making skills, and developing collaborative behaviors.

Outside consultants may be hard to find, states Mitchell. Few collaborative techniques are taught in teacher-preparation courses. Schools where SDM is working can be a good source of qualified experts. Mitchell also suggests visiting and networking with other schools to discover how they are implementing SDM.

Principals can assist staff in building a knowledge base in particular areas; they might share research on curricular trends and provide opportunities to discuss concepts (Huddleston and colleagues). Faculty meetings or retreats can be used for inservice workshops to share ideas or build skills.

Specific training models are sometimes used to prepare staff for SDM. Alvarez explains how Personalized Professional Growth Seminars helped teachers examine the culture and communication networks of their school and the norms and structures used for making decisions. Discussions provided a better sense of which decisions staff felt they should become involved in, and collaboration emerged as teachers shared ideas, materials, and plans. Perhaps the most important aspect of the seminars was the time they provided for practice and feedback. Before the seminars, the lack of adequate time to learn and understand the various roles in SDM had been a significant problem, Alvarez states.

John Russell and others describe how the Teacher Involvement and Participation Scale (TIPS 2) helps schools collect baseline data and identify issues that need attention. Another training model gives guidance on breaking problem-solving down into smaller units (Dianne Horgan). Fran Mayeski cites several leadership training programs for principals, such as the Blanchard Training and Development Model, which includes group observation forms for effective versus ineffective groups.

Learning by Doing: Informal Training

Oregon's school-improvement program, state Goldman and colleagues, has created a climate in which teachers and administrators can develop the skills and behaviors necessary for sharing decision-making responsibilities. Rather than provide formal training in problem-solving, consensus building, or communication skills, the participating schools offer staff "real reasons to solve problems, seek consensus, and communicate." When training in group-process skills is presented, "it can be applied immediately to real situations that have meaning and value to the participants."

Following skill training, whether formal or informal, staff members need a chance to practice new behaviors. "Much of the capacity to make good staff decisions and take responsibility for school outcomes," states Levin, "comes directly from practice or learning-by-doing. As school staff and community work at it, they become experts in the process."

Does SDM Really Work?

Advocates of SDM say it will create teacher satisfaction, improve student learning, and show principals a new way to lead. Does it deliver on these promises? While it is far too early to make definitive judgments, studies so far have shown reason for caution.

Does SDM Increase Teacher Satisfaction?

As promised, SDM does seem to result in greater teacher satisfaction. Many studies have found that teachers are pleased that their views can influence school decisions. One teacher interviewed by Gary Griffin put it this way:

> It was and continues to be so exciting to realize that my own judgments and beliefs and values are important enough to be used in making school rules and regs. In my 10 years of teaching I've always felt a bit like a chess piece, moved along because of someone else's goals or whims.

However, some studies also report ambivalence or dissatisfaction. Carol Weiss and colleagues have documented some of the reasons. For one thing, not everyone participates equally; those who hold back (often veteran teachers) may be dismayed to find enthusiastic rookies suddenly wielding major power. Collegial relationships also change; disagreements that could formerly be laughed off or politely ignored now have to be resolved.

Moreover, SDM often blurs the lines of authority, creating confusion over who has the right to make a decision.

Weiss and colleagues suggest that the ambivalence is a natural product of working with unfamiliar processes; they say it may be four or five years before participants are comfortable with their new roles and relationships. "What is needed is more than a change in formal structure; it requires a change in the culture of the school as well."

However, the learning curve is not smooth. Weiss (1993) says her team did not see "linear progression" in the SDM schools they studied. "Everywhere there were ups and downs, movement and relapse, optimism and disenchantment.... SDM is not a process that, once introduced, necessarily matures and flowers." Thus an apparent era of good feelings may turn sour when previously hidden conflicts bubble to the surface; teachers who were enthused about making decisions may begin to yearn for the simpler days when a benevolent principal listened to teachers and then made the decision.

These difficulties do not mean that SDM has failed. Weiss and colleagues note, "In the schools we studied, people complained a good deal about the aches and strains of shared decision making, but only one or two people said that they wanted to go back to the way things were in the past—and even they hedged." Rather, the problems merely underline the need to build the capacity for SDM; training is "fundamental, not a frill."

Does SDM Improve Student Learning?

As with any school reform, the ultimate purpose of SDM is to improve student learning. So far there is little evidence showing this to be the case (Edward Miller).

Of course, it may simply be too early to show results. If SDM requires four or five years to take hold, it may be a decade before it shows any measurable effect on student achievement. In fact, achievement may actually suffer for a time because teachers are absorbed with the new decision-making processes.

However, some researchers claim that SDM efforts are unlikely to have much of an effect on achievement because they seldom focus on the "core issues" of teaching and learning. Studies of SDM frequently mention a tendency to focus on "trivial" or "zero-impact" issues such as parking, bus supervision, and smoking in faculty lounges (Lew Allen and Carl Glickman; Peggy Kirby).

Weiss (1995) found that SDM schools adopted some significant reforms, but with one exception "the push toward innovation came from the principal—against the wish of a considerable bloc of the teachers."

Compared to non-SDM schools, teacher participation "acted as a brake on reform."

The rhetoric of SDM says that teachers, as "front-line" educators, are in the best position to make instructional reforms. So why don't teachers in SDM schools attack these issues more aggressively? The reasons appear to be complex.

The most obvious possibility is that shared decision-making is so different from the usual way of doing things that teachers' attention is initially absorbed by the *process*, leaving little energy for complex reforms. Weiss (1993) provides some support for this interpretation, observing that teachers in SDM schools spent considerable time making decisions about how to make decisions. She also noted that the one school in which teachers actively pursued significant reforms had been using SDM for over a decade.

Weiss (1995) also argues that SDM advocates may underestimate the power of school culture, especially at the high school level. She found that teachers were pragmatic about change, preferring to work through the existing structure rather than "fighting city hall." SDM was often regarded with skepticism as just another passing fad. Hence, teachers had little motivation to transfer their allegiance to the new way of doing things, especially since the high school's departmentalized structure already gave them a certain amount of autonomy.

Griffin emphasizes that teaching is a "culture of isolation" in which key instructional decisions are often made by individuals in the privacy of their own classrooms. The teachers he interviewed had a strong sense of their own competence; they believed they could make the right decisions and were inclined to let other teachers do the same. (Even if they had doubts about a particular colleague, the "live and let live" norms of teaching prevented them from raising the issue.) In fact, Griffin found that many teachers seemed to believe that no method could be considered better than any other; it was up to each teacher to determine the style that worked best for him or her.

Finally, Weiss (1993) suggests that teacher conservatism may be partly rooted in good sense. Teachers know better than anyone the complexities of the classroom, and experience has taught them to be cautious about "Ed School ideas."

Clearly, the mere existence of SDM will not nullify the strategies that teachers have developed to cope with a complex and demanding environment. Focusing SDM on worthwhile issues requires constant debate, dialogue, and dedication.

How Do Principals Lead with SDM?

In theory, SDM calls for new modes of leadership; in practice, the principal's new role is not well-defined. SDM broadens the base of decision-making but does not envision abdication of leadership; the decisions may be shared but in most schools the accountability comes back to one person.

Principals thus must walk a fine line. SDM calls for patient, low-key development of consensus; the existing system still issues mandates calling for quick action and measurable progress. If leaders wait for consensus to evolve, the process may stretch out interminably or may head in an unprofitable direction. If they try to nudge the process in a particular direction, they run the risk of undermining teacher participation. Not surprisingly, studies show that school leaders use a variety of strategies to deal with the conflicting demands.

In some cases, principals continue to exercise directive leadership in a sugar-coated form. In one school with a reputation for effective SDM, Angela Spaulding found that the principal was, in fact, consciously manipulating the process to move it in the direction he wanted by planting ideas, pressuring opponents, and showing favoritism to supporters. This principal characterized his approach as "going through the motions" of SDM but he still saw himself as the source of decisions.

Other school leaders show a strong commitment to shared governance. Joseph Blase and colleagues interviewed eight principals who sought to deepen teacher participation through strategies such as establishing trust, soliciting teacher opinions, building teams, providing information, and defending school values in confrontations with the central office. Yet even among these SDM supporters, there were those who took a more directive approach at key moments. One principal, concerned with the motivation behind a teacher decision, told the department chairperson:

> Even though you have taken a vote on it, and even though this is not necessarily democratic, I am being honest with you. I want you to take another hard look at it. If we're not going to do it for the best interests of the school, then I'm not going to be party to it.

Unfortunately, we have few studies showing how the different strategies affect the decision-making process. Since teachers are often skeptical that power will truly be shared, overtly manipulative leadership probably undermines the long-term development of shared governance. But it also seems possible that when principals consistently convey attitudes of trust and respect, teachers may accept principal assertiveness as a natural part of the process. Tony Wagner describes one principal whose faculty repeatedly reported feeling empowered, respected, and trusted:

> Ruben's leadership style is complex. He believes in teachers and knows that they cannot be "made" to change or grow, nor can meaningful programs be developed without teachers' active involvement. But.... Ruben doesn't sit and wait for teachers to come along with good ideas. He prods, he cajoles, he argues, he inspires, he sometimes even manipulates—all means to the end of encouraging teachers to rethink and reassess their work.

In short, SDM seems to be a complex process that does not lead to simple leadership strategies.

The Structure of SDM

Each school must gain "an explicit, shared vision of exactly what it intended to do with shared governance," say Allen and Glickman, who recount problems that arose in the process of implementing SDM in twenty-four Georgia schools that joined with the University of Georgia's Program for School Improvement (PSI) to form the League of Professional Schools. Problems and confusion arose when SDM was simply tacked onto existing power structures. Some schools ended up with several decision-making policies operating simultaneously, with SDM seen as just "another activity that some of the staff were doing" rather than "a fundamental change in the way schoolwide initiatives were generated and implemented."

Agreement must be reached about what decisions will be shared, what groups will be involved at what stage in the process, what time limits will be set for reaching decisions, how decisions will be made (majority vote or consensus), and who is responsible for carrying out the decisions.

A California school district that began SDM at the district level, instead of at school sites, developed "team agreements" during their training process that included groundrules and norms. "Taking the time to work out these agreements was critical for success," states Robert Kessler.

Who Will Be Involved?

Many schools develop one group, team, council, or committee to implement SDM; other schools use several groups or committees. In some cases, composition of the team is determined by mandate. Otherwise, schools need to decide who will be involved. Should students, parents, support staff, central-office staff, or outside consultants be included? What exactly should be the role of the principal? Should all teachers participate or only a select group?

One Michigan high school found it beneficial to involve students in the SDM process. The school reported improved attendance, a reduction in the number and severity of discipline referrals, and a more positive school culture after involving students in the decision-making process (Jay Newman). Some schools will want to include community members, as well as parents, in the SDM structure.

"The group must be large enough to be representative, yet small enough that it won't be cumbersome," states Stine. Groups of nine to seventeen members seem to work well. He suggests that half the members be teachers, with parents having the next largest representation. "Watch for special interest groups' attempts to 'pack' the council," cautions Stine. To avoid this, he recommends electing two-thirds of the council and having that group then appoint others "to ensure gender, ethnic, and special interest balance."

SDM can take a number of forms; it is important to adapt it to each school's own situation, history, needs, and intent. For example, Kirby examined four schools that had participated in Georgia's Program for School Improvement. One school had a self-selected group of concerned high school teachers that evolved into a highly formalized council, with each member representing a small group of faculty. Another school's faculty advisory group became a leadership team elected by the faculty. Still another school had an informal system the principal called the "Y'all come" approach; when an issue or concern arose, an informal meeting was held and anyone interested was invited to participate.

Who Makes Decisions and How

Should the SDM group make decisions or recommendations by voting or consensus? Will the principal have veto power or make decisions if the group can't agree on an issue? A number of groups choose to operate by consensus, which is very different from making decisions by voting. A Glenview, Illinois, school that has had success with SDM defines *consensus* as

> general agreement and concord. For consensus to exist, it is not necessary for every participant to agree in full, but it is necessary for every participant to be heard, and in the end, for none to believe that the situation violates his or her conviction. It is not necessary that every person consider the decision the best one. (Lifton)

Kessler describes how everyone listens carefully when a management team member objects to a proposal. Similarly, when members raise objections, they also offer suggestions. With the goal of consensus, everyone feels responsible for coming up with a solution instead of having the attitude, "It's not my problem, it's yours."

The decision-making sequence varies from school to school. For instance, Hall and Galluzzo note that preliminary work might be done by a task force. Or a committee might make recommendations to either the principal or the whole faculty. Or the committee's decision might be final. Some issues may be introduced by one group, endorsed by another, and approved by a third: "A schoolwide vision statement might be initiated by the leadership team, reviewed by individual faculty members and parent groups, and approved by the faculty at large" (Stine). Sorting through "this maze of stakeholders" may pose significant challenges for SDM groups. Whatever the configuration and sequence, it is important that everyone understand the details of the process *before* a decision is made.

Lessons Learned from Pioneers

A number of consultants and participants in SDM offer firsthand advice on what is necessary to implement and maintain the process and avoid pitfalls. Although these lessons are directed primarily to principals, they apply as well, in the collaborative spirit of SBM, to all participants.

Start Small, Go Slowly

Evidence on the adoption of innovations, state Hall and Galluzzo, suggests that SDM will be most successful if it is carried out in small steps instead of through "wholesale changes." Analyze your school's needs, then adapt selected processes that fit your local situation. Additional components can he added when staff are ready.

Begin by involving staff members who are willing to give time and assume responsibility for SDM. In this phase, you can build credibility for SDM and develop the skills of staff members who will be able to facilitate the process when the larger group becomes involved. When the time comes to involve all staff in decisions that have schoolwide impact, choose issues with low emotional content and those that have a high probability of being successfully implemented.

Provide Training

Training is a necessary preparatory step for SDM, as well as an ongoing need. Principals have a responsibility to provide training to all levels of staff. Lange believes inservice training should be given "simultaneously" to both central-office and school staff members.

Be Clear about Procedures

The need for clarity cannot be overemphasized. Steps for decision-making need to be carefully considered and articulated, and schools need to pinpoint the issues to be resolved. When Mayeski, a researcher, intervened in a Wyoming high school where there was staff unrest over SDM, she found confusion about roles. Teachers also complained that the decision-making process was rarely identified before a decision was made. During meetings Mayeski attended, "a standard procedure for decision-making was not followed." Not surprisingly, fewer than two-thirds of the decisions made by the Faculty Advisory Council were accepted and implemented by the faculty!

Likewise, in the League of Professional Schools, when the process was not clear, staff felt confused and, in some cases, angry. For example, even if staff members knew that they were to reach decisions by voting instead of consensus, they still needed more information, such as whether a simple majority or a two-thirds majority is needed, and so forth. "Unclear processes created confusion that fragmented people's actions and undermined the implementation of shared governance," note Allen and Glickman. "Clear processes empowered people by giving them all an equal understanding of how business was to be conducted."

B. J. Meadows, principal of Juchem Elementary School in Broomfield, Colorado, found it helpful to spell out the SDM process in writing. This clarified her own thinking, served as a starting point for discussions with staff, and became a way to "introduce new staff members to SDM."

Build Trust and Support

It is important to allow time for trust to develop among staff and the community, which Mitchell claims takes between two and seven years. Trust is so important to the process that if trust is absent, SDM will not work, no matter what formal programs or structures have been agreed upon (Lifton).

Support is also crucial, from both within and outside the school. A majority of respondents in the SEDL survey who listed "lack of hierarchical support" as one of the barriers to change stated that their school lacked "full system commitment" to SDM (Mutchler and Duttweiler). "If the culture outside the school does not change," state Hall and Galluzzo, "those inside the school will find it difficult to take charge of decision-making."

District office personnel, school board members, and state policymakers can help by relinquishing certain decisions, being willing to accept diverse decisions from different schools, and being flexible about changing or adapting many of the operating rules and regulations.

Principals can facilitate support for staff by providing adequate time for meetings, reducing teaching loads, providing waivers from contracts and regulations, and changing schedules to permit collegial work to occur.

Do Not Insist on Participation

It is unrealistic to expect all staff to want to be involved in SDM, and making participation mandatory is usually counterproductive. Larry Frase and Larry Sorensen found that teachers with "high growth needs" tend to welcome collegial opportunities; some teachers simply choose to place all their energies in the classroom. In third-year surveys of Dade County, Florida, schools using SDM, Strusinski noted the initial sense of urgency to get everyone involved had decreased. Schools were beginning to recognize that 100 percent involvement is unrealistic, especially considering the increased workload that accompanies SDM, which some teachers are unable or unwilling to undertake.

In the beginning, however, principals may have to "actively recruit" staff or community members to participate. If all else fails, they may have to appoint staff members to councils and enlist parents and others from community groups or booster clubs (Lange).

Focus on Significant Educational Issues

Why do many teachers, given access to schoolwide and curriculum decisions, choose to invest time and energy in "trivial" issues? In her study of four schools that had participated in the Georgia Program for School Improvement for at least two years, Kirby found that the school leadership teams often focused on issues such as smoking in faculty lounges, lunch-duty schedules, and student-discipline policies. More significant concerns were also addressed, including a comprehensive staff-development program, a school-within-a-school for at-risk students, and cross-grade-level planning.

Kirby offers four propositions regarding the focus of SDM teams or committees. First, the kinds of issues addressed by staff may change over time. SDM groups, Kirby asserts, may be more likely to address issues of greater significance if minor faculty concerns are resolved first; this fosters trust in the process and facilitates a more professional culture.

Second, SDM teams that limited the scope of their activities to schoolwide instructional topics were less likely to spend time on noninstructional issues. Initial clarity over roles and purposes may have kept the group on track and enabled them to focus their work "through formal structures for goal setting, determining agendas, and reaching decisions."

Third, issues addressed by SDM bodies may gradually focus more on global and instructional issues. For example, when faculty members at one middle school initially listed their concerns, they focused on managerial issues. A year later, when staff met in teams and developed priorities, each of the teams listed only curriculum and instruction issues. "Individual concerns are less likely to surface as priorities for shared governance when more people are involved in the task of prioritizing," states Kirby.

Finally, Kirby says knowledge plays a role in the kinds of issues staff choose to decide. Faculties willing to tackle schoolwide instructional concerns are more successful "when they engage in deliberate and thorough investigation of available alternatives, disseminate this information to others, and analyze consequences of preferred solutions before choosing among alternatives" (Kirby). It helps, therefore, to have a database, such as school-effectiveness criteria or literature reviews, that is both comprehensive and objective.

One way to get SDM teams to focus on student learning is for the school board to limit the teams' authority by school district policy. The National School Boards Association advises school boards against delegating "generic authority for managing the operations of individual schools." Instead, "Learning Improvement Teams" (their name reinforces their scope of authority) can be charged with the task of designing and implementing a plan for improving student learning. Even then, the building teams must conform their plans to the district's strategic plan.

Use Conflict Creatively

"Controlled conflict," when experienced in a supportive setting, can be a positive force. Meadows states, "Creative solutions involving many ideas are often the result of allowing some conflict to occur. If there is no opportunity to air conflict, destructive adversarial relationships may result." It is important for staff to affirm each other's individual worth. This facilitates an atmosphere of safety in which staff can disagree. Meadows' school welcomed different points of view "as long as we made decisions that benefited our students." Failing to resolve conflicts and placing blame on individuals or SDM does not benefit either students or the school.

Sheri Williams suggests that conflict can be "a healthy change tool." She recommends dealing with conflict as it arises, using the consensus model to resolve conflicts, agreeing on the rules for a "fair fight," recognizing cultural differences in conflict resolution, and looking at various methods groups use to solve problems.

View Failure as an Opportunity

Support in times of trouble is critical, state Huddleston and others. Principals need to remind staff that SDM is slower and often more frustrating than centralized decision-making. They should also involve staff in problem-solving to try to discover reasons for the failure and ways to avoid the problem in the future. Effective administrators demonstrate their support for participative decision-making even when the process is not working well.

On the other hand, Kirby found that success is a great motivator. One high school she studied dealt with issues that seemed trivial, but "early successes engendered further commitment and participation. Eventually, mounting success with shared governance began to create more demand for problem resolution." Therefore, use every opportunity available to build self-confidence with SDM.

Deal with the Issue of Time

One of the things most schools struggle with is finding the time to implement SDM. "The biggest problem in change is not needing more money; it is needing more time," one educator commented to Goldman and others. SEDL survey respondents, note Mutchler and Duttweiler, mentioned a desire to have more time for figuring out "'new ways of doing things,' time for training in new skills, time for decision-making bodies to meet, and time to 'play out the group dynamic' that is necessary" for effective SDM. Considering that teachers and administrators are already overloaded with work, the acute nature of the time barrier becomes evident.

Research on change, state Hall and Galluzzo, suggests that it takes three to five years for real change to occur: "To expect structural and procedural change in less time is unrealistic." For instance, local school councils need time "to struggle to identify the new roles and functions of their members."

What can be done? Mitchell suggests committing additional resources, such as part-time help, to ease the increased workload that accompanies SDM. Some Dade County, Florida, schools have initiated "modest supplements" to teachers involved with SDM, while other schools give compensatory time on teacher work days (Strusinski). "As roles change and time requirements become more demanding, matching salaries to new responsibilities must be evaluated," states Lange. He adds that meetings should be scheduled "to allow for meaningful discussion in a nonhurried way." Meetings should also be scheduled at a time when staff are not exhausted from a long school day (Amie Watson and others).

Facilitate, Yet Take Action

Principals must be *facilitative* yet *directive*. The need for facilitation is well established. Teachers come to SDM with a deeply rooted sense of territoriality: what happens in the classroom is their domain, and what happens anywhere else is the principal's responsibility. Even when teachers are interested in having a greater voice in school affairs, they often remain inclined to defer to the principal's wishes (Weiss 1993, Prestine).

Thus, principals must make a conscious effort not to dominate the process. The principals interviewed by Blase and colleagues offered a number of guidelines for participating actively but facilitatively:

1. Concentrate on keeping a steady flow of accurate information to all participants; full disclosure builds trust and kills rumors.

2. Keep the group from getting bogged down in irrelevant details; nothing kills energy like long, unproductive meetings. Principals are likely to have more group leadership skills than other participants and can suggest alternatives whenever meetings threaten to go off the track.

3. Resist becoming the problem-solver. When teachers say, "What should we do about this issue?," help them identify a number of alternatives, but make it clear that problem ownership stays with the group.

4. Use action research. When disagreements or uncertainties arise, gathering objective information is a neutral way of helping the group reach a decision.

5. Encourage openness and candor, and be willing to accept criticism calmly. One principal says, "If teachers are fearful that if they say something to you that you don't like, you're going to somehow retaliate against them, then that'll kill the process."

6. See that teachers are elected, not administratively appointed; have teachers serve as committee chairs.

7. Above all, trust others and be ready to take risks.

But even as they act facilitatively, principals must be ready to take direct action when necessary. This might happen if, for example, the site council starts to overstep the boundaries that have been laid down, or a group decision seems to violate key school values. As noted elsewhere in this chapter, principals may need to focus the group's attention on substantive issues.

When principals take this kind of assertive action, of course, they risk undermining the SDM process. How are some principals able to avoid this? The answer isn't completely clear, but the best guess is that in schools, as in marriages, strong relationships can handle disagreement, conflict, and raised voices. Prestine describes the ideal:

> What is called for is a close, trusting, and reciprocal relationship based on mutual respect and equality of contribution and commitment. This may be the most critical of all roles and the most difficult to achieve.

Share Accountability

Decision teams need to be held accountable for their performance. Will each team evaluate its own progress or will the superintendent do so, using criteria decided at the district level? The NSBA, favoring the latter course, lists several criteria that could be used:

- What are the results of the learning improvement plan?
- Has the team operated within its delegated authority?
- Does the team work well together? Has it used consensus decision-making practices?
- Has the team scheduled its work to accommodate the needs of both staff members and others on the team?
- Has the need for consistency and compatibility throughout the district been considered in team decisions?
- Does the team consider general community and staff reaction and satisfaction in its decisions?
- Has the team evaluated its own work?
- Does the team's work reflect the use of current education research?
- Does the team communicate well and as needed with other members of the school community?

Lange recommends developing a school profile based on indicators such as attendance rates, graduation rates, and test scores that can serve as "bottom line accountability" for each school. The profiles can serve as baseline data that can be used to evaluate the SDM process.

SDM, Kirby concludes, "may be an easy concept to sell; shared accountability is less appealing. Changing working relationships to include trust and respect may be a prerequisite for accepting the risk that accompanies accountability."

Conclusion

It looks as if SDM is destined to remain a primary school reform issue. Nonetheless, SDM is neither a panacea for all our educational problems nor a "quick fix." It involves major changes for principals, faculties, and school districts. As Bauer cautions, "You cannot expect miracles overnight."

At the same time, SDM "offers tremendous potential to improve schools," states Lange.

A premise of SDM, Lange says, is "to allow those closest to the problem (principals, teachers, support personnel, parents, and community members) to provide direct input into the design of the solution." Lange emphasizes, however, that this "valuable resource" should be considered "a piece of the larger puzzle" of restructuring that may help bring about the fundamental change that national, state, and local groups are demanding in our schools.

PART 4

The Skills

CHAPTER

10

Leading the Instructional Program

James Weber

It was once assumed that the principal was also captain of the ship. He or she not only steered the course and oversaw the actions of junior officers but made sure that the ship's purpose was being fulfilled—that the crew were doing their jobs. The organization was primarily hierarchical: layers of command over the captain, layers of command under the captain. The model was the Great Chain of Being, or perhaps the food chain, if cynics were to be believed.

Of course, this metaphor has never held quite as true for schools as for navies. Creative "insubordination" and individual vision play an enlivening and primarily positive role in a school's faculty, whereas they don't in a ship's crew. For the "captain" of a school, the looser organization means less direct control over staff and outcomes and more emphasis on organizational culture to achieve the positive outcomes.

Partly, these differences depend on semantics. To return to the image of the ship, who would we be talking about if we referred to the ship's leader? As Peter Senge has noted, there are a variety of possible identities for the "leader" of a ship. Besides the captain, the leader could be the navigator, who sets the direction, or the helmsman, who actually controls the direction, or the engineer or the chief cook. If the range of possible leaders depends on a single person's influence over the ship, we could go beyond captains and admirals and presidents—to the ship's designer. Senge points out that in organizations, design is rarely visible; it takes place behind the scenes. Its consequences may appear long after the work is done and have little to do with a desire for immediate control.

Recent studies of instructional leadership have likewise moved from describing ship-shape organizations whose instructional leaders were captains walking their bridges in lonely watch to describing organizations with multiple leaders drawn from the crew itself. Moreover, these leaders, drawn from the faculty, are being given increasing responsibilities in site-based-management schemes for areas of school governance previously reserved for administrators.

Thomas Sergiovanni replaces the idea of hierarchical schools with schools as communities that develop their own norms and identities. "Community norms," he believes, "provide the school with substitutes for direct leadership" (1992). In successful schools, the "crew" themselves, the teachers, adopt the values necessary for their success. Indeed, it is their professionalism that replaces a school's dependence on a single leader with the use of multiple centers of instructional leadership.

The faculty's professionalism is marked by four dimensions of commitment, according to Sergiovanni: (1) to practice their profession in an exemplary way (pushing for continuous improvement), (2) to practice toward valued social ends, (3) to value the profession itself (not just their own practice of it), and (4) to practice the ethic of caring. These sorts of commitments create the norms of a community that can carry on effective teaching with motivated, and largely self-managed, teachers.

This vision of the school is admittedly quite different from that in many an organizational chart or even leadership flowchart. And this is not a bad thing, according to Dennis Evans, who sees instructional leadership as an impossible task for principals. He and other observers, such as Keith Acheson, note that instructional supervision and instructional evaluation, two of the traditional roles of principals, are incompatible. Supervision is primarily formative and collegial, being concerned with improving teaching effectiveness. Evaluation is summative, involving role hierarchies, comparative judgments, legal concerns, and ultimately dismissal or retention of teachers. Evaluation and supervision are most effective when performed by different individuals. Principals are best placed for performing evaluations, but instructional leadership belongs to teachers, the district's specialists, or outside consultants.

Is the-principal-as-instructional-leader a misguided concept? Is it in jeopardy of becoming passé?

The Necessity of Leadership

The research suggests that even if an instructional leader were not packaged as a principal, it would still be necessary to designate such a leader. The leaderless-team approach to a school's instructional program has powerful appeal, but a large group of professionals still needs a single point of contact and an active advocate for teaching and learning.

Site-based management has introduced teachers to the world of specific decisions affecting their schools—scheduling, plant management, discipline, evaluation, and many others. In the process of shared decision-making, there may be seemingly endless hours of committee meetings, wrangling over decisions, and factionalizing of formerly quiet faculties. Although the increased involvement in school management may be positive for faculties, its time demands and potential for conflict can strain an instructional program. That strain may be lessened by a principal's leadership and advocacy.

Carol Weiss and colleagues observe that self-management gives rise to conflicts in faculties, as in communities, and that principals have active roles to play even in schools where the faculty is shouldering much of the burden of administrating or guiding the instructional program.

The leadership functions, then, are still present in schools, whether assumed by principals or other members of the staff. Communities, after all, need leaders just as navies do. And the larger communities—those that contain the schools—expect that someone in a school will at least oversee the critical leadership functions in instructional programs.

Table 1 provides a list of critical areas requiring attention in instructional programs. The table does not exhaust the areas where leadership may be needed, but it does provide an overview. Clearly, some areas are easily transferred to teachers and others: providing inservice training, setting and monitoring schoolwide standards, selecting teaching materials, balancing program goals with school goals, planning collaboratively, providing rewards and recognition, and setting high expectations and clear goals.

These and other areas may be excellent opportunities for empowering teachers to exercise their professionalism. Other areas, however, may remain primarily in the authority of principals, for reason of legality and policy: evaluating and selecting teachers, protecting instructional time, or specifying class size and composition.

For instance, a teacher who wants a change in class composition may be better served by an administrator than by a committee of faculty members.

Shared leadership, then, does not mean an absence of leadership. What research has been showing conclusively, it should be noted, is that where teachers are brought into more leadership roles, only a fully collaborative effort between principal and teachers will produce effective instruction. Where principals give teachers full administrative responsibilities in a school, without the benefit of information, active participation, or cooperation, mistakes will be made and wheels reinvented.

TABLE 1

Some Critical Functions of Instructional Leadership

- **Supervision**

  Observing classroom performance

  Providing feedback on instructional skills

  Giving direction and support for individual teachers to eliminate poor teaching performance

- **Providing Inservice Training**

  Arranging for inservices on instructional technique

  Collaborating with 272nservice needs and offerings

  Attending or being briefed about inservice sessions

- **Evaluating Teachers**

  Scheduling conferences before and after classroom observations

  Providing teachers guidance to analyze their own instructional processes

  Focusing on improving teaching rather than condemning teachers' habits or personalities

  Concentrating on issues "small in number, educationally vital, intellectually accessible to the teacher, and amenable to change" (Acheson 1985)

  Bringing in specific observations rather than general judgments

  Evaluating supervisors' techniques on the same bases used to evaluate teachers

- **Selecting Teachers**

  Contacting all references

  Observing and having others observe teaching of job candidates and new teachers

  Hiring different types of staff to reach all students

  Following up on new-hires with support and development opportunities

- **Protecting Instructional Time and Teacher Integrity**

  Supporting teachers' professional decisions and needs

  Eliminating disruptive "official" interruptions in class time over public-address systems or inclass announcements

- **Setting and Monitoring Schoolwide Academic Standards**

  Establishing academic requirements, consistent with and exceeding district guidelines

  Publicizing by word and print the high expectations of the school

  Providing counseling programs that challenge students

TABLE 1

Encouraging the use of standardized testing for improving academic performance

Keeping test results available for teachers' reference and goal-setting

- **Limiting Class Size and Controlling Class Composition**

  Assigning students to teachers on the basis of factors that may affect learning

  Experimenting with multiage grouping

  Avoiding "typing" students socially as the basis for assigning classes

- **Overseeing and Facilitating Selection of Teaching Materials**

  Matching objectives and materials

  Filling instructional priority areas fairly

  Helping teachers develop materials not commercially available

- **Balancing Specific Program Objectives with Overall School Goals**

  Ensuring scope and sequence in school instructional program by forming guidelines and checking department programs for consistency with guidelines

- **Helping Teachers and Students in Being Aware of School's Curricula**

- **Planning Collaboratively**

  Staffing committees with various viewpoints

  Expecting staff input on materials selection and evaluation

- **Providing Rewards and Recognition for Teaching and Learning Achievements**

  Setting up ongoing systems for recognizing academic success as well as athletic success

  Facilitating peer-group emotional support and incentives for teachers

- **Setting High Expectations and Clear Goals for Student and Teacher Performances**

  Requiring yearly instructional goals for each teacher

  Establishing policy on student promotion

  Analyzing program systematically to find general strengths and weaknesses

  Maintaining order and a pleasant environment to teach and learn

  Establishing and monitoring discipline

  Refusing to stereotype students

  Assigning staff and resources to promptly confront the violation of rules

Where responsibilities are accompanied by full faculty participation, communication and an organizational memory develop and problems are considered more as challenges than as barriers. Such an organization—collaborative and energetically devoted to instructional goals—is what Senge calls a "learning organization." That is, it is an organization that is self-correcting as well as self-managing and is always on the lookout for ways to improve itself.

Given the potential for sharing instructional leadership, what are the ways in which instructional leadership is expressed and how does it become effective? Whether a school chooses leaderless teams, works to make the inherited system more flexible, or stays with a strongly top-down system of management, instructional leadership appears to involve five domains of leadership: defining the school's instructional mission, managing curriculum and instruction, promoting a positive learning climate, observing and improving instruction, and assessing the instructional program.

Defining the School's Mission

Creating a common vision for an instructional program seems to be important in nearly all general research and advice about instructional leadership. In a study of 168 teachers from 9 urban schools, for instance, Kenneth Leithwood and colleagues found that teachers' commitment to change in instructional programs was affected the most by leadership that gave direction, purpose, and meaning to their work. Especially strong as influences were the vision-creating and consensus-building practices of school leaders. (At the bottom of the list of helpful influences were models of instruction and individualized support from principals.)

A vision and common goals, it is generally held, bind organizations together. In much of the research on instructional leadership, reaching a consensus on instructional goals is regarded as extremely important. "Articulating a theme, reminding people of the theme, and helping people to apply the theme to interpret their work," Karl Weick has asserted, "all are major tasks of administrators in loosely coupled systems," such as schools.

But what is meant by a *vision* for the instructional program? Teachers as a profession are notoriously maverick and self-motivating. Compared to their daily, or even yearly, concerns, programmatic visions as expressed in vision statements can look vague and huge. Unlike programmatic visions, however, teachers who build a shared vision collaborate like the members of a single team—bringing out interdisciplinary interests, encouraging individual creativity, and helping to ferret out and resolve conflicts among faculty, which is a useful tool for site-based management.

According to Senge, the learning organization builds shared vision by encouraging the sharing of personal visions (including the leader's) and by emphasizing positive over negative visions. The leaders in such organizations are skilled both in advocacy and in inquiry, that is, in listening and observing. A leader in an instructional program should be able to explain the reasoning and data that led to the group's view, invite others to test the view (to expose gaps in the reasoning or faulty data), and genuinely encourage others in their views. When inquiring into others' views, they need to actively test their understanding ("Am I understanding you to say that...?").

Although visions are by definition ideals, leaders may be able to bring them down to earth by listening to their staff; thus, general visions can become particular goals relevant to a content area. Take, for instance, a vision of a school that teaches students both life-enhancing skills and a disposition for life-long learning. When it is processed by math and English teachers into their lesson plans, what would you expect such a vision to look like? How would a school encourage life-long learning in math, for instance? Choosing a shared vision for a school in this instance could be less a matter of writing down an abstract vision statement and more a matter of getting staff to talk about what they value.

Senge also points out that bringing our mental models to the surface will help us to see where our assumptions conflict with actual practice. For the instructional leader, this is dangerous and yet potentially rewarding territory.

Sharon Bolster, in a study of seven elementary principals, found that some principals were not conveying the vision they thought they were. In one school, for instance, teachers thought that the principal valued discipline above all else. In fact, she regarded discipline as only one part of her vision. Another principal had changed emphasis in her vision, though teachers were still focusing on the old vision and were unaware of a new focus. These leaders' mental models of their values for the instructional program were divorced from actual practice in classrooms. Such examples also emphasize the danger in a principal inventing a vision for the school apart from input and daily contact with teachers' own personal visions.

Teachers, too, may hold views of the school's instructional program that they are not reflecting in their practice. Such discrepancies can be addressed in numerous ways—informally among colleagues or in formal observations of teachers. Outside consultants may reveal a conflict between espoused views and actual practice in an instructional program. An instructional leader, however, may most usefully devote energy to creating a climate in which people's defensiveness (including the school leaders') is recognized and defused.

Senge points out that those who are best at revealing and defusing defensiveness have a high degree of self-disclosure about their own defensiveness (for example, "I notice that I am feeling uneasy about this conversation. Can you help me see what I'm not understanding or what's threatening to me?").

Defining the school's mission is, then, a dynamic process, requiring cooperation to construct a workable vision and reflexive thinking to keep the mission clear and honest. A similar process, involving team-building and honest dealing with heterogeneous views, can strengthen the management of curriculum and instruction.

Managing Curriculum and Instruction

The implementation of a school's mission can be seen most clearly in curriculum and instruction. Here, the major task confronting an instructional leader may be in recognizing the options available and then selecting, with teachers, those that best fit the constraints provided by the school environment.

That instructional leaders need to know about instructional methods and trends is fairly obvious. A perceptive yet untrained observer may be able to see gaps in a teacher's presentation, but leaders need to provide informed advice and communicate priorities for improvement in a class or a program. At the very least, instructional leaders must share with teachers an understanding of instructional goals and a common language for describing and analyzing teaching practices.

An instructional leader's repertoire of useful skills undoubtedly varies from school to school. However, it may include certain basic trends in media and methods as well as areas of expertise in classroom supervision:

- Trends in Media and Methods, such as those in
  - Textbook Selection
  - New Technologies
  - Teacher-Developed Materials
  - Computer Software
  - Personalized Instruction
  - Direct Instruction
  - Mastery Learning
  - Cooperative Small-Group Learning
  - Study Skills
- Classroom Supervision Areas, such as
  - Teaching Styles

Class Size

Grouping Practices

Use of Time and Space

Instructional Strategies

Instructional Media/Materials

Homework

Clearly, no one person can be an expert in each of these areas. However, when training and opportunities for study are spread among both principals and teachers, a school can have both theoretical and working knowledge of most of these areas. Such collegiality, which Judith Warren Little defines as "recourse to other's knowledge and experience, and to shared work and discussion," has a profound effect on instructional success. Other recent research also emphasizes the shared approach to making and implementing decisions about curriculum, as well as to amending decisions from lessons learned in practice.

In their model of the curriculum process, for instance, Roger Niemeyer and Robert Hatfield advocate increasingly common views about the process of curriculum supervision. They note that it involves multiple participants and broad-based leadership, particularly drawn from the faculty. An evolving curriculum requires input from the whole school's instructional staff—and much of its support staff, such as librarians. Niemeyer and Hatfield recommend a decision-making structure that embraces administration and faculty, individual practitioners and teams, district and school input. They note that "decision making is most effective when done by a practitioner with a support team providing reinforcement and assistance needed to get the job done."

In the Niemeyer and Hatfield model, faculty curriculum teams contribute consistently to planning, implementation, staff development, instruction, and evaluation. They propose one teacher to lead a faculty team of five to six members. The team would comprise teachers from multiple grades (two to three levels) or from multiple subject matters (two to three areas).

Instructional teams, such as those used in the Niemeyer and Hatfield model, are currently adopting any of several patterns of organization and responsibility. Table 2, drawn up by Allan Glatthorn, lists some functions that instructional teams can—and do—perform.

Despite this encouragement to form decision-making teams, most teachers in a 1991 study reported being involved very little in such areas as student rights, reporting procedures, grading policies, teacher evaluations, selection of new teachers, budgeting, or student promotion policies (Conley, in Glatthorn). Incorporating teacher input into curriculum man-

TABLE 2

Functions of the Instructional Team

Functions	Examples
1. Plan	Exchange lesson plans Develop common plans Critique plans
2. Schedule	Allocate time Group students
3. Diagnose Student Problems	Identify and diagnose problems of learning, motivation, and discipline Make referrals
4. Teach	Exchange classes Present lessons together Assist in large-group sessions Lead small-group seminars
5. Assess Learning	Develop, administer, and evaluate alternative forms of assessment
6. Develop Curricula and Instructional Materials	Develop integrated units Develop enrichment and remediation materials
7. Identify Organizational Problems	Monitor learning and organizational climate Identify developing problems
8. Provide for Professional Development	Induct new teachers Use peer coaching Conduct action research Conduct professional dialogues

Source: *Teachers as Agents of Change: A New Look at School Improvement*, by Allan A. Glatthorn. Copyright 1992. Washington, D.C.: National Education Association. Reprinted by permission of the NEA Professional Library.

agement for many schools may require restructuring the school, in the corporate management sense of "restructuring," that is, remaking the decision-making lines of authority to include more of those professionals who actually carry out the curriculum policies in the classroom.

Such a restructuring involves certain assumptions: that teachers, supervisors, and administrators should have equal access to information and resources; that shared power does not dilute the effectiveness of an organization but concentrates it; that decisions should be made as close to the point of implementation as possible; that decisions should be made by those most expert at carrying them out, regardless of hierarchical level; and that, given the opportunity, most teachers will do what is best for the school (Patterson and others, in Niemeyer and Hatfield).

One principal profiled by Richard Sagor uses research as a way to resolve conflicts over curricular issues, such as tracking. The faculty instructional team in his school was deeply divided over the issue, citing differing opinions about the effects of the school's policy of tracking on students' attitudes and achievement. Some saw tracking as the source of the school's success, others as a restraint on experimentation. Through their research and informed discussion, the faculty agreed to replace tracking with heterogeneous grouping, with a focus on the disadvantaged learner. The faculty also created a paid academic coaching position to work with students at risk, much as a football coach might work with his team.

Making participation, and even leadership, accessible acknowledges that teachers' contributions are powerful in improving the instructional program.

Another principal, described by Lynn Liontos, regards the teachers as all capable of leadership in some respect, regardless of their position in a hierarchy. A department head at his school observes that this principal involves as many people as possible in decisions: "He's very good at getting people to come out and start becoming leaders in various committees." A school-improvement grant process, for instance, was codirected by two classroom teachers rather than administrators or department heads. Most of the collective decisions at this school related to instruction; leadership was shared on the basis of the staff's interests and expertise and as the needs in the situation dictated.

Promoting a Positive Learning Climate

The broader curriculum includes not only what is taught but what is learned, that is, not only teachers' experiences but students' as well. The issues in curriculum management, such as coverage and technique, intertwine with the areas of learning climate and program assessment.

Indeed, of all the important factors that appear to affect students' learning, perhaps having the greatest influence is the set of beliefs, values, and attitudes that administrators, teachers, and students hold about learning. So important is *learning climate* that it has been defined as "the norms, beliefs, and attitudes reflected in institutional patterns and behavior practices that enhance or impede student learning" (Lezotte and others).

The attitudes that students form about academic learning come, at least in part, from the adults in the school. In studies of both effective and ineffective schools, it is clear that the norms for learning come from the staff's requirements of students: the amount of time needed for studying, the amount of work assigned, the degree of independent work that students can do, the degree of preparedness students feel about the work given to them, the behaviors deemed appropriate for school, and the staff's judgments of whether students are capable of learning. All these variables are capable of being affected by the adults in the school. However, of the six variables, the most important remains the expectations and judgments about students' abilities to learn.

The research of Ronald Heck and George Marcoulides found that instructional leaders can take several kinds of actions to enhance the learning climate in their schools, among them:

- communicating instructional goals
- establishing high expectations for performance
- establishing an orderly, positive learning environment with a clear discipline code

Other research suggests a further action as well: working to increase teachers' commitment to the school. The following sections discuss each of these activities for improving a school's learning climate.

Communicating Goals and High Expectations

Whereas curricular goals and high academic expectations have most often been received from above in an organization, recent discussions of shared leadership advocate curricular goals that percolate up, from the classroom to the school and beyond. Recent studies have recommended that faculty be actively involved in determining those goals, not simply in an advisory role but as co-policy-makers. This could make curricular goals a less bureaucratic exercise than in the past.

Certainly, schools must adhere to state or district requirements in an instructional program. Often, however, these goals are minimums; schools are expected not to drop below the curricular goals. Beyond this baseline level, instructional goals are also found in individual schools, departments, and, of course, classrooms. It is in these areas of a school's life that shared goals and high expectations, as living instructional policies, have their greatest effect.

Instructional leaders perform like good coaches, setting goals and monitoring expectations with due consideration of their players' abilities and hopes. Like coaches, instructional leaders can prevent a school from falling into the trap of self-fulfilling low expectations.

In a school where expectations are low, the attitudes of teachers and students can form a vicious circle of failure, a destructive self-fulfilling prophecy: "Students probably can't get this, so why try?" or "Nobody's paying much attention to whether I learn this or not, so why try?" The power of self-fulfilling prophecies such as these is insidious. They are difficult to change because they generate the evidence to substantiate their own bias. Furthermore, when we make self-fulfilling prophecies, we often do so unconsciously, making them difficult to detect.

High expectations are the fulcrum point that instructional leaders can use to pry teachers, administrators, students, and parents away from unhelpful, unencouraging attitudes. According to William Brookover and colleagues, raising or lowering expectations has been shown to change a teacher's range of instructional activities. When teachers lower their expectations of students, they incorporate fewer of the following essential instructional elements in their teaching repertoires. When they raise their expectations, they use more of these elements:

- Amount and quality of praise for correct answers
- Actual amount of teaching that students receive
- Content covered
- Response opportunity factor—number of times students are called on, extent to which the questions are challenging, degree of cognitive demands
- Academic content (and less nonacademic activities)
- Verbal and nonverbal warmth and acceptance of the student in general
- Nonverbal cues—amount of eye contact, forward lean, affirmative head nods, smiles, physical contact
- General encouragement and support
- Teacher assistance and willingness to help
- Wait time (the amount of time a student is given to respond to a question before the teacher gives the answer or moves on to another student)
- High academic evaluations—reflected by percentage of students expected to master skills, complete high school or attend college, do A or B work
- Reinstruction of students in failure situations (that is, probing, restating questions, giving hints, and so forth, until student arrives at the correct answer)
- Evaluative feedback and constructive criticism of school work

- Academically oriented teacher role definitions (that is, lower expectations are associated with the belief that social control or other nonacademic goals are the appropriate teacher objectives)

Two general strategies demonstrate that instructional leaders are serious about high expectations: emphasizing time devoted to student learning and rewarding success in various school achievements.

Protecting Time for Learning

Studies show that time-on-task is highly related to student achievement. The more time students spend on learning, the better the outcomes. Students also gain more interest in subjects and a better attitude toward learning when they maximize time-on-task.

The National Educational Commission on Time and Learning (NECTL) recommends that U.S. schools double the time that students spend on core academic subjects, such as English, history, mathematics, and science. The NECTL observes that only half of the average U.S. school day is spent on core academic subjects, with the other half spent on electives, physical education, and other activities. By contrast, Japanese, German, and French students spend an average of five-and-one-half hours per day on core subjects.

But we must be careful here not to oversimplify the findings. As Lorin W. Anderson has pointed out, it is wrong to focus only on the "time" factor and to ignore the "on task" part. Simply providing more time for instruction will probably not raise achievement. The use of that time—that is, the quality of time spent in instructional activities—must also improve.

Moreover, some "elective" courses can effectively combine several instructional goals from core academic subjects and do so in a way that improves students' knowledge: for instance, role-playing situations in drama have been used to teach critical thinking skills, literature, and public speaking; architecture and art history have been used to teach mathematics, political and social history, and science. Thus, gauging effective use of instructional time is not so simple as limiting what or how students learn.

Instructional leaders can enhance useful time-on-task by enforcing tardiness rules, minimizing interruptions from visitors, and reserving 90 percent of classroom time for instruction. Teachers can prepare all materials before classes or make sure that students have succinct directions for work (see Lori Jo Oswald).

Effective use of instructional time also depends on a number of factors addressed in other parts of this chapter and book: keeping the school orderly, engaging teachers in their fields and helping them plan collaboratively, emphasizing the needs of students and adjusting the instructional programs accordingly, to name just a few.

Rewarding Success

Instructional leaders need to make certain that merit is recognized. Rewards for academic excellence—honor rolls, citations, and academic contests such as "college bowls"—make visible the underlying values in a school. They may also raise the level of camaraderie around academic pursuits, making schoolwork a competition and a problem-solving set of activities, which involves preparation, performance, and sportsmanship, with both group and individual efforts.

Appropriate rewards and recognition can honor a range of learning styles and intelligences. Drama awards can include recognition for dance and music, for instance, as well as technical theater arts such as sets and costuming. Athletic awards might include "most improved" recognition as well as that for best athletes.

Such rewards and recognition can enhance the sense of common effort that lightens the work of learning and teaching. Teachers working in less-effective schools have been observed to speak seldom of their work or the school with enthusiasm. William L. Rutherford described the environment in such schools as "placid and nonthreatening": "It placed few demands on teachers, but it was also ambiguous and without rewards." Students, too, have been found to suffer the same malaise of vague expectations and indifference.

Establishing an Orderly Learning Environment

When members of the public are asked about problems in schools, their responses paint a picture of an undisciplined rabble on the verge of riot. Control student misbehavior, the image suggests, and the benefits of an ordered life will become apparent. What impresses instructional leaders about discipline, however, is its contribution to a school climate in which learning is central.

According to Larry Hughes and Gerald Ubben, school discipline involves not only control of students but also helping students with academic advising and social-service referral. For maintaining positive student control, they advocate a preventive program of clearly understood rules and the defusing of tensions. A set of rules for student conduct should meet two tests for clarity and currency:

- The rules must be stated in a manner that ensures understanding by all affected.

- There must be regular and systematic evaluation of the need for and efficiency of the existing rules. Times change, needs change, and response patterns change. Therefore, it is important that rules be examined in view of whether or not they continue to serve their purpose in an efficient and effective manner.

Discipline problems can probably best be handled on a referral basis, say Hughes and Ubben. That is, a teacher will refer a problem to a faculty discipline team when the teacher needs advice or alternatives. Teams can usually determine if a teacher or student has misunderstood a rule or if the rule needs to be rewritten. The team would then refer the matter to the principal if it is serious and warrants school- or district-level action. A reporting system must exist for staff members to be made aware of disciplinary actions taken.

According to Hughes and Ubben, the key to keeping disciplinary issues from dominating a learning climate is to head them off before they happen. This could include resolving student-to-student conflicts with a mediator, involving students in developing rules, establishing an individual instructional plan for poor performers, and celebrating students' successes and activities, both inside and outside the classroom, with rewards and recognition.

Hughes and Ubben also recommend a student advising program, in which teachers advise a group of students on curricular decisions and learning goals. Such a program would supplement, not replace, the services of the school counselor, who deals with psychological testing and services and other student programs. Some schools include all the school's professional staff as advisers, including librarians, administrators, and specialists. Such an arrangement keeps the student-adviser ratio lower than when only teachers are advisers.

The adviser meets with individual students in the group regularly for ten or fifteen minutes to review the student's learning progress, set goals, and determine modifications in their personal instructional program. Although this model is designed for elementary schools, where teachers cover a range of subjects, it could also work for middle and secondary schools, with the appointment of departmental advisers or grade-level advising groups.

The advisers work closely with the school guidance counselor to refer students who need special help and to keep records. The guidance counselor also could provide staff development activities in group guidance and in diagnosing individual problems.

Finally, a successful discipline program will make use of resources available through the school district and the community. These include reading specialists and speech pathologists, hearing and vision specialists, special-education counselors, and attendance counselors. These resources are the tools that instructional leaders may use for making learning more accessible—or perhaps even possible—for more students.

Increasing Teacher Commitment

The sections above have repeatedly invoked the committed, participating teacher in describing plans for shared instructional leadership. What is teacher commitment and how important is it in broadening the base of instructional leadership? And how can teachers be motivated to greater commitment to their jobs?

In a study of urban elementary and middle schools, James Kushman looked into teacher commitment both to the organization and to student learning. Previous research had identified three kinds of commitments that teachers can show to the school itself: being willing to exert effort for the organization, wanting to continue working in the school, and accepting the school's major instructional values and goals.

A fourth kind of commitment, to student learning, can be recognized in three ways: a sense of teacher efficacy (the belief that a teacher can make a difference in student learning), the expectation that students will learn, and a willingness to put forth the effort required for student learning to occur.

Kushman points out a correlation between teacher commitment to student learning and gains in student achievement. He postulates that this linkage occurs in the following manner. Teachers' use of effective instructional behaviors in the classroom leads to increased student commitment to school, which in turn leads to increased student achievement.

How does a school and its leadership increase teachers' commitment to student learning? Work-related conditions must encourage teachers to go beyond the minimum and actively affirm the values that they seek to convey to students. Kushman has found four influences that decisively affect teacher commitment:

- Job stress is a powerful deterrent to teacher commitment. Burnout replaces enthusiasm. Kushman found two factors in particular that reduced teachers' stress and increased their enthusiasm. One was a sense of order and focus in schools—much the same as the liberating discipline discussed above. The other was opportunities for job renewal, that is, peer support, shared social activities, and staff development; particularly important was a schoolwide commitment to ongoing program and educational improvements.
- A second factor is a teacher's sense of professional fulfillment, which Kushman saw in frequent teacher collaborations on instruction and curriculum. He points to self-managing work teams, self-initiated leadership

among teachers in designing and implementing innovations, rotating leadership roles for teachers, professional growth opportunities within the school, and a value placed on a high quality of teaching and academics among teachers. Where teachers had to rely on rewards from student successes alone or on peer support and friendship, their commitment to the school suffered.

• More satisfied teachers also are actively involved in collaboration and leadership, which occurred both formally (as part of the school's institutional mechanisms) and informally. They were part of core decisions on discipline, school-improvement programs, scheduling, and personnel selection. In the school in which Kushman found these activities, the principal was also involved in the process, providing guidance, mediating conflicts, and reserving some decisions for herself. It is noteworthy that it was teachers' feeling of control over the teaching process, not over other ancillary roles such as counseling or administrating, that gave them their sense of empowerment.

Recent research suggests that providing teachers with time for professional development can address the three problems cited so far: burnout, a lack of fulfilling work, and the need for professional collaboration (see Gary Watts and Shari Castle in Oswald and Mary McCaslin and Thomas Good). Schools can increase professional-development time in a number of ways that involve varying degrees of change from the status quo: restructuring the school day, for instance, adding instructional time to the first days of the week and releasing students early on Friday for teacher development activities; scheduling a common time to allow the members of teaching teams to do their planning together; or giving teachers inservice credits for developing programs on their own time.

• Finally, Kushman found that teacher commitment was positively affected by a positive learning climate for students. Discipline, in particular, was clearly spelled out and swiftly handled in the school with the most committed teachers. Disruptions were dealt with in a formal process and student responsibilities were clear, rather than informally communicated. Teachers were not considered social workers or parents and could get on with the process of building a learning environment.

Observers often talk of the apparent "focus" of a school as it goes about its daily business of teaching and learning. Focus can be discerned in attitudes, time on task, and the importance of learning, to name just a few areas. The research suggests that school leaders can and do focus their schools: in communicating goals and expectations, keeping the learning climate orderly, and increasing teacher commitment. The effective leaders thus keep the purpose of schooling continually at the center of school life.

Observing and Improving Instruction

One of the most sensitive issues among teachers may be observation of their teaching. This presents a problem for instructional leaders who must monitor the quality of the instruction in the school, check for consistency in standards, and be available to help solve (or point out) the behavioral and academic problems that every teacher encounters. How should an instructional leader handle the monitoring of teachers?

To benefit, a teacher who is observed must be able to trust the observer in at least three ways: First, the teacher must believe that the observer intends no harm; second, the teacher must be convinced that the criteria and procedures of evaluation are predictable and open; and third, the teacher must have confidence that the observer will provide information to improve the nuts-and-bolts of his or her teaching.

When teachers are observed by uninterested administrators or teachers, there is the potential for the exercise to become a glib sidewalk superintendency. At its worst, observation of classroom teaching can actually erode the collegiality and norms of excellence that it was meant to fortify.

In 1985, Tom Bird and Judith Warren Little offered several requirements for successful observations. Their list applies as well to teacher-teacher observations as to administrator-teacher observations. It emphasizes the observation's potential for reciprocity—that is, the possibility of mutual learning rather than simply one-way communicating. An observer, they hold, should promise to report accurately to the teacher a description of the lesson that will shed new light on the teacher's practices. Praise should be as detailed and specific as criticisms. And observers themselves should attempt to learn something new, improving along with the teacher.

The observed teacher must, in turn, validate the observation process, affirming it as a valuable tool in improving her teaching, and take the observation as a learning opportunity.

For instructional leaders and for teachers, then, observations are opportunities for professional interactions, which means giving and taking information. Of course, this is not always possible, because a district or school requires teacher *evaluations* rather than simply interactions with an observer. However, it may be possible, even in an evaluative framework, to regard the evaluation as a facilitative observation. If the procedure is to be more than a turn of a phrase, how would it work?

At a minimum, the improvement of instruction would be a collaborative activity, of which classroom observation is only one part. With a sustained emphasis on everyone's continuous improvement, observations become *de rigeur* and not rare and fearful occasions. Moreover, observations then can be the grist for ongoing discussions of professional improvements and innovations.

Some instructional leaders provide research findings regularly to teachers—circulating copies of articles, for instance—and encourage teachers to initiate their own research (formal or informal) and attend conferences. Liontos reports on a high school that uses research as a way of providing current information to teachers, starting (or improving) discussions among teachers, and making informed decisions. The staff's own research and data-collecting have been vital in school decisions, such as schoolwide curricular goals. For instance, several departments integrated writing components in classes for the first time because of faculty discussions about research into writing across the curriculum.

The principal models the use of research by reading and bringing up new approaches to learning. He credits the emphasis on research-based decisions as the stimulus for considerable improvements in the instructional program: "I think that has been in the background of our changes and created a really solid foundation behind it. If you don't research or collect data, you're not operating from much of a base" (Liontos).

Assessing the Instructional Program

If studying other schools is essential to improving your school's instructional program, it is certainly at least as important to study your own program. Deliberate and ongoing assessment is an important part of instructional leadership. Indeed, program assessment shows why leadership is needed in an instructional program. Without leadership from within a school, program assessments often rely on surveys or quick reviews by consultants, district staff members, or other outside experts.

Although such assessments can provide valuable information, faculty participation is restricted only to the supply of data—not in planning, designing, and executing the assessment. Thus, the faculty may not claim a full stake in the results of the assessment. This deficit, in turn, can slow the implementation of program changes identified in the assessment.

Of course, informal assessments of the program take place all the time: in the faculty lounge, on playgrounds, or after school in the parking lot—wherever teachers, administrators, students, and parents sum up their impressions of a program. Although not all informal assessments are worth following up, others are insightful and timely. A complaint about the lack of copier paper, for instance, could be simply peevish or it could be a clue to greater dissatisfactions with a program: it could mean inappropriate or unhelpful textbooks (requiring a teacher to run off replacement materials) or bottlenecks in providing instructional supplies. What is needed is a formal, objective assessment that can also capture the valid gripes, insights, and trends of those involved in daily instruction.

A formal tool called a "concerns screen" can capture staff insights. It can be set up to gauge the status of formal program objectives and the use of resources. Developed by Susan Loucks-Horsley and M. Melle, the concerns screen ranks specific instructional and programmatic concerns according to their maturity and success. Table 3 summarizes teachers' perceptions of how their instructional concerns are faring. Whereas materials and inservices are progressing well, basic skills need to be more integrated into the curriculum.

Program assessment determines what the school is good at and what it is not. It provides information for planning, revising, or continuing parts of the program. Instructional leaders contribute to this process in a variety of ways, in planning, designing, and administering an assessment and in interpreting the outcomes.

Assessment depends not only on information about perceptions of how well the instructional program is doing; it also depends on facts about what is being taught overall. Occasionally, what is actually being taught differs from the intended or understood curriculum. Curriculum mapping may provide an overview of the emphasis in instruction in a department, school, or district.

The example in table 4 lists various topics in a science curriculum in one district and shows, for each grade, the total time devoted to each topic. Instructional leaders can thus see the breadth of the curriculum and its actual time priorities. In table 4, the science curriculum appears to orbit around four topics: magnetism, nutrition, solar systems, and the human body. A map such as this one can supply a basis on which to identify new curricular topics. For instance, a decision could be to include "optical illusions" in the curriculum, since it is not being done now.

A full model of a participative assessment, suitable for providing leadership opportunities at every level, is provided by Judy Carr and Douglas Harris.

Often, they note, the process starts in a school's curriculum committee, which has an overview of the instructional program. They can involve others in the assessment process via a curriculum-assessment planning team. This team can determine whether the special skills of an outside consultant are needed, as well as what are the budget and timetable of the assessment. The planning team also should draw up a list of goals for the program assessment. What is the purpose of the assessment? Is it to gauge how well the curriculum is meeting its goals? To inform parents or board members of the program's strengths and weaknesses? To allocate resources where they are needed? Perhaps all these purposes would be useful.

It is important at this point to know the questions, the sources of information, and the kinds of assessment that would best contribute to the

TABLE 3

Sample Building Summary Sheet

	1 — *Outside Intended Program*	2 — *Getting a Good Start*	3 — *Well on the Way*	4 — *Best Practice*	5 *Working*
1. Time is devoted to science	*** **	*	**	*	**
2. Science is taught according to R-1 Guide	*** ***	*** **			
3. Assessment of pupil learning	*** ***	*** **			
4. Integration of basic skills	*	***** ****	*		
5. The outdoor classroom is used as recommended		*** **	*** *	**	
6. Recommended materials, equipment, and media are available			*** **	*** *	**
7. Inservicing and financial arrangements have been made		*	*** **	*** **	
8. Long- and short-range planning		***	*** ***	**	
9. Use of class time	**	**	****	**	*
10. Teacher-pupil interaction facilitates progam	***	****	****		
11. Classroom environment facilitates program		***	***	***	**
12. Instruction is sequenced to facilitate the guided-inquiry-learning approach	**	**** *	****		

School: Winter Elementary. Teachers: All grade 3, 4, 5, 6 teachers.
* = one teacher

Source: Loucks-Horsley and Melle (1982). Reprinted by permission of S. Loucks-Horsley.

TABLE 4

Curriculum Mapping: Analysis of Data—Science Curriculum of Shady Grove Public Schools

TOPIC	K	1	2	3	4	5	6	7	8	9	10	11	12	*Total Time by Topic*
1. Simple machines	I/1	0	0	0	0	0	0	0	0	0	0	0	0	1.0
2. Work and energy	0	1/1	R/1	0	0	0	0	0	0	0	0	0	E/1	3.0
3. Locomotion	I/1	0	0	0	0	0	0	0	0	0	0	0	E/.2	1.2
4. Insects	0	0	0	0	0	I/1	0	0	0	0	0	0	0	1.0
5. Magnetism	0	I/1	R/1	E/1	0	0	E/1	0	0	R/1	0	R/.5	E/.2	5.7
6. Weather	I/1.5	0	0	E/1	0	0	0	0	E/.5	0	0	0	0	2.0
7. Kinetics	0	0	0	0	0	0	0	0	0	0	0	I/2	E/1	3.0
8. Temperature	I/1.5	R/1	R/1	0	0	0	0	E/.5	0	0	0	0	0	3.0
9. Nutrition	I/1.5	0	0	0	R/1	R/1	0	E/.5	0	0	E/2	0	0	5.0
10. Sex differences	I/1.1	0	0	0	0	0	0	0	0	0	E/2	0	0	2.1
11. Ecology	I/1.1	R/.1	R/.1	R/.1	R/1	0	0	0	0	0	0	0	0	2.4
12. Solar system	0	I/1	R/1	E/1	E/1	0	0	0	E/1	0	0	0	0	5.0
13. Gravity	0	0	0	I/1	0	0	0	0	0	0	0	0	E/.1	1.1
14. Radioactive dating	0	0	0	0	0	0	0	0	I/.5	0	0	0	E/.1	.6
15. Volume and mass	0	0	0	0	0	0	0	0	0	I/2	0	0	0	2.0
16. Bonding	0	0	0	0	0	0	0	0	0	0	0	0	I/.1	.1
17. Human body	0	0	0	0	0	I/1	E/1	E/1	0	0	E/2	0	0	5.0
18. Cells	0	0	0	0	0	I/.1	E/.2	E/.5	0	0	E/.5	0	0	1.3
18. Plants	0	0	0	R/1	0	R/1	E/1	0	0	0	0	0	0	3.0
20. Tobacco and drugs	0	0	0	0	0	0	0	E/1	0	0	0	0	0	1.0
21. Atom	0	0	0	0	0	0	0	0	0	I/1	0	0	I/.2	1.2
22. Friction	0	0	0	0	0	0	0	0	I/1	0	0	0	E/.1	1.1
23. Optical Illusions	0	0	0	0	0	0	0	0	0	0	0	0	0	0
24. Waves	0	0	0	0	I/.2	0	0	0	E/.5	0	0	0	R/.1	.8
25. Quantum theory	0	0	0	0	0	0	0	0	0	0	0	0	I/1	1.0
TOTAL TIME BY GRADE	8.7	4.1	4.1	5.1	3.2	4.1	3.2	3.5	3.5	4.0	6.5	2.5	4.1	

Legend: I=introduced; R=reinforced; E=expanded
Time Delineation: number equals hours per week per semester
Source: English (1980). Reprinted by permission of the Association for Supervision and Curriculum Development and Fenwick W. English.

ultimate audiences and uses of an assessment. Table 5, devised by Carr and Harris, shows the sorts of questions appropriate to assessments that include data on students, teachers, and programs. Carr and Harris distinguish the questions by three topics:

- *Inputs*—How available are resources for instruction—texts, supplies?
- *Process*—What is the nature of instruction in each particular area?
- *Outcome*—What are the results of instruction?

Using curriculum guidelines, the planning team can form assessment questions that bring out the inputs, processes, and outcomes in any area of the curriculum.

The next step is to determine what data would best answer each question. The available options may not be adequate to answer a question, so information will need to be gathered to fill in gaps. Generally, information is available from:

- standardized tests
- school-developed tests
- portfolios of student work
- observations
- interviews
- questionnaires
- reviews of records

These sources, say Carr and Harris, can provide the following sorts of information on inputs, processes, and outcomes of the instructional program:

- *Inputs*—supplies/equipment, time, teacher preparation, staffing, student/staff ratio, policies/procedures
- *Processes*—uses of supplies/equipment, uses of time, instructional activities, implementation of policies/procedures, classroom teaching/learning techniques
- *Outcomes*—individual achievement scores, group scores, student attitudes (toward self, learning, school, subjects), student attributes and behaviors, long-term outcomes (job readiness, for instance)

Carr and Harris remind us that assessment is not simply a review of outcomes, but a full understanding of resources and processes, as well. Instructional leadership again can be seen in terms of "generative learning," in Senge's phrase, that is, as opportunities for seeing whole systems that contribute to making the school what it is and that could be used in changing it into what it could be.

TABLE 5

Curricular and Instructional Assessment: A Relational Model

	Inputs	Processes	Outcomes
Student	Is the curriculum available to students? (texts, facilities, schedule, etc.)	Are learning experiences matched to the student and the tasks at hand? (learning styles, diagnostic assessment, etc.)	Is the student learning at an the acceptable rate? Is the assessment of performance based on goals? (knowledge, skills, attitudes, appreciation)
Teacher	Does instructional planning match the curriculum? (time allocation, selection of materials, staff development, etc.)	Do instructional strategies match the students and the task at hand? (management, methods, assessment)	Does the teacher's instruction lead to changes in student performance? (Formative) Is the teacher's level of performance acceptable? (Summative)
Program	Does the allocation of time, people, and resources match the curriculum? (budget, staffing, master schedule, etc.)	Do teaching strategies and learning activities match the curriculum? (time on task, interaction analysis, etc.)	Are the goals of the curriculum being reached? (Formative) Are they the right goals? (Summative)

Source: Carr and Harris (1993). Reprinted by permission of Allyn and Bacon.

Conclusion

An emerging model of instructional leadership includes both the traditional officers on deck—the administrators who have usually been responsible for leading the instructional program—and the faculty. It is a model in which leaders empower others to be leaders, as well. The structure of that leadership depends on the best configuration to achieve a learning organization—collaboratively managed, self-evaluating, and actively self-improving. Such instructional leadership has variously been called shared, cooperative, collaborative, or facilitative. It has been compared to a community of commonly directed professionals.

On the whole, the idea is of a distributed network of leaders within a school, leaders who share responsibility for conceiving, evaluating, and improving the instructional program. Their work as leaders encompasses the five major areas needing instructional leadership: defining the school's mission, managing curriculum and instruction, promoting a positive learning climate, observing teachers, and assessing the school's instructional program. Ideally, a network of leaders can cover these leadership areas more effectively than a single leader who is responsible for an entire school or department. Problems can often be raised and addressed by the same people, rather than the only alternative being to pass them on to a hierarchy of problem-solvers.

In a time of diminishing resources, rising expectations, and multiplying problems, this general approach to leadership may be unavoidable. Principals who resist sharing leadership with qualified, interested faculty may be missing the opportunity to tap into veins of professional expertise and commitment in their schools. No matter how high a profile the principal cuts in a school, it is difficult for his or her influence to be felt directly in the classroom.

A practical role for a principal may be as an agent of instructional support, a court of appeal, and an overseer of support functions. The roles for faculty appear to be varied—as originators and testers of ideas, as collaborators and assessors in building and renewing programs. Such leadership may mean involving a whole school—administrators, teachers, and students—in a pursuit of excellence in learning, a pursuit that can be contagious.

CHAPTER

11

Leading the Instructional Staff

Larry Nyland

"School improvement is first and foremost people improvement."
— Dennis Sparks and Stephanie Hirsh

School leaders increase student learning by encouraging teacher growth. Administrators who invest time, expertise, and energy in staff members increase staff capacity and thus improve student learning. Working with staff to obtain these results takes skill and patience. Administrators and teachers also must assume unfamiliar roles.

Over time, the concept of school leadership has changed. Two major shifts in how school leadership is exercised are noted by Ann Lieberman and Lynne Miller. In the first shift, school leaders moved from positional authority to instructional leadership. In the second, leaders moved from instructional leadership to capacity-building. Positional leaders use their authority to direct the instructional staff. Instructional leaders take bold actions, build coalitions, and obtain short-term results. Capacity-builders collaborate with staff, build people, assist in solving problems, and, working collaboratively with staff, achieve long-term results.

Needed today are leaders who encourage teacher growth in a community of learning. The National Staff Development Council defines *learning communities* as environments in which "all students and staff members are learners who continually improve their performance."

This chapter highlights four key elements of effective learning communities: collaborative goal-setting, professional development, teacher assessment, and sound personnel practices. Each section provides information on best practices and offers suggestions to administrators on building the capacity of staff.

Collaborative Goal-Setting

Goal-setting is one of the most effective pathways to the destination of improved performance. In a review of thousands of studies, Edwin Locke and others found that goal-setting increases performance when:

- goals are specific and understood
- goals are challenging but attainable
- employees have ability
- regular feedback is provided to show progress relative to the goal
- incentives are given for attainment
- the leader is supportive
- goals are accepted and valued by employees
- employees are confident of success

Goals improve performance by directing staff attention, mobilizing efforts to improve, increasing persistence, and encouraging the development of new strategies (Locke and others). According to Beverly Showers and others, "social cohesion and shared understanding" increase teachers' willingness to try new ideas.

Three types of goals work in concert to improve student learning: organizational goals, individual goals, and system goals. Organizational goals provide overall direction. Individual goals align individual efforts with the direction of the organization. System goals ensure various parts of the organization work together. Next, each type of goal is considered in detail.

Organizational Goals

One of the most popular ways of establishing organizational goals is through strategic planning. The process of strategic planning calls for the shared development of vision; mission; values, expectations, and beliefs; objectives; action plans; and performance outcomes.

Vision: The purpose of the school is stated briefly and memorably (in ten to fifteen words), repeated often, and practiced consistently.

Mission: A longer (up to half page) statement provides additional detail on how the school vision will be achieved.

Values, Expectations, Beliefs: Ten to twelve statements describe how people in the organization agree to treat each other. When statements have high internal agreement and are supported by the research, they become a permanent part of the school culture.

Objectives: Strategic objectives expand on the elements in the mission that describe how the vision will be achieved. Usually objectives take three to five years to accomplish and may remain permanent elements of the organization. Examples of objectives might be "To create a culture of continuous improvement" or "To increase parent involvement."

Action Plans: These are tactics that contribute to the success of the strategic objectives. An example of an action plan might be "To have 80 percent participation in a staff development program on shared decision-making" followed by the details of who will do what by when.

Performance Outcomes: In addition to the elements above, many experts advocate describing the skills students will actually be able to perform. Often envisioning outcomes helps to refine the intervening objectives and action steps.

The clarity of focus that comes from well-defined organizational goals is the first and most important principle for increasing student learning, according to William Spady. Of course, organizational goals alone are not sufficient to produce enhanced student learning. In many organizations strategic planning stalls for two reasons: individual goals or system goals needed to support the strategic plan are lacking.

Individual Goals

Focusing on organizational goals alone may fail to increase performance because individuals do not know what is expected of them. Gary Latham contends that organizations need to "identify critical behaviors within the control of the individual that will affect the desired outcomes." Individuals need to be aware of what behaviors to start, stop, or continue.

When goals are too general, individuals may fail to take personal responsibility. On the other hand, goals that are too specific often encourage activity for activity's sake. Organizational goals need to be clearly defined and understood by everyone. Instructional leaders who wish to take a direct approach might:

- model the new skill
- describe the new skill by telling what it is and what it is not
- develop a description (rubric) of the different stages of skill application
- assist each staff member in developing behavioral objectives for his or her performance

The capacity-builder works diligently with staff to ensure that organizational goals are shared and understood. Individual goals then are either selected jointly by the principal and the teacher or are self-selected by teachers actively engaged in professional decision-making aimed at achieving organizational goals.

System Goals

Individual staff members can only do so much—even when their individual goals are aligned with collaborative organizational goals. Even strong teachers are less successful in a nonsupportive culture. Consciously looking for the built-in systemic barriers to improvement—and then removing them—is one of the best ways to ensure that the system is supporting, rather than preventing, improvement.

Integrating and aligning goals increases the likelihood that the goals will be attained. Dennis Sparks suggests that goals, curriculum, instruction, assessment, staff development, and evaluation each be aligned around the vision of increased student performance. School improvement needs to be viewed as a long-term, multiyear process. Long-term goals need to be balanced with intermediate goals and timelines that can be celebrated along the way.

Goals are integral to increasing school and staff performance. Capacity-builders clarify and align goals. Only when leaders and staff members work together to create a system of interconnected elements that reinforce one another will more students learn better. The next section provides information on skill development and conditions that contribute to goal attainment.

Professional Development

Instructional leaders cannot become capacity-builders independently. Capacity-building increases the ability of the staff by increasing the number of teacher leaders in the building. Capacity-building requires a shift in focus from one-shot training to an ongoing, comprehensive program focused on continuous improvement of professional skills and organizational outcomes, all related to the goals and purpose of the school.

This section addresses three essential elements of professional development: collaboration, best practice, and teacher leadership. Collaboration and trust prepare staff to take the risks needed to improve performance. Focusing on best practice increases the likelihood of success. Finally, teacher leadership engages teachers in reflection on their performance, which can lead to increased student learning.

Collaborative Climate

When people work together, coordinating their efforts, they accomplish more than they could achieve alone. In schools, "collaborative norms enable teachers to request and offer advice and assistance in helping their colleagues improve," writes Susan Rosenholtz.

Initially, the school leader maintains primary responsibility for creating a collaborative climate. Over time, however, self-directed teams should gradually assume responsibility for creating the trust and collaboration needed to support high levels of performance.

Needed is a culture that supports both collaboration and continuous school improvement. Jon Saphier and Matthew King suggest that a culture that supports school improvement can be fostered through collegiality, experimentation, high expectations, trust, confidence, tangible support, appreciation and recognition, and involvement in decision-making.

Best Practice

Clear goals and a collaborative climate are necessary but not sufficient to increase student performance. Knowledge of best practices helps ensure that a selected course of action will make a positive difference for students.

At least four steps can be taken to ensure that the staff's efforts will have the greatest positive impact on performance. First, examine the research base to see if the innovation being considered is likely to improve student learning or to meet one of the strategic objectives of your school. One useful source is *Research on School Improvement* by Art Ellis and Jeffrey Fouts. Another good source is *Effective Teaching: Current Research* by Hersholt Waxman and Herbert Walberg.

Second, consider the underlying assumptions and values of the innovation to ensure that they are consistent with the vision and goals of the district and the school. For example, if a school has already invested heavily in ITIP (Instructional Theory Into Practice) and is now considering cooperative learning, make sure that the values of the two programs are compatible. Work by Thomas Guskey indicates that unless staff members clearly see the connection between innovations, they will abandon the older innovation in favor of the more recent innovation.

Third, network with those already implementing the same innovation. Conferences, publications, formal networks, and telephone surveys are all ways of learning more about what others are doing. After identifying schools that have incorporated the innovation, consider sending a team for a field visit. If possible, meet with one school that is in the early stages of implementation as well as one where the innovation has been fully implemented. Decide beforehand which questions to ask. Meet with a variety of people—parents, students, teachers—not just administrators. Ask what they learned, what they would and would not do again if they could start over. Sending a team models collaborative learning, provides more information on which to base a decision, and broadens ownership of the eventual decision.

Finally, the fourth way to increase the likelihood of successful implementation is to adapt the selected innovation through a program of action research. Action research includes nearly all the steps outlined in this chapter: goal setting, selection of best practices, gathering data, evaluating data, and then repeating the cycle based on what has been learned. One central tenet of action research is triangulation of data, that is, use of at least three data sources. Triangulation allows for use of traditional measures like test scores, inclusion of a variety of other measures of student performance, and consideration of more subjective data, such as staff members' feelings about the implementation process.

Innovations will have a better chance of succeeding if they are supported by research and are aligned with the school's vision. Networking with other schools that have implemented the innovation and using action research to adapt the innovation to meet the specific needs of a particular school can also increase the probability of successful implementation. The remainder of this section offers a brief overview of research findings that are relevant to improving student learning.

Effective Teaching and Learning

The research on effective teaching identifies specific teaching skills that seem to promote learning. The research on student learning examines how it is affected by teacher decision-making.

Teacher-effects research outlines specific classroom strategies used by effective teachers—the ones who see the most student growth on standardized test scores. Thomas Good and Mary McCaslin identify seven characteristics of effective teaching:

1. appropriate expectations
2. classroom management and organization
3. increased opportunity to learn
4. brisk pacing of curriculum
5. direct instruction
6. practice and application
7. supportive learning environment

Earlier, Benjamin Bloom (1984) argued that using multiple strategies can make group instruction as effective as individual tutoring. Advocates of a skill-based approach argue that investing in a multiyear program to build applicable skills is worthwhile. Doing so requires long-term commitment to ensure that the skills are effective and are used in the classroom. But critics point out that the research findings are merely correlational—that is, teachers who achieve good results use these skills. They contend that it is unclear whether other teachers can obtain equally good results if they employ these skills or if something not measured—for example, the way teachers make decisions on which skills to use—is responsible for student gains.

Another approach to making teaching more effective—improving the way teachers make decisions—is based on learning theory. Some researchers examine large chunks of classroom time to gain insight into the processes of cause and effect. What did the teacher do and why? How did it affect student learning and understanding? Learning, more than knowing, is the focus of this relatively new area.

Leaders should be familiar with the teacher-effects research and encourage teachers to become fluent in learning new skills. To build teacher effectiveness in decision-making, leaders can encourage teachers to reflect on and examine their own practices, either individually or in teams.

All these actions presuppose schoolwide adoption of best practices. Given teachers' history of functioning as independent practitioners, however, achieving this level of adoption can be challenging. As we move toward increased accountability for student performance, schoolwide implementation can help those involved to stick with practices long enough to learn new skills, reinforce learning methods for students, and learn what works and what doesn't. The following section provides more information on effective processes for delivering professional development.

Application of Learning

Simply providing staff development is no longer enough; these activities must have a meaningful impact on teaching and learning. This emphasis on outcomes requires increased teacher engagement and application of new concepts in the classroom. Furthermore, teachers must become leaders, actively making decisions about what will have the greatest impact on student learning in the classroom.

Objectives

What is to be accomplished determines how the objective is achieved. In *Planning for Effective Staff Development*, Meredith Gall and Roseanne Vojtek list eight types of staff development objectives. Five are teacher-centered objectives: knowledge, attitude, classroom skills, decision-making skills, and specialized role skills. There are also student-centered objectives, curriculum-centered objectives, and school-improvement-centered objectives. "When analyzing a staff development program, you should focus on determining its immediate objectives and the likelihood that they will be achieved," suggest Gall and Vojtek.

Processes

Adult learners, according to Janet Moore, learn best when they can direct their own learning, be actively involved in the learning process, collaborate with others, and see practical applications for what they are learning. In addition, effective professional development should take into consideration an understanding of systems and change theory, student outcome data, and the need for followup to ensure improvement (National Staff Development Council). Adult learners need time to think about and process new information.

Application

Teachers must teach well if all students are to learn well. Creating an organization of continuous learners who act on best knowledge and apply what they know requires attention to five elements of staff development identified by Bruce Joyce and Beverly Showers:

- *Theory*—Individuals need to know why they are doing what they're doing. Without an understanding of theory, people give up more quickly when they encounter problems.

- *Modeling*—It is useful to know what the innovation looks like in practice. It can be beneficial to see examples, role playing, and different modes of instruction. Teachers should envision themselves performing in new and successful ways.

- *Simulated Practice*—Opportunities to practice new techniques in small groups greatly improve implementation in the classroom.

- *Classroom Practice and Feedback*—New knowledge and skills must be applied in the classroom. Feedback through reflection, team discussion, peer observation, or other avenues is also important.

- *Qualitative Coaching*—Finally, positive and corrective feedback is important. "Coaching" can come from peers, trainers, or other expert practitioners.

When teachers assess their own performance, the standard should be whether all students are learning well. If they are not, then teachers must ask themselves what they can do to better serve students.

Stages of Professional Development

Seeking and applying practices that result in improved student learning involve several steps. First, identify effective practices in the research and prepare for schoolwide adoption. Second, build capacity by selecting inhouse experts. Third, train inhouse teacher experts to become trainers and facilitators among building staff. Fourth, provide training in small, timely increments, demonstrate techniques, and apply them immediately in the classroom. Fifth, create teacher teams to provide support, encouragement, and accountability in implementing and applying training. Sixth, consider a portfolio process that recognizes teacher leaders who continually learn new ways to increase student learning.

In conclusion, professional development requires establishing a collaborative culture of trust and continuous improvement, seeking out best practices in teaching and learning, and applying concepts in the classroom, where teachers can learn from their own decision-making. Doing so will increase the pool of teacher experts and teacher leaders, thus enhancing the capacity of the professional staff.

The next section examines the third essential ingredient for leading the professional staff—teacher assessment.

Teacher Assessment

Teacher assessment can build the capacity of teachers by encouraging professional growth. The two main types of teacher assessment are *formative* measures designed for teacher growth and school improvement and *summative* measures designed to increase accountability and student learning. Both forms of assessment focus not only on what teachers teach but on what students learn.

Shifts in Thinking About Evaluation

Effective evaluation of teachers involves five shifts in thinking, the first four of which are identified by Robert Starratt in his article "After Supervision."

1. Who does evaluation? *A shift from administrator to self-directed evaluation.* Historically, evaluation has been considered the responsibility of the supervisor, but in recent years many schools have been moving toward collaboration and partnership. Peer evaluation, self-evaluation, and portfolios, for example, give teachers a greater sense of ownership, involvement, and control over the evaluation process.

2. What should be evaluated? *A shift from summative to formative evaluation. A shift from knowing to reflective learning.* For the past two decades it has been the norm for principals to assess teachers on the basis of checklists of teacher traits. Some principals have shifted to characteristics of effective teaching or skill sets such as ITIP, TESA, or mastery learning.

Although such checklists have some value, especially for new teachers, it is essential to move beyond a deficit-skill model to a more reflective understanding of how teacher decision-making in the classroom improves student learning.

3. What is the focus of evaluation? *A shift from isolated pieces of learning to an understanding of learning systems.* Traditionally, the classroom has been considered the hub of learning and individual lessons the focus of observation. A larger "systems view" looks beyond the individual lessons to try to understand how student learning occurs and how teachers can improve their decision-making about student learning.

4. How should evaluation be conducted? *A shift from single measures and methods to multiple measures and methods.* "One size fits all" policies on teacher evaluation are prevalent in schools today. The stages of adult learning, however, suggest that beginning teachers and more experienced teachers benefit from different evaluation systems. New teachers, for example, generally need specific instruction and opportunities to ask questions, whereas veteran teachers are often open to alternative approaches, problem-solving, and application.

Finally, the issue of time should not be overlooked.

5. How important is evaluation? *A shift from management to learner-focused leadership.* Principals let others know what they value by how they spend their time. Strong instructional leaders spend 41 percent of their time involved in educational program improvement, whereas average principals spend only 27 percent of their time on this activity, according to Wilma Smith and Richard Andrews.

Capacity-builders apply adult-learning theory to engage teachers in their own professional growth. In restructured schools, states Linda Darling-Hammond, "teachers will be responsible for students, not just subject matter information, for understanding how learning is occurring, and for having tools to assess how students learn and think as well as what they know."

Evaluation Options

Many states still require traditional checklists and other summative-evaluation models that tally specific teacher traits or behaviors. Growing in favor with many educators, however, are evaluation systems that rely on more formative, self-directed processes.

Summative Evaluation

Summative evaluations usually require supervisors to rate teachers against a fixed scale of traits, standards, or behaviors. Usually, the purpose is to assess competency and ensure accountability. Summative measures can be quicker, more objective, and easier to use than other evaluation processes. They are not, however, likely to change teacher behavior. According to Thomas McGreal, difficulties with summative evaluations include low teacher involvement, a focus on minimum standards, minimal time investment, and a poor teacher attitude toward summative evaluation. Because the results are final, teachers often feel that they can't do much about improvement.

Formative Evaluation

Most researchers now urge the addition of or transition to a more formative approach to evaluation. Some believe summative and formative approaches can be blended. Others, like Daniel Duke, call for a clear separation between summative evaluation for accountability purposes and formative, growth-oriented supervision for developmental purposes. Still others, like Starratt, argue for the abolition of supervision because it is counterproductive as currently practiced. As Susan Black notes, administrators must decide whether they want others to see them as the "sole authorities on teacher effectiveness" or as "mentors, coaches, and helpers."

Outlined below are several formative elements administrators may want to add to their existing evaluation repertoire.

Clinical Supervision

Clinical supervision, as conceived by Goldhammer and Cogan, is a collegial process that emphasizes data collection and feedback and focuses on improvement of instruction. Carl Glickman describes the clinical-supervision model as including a preconference with the teacher, classroom observation, data analysis, a postobservation conference with the teacher, and postconference analysis. During the preconference, the teacher and supervisor reach agreement on the purposes, methods, and time of the observation. The supervisor observes the classroom to gather objective data related to the agreed-on purposes and then tabulates and analyzes the data. The postobservation conference provides time for discussion of the data and reflection on next steps.

"Thinking," according to Glickman, "improves when people interact with each other, when they break routine by experimenting, when they observe others at work, and when they assess and revise their own options." The goal in clinical supervision is to think together as partners, with the teacher becoming the ultimate decision-maker. The supervisor can facilitate this process by making every effort to build collaboration and trust. Take accurate, objective notes that can be examined with the observed teacher. Avoid the temptation to be directive or offer suggestions.

Collaborative Goal-Setting

Clear goals go a long way toward improving performance. Over time, there has been a shift from supervisor-initiated goals to jointly initiated goals to teacher-initiated goals. The goal-based approach, according to McGreal, reduces stress and enhances teacher professionalism. Edward Iwanicki reports that goal-based evaluation promotes growth, corrects weaknesses, enhances strengths, meets the unique needs of each teacher, and integrates individual and school goals.

Weaknesses of the goal-setting approach, according to Iwanicki, are the time and paperwork required. Recent legislation in the state of Washington addresses the time problem by allowing experienced teachers to participate in a "professional growth option" once every three years. During a teacher's year of growth the supervisor is able to spend more time with the individual for evaluation.

Portfolios

Some teachers and supervisors are pioneering the use of portfolios as a tool for professional development. Portfolios provide opportunity for reflection, analysis, and teacher-directed learning. To make the best use of portfolios, give consideration to purpose, format, and implementation. Mary Dietz identifies four basic types of professional portfolios:

- *Presentation Portfolios* represent "accomplishments, learnings, strengths and expertise."
- *Working Portfolios* provide evidence that "fulfills prescribed competencies, standards, or outcomes."
- *Learner Portfolios* provide a framework on which to "focus learning, collect evidence and describe learning outcomes."
- *Professional Development Portfolios* combine elements of the working portfolios and the learner portfolios to create a "framework for facilitating professional development goals."

Avoid making the portfolio format too prescriptive or too open-ended. Being unnecessarily prescriptive dampens the learning process; being too open-ended wastes precious time in setting direction.

These features should be considered prior to deciding what to include in the portfolio process:

1. *Philosophy*—values and principles that are important to the teacher

2. *Purpose/Focus*—explanation of the project and why it is being undertaken
3. *Process*—methods of learning to be used
4. *Outcomes*—exhibits of learning accompanied by explanations of what has been learned

When implementing the use of portfolios, start small. Don't get caught in an activity trap. The National Board for Professional Teaching Standards advises teachers to focus on one class for a three-week period: videotape lessons, keep samples of student work, and reflect on the experience. Use portfolios initially only for professional growth. Later, after refining the process, portfolios may be incorporated into the teacher-evaluation process.

Peer Assessment

Peer supervision, more than most other forms of evaluation, symbolizes the shift to teacher leadership and team learning. Peer evaluations can be as objective as evaluations conducted by supervisors, but colleagues may have to invest considerable time to develop trust, "address process concerns, and explore learning possibilities," says Elizabeth Walen. Peer supervision frees up principal time, provides teachers with current practitioner feedback, and, according to Marjorie Hanson, improves teachers' attitudes.

Peer assessment can be modified to fit individual needs. Use a team approach, including two teachers who will observe and evaluate each other. Encourage teachers to work in groups on action-research projects. Or combine peer-assessment data with other information, such as student achievement data, student ratings of teacher performance, or self-evaluations.

"Implementation of a collegial model will be time consuming but ultimately worthwhile," says Donald Haefele, because it is better than the "traditional deficit model of teacher evaluation in which principals judge teachers' faults."

Artistic Supervision

Artistic supervision promotes growth by helping teachers reflect on their decision-making processes. This approach looks at learning as a whole rather than breaking teaching down into its component parts. Case studies, profiles, ethnographic studies, and reflective supervision are recent examples of artistic supervision. By extension, reflective journals, action-research projects, portfolios, self-evaluations, or even clinical-supervision models can incorporate elements that encourage professional growth through a process whereby the teacher and supervisor reflect together on teacher decision-making and student learning. Regardless of method, the goal is for teachers to better understand the relationship between teaching and learning and, as a result, make better decisions about how to foster student learning.

Differentiated Supervision

Differentiated supervision uses different supervision methods to meet the variable needs of teachers. Differentiated supervision can include any of the supervision methods mentioned in this section. Pam Robbins and Harvey Alvy recommend consideration of cognitive coaching, videotaped lessons, drop-in visits, artifacts, reflective journals, and action-research projects. Beginning teachers, according to Allan Glatthorn, benefit more from direct supervision, whereas experienced staff can be more self-directed.

Student Performance

Noting that "most teacher evaluation does not examine what students actually learn from the teacher," John McMurtry recommends that teachers' effectiveness be evaluated through performance appraisals written by students. Calls from the public for accountability have encouraged merit-pay plans and other evaluations based on how well students perform. Oregon requires evidence of student learning for teacher certification while South Carolina, Arizona, and Utah require student-achievement data to be included as a part of teacher evaluations.

Despite problems of controlling for class size, readiness to learn, and other variables, teachers and school leaders may be called upon to provide evidence of what students have actually learned.

Principles

Teacher evaluation poses a dilemma for school administrators, who must encourage thoughtful reflection by staff while concurrently delivering concrete student-learning results to the public. When developing an evaluation system, it may be helpful to keep the following principles in mind:

- Make teacher assessment and student learning a priority—spend time on it.
- Develop a shared understanding of the purposes, objectives, expectations, and processes of your evaluation system.
- Build a climate of trust, growth, and risk-taking.

- Use multiple data sources, including student learning.
- Provide prompt, specific feedback.
- Facilitate continuous teacher growth.
- Recognize and involve teachers as leaders and experts.
- Support self-directed reflection and decision-making.
- Recognize different supervision needs—use differentiated supervision approaches.
- Apply what is known about adult learners.

In summary, this section outlined the need for school leaders to become reflective practitioners—to consider the evaluation targets, measures, and processes most likely to generate increased student learning. Teacher assessment for teacher growth is the third essential ingredient for building the capacity of the instructional staff.

Goals, professional development, and evaluation work together to create a system of learning that pays dividends for staff and students. Each step informs the others and requires constant assessment and adjustment by the leader working together with the professional staff. The final section in this chapter turns from leadership to the logistics of managing basic personnel functions.

Personnel Practices

Leading and developing the capacity of the professional staff is more than goals, professional development, and teacher assessment. The tasks of recruiting, interviewing, selecting, inducting, and mentoring new staff members together with the potential of remediating and/or dismissing those who fail to perform up to standards determine to a large extent the quality of the professional team that exists in a particular school. These actions, while not sufficient alone to build a high-performing professional staff, are necessary if the goal of improving student learning is to be met.*

Recruiting Teachers

Recruiting and selecting teachers are two of the most important tasks that school administrators face. Each time a new teacher is hired, there is an opportunity to improve the instructional program. Likewise, if teacher selection is mishandled, there can be costly, long-term consequences. Re-

* This section is a condensed and revised version of "Leading the Instructional Staff," by Mary Cihak Jensen, which appeared in this book's second edition.

cruiting involves much more than simply posting employment-opportunity notices.

As competition for quality candidates increases, administrators seek quantity, quality, and speed in gaining an edge on selecting the best candidates. The quantity of applicants can be increased by streamlining the application process, updating application packets, and attending job fairs.

Mark Anderson, assistant superintendent for human resources in Spokane, Washington, enlists "district ambassadors" to recommend and recruit promising candidates. The quality of applicants can also be improved by getting referrals from professors who prepare teachers, contacting previous applicants who looked promising, and interviewing excellent substitute teachers. Some districts encourage ample notice of retirement and aggressively push the timelines for posting, closing, and interviewing. These strategies help administrators to tap the job market while the best candidates are still available. Using an "open until filled" posting can also help expand the pool of candidates.

Hiring credentialed minority teachers has become more difficult as the number of minorities entering the field of education has decreased. Short-term efforts to increase minority hiring can include expanding the geographic scope of the search and starting recruiting efforts. Unfortunately, neither of these efforts increases the pool of minority candidates.

One way to increase the pool of capable minority candidates is to promote from within. Seattle Public Schools, for example, partnered with Seattle Pacific University to provide a two-year preservice teacher-certification program for minority paraprofessionals already employed by the district.

Selecting Teachers

School districts do not always select the best teachers. Larry Frase suggests that "if hiring the best teachers is the top priority, teaching must be the focus" of the selection process. Finding the best candidates requires a comprehensive process that includes an analysis of position needs, careful screening of application materials, structured interviews, a review of candidates' work, and a final decision and an offer. Each step is reviewed in greater detail below.

Position Requirements

To find the right person for the job, administrators must know what they are looking for. Therefore, carefully considering the skills required to do the job should be the first step in selecting the best candidate.

Dale Bolton suggests that it is wise to distinguish between the characteristics that can be acquired through training and those that cannot. For example, an administrator may decide to hire "teachers who like students and can work well on teams," because these qualities are difficult to impart through training. Or a decision might be made to pass over the person trained in a specific innovation in favor of the candidate who is a quick learner, who can be trained for the current innovation as well as future innovations.

Careful discussions of job requirements with those who will work with the person who fills the position or who have held the position before can help determine job criteria. These criteria, in turn, should become the basis for interview questions and selection decisions.

Paper Screening

Applications should be screened to sort out candidates who meet the criteria from those who don't. Clerical staff can screen out those with incomplete applications and those who do not meet minimum required levels of experience. The interview team can complete the next round of screening with a score sheet based on the job criteria. They may consider qualifications such as grade-point average, work samples, experience, and letters of recommendation. This step can also be done independently by tabulating ratings after all team members have completed their screening.

The Interview

Although the interview is the most common selection technique used in the hiring process, Terry Caldwell found that interviews are often too unstructured and inconsistent to provide an accurate measure of a teacher's competence. To get the most value from the interview, focus on the job criteria, select interview questions in advance, use and train an interview team, and ask probing questions. Structured interviews with written questions related to each of the job criteria ensure fair, consistent interviews that focus on the most important criteria. Using an interview team provides a broader perspective and lessens the likelihood of bias or favoritism.

Meet beforehand with the interview team to clarify the job criteria, go over the questions, decide who will ask the questions, review the rating scales, and talk about the process. After general questions to put the candidate at ease, follow with open-ended questions that will challenge and stretch the candidate.

Finally, telling the candidate what to expect before and after the interview is a courtesy that makes the interview go more smoothly. Ensuring a good interview experience may determine whether the top candidate accepts your offer.

Teaching Skills

Districts that want to hire the best teachers ask candidates to demonstrate their teaching skills by teaching a sample lesson, providing a video sample, or designing a written lesson. Some districts ask candidates to provide portfolios of their work and/or samples of their students' work. Writing samples can be used to assess the candidate's philosophy, knowledge of content or pedagogy, handwriting, or problem-solving ability. Finally, the Teacher Perceiver instrument measures teachers' empathy for students and can help screen out candidates who dislike students.

References

None of the above—applications, writing samples, grade-point average, interviews, portfolios—provides assurance that the candidate can teach well. Talking with applicants' references, while also not a guarantee, can give employers a better idea of whether the person is an effective teacher. If this step is passed, schools and districts run the risk of "negligent hiring"—hiring someone who has a history of poor evaluations, criminal convictions, or student-abuse allegations.

Always contact previous supervisors, even if they are not listed as references. As in the interview, ask each reference a similar set of job-related questions. Two useful questions to include are "Would you hire this teacher again?" and "Who else can tell me about the work of this teacher?"

The Decision

Finally, the process is complete; interviews, work samples, and references have been rated. If the process was initiated at the building level, the district personnel office will likely want final approval. If it was conducted at the district level, the building will want to be involved in the final decision-making process. Keep in mind during the selection process that even if the individual is being hired for a specific building he or she will probably remain in the district for many years and therefore need to fit well in any school in the district.

Use caution in the final notification. Make sure the top candidate has accepted the position before notifying the other candidates. When the other candidates are informed, they should be thanked for their interest in the district and invited to apply for other positions in the future.

In summary, selecting the best candidate is not easy. Design the selection process carefully and follow up to see how the new employee is performing on the job. Use what is learned to improve the selection process.

Inducting Teachers

Nearly 35 percent of new teachers nationwide leave teaching after three years. Jensen suggests that many of the most capable teachers are among those who choose to leave the profession. According to Phillip Schlechty, new teachers often need help in two areas: learning the school culture and refining their job skills.

School Culture

The first year for new teachers is often traumatic. New teachers are most likely to experience difficulties in the areas of discipline and classroom management. Often, new teachers are given teaching assignments equal to or more difficult than those assigned to veteran staff members. Beginning teachers will learn to teach more effectively, according to Leslie Huling-Austin, if their teaching loads are lighter and if they are provided with opportunities to teach the same content.

Without assistance, new teachers must learn exclusively through trial and error. Two barriers inhibit open communication: newcomers are often reluctant to ask for help, and experienced teachers are hesitant to interfere. Principals can help new teachers survive the first few years successfully by providing support, feedback, and assistance.

Job Skills

Districts with induction programs often use one or more of three formats to support new teachers: mentor teachers, increased supervision and training, and support groups.

Mentor Teachers—Mentors can assist new teachers in their instructional skills as well as in learning the school culture. Gary DeBolt found that effective mentors need to possess professional skills and commitment, communication skills, and organizational skills. In addition, mentors need training in how to provide support, encouragement, feedback, and problem-solving assistance to new teachers.

Supervision and Coaching—Increased supervision during the first year of teaching can reinforce strengths and address weaknesses. However, supervisors must emphasize collegiality and formative supervision with new teachers. Otherwise, increased supervision during the first year may provoke anxiety rather than encourage new teachers.

To reduce anxiety and emphasize support, some districts separate supervision from coaching by assigning the induction process to the staff development department. One large suburban district assigns all teachers new to the district to a staff development specialist who becomes their "coach." Coaches provide support, individualized staff development plans, classroom observation and feedback, demonstration teaching, team teaching, and joint observations of other teachers.

Inservice Training—Many districts offer formal workshops to new teachers during their first year. Topics often address common needs and concerns of first-year teachers. Jensen emphasizes the importance of making the most of teachers' time by addressing the most pressing needs first and providing them with release time.

Support Groups—Support groups can help new teachers address the disillusionment that accompanies entry into any organization. Building informal district programs around the expressed needs of staff members is one of the best ways to meet newcomers' needs. Providing supportive relationships with other teachers and administrators is also helpful.

William Bridges suggests that all transitions include endings, a neutral zone, and then new beginnings. Giving teachers time to talk about their "endings" can help them make the transition to a successful beginning in a new school.

Correcting Problem Behavior

Most staff members work hard, do their best, and are open to suggestions for improvement. Goals, professional development, evaluation, and personnel actions need to emphasize ongoing improvement. Building systems around minimum expectations discourages and demoralizes the top performers. Ignoring problem behavior can lower the morale of those who are trying hard to perform. This section outlines four strategies for correcting problem behavior: interventions, discipline without punishment, investigations, and progressive discipline.

Overcoming Denial

When faced with loss—of a job or a loved one—most of us go through several predictable phases—denial, anger, negotiation, and depression—before we eventually reach some level of acceptance. Most individuals cannot process fully information presented with bad news. Having a trusted colleague, building representative, or union official present during remediation sessions to ask questions and clarify consequences can help the individual break through denial and see his or her situation more clearly.

Direct confrontation is another way to move an employee out of denial. If several people state specific consequences at the same meeting, this often has a stronger impact than individual confrontations.

Discipline Without Punishment

The word *discipline* comes from the same root word as disciple—a learner who learns from instruction, training, self-control, or discipline. Since punishment destroys trust, lessens employee ownership, and increases resistance, other strategies, like training and instruction, are often more effective.

Richard Grote, in *Discipline Without Punishment*, promotes an enlightened alternative that puts more responsibility on the employee. He recommends oral "reminders," instead of warnings, to encourage employee participation in correcting behaviors. If oral and written reminders are insufficient, he follows with a one-day "decision leave," inviting the employee to return with either a commitment to improve or a resignation. The process treats employees as responsible adults, lessens adversarial confrontation, and focuses on the problem that needs to be corrected.

Investigations

For those job-related issues that pose a more immediate threat—such as sexual harassment, financial irregularities, physical or emotional abuse, substance abuse, criminal allegations—investigations are often the best way to uncover the truth. Always investigate before administering formal discipline. Start small and expand the investigation as needed. If the allegations are serious, begin the investigation immediately and consider suspending the employee with pay while the investigation is under way. Failing to initially suspend the employee may prevent administrators from later opting for more severe discipline. Courts often rule that serious sanctions are unwarranted if administrators initially appear unconcerned about the issue.

To be fair, witnesses should be interviewed separately and asked similar, nonleading questions. Expect variations in testimony. Look for similarities in response patterns instead. But if the responses are too similar, it may indicate that witnesses are comparing their stories. Finally, keep an open mind. Be ready to terminate the investigation if substantiation is not found. And be equally ready to expand the investigation if wrongdoing surfaces.

Progressive Discipline

Courts expect districts to use progressive discipline—applying lesser disciplinary actions first and gradually progressing to more severe discipline if necessary. Although the exact progression may vary somewhat, the following steps are typical:

• *Oral Reprimand*: Clarify the rules, the expectation that the rules be followed, and the consequences if the rules are not followed.

• *Written Reprimand*: Provide written documentation of the same items as above: the rule violated, the expectation of corrective action, and warning of consequences.

• *Suspension*: Remove employee from the workplace, most often with pay, while an investigation is under way or to provide a cooling-off period.

• *Demotion*: Move employee to another position where lack of job skills is less of a problem.

• *Dismissal*: Provide a notice of dismissal clearly specifying reasons (behavior and history) for the discharge. Due process and just cause, discussed below, must be followed.

Due process and just cause have evolved from case law. These two phrases are likely to be found in state law, district policy, and any negotiated contracts. Most forms of discipline are subject to these two principles of law. The more severe the punishment, the stricter the courts will be in their efforts to ensure these principles are followed. Each term includes many safeguards for employees facing disciplinary action.

Due Process

Districts must publish and follow their own rules. They must also provide a hearing before enforcing the rules. At a minimum, due process generally requires three elements—notice, hearing, and procedure.

• *Notice*: The employees must know in advance the rules and the consequences. This can be done verbally, through a handbook, or through an earlier warning.

• *Hearing*: Employees are entitled to prenotification of a hearing, notice of charges, time to prepare, the right to have a representative present, the right to confront their accuser, and the opportunity to tell their side of the story.

• *Procedures*: The district must follow the rules (laws, policies, contracts).

Just Cause

The district must show that the punishment is justified. Just cause is usually considered to include the following elements:

• *Warning*: The employee must receive oral or written warnings (except for very serious offenses).

• *Reasonable Rules*: There must be a job related reason for the rule.

• *Investigation*: An investigation must precede discipline.

• *Fairness*: The investigation must be fair and objective.

- *Evidence*: There must be substantial (not necessarily conclusive) evidence.
- *Even-Handedness*: The rules must be consistently enforced.
- *Past Record*: Consideration must be given to past performance.

Remediation Through Probation

Failure to follow school district rules is most often dealt with through progressive disciplinary procedures as outlined above. In contrast, incompetent job performance is generally seen as an area for remediation—through evaluation and, if necessary, through probation. Terms of probation are often defined in law or in the negotiated agreement. Meeting the requirements for probation, therefore, requires meeting both procedural due-process requirements (including all the timelines) as well as proving incompetence.

Employees must know what is expected of them. Job descriptions and evaluation criteria should be determined in advance and given to employees. Most often, employees must be evaluated formally to determine whether or not their performance is satisfactory.

Employees with unsatisfactory performance should be notified in writing in accordance with the legal requirements. This notice usually must state specific areas of deficiency related to the evaluation criteria, include a program of recommended strategies for improvement, and specify a period of "probation" consistent with state or district timelines. During the probationary period, supervision is usually intensified. One state requires observations twice each month, followed by a written evaluation and employee conference.

When an employee's performance remains unsatisfactory, documented deficiencies from the probationary period constitute grounds for "probable cause" for nonrenewal. The district may then elect not to renew the employee's contract for the coming year.

Teacher Support

Additional teacher support is needed to make probation an effective remediation tool. Denial often yields to anger at this stage, making it more difficult for the supervisor to be seen as supportive. Work by Douglas Herman shows that plans of assistance are more likely to be effective when the teacher, principal, and educational association work together as a team. Resources for the support team to meet with or visit in the employee's classroom and release time for teacher-training opportunities or observing skilled professionals can also be helpful.

Supervisor Support

Probation is also time-consuming and stressful for the supervisor. This is especially true if the supervisor or the district is going through this process for the first time. Supervisors should seek support from colleagues and from the district. Colleagues who have been through the process can often provide useful advice.

The district can provide access to resources, advice, and the district's attorney. It is wise for the supervisor to meet frequently with personnel at the district level to ensure that the district remains supportive. District failure to proceed with an action recommended by a supervisor could result in many hours of wasted effort and create an impression of condoning substandard performance.

Follow Procedures

Districts must meet every timeline or they will fail to meet the procedural due-process standards. Two meetings per month means two meetings per month. Document everything. Keep copies of notices. Make special note of dates—especially the ones with deadlines. The stress of the probation process may cause the employee to miss work on days scheduled for observations. Plan to meet deadlines early. Always allow extra time for emergencies and rescheduling.

Managing Expectations

The bimonthly meetings between the employee and the supervisor are likely to be tense. After all, the employee's job is on the line. In an effort to reduce the tension, the supervisor may be tempted to gloss over the seriousness of the process. That may be appropriate early in the probation period, but if improvement is not forthcoming the supervisor should work hard to emphasize the seriousness of the consequences. The biggest danger is for the supervisor to conclude that there is probable cause for nonrenewal while the employee continues to feel that everything is going to work out. The larger the gap between employee and supervisor expectations at the end of the process, the more likely arbitration or legal action will be initiated by the employee.

Deciding not to renew a contract is a serious step—for the employee and for the district. The final outcome will likely be determined by an arbitrator, a hearings officer, or a judge. Success or failure on the part of the district will have impact on the district as a whole, sending a message about whether or not the district has high expectations for job performance. Therefore, it is important to ensure that all the tough questions are raised before the probation decision is made. It is better to take a smaller step and be assured of success than to take a larger step and face possible reversal.

In summary, sound personnel practices build a firm foundation for your professional staff. Hiring and supporting competent staff, combined with remediating and, if necessary, removing marginal staff members, will help build a professional school community that will work together for school improvement.

Conclusion

Building the capacity of the professional staff requires the development of clear and compelling goals, sound professional development practices, careful supervision and evaluation, and sound personnel practices. Each of these areas contributes to the development of a culture of continuous improvement and a commitment to student learning.

As for the best leaders,
the people do not notice their existence.
The next best,
the people honor and praise.
The next, people fear
and the next the people hate.
When the best leader's work is done,
the people say, we did it ourselves.

—Lao-Tzu, Sixth Century, B.C.

CHAPTER

12

Communicating

David Coursen, Karen Irmsher, John Thomas

"If I had to name a single, all-purpose instrument of leadership, it would be communication."— John Gardner

Whether outlining rules to nineteenth-century school children in a one-room school, or explaining site-based management to contemporary parents, school administrators have always needed to be effective communicators.

By *communication*, we mean the art of listening carefully and expressing views clearly and concisely—skills essential for anyone in a leadership position. High-level administrators of successful businesses, for example, say that the most valuable managers in their organizations are those who excel in communication skills such as giving employees timely feedback about their performance, accepting criticism without being defensive, speaking clearly and succinctly, and being good listeners. Interviewed by Susan Glaser and Anna Eblen, the top-level executives also said they valued managers who expressed their "feelings, opinions, and ideas openly." These communication skills are as valued in educational organizations as they are in the business world.

This chapter offers some suggestions for administrators who want to learn how to communicate more effectively with people both within and outside the school. Divided into two major sections, the chapter first discusses principles and skills of effective interpersonal communication, then recommends strategies for communicating with the public.

Learning To Communicate

Most people believe that if they speak or write clearly, they are communicating successfully. However, in a basic sense, communication is a two-way process, a sharing of information. This means that communication is listening as well as speaking, understanding as well as being understood.

Research indicates that, on average, leaders are engaged in some form of communication during about 70 percent of the time they are awake. According to Frank Freshour, 10 to 15 percent of that time is spent on writing, 20 to 40 percent on speaking, and 45 to 65 percent on listening. Steven Covey believes the best communicators are people who make listening and understanding their first priority.

Communicating for Understanding

"Seek first to understand, then to be understood," directs Stephen R. Covey in his best-selling book, *The Seven Habits of Highly Effective People.* He believes this to be the single most important principle in the field of interpersonal relations. If you want to interact effectively with anyone—teachers, students, community members, even family members—you need first to understand where that person is coming from.

If all the air were suddenly sucked out of the room, would you continue reading this book? No way. Your only concern would be getting air. But right now, you've got plenty of air. Getting more wouldn't motivate you. Satisfied needs do not motivate, notes Covey. Nor do somebody else's concerns and priorities. But, he says, "next to human survival, the greatest need of a human being is psychological survival—to be understood, to be affirmed, to be validated, to be appreciated."

When you listen carefully to another person, you give that person psychological air. Once that vital need is met, you can then focus on influencing or problem-solving. The inverse is also true. Principals focused on communicating their own rightness become isolated, ineffectual leaders, according to a compilation of leadership communication studies by Karen Osterman.

As we inquire further into the communication process, we will see that this theme of communicating for mutual understanding appears again and again. Next we examine the components of the communication process, before discussing some particular communication skills.

How the Communication Process Works

Communication can be broken down into five components, says Kristen Amundson: source, message, channel, receiver, and effect or reaction. Communications can go awry anywhere along this continuum, so understanding the points of potential interference in each component is essential.

Source. How the source is seen is very important. A principal who is consistently helpful and treats others with respect will have higher credibility than one who is alternately friendly and caustic.

Message. All messages are more easily understood when they are delivered in clear, grammatical language, free of jargon and "loaded" words.

Channel. The medium should be chosen with an eye to reaching the desired audience. Face-to-face contact allows for direct feedback, so it is generally the best. Several media can be used simultaneously so that people missed by one will be reached by another.

Receiver. Any message will be received with a certain number of preconceptions and prejudices. A school leader should never forget this. By understanding his or her receivers, the principal can try to construct messages that will not alienate them.

Reactions. There still may be unexpected reactions. Anticipate as many as you can, and try to plan for them.

Nonverbal Communication

Ralph Waldo Emerson once said, "What you are speaks so loudly, I can't hear what you say." Whether you're talking one-to-one, or addressing a group, body language, gestures, and facial expressions send nonverbal messages to your audience. Amundson notes that one study found 93 percent of a message is sent nonverbally, and only 7 percent through what is said. The following pointers are compiled from Amundson, Freshour, Mary Alice Griffin, and Doreen S. Geddes:

Body position. Use body language to convey energy and openness. Look alert. Lean slightly toward the listener to emphasize interest. Tightly crossed arms and legs say you are closed to other ideas.

Use of space. Four to seven feet is a comfortable distance among people working together. Staying behind your desk when someone comes to visit gives the impression that you are unapproachable.

Eye Contact. Maintaining eye contact 40-70 percent of the time conveys openness, receptivity, sincerity, and honesty. A principal who avoids eye contact may give the impression of feeling superior. But 100 percent eye contact is intimidating.

Facial expression. An open face, genuine smile, and raised eyebrows project warmth and interest. Exaggerated facial expressions as well as a neutral, masking face often belie hidden feelings.

Gestures. Appropriate gestures add strength to your message and project self-confidence. Others can be distracting, such as fussing with your hair, tapping your fingers on the table, or picking lint off your clothes.

Personal appearance. Clothes, posture, and grooming—usually the first things people notice about you—send messages about your status, attitudes, and how you feel about yourself and others.

Voice. Through tone of voice we can communicate warmth, coldness, interest, disinterest, confidence, uncertainty, openness, lack of openness, sadness, happiness, snobbishness, superiority, and other attitudes. Speaking softly may be seen as a lack of confidence. Speaking loudly may be perceived as aggressive or offensive, and speaking very quickly may give the impression of curtness.

Since there is always an element of risk in communicating openly, trust is particularly important. Several experts list responses that increase trust and engender open communication:

- giving the speaker your undivided attention
- listening actively—nodding, saying "uh-huh," and so forth
- paraphrasing, checking impressions of the other's meaning
- seeking additional information to understand better
- offering relevant information
- describing observable behaviors that influence your feelings
- sharing your own feelings
- offering opinions, stating your value position

These authors also list responses that reduce trust and openness:

- getting distracted or changing the subject without explanation
- focusing on and criticizing things that are unchangeable
- trying to advise and persuade
- vigorously agreeing or strongly objecting
- approving someone for conforming to your own standards
- commanding or demanding to be commanded (Doreen Geddes, Richard Schmuck and Philip Runkel)

Communication Skills

A number of skills are important for the effective communicator to understand and master. The skills that we highlight here are listening, asking questions, giving feedback (includes perception-checking, paraphrasing, and I-messages), and agreeing and disagreeing.

Listening

To really listen, says Abby Bergman, "you must move beyond simply hearing the content of what is said. You must hear some of the emotion, concern, and passion with which points are made." Good listeners, says Richard Gemmet:

- Don't interrupt, especially to correct mistakes or make points.
- Don't judge.
- Think before answering.
- Face the speaker.
- Are close enough to hear.
- Watch nonverbal behavior.
- Are aware of biases or values that distort what they hear.
- Look for the feelings and basic assumptions underlying remarks.
- Concentrate on what is being said.
- Avoid rehearsing answers while the other person is talking.
- Never start mental combat or tune out because of "red flag" words.
- Don't insist on having the last word.

One masters the art of listening, Gemmet notes, by developing "the attitude of wanting to listen, then the skills to help you express that attitude."

Listening skills can be improved by learning techniques to keep the mind from wandering. Frank Freshour mentions five approaches good listeners use:

> *Visualizing*—For example, picturing themselves as being in the speaker's shoes or engaging in the activity the speaker is talking about.
>
> *Analyzing*—Asking yourself, Does it make sense? Is it logical? What evidence does the speaker provide? Is the communication fact or opinion?
>
> *Summarizing*—Recapitulating the main points and supporting details.
>
> *Note-taking*—Freshour suggests drawing a line down the middle of the paper, writing main ideas on the left, and supporting details on the right.
>
> *Anticipating* what the speaker is going to say. If correct, you learn by repetition. If off the target, you learn by comparison and contrast.

Asking Questions

Question asking is an excellent way to begin communication, because it tends to make the other persons feel you're paying attention and interested in their response. Susan Glaser and Anthony Biglan suggest the following three tactics:

- Ask open-ended questions that can't be answered with a single word.
- Ask focused questions that aren't too broad to be answered.
- Ask for additional details, examples, impressions.

Giving Feedback

Feedback comes in a variety of forms. Some of the most common are paraphrasing, perception-checking, describing behavior, and "I-messages."

Feedback is a way to share understanding about behavior, feelings, and motivations. In giving it, say Charles Jung and associates, it is useful to describe observed behaviors, as well as the reactions they caused. When giving feedback, follow these guidelines:

- The receiver should be ready to receive feedback.
- Comments should describe, rather than interpret, action.
- Feedback should focus on recent events or actions.
- It should focus on things that can be changed.
- It should not be used to try to force people to change.
- It should be offered out of a sincere interest and concern for the other person.

When you want feedback, state what you want feedback about, then check what you have heard, and share your reactions.

One especially important kind of feedback for administrators is letting staff members know how well they are doing their jobs. In Glaser and Eblen's study, the managers who were most valued by high-level business executives gave their employees plenty of timely, positive feedback about their work. In contrast, ineffective managers stressed poor performance and rarely gave positive reinforcement. "These managers were not there to compliment, but were usually there if something went wrong," the researchers say.

Effective managers gave negative feedback privately, without anger or personal attack. They accepted criticism without becoming defensive and used negative feedback about their own performance to learn and change.

Paraphrasing

One way to avoid misunderstanding is paraphrasing—repeating what you just heard in an effort to show the other person what his or her words mean to you. Paraphrasing allows you to confirm your perceptions and assumptions. In this way, you not only clarify the meaning of the message, but you show genuine interest and concern about better understanding.

Jung and his colleagues stress that the real purpose of paraphrasing is not to show what the other person actually meant (which would require mind-reading skills) but to show what it meant to you. This may mean restating the original statement in more specific terms, using an example to show what it meant to you, or restating it in more general terms.

Glaser and Biglan warn against overusing this technique. People who paraphrase constantly end up sounding like parrots and are often regarded as tedious.

Perception-Checking

Perception-checking is an effort to understand the feelings behind the words. One way of checking perceptions is simply to describe your impressions of another person's feelings at a given time. It should be done in a way that avoids any expression of approval or disapproval.

Describing Behavior

When talking about what someone is doing, it's important to distinguish between describing and evaluating. Useful behavior description, according to Jung and his associates, reports specific, observable actions without placing a value on them as right or wrong, bad or good, and without making accusations or generalizations about motives, attitudes, or personality traits. "You've disagreed with almost everything he's said" is preferable to "You're being stubborn."

"I" Messages

This feedback pattern works well as a nonaccusatory method of requesting behavior change. One form it takes is as a three-part message stating: (1) the problem or situation, (2) your feelings about the issue, and (3) the reason for the concern. For example, "When you miss coming to staff meetings, I get concerned that we're making plans without your input." Osterman calls the I-message "an extremely powerful technique.... Because the statement reflects only one's own views and relies on description rather than criticism, blame, or prescription, the message is less likely to prompt defensive reactions or roadblocks and more likely to be heard by the recipient."

Jung and colleagues recommend using a simpler form of the I-message to describe feelings. You can refer directly to feelings ("I'm angry"), use similes, ("I feel like a fish out of water"), or describe what you'd like to do ("I'd like to leave the room now.")

Glaser and Eblen suggest you determine your outcome goal before you speak. For instance, you may want Mona to speak less in meetings. Then state your concern, using "I" language plus a feeling statement: "I like hearing your opinions in meetings, but lately I've felt out of touch with what some of the other teachers are thinking." Finally, give a preference statement telling your intention: "I'd like you to self-monitor the percentage of air-time you take at meetings, and help insure that everyone gets a chance to express their opinions."

As in most aspects of communication, openness and honesty are crucial. Feelings should be offered as pieces of information, not efforts to make the other person act differently. Again, nonverbal cues—facial expression, tone of voice, and body language—should agree with words. Another way to let others know how we feel is by agreeing or disagreeing.

Agreeing and Disagreeing

Taking a stand, say Glaser and Biglan, allows us to respond actively. Even disagreement, when done effectively, contains an element of agreement. The school leader who has learned to agree directly and clearly will find it much easier to disagree productively. Geddes points out that "someone who violently disagrees with you should not necessarily be viewed as the enemy but could also be seen as someone who greatly cares about the issue."

Social psychologists have found that people who agree about important things find it much easier to work together amiably. Agreement puts the other person at ease and establishes rapport quickly. It is not necessary to avoid disagreement when you do not agree, the authors say, but indicating points of commonality with the other persons will make it easier for them to accept your opinions. Disagreement, in fact, may make your agreement more meaningful. The authors add that it is particularly important to express agreement with new acquaintances.

Exercises for Improvement

Several exercises can help leaders develop or refine the above skills (suggested by Schmuck and Runkel, Glaser and Eblen):

Paraphrasing. Divide into small groups. One person asks a question; the next paraphrases before answering.

Impression Checking. Divide into pairs; one person conveys feelings through gestures, expressions, nonsense language, while the other person tries to interpret these cues. The two discuss the accuracy of the interpretations.

Behavior Description. Describe the behavior observed during any nonverbal exercise.

Describing Feelings. Each person is given a written list of statements and told to identify which describe feelings and which do not (for example, "I feel angry" does, but "I feel it's going to rain" does not).

I-messages. Each person requests a change in someone else's behavior using the I-message to express feelings, concerns, and preferences.

Giving and Receiving Feedback. Divide into trios. One person describes two helpful and two unhelpful behaviors of the second, who paraphrases the descriptions; the third person acts as an observer, making sure the other two are using communication skills correctly.

The same authors also describe exercises that clarify communication in meetings:

Right to Listen. Each speaker is required to paraphrase the terms of the discussion up to that point before speaking.

Time Tokens. Each person pays a poker chip each time he or she talks. This clarifies who talks how often.

High Talker Tapout. Signal when each speaker uses up an allotted amount of time; at the end, discuss the reasons some people talk more than others.

Take a Survey. Ask each person for an opinion about a certain question. Everyone contributes, if only to admit having nothing to say.

Schmuck and Runkel say circular seating for groups has two advantages: (1) nonverbal behaviors are most apparent when everyone can be clearly seen, and (2) equal participation is encouraged when there is no podium or head-of-the-table to suggest someone is "in charge." In certain circumstances, they add, videotaping or audio recording may be useful (if someone with skills and experience is available to judge what to record and when to play it back).

The Principal's Responsibility

Because of the principal's key role in influencing the human-relations atmosphere of a school and local community, it's crucial that he or she communicate effectively. Two national studies conducted by the National

Association of Secondary School Principals concluded that "the one constant of able principals in a broad variety of settings was strong interpersonal relationships with colleagues and constituents."

Vision, praise, accessibility, team-building skills, and humor all play important roles in building a positive emotional climate.

Vision

During the 1992 presidential campaign, recalls Allan Vann (1994), candidate Bill Clinton said he had a vision of where he wanted to lead the country. And a vision, too, of how he would deal with the economy. His opponent, President Bush, grumbled, "What is this vision thing, anyway?" Many political analysts saw Bush's defeat as being due, in part, to his failure to appreciate the importance of the "vision thing."

A principal's ability to lead and motivate is equally dependent on the "vision thing." Vann observes that "principals earn staff respect by articulating a clear vision of their school's mission, and working collegially to accomplish agreed-on goals and objectives." An elementary school principal, Vann begins collaborating with teachers before school starts each year to ensure that the staff shares a vision everyone can get behind. To keep the vision fresh in everyone's mind, he uses weekly discussions on the public-address system, meets regularly with the school council, and puts out a weekly staff bulletin. Public meetings and informal discussions reach parents and board members.

Removing Barriers

Faulty communications between principals and teachers rob a school of its effectiveness, say Patricia First and David Carr. Communication barriers can deplete team energy and isolate individuals who may then proceed on the basis of faulty assumptions regarding personalities or goals. In this type of situation, trust between principal and faculty—as well as overall morale—can be seriously inhibited.

Increased contact, then, would seem to be the logical remover of such barriers. First and Carr suggest that teachers be involved early in any decision, and they be kept up-to-date about whatever is going on. Meetings and various inhouse communiqués are often used for this purpose. Private discussions provide the kind of frankness and openness needed to clear the air, while removing interpersonal barriers before they become larger problems. Such meetings can also be the occasion for praise and compliments for good work, say the authors.

Giving Praise

Robert Major urges that principals use sincere praise whenever possible to create a more constructive atmosphere in schools. One principal, after observing a class, leaves a note mentioning only positive things. Later, if she has any criticisms to make, she meets with the teacher so she can make them face-to-face.

An indirect way of giving praise is through telling others stories about people at your school who are doing remarkable things. Coleen Armstrong recommends building and polishing a story arsenal for use at meetings and other occasions. It can include stories that highlight people at their best, such as "The Kid Who Succeeded Despite Incredible Odds," "The Community Leader Who Taught for a Day," "The Classroom Materials Purchased out of Teachers' Own Pocketbooks," and "The Custodian Who Everyone Likes to Talk to."

Being Accessible

The principal must be certain communication channels are open both ways. One of the most important things a principal can do to improve relations with the school community is to be open and accessible. It's important for people to feel you are available and welcome personal contact with them. Spend time with various faculty members over lunch, during coffee breaks, in the faculty lounge, or at informal teacher "hangouts." Ask people about their families and call them by their first names. An administrator who takes the time to get to know the staff will be able to identify, develop, and make best use of each staff member's capabilities.

Building Teamwork

A good communications climate leads to effective teamwork. With many schools moving toward site-based management, open communication becomes even more essential. Good teamwork in a stimulating environment grows out of an earnest effort to help each staff member achieve his or her potential, and the prime mover is the administrator. A supportive, encouraging, open climate can head off the problems related to misinformation and misunderstanding.

Using Humor

Various researchers have shown humor to be the seventh sense necessary for effective school leadership. Results of a study by Patricia Pierson and Paul Bredeson suggest that principals use humor for four major purposes: (1) creating and improving school climate; (2) relating to teachers the principal's understanding of the complexities and demands of their professional worklife; (3) breaking down the rigidity of bureaucratic structures by humanizing and personalizing interpersonal communications; and (4) when appropriate, delivering sanctions and other necessary unpleasantries.

Communicating in Small Groups

Administrators must frequently communicate with groups of staff members, parents, and students. Group meetings have increased with the spread of shared decision-making. Successfully meshing the various human factions in such groups can be a difficult task, requiring a delicate touch. Group members have three primary needs:

- Inclusion (or belonging)
- Control (or power)
- Affection (or friendship)

These needs must be satisfied if the group is to be successful, and they must be met adequately, but not excessively.

Inclusion

Inclusion is particularly important when a group is first forming. Introductions and the sharing of brief, pertinent biographies about each member can often help meet this need. Assigning a "greeter" at meetings, passing out name tags to members, and organizing get-acquainted activities or social events can also help.

Control

In traditional groups, members are given influence in decisions through such activities as exercise of voting power, election of officers, and the establishment of authoritarian hierarchies. To make sure control is evenly distributed, groups may want to study their decision-making process and practice role-switching. By giving each member a turn as the dominant member, the group can foster an equitable distribution of control.

Affection

An interpersonal element must be present for the group to succeed. Group members must relate to each other with sufficient warmth and closeness to further the group process. The need for affection can often be satisfied by allowing group members to talk briefly and informally during their work, meet for coffee after the business of the meeting, and bring refreshments to the meetings.

Like inclusion and control, affection is best used in moderation. Too much closeness in a group can interfere with its ability to serve its primary purpose. It can also lead to the personalizing of issues within the group, where an issue otherwise regarded as good or bad can be decided (accepted or rejected) by the group on the basis of the popularity of the member identified most strongly with the issue. To avoid this problem, rules should be adopted early in the group's existence about fraternization, agendas, and other procedural techniques.

Meeting Criticism and Attacks

Controversy, both internal and external, is no stranger to the public schools. Any number of situations, from the closing of a school to a book in the library, can become rallying points for angry groups. How should the school administrator respond?

In the case of controversial or heated issues, say Susan and Peter Glaser, it's important to pick the time and place for the interaction and to think before you speak. Make sure that you are clear about what you want from the interaction. This phase is crucial, for you do not want to jeopardize goals you may want to achieve with the group later, after the controversy has passed.

Begin by finding some common ground—something about which you and the group's spokesperson can agree. A good way to do this is to ask questions, then paraphrase the person's response. This gives you important additional details, and helps you listen effectively.

Once you know the other person's or group's general point-of-view, you can get additional information by asking for specific examples likely to be behind these views. (There is at least one good reason behind every strong feeling.) Find out why the group feels the way it does and why it thinks something is an important issue. At times, you can guess about specific instances and let them tell you if you're right. This will open a dialogue between you, say the Glasers, and often defuse any tension in troublesome situations.

Next, it is important to agree with them. There are always two aspects of any issue with which you can agree: (1) the facts of a situation and (2) the other person's sincerely held perception of those facts.

This doesn't mean you must cave in to a different point-of-view. You can easily maintain your own stand and simultaneously acknowledge that, yes, X incident did take place, and yes, the group feels strongly about it.

At this point, the Glasers say, there are four basic ways to respond to suggestions or demands relative to the issue:

- Say "yes" and implement as soon as possible.
- Say "no" but tell them why.
- Table the suggestion while you study the issue further. It's important to set a time limit on this phase. Never allow things to simply float.
- Ask for more information from the group, or appoint a subgroup to study the situation further.

You don't have to agree or implement suggestions or demands from every group to maintain a successful relationship with the community, but some response is vital.

Moving from general to specific, this section outlined elements of the communication process, described pertinent communication skills as well as ways to develop those skills, discussed the principal's responsibility for establishing positive communications in the school, and then covered principles of communicating in small groups and with angry groups. Now our attention shifts to another important focus for school leaders—communicating with the public.

Reaching the Public

"Talk to us."

In a nutshell, that's what public relations is all about, say Larry Hughes and Gerald Ubben. "Listen to us" finishes out the equation.

Until fairly recently, school officials were reluctant to commit staff and funds to public relations. According to Don Bagin and colleagues, they felt that "public relations" carried a stigma—it was perceived as a deodorant for covering up problems. Some school administrators still believe that doing their job well makes public relations unnecessary.

Their view overlooks a basic fact, according to Lew Armistead. Every school has a public-relations program, formal or not, that operates whenever the staff or students come in contact with the surrounding public. When a parent meets with a school official, when a child describes what went on in class during the day, or when a caller is greeted courteously, the school is communicating something to the public. If that caller is put on hold and forgotten, the school is also communicating something.

"We can't turn those messages on and off like a water faucet," says Armistead, "so our challenge and opportunity is to make those messages more positive than negative."

The question to ask about school public-relations efforts is not, then, whether to develop a program but how.

Planning the Public-Relations Program

What would an ideal public-relations program look like? Its elements are contained in this definition by the NSPRA:

> a planned and systematic two-way process of communication between an education organization and its internal and external publics . . . to stimulate a better understanding of the role, objectives, accomplishments, and needs of the organization.

As this definition suggests, planning is essential if the public-relations program is to have a solidly positive outcome. Public-relations textbooks, according to Armistead, break public-relations efforts into a four-part process: research, planning, communication, and evaluation. These steps apply to your overall strategies as well as to individual public-relations projects.

Research

Just as listening was seen as a crucial first step earlier in this chapter, studying the intended audience(s) is essential before developing a public-relations program. Bagin and colleagues recommend that school districts take an inventory of the community's sociological characteristics, the nature and influence of its power structure, and the way in which people think and feel about education and the programs provided by their schools. Do parents and other members of the community think students get away with too much or do the schools keep them on track? Are teachers dedicated professionals or are they basically there to collect a paycheck? Attitudes in these and many other areas can affect the effectiveness of your school, notes Armistead.

Bagin and colleagues warn against making this an overwhelming and burdensome process. They suggest limiting the inventory to those selected characteristics that feed directly into the planning process, concentrating on customs and traditions, population characteristics, communication channels, community groups, leadership, economic conditions, political structure, social tensions, and previous community efforts. Much of this information may already be available in school records, or may be gained by taking an annual or biennial census of the community.

One way to find out what the public thinks or wants from schools is the opinion survey. When most of us hear the word *survey,* we tend to think of the national polls like Harris and Gallup. Technically, however, a poll can also be a show of hands from an audience in your auditorium. One Oregon principal makes it a point to provide a generous supply of number 2 pencils at all breakfast meetings. She invites those attending to write down any ideas or comments relating to the agenda and business at hand, then to turn them in, coffee stains and all. Many schools include a space for parents' comments on their report cards. Others regularly place questionnaires in their own newsletters, school paper, or the community newspaper.

Carolyn Warner suggests sending questionnaires to members of targeted groups, accompanied by a stamped, self-addressed envelope. Topics can range from single issues, such as AIDS education or changes in the length of the school day, to a more elaborate climate survey. Many schools use the NASSP Comprehensive Assessment of School Environments or other prepared surveys. If you find a survey from another school that fits your needs, ask permission to adapt it to your purposes.

Bagin and colleagues note that surveys can also be conducted through personal and telephone interviews, dropoff and pickup questionnaires, or informal polling of key communicators. Forums, advisory committees, and panels are other options.

Once a survey strategy has been chosen, the next step is to define whom to survey, what type of survey to use, and what questions to ask. The best, most reliable, and economical survey will be an ongoing program that keeps schools and public constantly informed about each other.

Planning

A key step in planning a public-relations program is to decide what objectives the school wants to meet. Possible objectives cited by Bagin and colleagues include the following:

- promoting cooperation between the school and community
- securing adequate financial support for a sound educational program
- bringing about public realization of the need for change
- involving citizens in the work of the school
- earning the good will, respect, and confidence of the public
- developing intelligent public understanding of the school

- helping citizens feel more responsibility for the quality of education

Timelines, responsibilities, and dates should be established during the planning stage. It's important that communications be received throughout the year, not just when an election is coming up.

Communication

The channels and events for enhancing your image are endless. Among them are the typical community meetings, press releases, and newsletters. Warner suggests a speaker's bureau, staff involvement in the community, "ask the principal" sessions, civic projects, cultural/art festival, community awareness day, feature articles in the local paper, radio shows, advertisements, and holding classes in the local shopping mall for a day.

Evaluation

This last, often overlooked, step can help you see if what you did was effective. You mailed twenty-five press releases. Were any used? If we do not evaluate PR efforts, we stand the chance of making the same mistake year after year. Interviews and short surveys can provide essential feedback.

Attending to Informal Messages

School contact with the public can be divided into three classes:

- public and formal
- private and formal
- private and informal

The first two—covering a school's official business from report cards to press releases—are generally recognized as public-relations concerns. But the often-neglected third type is by far the most important.

Communication takes place whenever anyone associated with a school gives the public any kind of message about the school. These messages can be conveyed by students, volunteers, or employees. Many people see all school employees as "insiders" with special knowledge or information about school operations. Traditionally, says Armistead, the top four sources are professional support personnel: secretaries, custodians, bus drivers, and food-service personnel. The message people transmit may be verbal (a rumor or comment about policy) or nonverbal (litter on a school neighbor's lawn, or students helping a motorist change a flat tire). Because many of these exchanges are beyond a principal's control, a well-run school with a satisfied, well-informed staff and student body are essential to any public-relations effort.

Fostering Two-Way Communications

Two-way communication is vital. School administrators should never get so caught up in their efforts as to lose sight of primary goals. A classic example of bad public relations is the school district breaking its back to communicate with the public and not getting any feedback from that public, writes Philip Dahlinger. Administrators should daily remind themselves that they work for and with the community and its children. They should remain open, accessible, and receptive at all costs. Moreover, he says, they should be willing and able to take action quickly, correcting errors and resolving problems as soon as possible.

The Media

In cops and robbers movies of the 1930s, slick people generally dealt with bedraggled reporters by barking, "No comment." In reality, say Pat Ordovensky and Gary Marx, "these two words imply that the speaker has something to hide or is being condescending." "No comment" doesn't cut it, agrees Tripp Frohlichstein. It is seen as "a virtual admission of guilt—at least that is the way the public perceives it."

Reporters can have tremendous impact on the public consciousness. They are seen, heard, or read by large numbers of people at the same time, and their news has a certain built-in credibility. Not all questions can, or should, be answered on the spot, but a courteous, thoughtful, and honest reply will serve your school much better than the curt brushoff. "The key is to make any media encounter a win-win situation," says Frohlichstein. "The media must win by getting a story; the administrator must also win by getting his or her message across. Then the real winner is the public, which will have a better sense of the real story."

The media—print and broadcast—remains the best way to reach a large number of people in a short time, but the form that a story takes is beyond your control. Coverage can be negative or positive, a fact that can be intimidating to administrators. The right of the press to cover news and the public's right to know it, however, dictate the reporting of newsworthy events in schools. Thus it is the administrator's job to work with the media and see that coverage is as fair and accurate as possible.

Ordovensky and Marx offer the following ground rules for working with the media:

- Whatever you say, be sure it's true and accurate.
- Know your audience and address it.
- Remember that brevity is a virtue.
- Avoid education jargon.

- Stick to the story.
- Don't blame reporters for things they can't control (such as headlines).
- Know what is public information.
- Return calls promptly.
- Assume that no conversation with a reporter is off-the-record.
- Look for news pegs—stories that will grab reader interest.
- Be sensitive to deadlines.
- Never ask a reporter to show you a story before it is published.

In working with the media, the biggest problem for school leaders is the alarmingly easy way misunderstandings develop between school and media. This is inevitable to a certain extent, because of the tension between the school's and the media's objectives. Schools want reporting that promotes their objectives and avoids trouble. The media wants stories to interest viewers or readers. School officials thus may perceive the media to be distorting or sensationalizing events, taking comments out of context, or reporting facts inaccurately. The media may see administrators as refusing to "come clean" or limiting media access to information and offering them material that is little more than puffery.

Striking the right balance is easier when schools are accessible to the media and accept the need for the coverage of news—good and bad—advise Bagin and colleagues. Schools need to recognize the media's legitimate function as eyes, ears, and voice of its community.

A working relationship based on trust, mutual respect, and understanding can be promoted by the school's willingness to give the press a diet of news steadily—not just at budget time. It's also helpful for school officials to get to know reporters personally, always keeping in mind that reporters are paid to cover the news. Friendships will never prevent the reporting of unfavorable events. Although most reporters are conscientious and careful, many are so overworked and burdened by deadline pressure that some honest mistakes are inevitable. Don't take negative coverage or mistakes personally.

Bagin and colleagues also suggest that school leaders:

- provide the media with calendars of newsworthy events, agendas of meetings, and lists of key personnel and their phone numbers
- call press conferences and be available when negative news occurs
- alert the press to potential announcements and stories
- treat all reporters with the same professional respect
- cultivate relations with broadcast, as well as print, media

The Local Newspaper

Of all media outlets, says Armistead, probably the quickest, cheapest way to reach large numbers of people is through the community newspaper. Many citizens get their information about schools this way.

If you have access to such resources, Armistead advises using the school district's public-relations and media professionals: they have the skills, experience, contacts, and time to obtain the needed coverage. If you don't have access to a public-relations staff, he says, write your own news releases and send them from the school. Editors like material that is timely and new. Being part of a school gives you an almost unlimited source of possibilities. A good rule of thumb is that any event involving a large number of people has news potential.

Nicholas Criscuolo also stresses the value of regular, personal contact between educators and reporters. Such relationships pave the way to increasing both the amount and quality of news coverage. He suggests meeting with them to discuss past, present, and future coverage, and scheduling news conferences often enough not to disappear from the public mind. Most newspapers, and many television stations, have reporters assigned to the "education beat." Criscuolo suggests making a special effort to invite these people to observe various events and activities. Even if they were already planning to attend, it creates a friendly, open impression.

Criscuolo also recommends making use of your staff's writing talents. Encourage them to contribute articles for newspaper publication, or do it yourself. You or another staff member could volunteer to write a regular newspaper column or editorial-page feature about various school-related topics, especially if the newspaper doesn't have a regular education reporter.

Radio and Television

Many people who would not take the time to read a newsletter or newspaper or come to a meeting might very well receive a radio or television message. Most stations have standardized procedures for use of "PSAs"—public service announcements—developed from information supplied to them by various organizations and institutions, including schools. You should not expect these opportunities to be volunteered, warns Armistead. Your best course, again, is regular, personal contact with the news director or program director. Simply pick up the phone and ask.

Bagin and colleagues list the following radio opportunities: spot announcements, newscasts, infomercials, questions of the day, sports programs, music programs, discussion programs, documentaries, and talk shows. The station's program director can give you necessary information about details, restrictions (if any), and deadlines.

Television will be more selective than newspapers or even radio, says Armistead, but an administrator who remembers to "think visually" will seldom have much trouble. Always keep in mind this medium's need to have something they can show their audience.

Your Own Resources—Inhouse Media

School-based media are another way of reaching various groups. These media allow school leaders to say exactly what they want in a form that is under their control. Those who develop a publication of this type should keep its primary purpose in mind, understand its intended audience, and make certain the benefits justify the costs. All written material, from letters to brochures, should strive for clarity in writing, format, design, and graphics.

Printed material should be distributed by mail. Sending it home by students may be cheaper, but the U.S. Postal Service is considerably more reliable!

A 1980 Michigan survey of parents showed that roughly 80 percent of them got their school news from the humble newsletter. Others reported that notes, comments on school papers, memos, and other similar material generated by the school were regular sources of the same kind of information. The underlying message, says Armistead, is that you should never underestimate the value or importance of your school's newsletter. They are much more widely read than you may have thought.

In preparing a newsletter, says Armistead, it's important to avoid the appearance that you only publish when you want something from its readers. The sudden arrival of a newsletter or some other school publication, bristling with budget figures and your interpretation of them, plus your arguments for approval of the overall budget—all coincidentally a week before the big budget election—is likely to generate more suspicion than support. Instead, says Armistead:

- Write frequently.
- Write in language that your readers will understand.
- Write about things that will interest them.

Lack of funds needn't keep you from having a newsletter. Local businesses may be willing to support part or all of such publications in exchange for mention or credit as sponsors.

Writing should be done by people who know how to put facts and ideas into simple, readable language, say Bagin and colleagues. Sentence length should rarely exceed seventeen to twenty words, and the two-syllable word is clearly preferable to the five-syllable word. Have someone else read everything before you mail it to the community. Those tales in *Readers Digest* about embarrassing typos are amusing but all too familiar. Printed materials should showcase your professionalism and expertise as they build community confidence.

Staff bulletins may be your best method of keeping everyone current on inhouse information. These bulletins don't need to be fancy, literary, or particularly artistic, says Armistead, but they need to serve their primary function, come out regularly, and go to everyone. They should have information the staff needs and wants to know in language that will make it clear to them.

In some schools, staff bulletins are also sent to people outside the school—the president of the local parent-teacher organization, chairs of advisory groups, booster clubs, and sometimes even the media. If your staff bulletin can be used this way as well, you have an excellent method of informing additional groups about your school without additional cost in time and money.

Publications such as letters, annual reports, budget proposals, and other documents can sometimes serve the same purpose. Announcement boards, public exhibits, showcases, wall displays, and the like can also get the school's message across in a simple, relatively painless way.

Conferences and other programs reach audiences in much the same manner. In some cases, the impact, because of their simplicity and low-keyed quality, can be even more effective than more elaborate undertakings. An audience motivated to attend school programs may not always come predisposed to support you or the school, but they can often be won over by an effective, well-documented, well-presented program. At least, you can count on such audiences to listen attentively.

And don't overlook electronic forms of communication. A site on the World Wide Web can convey important information about your district and its schools both to parents down the street and to families thousands of miles away who plan to move to your community. A Web site has the added advantage of permitting two-way communication. In addition to displaying pertinent information about your schools, you can solicit comments from those who log on to it.

Legislative Relationships

Many legislators view educators as whiners who only show up when they want more money. President Lyndon Johnson was fond of saying that the time to make friends is before you need them. David Turner says that the same holds true in building relationships with representatives and senators. He suggests being present when they hold "town meetings"; sending them clippings of your school's successes; and sending notes of congratulation and notes of thanks for support. When you lobby them, make your position clear. Explain how the issue would affect your school programs and students. Be accurate and concise. Offer to serve as a resource for education information.

In sum, the key to good public relations starts with determining what your target audiences know, want to know, and need to know, then getting them the information they need in a way they can digest it.

A Time-Saving Suggestion

An effective public-relations program is essential to a school, but it takes time, one commodity no principal has enough of. One solution to this problem is to assess the situation, decide on a suitable public-relations approach, and devote five minutes a day to implementing it. If the first day's task takes more than five minutes, the time can be credited to future days. As a result, there will be a systematic and ongoing effort to improve public relations that does not make unreasonable demands on your time. It is surprising how much can be accomplished with even this modest investment of time.

Conclusion

Communicating can be a complex, difficult (as well as occasionally frustrating) business. Yet for the school leader who perseveres in understanding and communicating with students, parents, staff members, other administrators, and the community, there is a rich payoff. Effective communication with these groups can produce a positive school climate and good school-community relations.

CHAPTER

13

Building Coalitions

John Thomas, Thomas E. Hart,
David Peterson-del Mar, Stuart C. Smith

Schools today cannot fulfill their mission in isolation from other community organizations and resources. Schools confront unique pressures. Perhaps no other institution faces such high and steadily growing expectations, expectations that become increasingly difficult to meet as budgets plateau or decline.

But many other groups and institutions share the difficulties that schools face. Poverty, drug use, family fragmentation, a changing job market, and declining social-service budgets affect all of society. "Schools, families, communities, organizations and agencies. . . are all part of the problem," writes Don Davies. "An ecological solution to an ecological disaster requires that they all must participate in solving the problem," he says. In other words, coalition-building is a critical part of school success and community success.

Coalitions and the process of forming them vary greatly from place to place. They can be formal or informal, temporary or permanent. They may meet regularly or not at all, address one issue or many. In some instances, coalitions represent a broad-based community effort to improve the school system as a whole, such as school reform or restructuring efforts. In other cases, coalitions treat more limited objectives, such as improved public relations with the community or coordinated social-services delivery.

This chapter is addressed to school leaders considering a broad range of coalitions with people and groups. After discussing the advantages of coalitions and some examples of them, the chapter discusses how to initiate and operate them. The final section advises leaders how to build coalitions with some central groups: parents, the community and its power structure, advisory councils, key communicators, local businesses, social-service agencies, school boards, and government agencies.

Some Advantages of Coalitions

The most obvious advantage of coalition-building is mentioned above: Close relations with people and groups outside the school are virtually essential when schools are expected to do more with shrinking resources. But coalitions bring other, more subtle advantages as well.

Coalition-building can greatly expand the number of people who feel like shareholders in the schools. Community members who serve on an advisory committee or business people who offer structured work experiences become insiders, not simply users. This is particularly true of schools that distribute substantial authority to parents and other community members. Ameetha Palanki, Patricia Burch, and Don Davies note that such efforts have "the potential to give families and communities access to the resources needed to participate in the real improvement of school programs." People outside the school have the opportunity to become part of it much more fully than before.

Widespread community participation benefits students and educators as well as community members. Educators frustrated by the stubborn problems of individual students may see these problems abate when social-service agencies collaborate with them on a plan for the entire family. High schools plagued by truancy, high dropout rates, and apathy may be energized by coalitions with local businesses that make the curriculum more interesting and relevant to students' vocational needs. Parents may throw their support behind restructuring efforts or serve as tutors or mentors to lagging or troubled students.

Coalitions with the business community can bring very substantial rewards. Frederick S. Edelstein, Esther F. Schaeffer, and Richard J. Kenney list several services available from local businesses:

- Training in management, such as developing goals and objectives and long-term planning
- Advocacy in the community
- Staff development of both teachers and administrators
- Research and development to foster creative new approaches to stubborn problems
- Applying new technology that may be unavailable to schools otherwise

In sum, coalitions bring to the school skills and perspectives that may not otherwise be utilized.

Examples of Coalitions

Coalitions can assume a wide variety of forms and roles. Cooperative coalitions entail two or more groups working together without fundamentally changing the nature of each group. Collaborative coalitions are more far-reaching, for they entail sharing basic resources. Both sorts of coalitions can include many different sorts of organizations and pursue a wide range of goals.

The faculty at one innercity elementary school serving an ethnically diverse and poverty-stricken community decided that closely involving parents in their children's education was a key part of reform. "In practice," notes Calvin Stone, "this has meant that the school would become site managed and be guided by parent participation in school decisions." This coalition has born ample fruit. Monthly meetings on school decisions draw up to 200 parents. Parent concerns over their children's learning spawned an afterschool program to improve reading and math that is run by community organizations. Parents have also provided most of the staff for a preschool, organized school fundraisers, and formed work parties to clean the school grounds. Coalitions with parents have been at the center of this school's intensive improvement efforts.

Schools in Hermiston, Oregon, have benefited from a very different sort of coalition. Their coalition was formed largely through the initiative of social-service personnel who felt frustrated that troubled families received fragmented and ineffective care. They sought, in the words of Twila Schell of the Oregon Department of Human Resources, "to do a better job for clients with the same resources we've got." The coalition created a center where agencies meet together to coordinate services for families in crisis and where families work with social workers to identify broad solutions to their problems.

Schell reported that local schools participate by identifying "families before they get into really bad situations," by telling social workers what is working, and by helping to coordinate services. Teachers note that children served by the program are doing much better in school.

Another effort to pool resources for the benefit of families is run by the Mayor's Office in Owensboro, Kentucky. Betty E. Steffy and Jane Clark Lindle report that Project Parent enlists businesses and community organizations to expand "social capital" (the support system for parents and kids) and "educational capacity." For example, a civic club supports a child-care unit, a bank sponsors lunchtime seminars for parents, and two businesses host a dinner to recognize schools and parents. The Mayor's Office plans acts of celebration throughout the year to draw attention to the program and strengthen the commitment of both families and contributors.

Sprague High School in Salem, Oregon, features a variety of school-business coalitions. Representatives from local businesses sit on advisory committees, offer job shadowing and structured work experiences to students, come into classrooms to teach topics like marketing, and even have a branch bank at the high school. Giving students these kinds of experiences opens their eyes to careers they may not be aware of. Coalitions with business can make high school education, in particular, much more interesting and relevant.

Initiating a Coalition

In every community, many disparate groups are in a position to abet or hinder the formation of a productive coalition. An effective coalition requires participants able to work skillfully and harmoniously with others. Therefore, school leaders should carefully choose the groups and people to be invited into the coalition.

Terry R. Black notes that school leaders can begin the coalition-building process by listing three groups of potential participants:

- All the "natural" allies—individuals, groups, types of people—who will probably share the leader's concern
- All the groups and organizations likely to be affected by the concern
- All potentially interested, civic-minded groups who might stand to gain indirectly by participating

School leaders can use questionnaires to gather data about political, social, and economic power bases in their district. The Michigan State Board of Education recommends that districts compile fact sheets displaying:

- Community demography, including the formation and development of neighborhoods and their styles, patterns of land use and zoning, and general population statistics
- Community power structure, that is, the persons or groups that influence community decisions
- Community support systems, such as communication, culture, housing, law, and recreation

This information can be the starting point for determining where to begin in recruiting coalition members.

The Allegheny Policy Council for Youth and Workforce Development is an example of how an urban coalition might be constituted. It has enjoyed the cooperation of business and civic leaders, members of the Pittsburgh Board of Education, past and present school superintendents, district administrators, the Pittsburgh Federation of Teachers' leadership, teachers, principals, and students.

Coalitions in smaller cities, towns, or communities will of course be less likely to include corporate presidents or university deans. But the same principle of inclusiveness applies, for even the smallest districts contain people interested in working with others to improve their schools.

Contacting and Recruiting Members

Once potential coalition members are identified, the next step, in Black's words, is "to develop a strategy for selling" the coalition to them. Black emphasizes that leaders must clearly understand and be able to appeal to the potential participants' self-interest, for the "pursuit of self-interest is fundamental to effective political action."

When taking their case to the key persons in targeted organizations, coalition organizers should actively welcome ideas, not just ask for help, advises Black. This will help all participants to feel a sense of ownership in the coalition from its inception.

The final step in forming the coalition, Black says, is "to invite representatives of all allied organizations to an area-wide meeting to make a formal/official decision about whether to form a coalition, how the coalition should be structured, and what coalition strategies and activities to initiate."

Lynda Martin-McCormick and her colleagues suggest a three-step alternative process of recruitment that gives school leaders more control. First, a member of the recruitment committee telephones prospective members to find out if they are interested in joining. Second, given a positive answer, the committee sends a letter inviting the group or organization to join the coalition. The letter outlines exactly what will be expected of them. Third, the committee meets with the new member, where they discuss how they can work together. This meeting may be followed by a formal letter of acceptance and commitment to participate in the coalition's work.

Lynn Balster Liontos presents another three-step approach. Leaders should first "reach out to the community—don't wait for them to come to you." School leaders should also "get involved in community groups and activities" so they can find out where community power is and go to it. Third, school leaders should recognize that they "are, in fact, community leaders." Lines that separate school and community leaders are artificial and should be crossed.

Coalitions have a purpose, and they are most likely to succeed when that purpose is widely understood. Davies points out that reform is most likely to succeed "where the felt need is more broadly owned and where substantial numbers of teachers, staff, parents, and other community members can agree on the nature of the problems and needs to be addressed." Recruitment can serve in part as a means of infusing community members and groups with a vision of how a given problem is harming the schools and how it might be addressed.

Establishing a Governing Board

Formally organized coalitions have governing boards that establish policy and, if necessary, generate funds. A board that represents all major segments of the community will of course have greater credibility. If there is a large industrial base, then industrial leaders should be included; if there is a university, then university faculty, administrators, or staff should be invited; if the district is dominated by farmers, then farmers should sit on the board.

Most boards include members from area churches, banks, chambers of commerce, and civic groups. But do not overlook leaders of labor unions or parent groups. The school district itself can be represented by a school board member, the superintendent, a principal, a teacher, and other staff members.

District representatives may not be a substantial proportion of the board membership in independent coalitions. Yet this situation need not alarm school-district personnel. The purpose of such coalitions is to locate additional sources of expertise for the district. In some coalitions, superintendents may serve on the board but not as an officer. Local conditions will dictate the coalition's composition and leadership.

Once boards are established, they commonly form committees to oversee coalition projects. This serves to divide the work into manageable parts and to enlist participation from additional people. One committee might devote itself to drawing up bylaws or regulations, steps that must be taken if the coalition decides to become involved in fundraising. Bylaws are a required part of the 501(c)(3) application, which is a request to the Internal Revenue Service for a letter identifying the organization's nonprofit status for tax purposes. A lawyer should file the articles of incorporation and handle the (501)(c)(3) application.

Not every coalition requires such a formal structure, of course. But newly formed organizations should discuss this matter early in their history to determine what legal steps they may need to take.

Writing a Mission Statement

A brief statement of the coalition's mission serves several purposes. It tells all the members and their constituents why the coalition exists. It expresses the partners' commitment to the project and defines their roles and responsibilities. It provides the basis for planning the coalition's activities. And it serves as an anchor to keep the coalition from drifting away from its intended purpose. If members begin to push their own agendas, the mission statement calls them back to serve the collective vision.

Steffy and Lindle suggest several guidelines for developing a mission statement:

- Identify the community's major stakeholders in the development of the mission statement.
- Formulate a plan that involves these major stakeholders in the strategic planning process.
- If the group developing the strategic plan is different from the initial advisory group that initated plans for this community collaborative effort, devise a mechanism to keep the advisory group informed about the progress of the planning process.
- Focus on areas of agreement, not areas of disagreement.
- Keep the statement short, simple, and easy to understand and remember.

Steffy and Lindle recommend that coalition members review the mission statement periodically to ensure it continues to reflect their common goals.

Operating the Coalition

Coalitions by their very nature bring together disparate groups and individuals who do not have a history of working together. Few coalitions, then, are initially prepared to function efficiently and harmoniously. Nor should it be assumed that coalitions will automatically work smoothly with the school districts they serve. Productive, useful coalitions seldom emerge without considerable attention to managing conflict and promoting communication.

Anticipating and Dealing with Conflict

"Change is personal," remarked a principal at an urban high school, and fear of change is therefore natural. School leaders will be best prepared to confront fear and conflict if they anticipate resistance to the coalition-building process.

Resistance is apt to be highest when staff members are excluded from coalitions. Stone cites an example in which teachers perceived a school-based social-services center as "the superintendent's pet project" that enjoyed more support than the school itself did. Likewise, Atelia I. Melaville and Martin J. Blank discuss a school in which the district had collaborated with a community agency to address dropout prevention without working with the school's principal and staff. The agency and school ended up working at cross-purposes; school personnel even refused to make attendance information available to the agency counselors.

Teachers may particularly fear coalitions with businesses. Many educators, as David T. Conley notes, "have strong feelings that their central purpose should not be to prepare workers." Teachers in the humanities, in particular, may feel that coalitions with businesses may lead to the disappearance of courses in art, music, or literature. A broad variety of district staff may fear that coalition-building will simply mean a more taxing workload in both the short and long term.

District administrators may also be apprehensive of coalitions. Working with groups outside the district commonly means distributing real power to such groups. Central-office personnel and principals may consequently feel increasingly marginalized.

School boards and superintendents must address the concerns that teachers and administrators may have over coalition-building. Staff, in the words of Conley, must "understand how they will be able to survive and succeed in the new environment." Administrators, for example, must recognize that their jobs will entail less solitary decision-making and more collaboration and coordination. Effective managers will be able to see and articulate the big picture and to help a broad variety of people work toward its realization.

Jan Baxter, the principal at Gresham, Oregon's Hollydale School, has taken particular pains to be sensitive to staff concerns over coalition-building. Her school has been an early participant in Oregon's program of creating school councils that include at least one parent representative. "You can't have someone come in who is going to try and run the school," Baxter said. Hence she works carefully to ensure that parent representatives are people who respect school staff and can work well with them.

Even the meeting site can be a source of friction for coalition members. A neutral site may be preferable. The Public Education Fund Network suggests that coalitions establish distinct physical presences in their communities by having offices and meeting places outside the schools.

Another idea is to rotate meeting sites among the offices of each agency or group included. "This practice," say Steffy and Lindle, "enables team members to become familiar with other members' workplaces." The agenda could include an overview of how the host organization operates and how its mission relates to the coalition's mission. Such meetings also help coalition members to learn each group's unique vocabulary. "Eventually the team members will develop a common language," the authors say.

Coalition members should anticipate the tensions inherent to group decision-making. Training in interpersonal communications and conflict resolution is an excellent way to begin the group process, and it pays handsome long-term dividends.

Members may also be insensitive to cultural differences within the group. The California State Department of Education offers the following recommendations:

- Create an environment supportive of differences in attitudes and appearances.
- Appreciate verbal and nonverbal forms of expression based on ethnic, religious, socioeconomic, and other differences.
- Be attuned to subtle signs of disaffection or lack of participation that may be related to group differences.

At a time when the nation's schools are becoming increasingly diverse, coalition members can model how to recognize and respect cultural differences.

Black advises coalition members to "pull together rather than work on a hierarchical basis." A coalition can be likened to a small United Nations of sovereign states. Hence decisions should be made through all participants' consent whenever possible. To help build unity, component organizations should periodically express their commitment to the coalition's work and goals.

The very process of being part of an effective coalition can defuse conflict. "The best way to end power struggles," said George Dyer, a high school principal, "is to empower people." Teachers, parents, and other community members who may have always felt on the outside of district or school policy-making have, in coalitions, a vehicle for wielding influence positively. Exercising power in an open, broadly democratic decision-making process depends largely on the quality of participants' ideas and their ability to work well with others, not simply on their titles.

Although close interpersonal relationships can help the coalition to function smoothly, members must realize that the coalition is not a club. Its members represent their respective organizations, Black points out, and therefore they must state their organizations' opinions on given issues, even if they do not conform to their own views. Furthermore, members should not take for granted how other members might vote. They should instead sound out each member's opinion and work toward consensus and compromise.

Communication Between District and Coalition

Coalition-building requires a "huge investment of time," noted Billie Bagger, Oregon's Adult and Family Services representative for service integration. Communication is perhaps the prime reason why coalition-building is so time-consuming. Yet this investment is crucial, even essential.

Communication is particularly necessary among participants accustomed to working within varying timeframes. Business people are typically used to fast-paced meetings and quick decisions. They may have to learn to be patient with the more deliberate pace of education reform. By the same token, district personnel must recognize that many coalition members are extremely busy people who are not necessarily being paid to sit on coalition committees. Mutual communication and understanding of such differences engenders mutual tolerance and respect.

"Linkage agents" can facilitate communication between coalitions and districts. These district employees establish regular contacts between coalitions and district members. In small communities the superintendent or another single administrator might be able to perform this function. In larger settings, where coalitions include many different groups, the task must often be shared among several people. In one large school district, for example, school principals take turns attending meetings of neighborhood associations and write up meeting summaries to distribute to other district administrators.

These linkage agents, whether one or many, must be committed to bridging the gap between the school district and the community. The agent must also bear in mind that the coalition and the groups represented in it are not part of a district's official administrative structure. Hence she or he must be able to perceive and respect often complex organizational networks and boundaries.

This chapter has so far surveyed the general purpose and nature of coalitions and how they are initiated. Attention now turns to a more detailed consideration of how school leaders can interact with particular constituencies whose support is critical to school success.

Obtaining the Support of Key Groups

School leaders are going into their communities for help in the hard work of school improvement. Communities that are already concerned about the quality of their educational systems generally welcome an opportunity to assist their schools. When such concern is lacking, school leaders can generate support through many of the suggestions presented here. The following sections explain how to contact and elicit support from parents, the general community, members of the community power structure, school advisory councils, key communicators in the community, businesses, social-service agencies, school board members, and government agencies.

Parents

Parents are undoubtedly the group most affected by schools and the group most likely to lend their support to them. David Green calls parent/teacher organizations "gold mines" from which skillful school leaders can extract much ore.

A good way to begin increasing parent involvement in the schools is to make the school a community center of sorts. Green notes that a Connecticut grade school built a strong supportive partnership with its parents by creating an advanced reading program, computer-literacy assistance, minicourses, and a school beautification program. Such projects require schools to commit resources to parents as well as to their children, but these commitments may repay themselves several times over.

Other schools initiate stronger relations with parents by sponsoring child-centered educational or recreational activities. Parent conferences, open houses, and musical, dramatic, or sporting events are traditional ways to enhance parent involvement. Other possibilities include carnivals and parent-education nights that cover topics like positive discipline or gang awareness.

Episodic contacts can lead to more substantial relationships. One midsized high school uses parents as hall monitors, tutors, and mentors. According to George Dyer, the school's principal, parents consequently "feel they know what is going on in the school"; they can drop by and talk with teachers, administrators, and other staff. Dyer also meets monthly with a focus group of about ten parents who discuss community developments and offer suggestions. Two parents also serve on the school council, which wields substantial and growing power in school decision-making. "Parental involvement as a whole has made this school successful," Dyer concludes.

Parents can play an active role at all levels of reform. At one elementary school, parents serve on committees that set new goals and policies in making their children's education more experiential and process-oriented. Parents are also implementing these changes. For example, they create a weekly newspaper that identifies weekly learning activities students will need their parents' cooperation to complete. All parents are expected to participate by working alongside their children on these assignments.

Parent-school coalitions can assume widely varying levels of formality and responsibility, from serving on powerful committees to working on a take-home science project. Parents are a vast resource whose potential remains largely untapped.

The Community

Parents have a direct stake in the success of their schools, but other community members may have to be convinced that a strong educational system is in their best interest. By reaching out to segments of the community that have direct ties to schools, school leaders can turn apathy or even opposition into active support.

Schools that have succeeded in forging strong ties with their communities have used five major strategies, say Bruce L. Wilson and Gretchen B. Rossman, who examined data collected by the U.S. Department of Education's Secondary Schools Recognition Program.

1. They actively recruit human resources. The schools seek volunteers to perform clerical duties, serve as nursing assistants, and teach special skills.
2. They have aggressive public relations programs.
3. They use staff members who are also good communicators and fundraisers.
4. They invite the community into classrooms and send staff and students into the community. Students visit nursing homes, assist local charities, and stage musical performances for local recreation departments. In turn, school facilities are open to numerous community social activities.
5. They establish an identity for the school. Schools use signs at roadsides, fly school flags all over town, and use other means to identify the school with the community.

The outcome of these strategies, say Wilson and Rossman, is a general strengthening of the school. It is able to tap an enormous pool of expertise, multiply its resources, and often greatly improve programs at little or no extra cost.

Larry Hughes and Gerald Ubben also advise school leaders to let the community into the school. A series of properly organized seminars, attended by people from a cross-section of attitudes and orientations in the community, may be a good way to begin, even if they are at first "gripe sessions." Once under way, this approach lays the groundwork for more sophisticated community-involvement programs, and the principal doesn't have to do it all: The discussions can be led by well-informed, well-briefed staff members who are effective and tactful moderators.

Committees of citizens, students, and staff can work simultaneously on various educational issues without impinging on the power of either the principal or the school board. This type of citizen involvement eases professional workload, dispels apathy, and often leads to valuable solutions.

School leaders who successfully involve their communities must be able to make sensitive use of people and their talents. It takes a good eye to pick effective leaders out of groups of parents, advocates, public agencies and services, clubs, organizations, schools, health facilities, the clergy, businesses, and professionals—people who influence decisions and who instigate and support action for programs.

The Power Structure

Power, a necessary function in society, is distributed unequally throughout communities both informally and formally. Informal power is often held by an elite at the top of their respective social and occupational hierarchies. These are the people to see if you are trying to promote some community program. Without their help, any such project would be risky. Formal power generally resides in elected or appointed officials. People with informal community power—although they would not seek or hold an office—influence office holders.

According to Hughes and Ubben, a community's power structure is dynamic, not static. Yet power relationships are not random. They have enough stability that an experienced observer can generally predict them.

Don Bagin, Donald Ferguson, and Gary Marx describe three levels of community leadership that school leaders should be sensitive to:

1. *Visible Leaders*—easiest to identify, include people always on committees, councils, drives, plus elected officials.
2. *Invisible Leaders*—harder to identify, often behind the scenes, such as with large financial interests in the community, or with influence in significant political groups within the community; not usually office seekers but involved in getting others elected; selective in allowing their names to be used for endorsements.

3. *Emerging Leaders*—"heirs apparent" who will assume control when current leaders complete terms of office. Many communities recruit, train, and mentor these people as a "good investment" in the future.

Educators should be the community's intellectual leaders, Bagin and his colleagues believe, and create a strong connection in the community's collective mind between learning and people in schools. Educators should participate in such things as the local chamber of commerce, charity drives, boards, commissions, and the political system to identify community leaders and work with them to build a positive relationship, they say. In the process, there will be ample opportunity for educators to show citizens how the schools can help improve the community and how various proposed changes will affect schools. This sort of coalition-building means that the educator will be able in times of need to turn to colleagues, not complete strangers.

Advisory Councils

Advisory councils are mandated in many school districts. Some government programs require community participation in school decision-making. Some councils wield substantial formal power; others are strictly advisory. In either case, introducing citizen committees into the schools' decision process represents a major change that may annoy some administrators. Along with extra work and potential frustration, however, advisory councils bring some clear benefits to administrators seeking public support.

Every community evaluates its schools. The advantage of an advisory council is that it channels public evaluation toward a constructive end. Criticism—based, as it often is, on vague or incomplete understanding—can be reduced when school administrators have a forum where they can respond. Council members with clear facts about the school's strengths and weaknesses can use this same forum to pass information along to the rest of the community.

But advisory councils or ad hoc committees are much more than mere arenas for disseminating school policy or airing collective gripes. The functions of such groups range from determining and prioritizing school objectives to evaluating progress, investigating facility use, and revising curriculum.

Advisory groups also provide a formal process by which opinions from the community can be incorporated into school decisions. Administrators with current, accurate information about community needs and expectations are in a better position to make sound choices.

Advisory councils are most helpful when they represent a cross-section of the community. Diversity is not only desirable, it is essential.

Many councils suffer from shortages of minority, low-income, student, nonparent, and (except in leadership positions) male representation. Past experiences may have made people in these groups reluctant to participate in school affairs. Some people lack confidence in their communication skills when placed alongside more affluent or educated people. Yet their participation is a high priority, and the schools must be prepared to recruit them.

It is also important to recruit individuals with expertise in areas the council will be considering. All participants should be interested, available, and able to work well with others.

The best way to attract and keep council members is to appeal to both their self-interest and their desire to make a difference. Simply asking people to serve on a council or run for an office is often enough to demonstrate that their services are needed and valued.

Convening an advisory council will thoroughly test any principal's leadership skills. The principal's most important function will be, on the one hand, to keep the level of participation up, to generate enthusiasm, energy, and activity. On the other hand, the principal must alert the council to its limits and responsibilities, not just to its possibilities. Governing a citizens' advisory council requires skills in leading meetings, managing conflict, sharing power, and communicating effectively.

Key Communicators

Every community has people who are asked questions about everything—city government, elections, investments, rising prices, and the local schools. They have community members' respect, and educators need to keep them informed of school issues and events. Lew Armistead suggests inviting these leaders to school events—an award assembly, a musical or dramatic performance, an athletic event, or a school meeting—as well as putting them on your mailing list. Some schools recruit them to community-relations committees.

These "key communicators" talk to many others. They are people who other people believe and trust. Key communicators do not necessarily have a lot of formal status and power. They are found in the ranks of all professions and trades, at many levels in the community. They can be barbers and day-care providers or mayors and physicians.

Key communicators are also found throughout schools and districts. They can be members of the student body or your own staff. Make sure these people have accurate information before they share it with those outside the school, Bagin and colleagues advise, for these key people can "identify the sparks before they become fires" and reduce rumors and other misinformation. Although it takes time to set up a network of key communicators, most administrators agree that it saves time in the long run.

Few school leaders have the time to meet personally with members of the larger public. Working with key communicators can save a lot of time. Superintendents and principals can cultivate these people informally—with periodic telephone calls to discuss district affairs or invitations to lunch at school—or by establishing a formal group and meeting with it regularly.

Because they can generally reach a lot of people quickly, timely contact with key communicators during potential crises can help defuse controversies and problems. It can quickly and effectively address misconceptions about the school before they become widespread.

Because communication is a two-way process, key communicators also bring in information: accurate and prompt feedback on how the community is responding to the school. This feedback can give administrators new perspectives on their schools and their own management styles, can make it easier to identify potential problems and dissension. These people can also serve as sounding boards, helping administrators to test public reaction to new ideas.

Local Businesses

Long-term economic growth is tied directly to the performance of public education. Indeed, much of the recent impetus for educational reform has come from business leaders who are concerned that the work force lacks the skills necessary to compete successfully in the modern global economy. Edelstein and his colleagues cite the example of an electronics firm in the U.S. that spends $250 per employee in quality-control training, some 500 times the amount that its Japanese competitors have to invest in that activity.

Educators should not be shy about pointing out to business people that joining in coalitions is in their best interest. Businesses largely rely on public education to prepare people for jobs. Hence stronger schools will create better employees. Business participation in school-improvement efforts can also bring more particular advantages. For instance, a financial institution that trains several thousand students a year in partnership with the Los Angeles Unified School District has first choice at recruiting the students it helped train. The company has hired about 20 percent of the students after they graduated.

Bagin and colleagues argue that educational leaders should approach coalitions with businesses in a careful, systematic manner:

- Determine what local businesses expect from schools.
- Survey businesses in the area.
- Learn local business people's perception of the school's strengths and weaknesses.
- Find out what skills graduates will need to get available jobs.

Bagin and his coauthors recommend an early investigation based on a single basic question: What can you do for them? Businesses can assist schools in many ways. These include:

- Recognizing and awarding special student achievements
- Teaching specialized courses in topics like marketing
- Offering specialized management training to district administrators
- Serving on school-oversight committees
- Serving on curriculum-reform committees
- Providing a broad array of work-experience opportunities, including job shadows, supervised work experiences, apprenticeships, and internships

These possibilities by no means exhaust the range of available school-business collaborations, but they indicate their broad scope.

Business people and educators must often overcome misconceptions to work together successfully. Edelstein and his colleagues advise business people to be cautious; they "must ask themselves whether their own methods and strategies would fit in the management of public education." Education by its very nature often cannot divest itself of activities considered unprofitable, and it has very little control over its raw materials (incoming students). By the same token, educators should beware of stereotyping business people as shallow pragmatists incapable of rising above narrow self-interest.

Bagin and his colleagues warn against too great a dependence on business support. The bulk of school funding should come from taxpayers. Hence businesses should supplement, not supplant, financial support from the broader community.

Yet corporations and smaller companies represent a vast and diverse resource that schools are increasingly turning to their advantage. In a time when education is under fire for not keeping up with the requirements of the modern workplace, coalitions with business are likely to become both more numerous and more necessary.

Social-Service Agencies

Among the most difficult challenges facing school leaders is the need to address increasingly acute family difficulties. Until fairly recently, most schools did not feel much pressure to treat issues like poverty, unemployment, family violence, or drug abuse. But many of these problems have become so large that effective education cannot occur until they are defused.

In any given community, no school or agency has the resources to address all the needs of a troubled family. Indeed, family fragmentation appears to be growing much more rapidly than school or agency budgets, which commonly are not even keeping pace with inflation. Hence schools and social agencies are creating coalitions to address complex, systemic problems. Wendy del Mar, social worker in an urban district, said that a coalition of service providers and staff in her district quickly decided to work cooperatively because "nobody had extra funds." "Everyone was so frustrated in their agencies because of how things weren't working," she notes.

The coalition members in del Mar's area decided on a "one-stop shopping format" that puts social workers from several agencies in three elementary schools. Parents can therefore visit representatives from a wide variety of agencies in one place. Furthermore, the very process of sharing office space encourages collaboration among care providers. Professionals find themselves working together, along with clients, to create comprehensive treatment plans for the entire family, not just for one aspect of a child's life.

Coalitions in less populous areas may not be able to set up and continually staff offices in schools, but they are still able to serve entire families. In one rural area, for example, agency representatives and school staff meet weekly to plan intensive services for specific families.

Billie Bagger, Oregon's Adult and Family Services representative for such coalitions, urges social workers and school staff to create their own programs. "Don't try to take a project that worked somewhere else and try to duplicate it," she said. The collaborative process itself will produce the program best suited to a particular area's needs.

Schools are not necessarily the leaders of these coalitions. Social workers from many types of agencies are frustrated by the lack of coordination of service provision. But schools are a crucial part of these collaborative organizations. More than any other institution, they offer a context in which the entire family's needs may be comprehensively addressed.

School Boards

School leaders seeking to build support for education should not overlook school board members, who are important elements in the coalition-building process. School leaders naturally want to build goodwill between the board and the schools.

Board members, as elected representatives, have their own followings, and, if conscientious, are aware of their constituents' views. Hence administrators can use the board to sound out public opinion and to serve as a conduit for presenting school needs to particular segments of the community.

School boards can communicate effectively with other governing bodies. For example, a board of education could meet occasionally with the city council and the county board of commissioners to coordinate policies and increase community involvement in the schools.

Government Agencies

Contact with elected officials has become important not only for the school board but for school and district administrators. Government affects education—whether it is an agency providing federal money, a regulation that causes chronic problems, or a state action that facilitates providing quality education. Either way—curse or blessing—government relations have become a top priority for administrators.

Bagin, Ferguson, and Marx provide some helpful guidelines for administrators who take seriously their role of influencing the public decision-making process. They argue that a district should rely on a single administrator to handle key legislative or governmental relations. Yet professional associations and unions also play a crucial role in government relations. All school employees should shoulder part of the load.

According to Bagin and his coauthors, government relations entails a variety of efforts:

- Developing cooperative relationships with organizations that share a concern about legislative issues affecting education
- Providing leadership in issues that affect schools
- Working with regulatory agencies and various members of local, state, and federal bureaucracies

- Lobbying at the grassroots level
- Forming coalitions focused on issues that government is concerned with
- Working with nonlegislative groups interested in legislation affecting schools
- Responding to media inquiries about issues before legislative bodies
- Maintaining contact with political leaders to know their stands on educational issues
- Monitoring legislative trends in other communities
- Allying with professional associations and unions for a stronger voice in educational policy-making

The school system's goal may be to influence, mitigate, or even lead government policy and programs related to education, say Bagin and colleagues. Often, however, educational institutions wait until they are in a reactive position, when they can only try to limit and repair damage already done. Because of this, say the authors, educators should stay abreast of possible legislation and policy and maintain contacts with elected and appointed officials. The authors suggest conducting periodic surveys and generally "keeping an ear to the ground." They should stay informed of issues that could trigger legislative action. It is better, the authors suggest, to have a hand in shaping educational policy than to simply react to it.

A proactive government-relations program could include:

- Initiating legislation cooperatively with elected officials or governmental departments
- Negotiating with other groups, governmental departments, and decision-makers toward consensus
- Researching potential effects of specific legislation and regulations
- Working closely with regulators after the legislative decision is made
- Providing expert information and analysis on issues under consideration by government officials
- Preparing, coordinating, and providing testimony

School administrators, board members, and parent-group representatives can take active roles in this legislative process, say the authors.

Although "lobbying" may have an unsavory reputation and be associated with graft, bribery, and corruption, its primary purpose is "to provide elected and appointed decision-makers with the information they need to make sound decisions," say Bagin and his coauthors. The lobbyist should avoid or minimize "intuitive decision-making" on governmental issues

("Let me tell you what I think my people would say about this") and instead convey knowledge of the subject, process, and constituency. Organized and trained volunteers and a strong communications network are essential, they say.

The authors recommend following these steps in presenting official positions with supportable evidence:

> *Analyze the issue:* What is its potential impact on the school district and programs? Can the impact be measured? What will it mean in terms of funds, staffing programs, and the like?
>
> *Analyze the players:* What other groups will be affected? Who is the opposition? What are its positions, strengths, weaknesses? Who are the people behind the issues, and what are their voting records on similar issues? Who are the allies and potential members of coalitions? What is necessary for success? What do you risk losing by fighting and winning?
>
> *Know the process and laws:* What is the decision-making process for the group with which you are working? What steps do proposals go through? What happens if it is killed along the way?

Bagin and his colleagues remind us that the process is not over when a particular issue is resolved, a bill passed, or a law changed. Working with government officials or agencies should be part of a long-term relationship, much like other groups already discussed in this chapter. Maintain the contact, say the authors, and the relationship will move more smoothly. Invite them to come see you, and go to see them regularly. Write to them. Make sure that they know your school and what it faces.

Conclusion

This chapter has outlined several types of coalitions. These coalitions can be divided roughly into two major types. One consists of large organizations of diverse groups who share a commitment to strengthening a community's public education system. School leaders in such coalitions have considerable responsibility. They will recruit members, establish a governing board, and typically take the lead in helping the members work together harmoniously.

Formalized, highly organized coalitions can be very powerful. These groups should include the community's most influential leaders and representatives from a broad cross-section of its residents. They can carry out projects that are well beyond the reach of what schools could normally attain. But such coalitions require a lot of time and effort, both to form and to operate, and there is of course no guarantee that this substantial investment will bring a substantial return.

An alternative type of coalition is more limited. School leaders in these enterprises typically reach out to particular segments of the community for relatively limited objectives. Coalitions with parents can be a key part of more fully involving them in their children's education. Coalitions with businesses can reform and reenergize high school curriculums. Coalitions with social-service agencies can greatly enhance the larger learning environment of children from troubled families.

These more limited types of coalitions can be highly structured. But they can also be relatively informal: A principal can get together over coffee once a month with groups of parents, or a superintendent can telephone a local state legislator every few months.

Not every school district or school has the resources to begin a comprehensive and highly structured program of coalition-building. But in this time of rising expectations and diminishing resources, few leaders can neglect the many opportunities to work together with community groups whose support can help to build a stronger, more effective educational system.

CHAPTER

14

Leading Meetings

John Lindelow, Karen Irmsher, James Heynderickx

"Our meetings are so boring! We never seem to get anything done."

"The same people make the decisions all the time, and no one else gets involved."

"Why should we bother when most of our decisions never get carried through. No one remembers who's responsible for what and our plans are forgotten."

"As often as the principal says he wants us to be involved, he always seems to have things work out his way."

If any or all of these meeting-related commentaries strike a familiar chord, you're not alone. Research indicates that poorly run meetings are a frequent source of dissatisfaction in schools and other organizations.

Michael Doyle and David Straus note that meetings are the only time staff members actually consider themselves a group. Consequently, these group experiences directly affect their feelings about the group, their commitment to decisions, and how well they work as a team or individually. What takes place in meetings can generate a "ripple effect" on the rest of the organization. "A meeting of fifteen people," say Doyle and Straus, "can affect how 300 people work—or don't work—for the rest of the day or week or even permanently."

Just as meetings can be boring and frustrating, they can also be stimulating and satisfying. "There is a certain amount of magic when people come together for a meeting," says the 3M Meeting Management Team. It's created by the interplay of ideas and personalities that takes place in the meeting room. Part of the magic, they note, is that a meeting can be so many things at once: "a communication device, a cauldron of creativity in which new ideas are born, and an anvil on which solid plans are forged."

Well-run meetings can ease the loneliness and burden of responsibility by allowing people to work together on problems and decisions. Groups usually produce more ideas, stimulate more creative thought, develop more realistic forecasts of the consequences of decisions, and produce bolder plans than the average individual working alone. They can satisfy the need for ownership, recognition, and affiliation while engendering a sense of collaboration based on common understanding. Well-run meetings can rejuvenate an organization, leading to improved teamwork, communication, and morale on many levels.

So what gets in the way of this magical synergy? Often it's a simple lack of organizational and human-relations skills. Most of these skills are as old as meetings themselves, such as dealing with the long-winded participant, creating an agenda and sticking to it, and ensuring that responsibilities are assigned and deadlines set.

Robert Maidment and William Bullock, Jr. note that the primary distinction between efficiency and effectiveness is that of "doing the job right" and "doing the right job." Unfortunately, the first does not ensure the latter, as proved by the occurrence of "efficient meetings that yielded totally ineffective outcomes." For decades social scientists in the field of group dynamics have studied the interactions of group members to determine how the communications process can be improved. And in the behavioral sciences, a procedure called *organizational development* examines the communications structure of an organization. Both these fields have shed light on ways to make meetings more effective.

This chapter helps educators to improve their performance in meetings, both as group leaders and as participants. Before attending to practical aspects of meeting management, the leader must first establish clear-cut goals.

Goals and Values of Meetings

Begin by asking: "What do I want to accomplish with this meeting? What goals and objectives do I wish to reach? Is a meeting the best route to my goal, or might another form of communication be more efficient? What are the other benefits to be gained by scheduling a meeting, in addition to the obvious practical ends it might achieve? What will happen if I don't call a meeting? Each of these questions will be considered in turn.

Meetings with Purpose

"No wind favors him who has no destined port," goes the old saying. Yet many meetings seem to drift pointlessly with no clear goals or purposes to guide them. Every meeting should have one or more definite purposes known to all group members, and it is best when members are actively involved in determining what those purposes will be.

Most meetings take place for one or more of the following reasons:

- to exchange information
- to make a decision together
- to define, analyze, or solve a problem
- to reconcile conflicts
- to express feelings

Perhaps the most common complaint concerning meetings is that there are too many of them. Participants begin to believe they are present only to take part in an organizational ritual. "One-way, information-giving meetings," states Jack Whitehead, Jr., "can seldom be justified as either efficient or effective." The most important purposes of any meeting may be those of stimulating involvement, exchanging information and opinions, and obtaining commitments for action.

When setting a meeting's objective, consider especially the context of the meeting. How closely do the subjects proposed for discussion relate to the mission of the school? Will the decisions or actions taken make the school more effective? Donald K. Lemon, professor of educational administration at the University of North Dakota, says teachers quickly tire of talking about the business of the school. But they hunger for intellectual stimulation. Teachers do not tire of talking about teaching, says Lemon (in Jones).

Imparting Information

Meetings designed primarily for the exchange of information among participants can be set up several ways. The meeting leader may want to brief or instruct members, as in a training session. Conversely, the leader may want to receive reports from participants. In this type of meeting, a more autocratic leadership style is usually the most efficient.

The advantage of an information meeting over a memo or written report is that reaction and feedback can be immediate. Every member can hear the information presented and the reaction of all other members to it. But, notes Nicholas Criscuolo, too many information meetings can cause teachers to complain, especially when meetings relate routine announcements that could easily be presented in a bulletin or via the school's public-address system.

Another problem with information meetings, say Barbara and Kenneth Palmer, is that too many meeting leaders fail to recognize the importance of personalizing the content. In dealing with complex information, it's vital to provide concrete illustrations of how changes will affect students or the working atmosphere of the school. Role plays are one way to stimulate interest and reduce confusion.

Decision-Making

Decision-making modes range from autocratic to fully democratic. A single person may simply wish to get some input from participants before making a decision; the majority may overrule the minority; or the total group may reach consensus after discussion and debate.

Many decisions are best made by one person or a small group, but if committed action by most or all members of the group is required, it is best to get consensus. "Indeed," say Richard Schmuck and Philip Runkel, "when nonsupport or sabotage by one or more members could seriously damage an undertaking that requires total group support, a decision by majority vote could be dangerous."

Problem-Solving

Several heads are usually better than one, particularly for defining, analyzing, and solving problems. In a problem-solving session, a group can combine the bits and pieces of experience and insight that may lead to a common understanding. According to the 3M Meeting Management Team, the best results come through interaction. Therefore, an effective problem-solving group process must engender "a well-balanced interplay of ideas, experiences, facts, contradictions and insights." An effective group may be flexible and wide-ranging in its thought, but at the same time sift out impractical or far-flung ideas.

Leadership styles can vary widely in problem-solving meetings, depending on the nature of the problem, time limitations, and other variables. For example, a brainstorming session might be called to foster ideas for increasing community awareness of certain school programs. In such a session, a very informal, democratic atmosphere would be needed to stimulate a variety of ideas. If, on the other hand, the analysis of a problem calls for an orderly presentation of data and some hard thinking, a more leader-controlled meeting would be more efficient.

Reconciling Conflicts

A meeting is often the best format for exploring sharp differences of opinion and negotiating some kind of compromise. Ernest and Nancy Bormann recommend putting the conflict on the agenda as a first step, and making certain to allocate adequate time for it. This type of meeting requires tight control so tempers do not flare. If the conflict does not directly affect the group leader, he or she can serve primarily as a facilitator, bringing out and clarifying points of contention, making sure that each side's position is fully heard, and hammering out compromises. When the group leader is one of the principal contenders, it is necessary (and sometimes required by law) to appoint a neutral third party to manage the conflict.

The goal is to reach agreement, say Maria Shelton and Laurie Bauer. But the process begins by allowing participants to speak their minds. People exhibiting closed body language, anger, disagreement, or boredom should be especially encouraged to express their feelings. "Once the cards are out on the table, and everyone has the chance to voice concerns, then it is possible to brainstorm solutions."

The three primary channels for resolving conflict, according to the Palmers, are force, arbitration, and mediation or negotiation. If a conflict in a meeting is limited to only a few people, or concerns a minor issue, the group leader might use the force of his or her authority to settle the matter without further discussion. When a meeting's participants voice sharply different ideas and viewpoints on an important issue, the Palmers say the only fair and efficient way to resolve conflict is through mediation or negotiation. Time must be invested "to explore all aspects of the dispute or conflict, look at a full range of alternatives for resolving the conflict, and work toward a mutually agreeable decision," they state. When a leader is perceived to be less than absolutely neutral in a decision, more democratic channels for resolution should be used.

The resolution of personal conflicts should not be attempted during meetings, nor should the group leader discipline or reprimand organizational members while a meeting is in progress. Such actions, when necessary, are best carried out through individual meetings and actions.

Expressing Feelings

It is often useful to hold gripe sessions or rap sessions with staff members to sound out their feelings about the organization and its administration. Such meetings should be as permissive and unstructured as possible, for they are important steam valves for an organization. The leader should remain in the background and allow members to contribute spontaneously. At the same time, it's helpful to set guidelines for expression, to prevent the meeting from turning into a boxing match.

One way to describe a feeling, say Schmuck and Runkel, is to use "I" statements, such as "I'm worried," or "I feel annoyed," and go on to detail the action that's bothering you. For example, "I feel annoyed when you come to meetings 15 minutes late." The aim should be to open a dialogue that will improve the relationship, not to coerce the other person into changing.

When teachers believe meetings they attend are meaningless or boring, Criscuolo suggests that administrators involve them in setting agenda topics. One way is to form a committee to generate agenda topics and themes felt to be of particular importance. Even a simple action, such as placing a blackboard or clipboard in the faculty lounge for teachers to write down possible topics or issues, can encourage participation in planning. The strategic placement of favored topics can help maintain interest and involvement during mundane but necessary items on the agenda.

Is a Meeting Necessary?

The best way to reduce wasted time in meetings is to ask whether the goals of the meeting might be reached in some other, more efficient way. Too many meetings are called simply because it's a certain time of the week or month. An effective leader, Whitehead notes, will consider whether six ten-minute face-to-face meetings with individuals would be more effective than gathering them all together. Memos, e-mail, staff bulletins, computer network bulletin boards, or telephone calls (individual or conference) can often accomplish the communication desired without the time and expense of a meeting.

Generally, says the 3M Meeting Management Team, meetings should only be called when a situation requires group action or participation. "If this common denominator can't be found, then the meeting probably shouldn't be called and alternate means of communication should be investigated."

On the other hand, group decisions are more likely to be on target than individual decisions. It's also sensible to reveal as much of the reasoning process as possible to public scrutiny in this era of increasing accountability.

Hidden Values of Meetings

Most meetings can achieve more than the organizational goals stated on the agenda. Well-run, effective, purposeful meetings can satisfy the personal and emotional needs of individual members, especially those of participation, belonging, achievement, and power. Participants interact, develop roles, and share their experiences, problems, and successes.

Meetings also play an important role in building the cohesiveness of an organization. "In the simplest and most basic way," states Antony Jay, "a meeting defines the team, the group, or the unit. Those present belong to it; those absent do not. Everyone is able to look around and perceive the whole group and sense the collective identity of which he or she forms a part."

Schmuck and Runkel characterize the values of school meetings as follows:

> Meetings provide an opportunity for participation not found in memos, newsletters, loudspeaker announcements, and the like. They enable us to check reactions immediately to a speaker's contribution and to our own utterances as well. If managed effectively, meetings can be the principal channel for bringing staff members into collaboration to reach common understandings, and for that reason can be highly productive and satisfying events in the life of the educational organization.

Basics of Meeting Planning

Conducting a meeting without a plan is a lot like trying to build a house without blueprints. It can be done, but the process is likely to be a frustrating waste of time and the end result disappointing. The time spent planning a meeting, notes Cindy Morley, reduces the actual meeting time. "It makes a lot of sense for you to spend an additional planning hour to reduce one hour of a meeting involving ten people's time!"

To start, ask yourself, "What are the reasons for the meeting?" Put the purposes in statements that begin with the word "to," and continue with a verb and pertinent details. For instance, "to decide how teachers will share the computer lab." The next step is to state the desired outcome. The outcome for the purpose stated above might be "a decision on, and schedule for, use of the computer lab."

The meeting planner should try to imagine what is likely to happen in the meeting from beginning to end, especially barriers that may impede progress. The purpose of the meeting generally provides a preliminary idea of who will be attending and what might transpire. From that point, the planner should consider the stakes the meeting participants have in the matters to discuss. How will their personalities and positions affect the course of discussion? What conflicts are likely to develop among participants? Who will be asked to change or adjust, and how might they react?

If the meeting is called to solve targeted problems, make sure the necessary skills and information are on hand. If the requisite skills are not available within the organization, consider inviting experts. Once the critical issues on which a decision might hinge are identified, a range of possible compromises can be generated. Every situation is different, but most decisions are made by determining what can and cannot be traded off.

Other important facets of meeting planning include writing up the agenda, allotting time for each item, deciding who will attend, arranging the seating, and selecting the meeting room.

The Agenda and Time Considerations

The agenda is a meeting's blueprint. Its purpose is to make sure that all topics are covered, that the meeting moves along from point to point, and that something is accomplished.

Agendas can be written up beforehand or generated at the beginning of a meeting. Many meeting leaders combine both methods of input.

Before a meeting, it's wise to consult with meeting participants to determine what topics need to be covered. Premeeting discussions can sometimes eliminate the need to put a topic on the agenda, saving everyone's time. Early consultation can also stimulate participants to properly prepare for the meeting.

Preset agendas should be distributed to meeting participants from one to three days before the meeting. This allows time for careful consideration of meeting topics, but is not so far in advance that participants forget it or lose it. When a meeting is called on short notice, advance distribution of the agenda may be impossible. On the other hand, earlier circulation of an agenda may be necessary for an elaborate meeting or one requiring detailed preparation.

Any necessary background information should be distributed to participants before the meeting, along with the agenda. "High quality information leads to high quality decisions," says Barry Maude, and prevents a discussion from becoming a mere pooling of ignorance. Brief and concise background information allows participants to consider matters carefully in advance and formulate useful questions.

The agenda should include definite starting and ending times. Participants have other commitments and it is common courtesy to let them know when the meeting will be over.

Meetings should also have an internal structuring of time. This, too, can be done before or at the beginning of the meeting. Whitehead says meetings often correspond to "a type of Parkinson's Law in which the length of time it takes to reach a decision expands to the amount of time available." Simple topics need only a few minutes, and all should agree to limit useless discussion and avoid any superfluous additions.

When a meeting is held to resolve a complex problem, the group can avoid wasting a lot of time if it agrees in advance to follow a particular problem-solving strategy. For instance, Ken Blanchard outlines the "Ross Four-Step Agenda" developed by Ray Ross:

1. Define and limit the problem.
2. Determine the nature of the problem and its causes.
3. Establish and rank the criteria for solutions.
4. Evaluate and select solutions.

Such a systematic process helps the group to focus objectively on the clarification and solution of a problem.

The order of agenda items is another aspect of meeting design that can be arranged to achieve desired ends. Urgent items, of course, need to come before those that can wait. But if some items might divide members, and others might unite them, the meeting planner can vary their order to produce, hopefully, a smoother running meeting. In any case, it's always a good idea to end each meeting with a unifying item.

Antony Jay makes these suggestions concerning the order of agenda items:

> The early part of a meeting tends to be more lively and creative than the end of it, so if an item needs mental energy, bright ideas, and clear heads, it may be better to put it high up on the list. Equally, if there is one item of great interest and concern to everyone, it may be a good idea to hold it back for a while and get some other useful work done first. Then the star item can be introduced to carry the meeting over the attention lag that sets in after the first 15 to 20 minutes of the meeting.

The overall length of meetings can also affect the quality of decision-making that takes place. Meetings scheduled to last longer than an hour may best be separated into a set of shorter meetings. Similar topics can be clustered in each meeting, allowing a smaller number of participants.

Meetings are not likely to remain productive after two hours. Thinking begins to falter and emotions take over, opening the door to dissension. The ideal length seems to be from an hour to an hour and a half. If a meeting must go longer, be sure to provide coffee and fresh-air breaks.

In addition to the meeting date, location, and starting and ending times, the agenda should contain a brief description of each topic, the outcome desired for each topic (for example, decision, discussion, information), the name of the person responsible for introducing each topic, and the estimated time allocated to each.

Although a firm structure is desirable for effective meetings, the planner should not overstructure the meeting. Meetings fully and rigidly planned may give participants the impression they are merely assembling to hear proclamations. Involving participants in agenda-setting shows them you value their views, information, and problem-solving talents. So within the structure of the agenda, a good bit of flexibility is advised.

Who Shall Attend?

Once the desired goals of a meeting are determined, the question of who should participate will be half answered. The search then begins for those who are most affected by the issues to be discussed, those who have to give or receive information at the meeting, and those whose presence is necessary or desirable for decision-making purposes.

It is most important, according to Maude, that meeting participants be chosen from the organizational level most appropriate to deal with the problem. Experienced, upperlevel administrators, for example, should be involved in deciding long-term policy issues, since they "have the experience and overview to grasp the financial implications of a particular decision and to overcome the inherent uncertainty of this kind of long-term decision-making."

By the same token, middle-level managerial decisions and day-to-day operating decisions should also be made at the appropriate level. Maude warns against inviting people to meetings simply because of their high status in the organization. One secret of making meetings more efficient, he states, is to "push decisionmaking as far down the organization as it will go, i.e. to the lowest level competent to handle the problem."

Depending on the goals of your meeting, you can invite either a group with diverse personalities or a more like-minded group. Maude cites evidence that

> meetings made up of people of unlike personalities often produce better solutions than like-minded groups. The reason may be the wide range of ideas that is likely; or simply that different-minded people tend to disagree and this prevents over-hasty decisions being made.

For creative problem-solving sessions, it may pay to invite a range of people from different levels and backgrounds, perhaps even some "outsiders."

Once the people who might either do the meeting some good or gain something from it are identified, the next step is to pare down the attendee list so it includes only those members whose presence is absolutely necessary. Meeting-improvement experts all agree that poor meetings are more likely to occur when too many people have been invited.

Although the philosophy of the public sector necessitates the use of participative decision-making for important decisions, a gathering of twenty or thirty people to touch all the bases usually results in unproductive or stagnant meetings. Productive meetings are the result of the right persons discussing one subject at a time. As Whitehead puts it, a single conversation is difficult to maintain when a meeting has more than eleven members. The most common outcome is that several conversations will start up simultaneously, and the group will deteriorate into several smaller groups.

To preserve a flow of interaction, Whitehead suggests seven or eight members as being the best number. Jay states "between 4 and 7 is generally ideal, 10 is tolerable, and 12 is the outside limit." If a meeting must involve a large number of participants, it may be desirable to create committees or subgroups to work on particular topics. Groups of four or fewer are more prone to biased decisions, and they lack the "breadth of experience and thinking to deal adequately with complex problems," says Maude. On the other hand, when groups grow to over ten, "an increasing number of people are scared into silence" and "intimate face-to-face contact between all members becomes impossible."

The optimum number for a particular working group is best found through experimentation. The ideal size is large enough to provide the needed expertise to solve a problem, yet small enough to prevent communication and control problems.

Seating Arrangements

The meeting objectives should be taken into account in determining the seating arrangement, as well as the leadership style. Another factor is whether the meeting planner wishes to promote or prevent conflict among individuals.

Meetings on important issues tend to produce the most conflict among participants. This, in turn, often results in a deadlock between two groups in the meeting with no resolution. Kermit Moore researched this phenomenon in a large Philadelphia high school and found without exception that "opposing groups consistently sat together on opposite sides of a large rectangular table." The table was the "no man's land" across which the two opposing factions would repeatedly face off. Individuals voted as blocks, instead of following the logic of others' arguments and changing points of view.

The solution is to intersperse the opposing groups around a circular table. This eliminates the competitive "face off" and reduces the space between the participants from a public to a personal distance. It fosters cooperation rather than competition, according to Moore.

A group leader can also increase, or decrease, his or her control of the meeting by his position at the table. In placing opposing groups around a circular table, the leader may choose to seat the most disruptive members next to him, since proximity increases control. Seating near the leader is also one of the best ways to encourage the participation of quiet or shy participants who have intelligent viewpoints and ideas but rarely make them known.

When it is essential for the meeting to be "leader-central," the symbolism is strongest if the leader sits at the head of a long, narrow table. To decrease the chance of verbal tennis matches that can occur with a rectangular table, a recommended variation is to have the leader sit at the middle of a U-shaped arrangement.

When a gathering, such as an information-giving meeting, does not involve social interaction, the leader can emphasize his or her authority through position, height, and density. The classic arrangement is to place the leader at the front of the room with all other chairs facing the front. This arrangement may be enhanced if the leader is elevated, since "North Americans tend to associate height with status," says Moore.

You can increase the energy level by seating group members close together, rather than allowing them to spread out in a large number of chairs. "To increase audience interest and involvement," Moore suggests, "jam people together in a space that's confining enough to create mild (but no more than mild) irritation in the members of the audience."

In general, however, the meeting planner will want to increase interaction and eye contact among meeting participants. When participants can see one another's faces and read their body language, their mutual understanding will grow. For greatest eye contact, use a U-shaped or circular table.

The Meeting Room

"Leaders usually get their best results when the participants feel comfortable in their surroundings," says the 3M Meeting Management Team.

This may seem like common sense, yet how many meetings have you attended where something disturbed your concentration, such as an uncomfortable chair, a burnt-out projector bulb, a hot, overcrowded room, or a dance class meeting on the floor directly above? Attention to the physical setting of a meeting may not guarantee a good meeting, but it can prevent a bad one.

The location of your meeting depends on its purpose. For an instructional meeting, a classroom may be the best place. A ritualistic meeting, such as one held to celebrate some success, or the first meeting of the school year, should probably be held in the best conference room available. Problem-solving or decision-making meetings need only a simple meeting room. A leader may choose to hold private meetings in his or her own office to gain a "home court" advantage. But a leader should be cautious about holding a decision-making meeting in her office. The surrounding symbolism is bound to overwhelm some people, thus inhibiting free communication.

The size of the meeting room should match the size of the group. Maude reports that "the size of the room preferred by most participants is one that gives the impression of being comfortably full—not crowded—when everyone is present and sitting around the table."

Chairs should be comfortable, but not so comfortable participants doze off. Electrical sockets should be available for projectors, recorders, and so forth, and the meeting planner should make sure the correct audiovisual equipment is available and in working order. Paper and pencils should be in ample supply, and a coffee pot should be nearby. Since teachers are likely to be tired and hungry after a long school day, Maidment and Bullock suggest simply to "feed the troops." An inexpensive tray of carrot sticks and other snacks can supply surprising motivation.

Good acoustics, lighting, and ventilation are other common-sense necessities for a good meeting. A room with poor acoustics or lighting may lull participants to sleep or frustrate them. Poor ventilation can also make group members irritable, especially if there is antagonism between smoking and nonsmoking participants. The best remedy is to restrict smoking during the meeting altogether.

Incoming telephone calls, late-comers, and outside noises are also common meeting distractions. All but emergency calls to meeting participants should be held. If the meeting room has two or more entrances, only one should be used, to minimize interruption by late-comers. And the meeting should be held in a room not usually subject to outside noises.

It's impossible, of course, to meet in an ideal room every time, but by paying attention to environmental factors that can be altered, you can usually ensure that the meeting environment will be comfortable and conducive to good communication.

The Art of Leading a Meeting

"The root word of facilitate is *facil*," notes Morley, "which means to make things easy. As a meeting leader, your role is to make participation in the meeting easy and to make reaching the desired outcomes achievable."

Even with the best planning, meetings can go awry. Half of the leader's job is planning and preparation. The other half consists of successfully managing the human energy during the meeting.

The concept of leadership has changed rapidly in recent decades. It was once recommended that the leader be the master and controller of the group, acting like the captain of a ship. Now it is more common for the meeting leader to be a manager and facilitator whose primary function is to foster a democratic and cooperative group process among participants. The suggestions in this section are designed more for the leader as facilitator and less for the leader as captain.

The What and How of Meeting Management

Trained meeting observers and perceptive meeting participants are aware of three distinct sets of activities that take place in every working session. The first set, called the "task"or "content" activities of the group, has to do with what the group is doing. The second set, called "maintenance" or "process" activities, has to do with how the group is doing it. The third set, called "team building" activities, involves ways the group is improving its cohesiveness and expanding its effectiveness. The group leader should be aware of and facilitate all three activities.

Task activities relate to the stated goals of the meeting. Examples include setting goals, listing priorities, using background and history, examining consequences, linking with other issues, setting assignments, and agreeing on time limits.

Maintenance activities, states Nicholas DeLuca, "focus on keeping the group in functioning order by attending to process and group interactions." They involve the personal, usually unstated, goals of each member, to feel acceptance and affiliation, to achieve, and to have power. Schmuck and Runkel list the following as typical process activities: ensuring that others have a chance to speak, reconciling disagreements, and sensing group mood.

Maintenance activities can be evaluated by watching the eruption of conflict and how it is handled, the participants' body language, the relevance of inputs from each participant, the expression of emotion by participants (such as anger, irritation, resentment, apathy, boredom, warmth, appreciation, or satisfaction), and the mixture of seriousness and playfulness in the group.

When emotions start surfacing, it is time for the group leader and other sensitive meeting participants to start "maintaining" the human relations in the group. Once calm is restored, the meeting leader can guide the group back into task activities.

Shelton and Bauer suggest developing three communication skills for use in conflict management: disarming, empathy, and inquiry. *Disarming,* they say, is the most difficult but also the most powerful: "You simply listen and then find something to agree with in what the other person is saying. This can defuse a potentially volatile situation." *Empathy* "requires that you put yourself in the other person's shoes and look at the world through his or her eyes, either by paraphrasing what the individual says or by identifying with his or her feelings." *Inquiry* "allows you to ask gentle, probing questions to determine what is going on." Gathering additional insight allows you to work with the conflict.

Team-building activities, says DeLuca, "are designed to strengthen the group's capacity to act in the future." Considered collectively, team-building activities involve motivation functions, training functions, and celebration functions that serve to enhance the cohesiveness of the group as well as expand individual abilities and effectiveness. As team commitment grows stronger, the expertise and devotion of each participant coheres into a powerful force for success, allowing the leader to become more a facilitator than a leader.

Task Functions

The agenda is the primary tool the group leader has to help a group toward its goals. It defines the topics and objectives of the meeting and structures the time within the meeting. The agenda lists the work items of the meeting, the roadmap to its goals.

Topic number 1 on any agenda should be the approval of the agenda itself. This activity allows participants to review the "meeting menu" and suggest any changes they believe are necessary. For example, some members might believe that a topic deserves more time in light of recent events, or that a certain topic should be talked about first. Even if no changes are made, the agenda review and approval are valuable for setting the stage for the meeting and allowing members to consider the topics collectively, before individually.

Whenever possible, the meeting leader's introduction to each topic should include a brief summation of its purpose and issues, aspects agreed upon in earlier discussions, and points of disagreement. The information can set the stage for immediate discussion and action.

During the course of the meeting, the leader is responsible for monitoring the discussion in relation to its plan, the agenda. If the conversation gets off track, the leader should correct the direction of discussion. Questions can be a useful way to redirect the course of a meeting. For example, the leader may ask, "Just a moment, please. How does this relate to the point Janet made earlier?" A more direct approach, however, is sometimes needed: "This is interesting, but we're getting off the subject. Let's get back to the main topic."

The repetition of ideas or a general loss of interest indicate that a subject has been discussed enough and that it is time to move to the next topic. But it's also important that the leader be flexible and not hurry the meeting along too fast in the interest of sticking to the agenda. Says Maude: "Meetings need time to deal with complex problems: under pressure, they settle for quick but unsound decisions." For simple and routine decisions, it's best to decide them quickly, allowing time for more important decisions. This is best accomplished when the group sets its own time allotments and sticks to them.

A good way to round off the discussion of a topic is to summarize the main points that were made. The leader can then gracefully move to the next topic. This may be done by simply introducing the group member listed on the agenda as responsible for the topic. Or the leader may give background information, then solicit group members' ideas.

At times it may become obvious that a different approach is needed to solve a problem. The leader should stop the discussion, suggest a new strategy, and ask what the group thinks of the change. Such restructurings of the group process can save time and prevent unnecessary conflict.

Another frequent problem is that some members are more aggressive than others in their presentation of ideas. More timid members may have good ideas, but their ideas may only get half-stated or half-heard. It is up to the meeting leader to assume the role of "best listener"—to draw out ideas and help elaborate them for the group. When the focus of a discussion is a decision, the leader should step in when he or she senses there may be a consensus, and ask if the group is in substantial agreement. If no consensus is in sight and the discussion is not progressing, the leader can call for a vote. If consensus is necessary, however, the leader may have to think of a new method for resolving the remaining conflicts.

When a decision is made, the meeting leader should clarify what the decision is and how it will be implemented. This solid information should be entered at once into the minutes and recorded by the participants who have agreed to the tasks. An action plan, writes Morley, should answer these questions:

What is the task (or action step) to be completed?

Who is going to do it?

By when will it be done?

At the conclusion of the meeting, the leader should sum up the entire meeting, restating its decisions and assignments of responsibility. Just before the meeting adjourns may be a good time to schedule the next meeting with group members.

Maintenance Functions

Maintenance functions concern the way people feel, think, and act while they're immersed in the task. The importance of these functions can equal that of task functions, according to Leland Bradford, since "without attention to moods, feelings, and interpersonal relationships, a group chokes its lifeline of energy and motivation to complete the task." The amount of personal reward members feel influences both their willingness to participate and their satisfaction with group outcomes.

The meeting leader must attend to maintenance functions, then, to create a group in which members feel involved, nonthreatened, and satisfied in their personal needs. As negative interpersonal conflicts fade, the natural tendencies of humans to cooperate and solve mutual problems will emerge.

Drawing out and encouraging the more timid members of a group is one maintenance function already mentioned. Doing this not only increases the group's idea pool but prevents the withdrawal of timid members from active participation. Withdrawn members can cause trouble for a meeting in two ways. First, they are dead weight on the group's shoulders, contributing little to the meeting's productivity. Second, out of resentment, they may sabotage group decisions by "forgetting" to do things or by working actively against implementation of decisions in which they felt they had no say.

Group members who feel they and their ideas are valuable to the group will work for the group instead of against it, because they have gotten something positive from the group: acceptance, identity, and a feeling of belonging. Thus, the group leader should encourage participation from all members and ensure the quieter members are not overlooked.

One way to open verbal space for the timid or unheard member is to take action against domineering participants, especially those who are long-winded. The Palmers offer four suggestions for dealing with the disruptive participant:

- Don't yield the floor to them again when they finally yield it to another person.
- Direct the conversation to another: "John, I know this is a concern of yours as well; what do you think?"

- Summarize for them: "Let me see if I understand what you're saying before we go any further."
- Take the direct approach: "Jane, we don't have a lot of time. . . ." or "I'm sorry to interrupt, but we still have to deal with. . . ."

It's also the leader's role to be a harmonizer when conflict breaks out in a meeting, as it inevitably will. "Harmonizing," says Bradford, "is negotiation between opposing sides in which one member serves as a third-party peacemaker, trying to retrieve the best ideas of both sides."

A certain degree of conflict, however, is part of a healthy group process. "When overdone," Bradford also warns, "harmonizing dulls the flash of creativity that confrontation can produce." But when conflict is extreme and egos are involved, the process can come to a complete standstill.

To decrease personal conflicts, it is important to distinguish clearly between ideas and individuals. Ideas, not individuals, should be evaluated by the group, stresses Bradford. "An individual may feel that a critical evaluation of his contribution is a rejection of himself. Such individuals, unable to separate their ideas from themselves, may withdraw. Others may fight, creating polarization and conflict in the group."

It's no easy task getting participants to keep their minds on ideas instead of individuals, but reminders from the leader at critical times can help. One useful way to emphasize the distinction is to have each member write down his or her ideas for the solution of the problem. Collect the ideas and emphasize they have become group property. Then have the group evaluate the ideas one by one.

If possible, the leader should not take sides in an argument. When questioned about his or her opinion, the leader should relay the question back to the group: "That is a tough problem. Can someone take a crack at it?" A leader who answers questions about substantive measures is likely to be drawn into conflict. Once part of the fight, she loses control of the meeting. The leader who tries to both lead the meeting and take an active part in it may monopolize the meeting.

Indeed, monopolizing the meeting is usually what a traditional-style leader does when conflict is brewing. Yet one cannot both lead a meeting in which a personal stake is held and facilitate the meeting, as if neutral. One solution, discussed in the next section, is to train several or all members in facilitating meetings. Then when conflict erupts, the person neutral on the issue can referee. Another approach, discussed later in this chapter, is to have a neutral person from outside the group facilitate the entire meeting (see "The Interaction Method").

Team-Building Functions

In his best-selling book *The 7 Habits of Highly Effective People,* Steven Covey defines the word *synergy*:

> It means that the whole is greater than the sum of its parts. It means that the relationship which the parts have to each other is a part in and of itself. It is not only a part, but the most catalytic, the most empowering, the most unifying, and the most exciting part.

The object of team-building activities is to nurture synergy—to continually refine and add to meeting members' skills while increasing their motivation and cohesiveness as a group. Team-building activities are a combination of task and maintenance activities, because they provide work items on the agenda that focus on the needs and abilities of group members.

Team-building activities may include specific training activities that add to participants' communication skills, thus increasing their ability to work as a team. For instance, if all group members learn meeting-facilitation skills or conflict-management skills, discussions can progress more smoothly and decisions can be made more quickly.

Motivation and celebration activities can be equally important ways to build team cohesiveness and interaction. Motivation activities, says DeLuca, "reinforce group membership and participation in the organization." One sure-fire way to provide motivation for group members is to recognize organizational and individual achievements. If an individual creates a successful new disciplinary plan, that person should be singled out in a meeting and applauded. If a group of teachers devises a new materials-distribution plan more efficient than the old one, a significant part of the group's next meeting should be spent celebrating that achievement. Whether it be food and drink in the meeting room or a gathering at a restaurant after the meeting, participants should be allowed to step away from issues and ideas for a while and enjoy their accomplishments.

You as a Participant

A meeting's success is not, of course, solely dependent on the leader's capabilities. Participants are also responsible for making meetings work.

The first rule for meeting participants is to come prepared. Read the agenda, think about the topics to be discussed, and make sure you understand the issues. Review the background information provided with the agenda, formulate your own views and opinions, and imagine what other points of view might be presented.

When you have a presentation to make at a meeting, prepare yourself fully: make an outline, prepare any visual aids you need, and rehearse your presentation. If your proposals are controversial, discuss them with key people before the meeting.

Once the meeting begins, use good manners: try not to shuffle papers or engage in side conversations. Participants are obligated to attend each meeting with a good "discussion attitude," say the Palmers, which "means being open-minded, willing to consider compromise, accepting of disagreement and criticism, objective and realistic about your own contributions, and respectful of the contributions of others." Ask clarifying questions when there appears to be confusion. Speak up when you have knowledge or ideas to share, but don't overparticipate—remember that you are part of an active group process.

The 3M Meeting Management Team notes that "good participants" also speak only when they have something to say that adds to what has been said and bears directly on the topic; avoid haggling over small, unimportant details; and do not interrupt a speaker in the middle of a thought. They help the leader by sticking to agenda topics and time limits, drawing out the ideas of others, facilitating the resolution of conflicts, and criticizing ideas instead of people. And they make it a point of respect to arrive on time.

Utilizing Minutes

Minutes were invented to prevent conflict as much as to provide records. Memory, unfortunately, can be as fleeting as time itself. While you're in the meeting, it's easy to assume that everyone will remember what the final outcome of a discussion was and what assignments were made. Later, participants may find themselves asking each other, "Didn't we deal with that last week?" or "Wasn't Alice supposed to get that information to us for the next meeting?"

Thus, an important principle for making meetings more effective is to document the results. Promptly recording the decisions and required actions will help ensure they are both remembered and implemented properly.

Minutes may consist of a few simple statements outlining the major decisions of a meeting. At the very least they should answer these questions: What action is required, and how will it take place? Who is responsible for taking action? When should these actions be completed? It is also advisable to note motions that didn't pass.

The information can be recorded by a group member or the group leader. Once a decision is reached, the minute-taker should record the decision and all its details, then immediately read it back to the group for confirmation.

Because meeting topics change from meeting to meeting, it may be wise to have a different person take notes at every meeting. "Choose someone who is unlikely to become involved in the meeting's controversies," suggests Oswald Ratteray. If an experienced and articulate writer is not available within the group, or absolute impartiality is required, it may be best to hire a formal minute taker.

One way to speed up this process is by using a tape recorder and extracting the necessary information after the meeting. "If your meeting is dynamic," states Ratteray, "participants will soon forget the equipment. When they know why it's there, they'll talk 'for the record' as much as to each other." Part of the stated policy of using a tape recorder should be to erase tapes as soon as the information is transcribed.

In addition to being time-consuming, another disadvantage of taking minutes on the traditional notepad is that others at the table cannot refer to past key points. Many facilitators now track the proceedings of a meeting on large pieces of paper taped to the wall, or on large pads at an easel. Participants can see the past flow of ideas in the meeting and won't feel as compelled to repeat their thoughts. This method also serves to depersonalize ideas. Once written on the pad, ideas become the property of the group, not the individual.

After the meeting, Ratteray recommends that the notes or recording of the meeting becomes the basis of an executive summary "that systematically helps sort the wheat from the chaff." Under each topic or subject, a concise digest of what was discussed should be presented, perhaps focusing only on new information gained in the meeting and significant feedback. The summary should then be distributed to participants or published in the faculty newsletter.

The rewards of summarizing meetings will become apparent in future meetings. A concise record of previous discussions can help participants prepare for the next meeting. Ratteray suggests, further, that meeting summaries be indexed under topic headings. Such archives can be used to resolve future problems and conflicts.

The Interaction Method

Another way to solve the leader/facilitator conflict mentioned earlier is to have a person from outside the group do the facilitating. In this arrangement, the leader is free to concentrate on the "what" of the meeting (the task functions), while the facilitator takes care of the "how" of the meeting (the maintenance functions). This is the approach proposed by Michael Doyle and David Straus in *How to Make Meetings Work.*

Dubbed the "Interaction Method," the process actually involves four separate roles that "collectively form a self-correcting system of checks and balances." The *facilitator* is "a neutral servant of the group and does not evaluate or contribute ideas." The facilitator suggests methods and procedures for the meeting, protects members of the group from personal attack, and makes sure everyone has an opportunity to speak. In short, "the facilitator serves as a combination of tool guide, traffic officer, and meeting chauffeur." He or she also takes charge of premeeting and postmeeting logistics.

The *recorder,* or minute taker, is also neutral and nonevaluating. The recorder writes the group's ideas on large sheets of paper on the walls, using, whenever possible, the actual words of each speaker. The advantages of this approach, according to the authors, are that "the act of recording does not significantly slow down the process of the meeting," and the written record (the "group memory") serves as "an accepted record of what is happening as it is happening."

The *group member* is the role played by the active participants in the meeting. The group members "keep the facilitator and recorder in their neutral roles" and make sure ideas are recorded accurately. Group members can also "make procedural suggestions" and "overrule the suggestions of the facilitators." Other than these functions, their main focus is the agenda and the tasks to be accomplished.

The fourth and final role is that of the *manager/chairperson,* who is an active participant in the group yet retains the powers and responsibilities of the traditional leadership position. The manager "makes all final decisions," controls the progress of the meeting, sets the agenda, "argues actively for his or her points of view," and "urges group members to accept tasks and deadlines."

Even though the Interaction Method was built around an autocratic leadership style, it is now a prescribed technique in the area of participative decision-making. The alterations needed to adjust the method to a more democratic style, or even a leaderless group, are very simple. The most important changes involve the manager / chairperson. While continuing to define the limits of the group's authority, he or she does not usurp the roles of the facilitator or the recorder.

Many organizations have implemented the Interaction Method and report widespread success. Doyle and Straus's book contains a complete description of the method as well as a wealth of techniques for improving meetings.

Tools for Evaluating and Improving Meetings

According to a survey by Richard Gorton and James Burns, teachers believe the minimal requirements of meeting planning, group interaction, and follow-through are often not fulfilled. A majority of teachers surveyed in eleven school systems expressed disappointment with the way meetings were conducted in their schools. Major areas of discontent included unavailability of background information, irregular planning procedures, control of meetings by a minority of members while others are silent, and unavailable or poorly summarized minutes.

Gorton and Burns concluded, "If teachers are not adequately involved during the meetings in productive problem solving and consensus seeking, they are likely to view their meetings as boring, unimportant, and administrator dominated."

When discontent among meeting members arises in a school, it is the group leader's responsibility to isolate the main problems and attempt to solve them. Literature on group dynamics and organizational development is replete with exercises, techniques, and "structured experiences" for evaluating and improving meetings. Some can be implemented easily and do not require special training, whereas others require considerable preparation and followup and work best with a meeting consultant.

As an example of the former, the Bormanns provide three checklists for meeting improvement. The first is used to evaluate how well the group communicated. It asks questions such as "How good were the members' basic discussion skills?," "How effective and rewarding was the group process?," and "Were agreements productive or non-productive?" The second checklist is designed for evaluating a meeting by a participant or an observer. Questions include "Was the preparation for the meeting adequate?," "Was a permissive social climate established?," and "Did the leader exercise the right amount of control?" The final checklist is designed for the leader to evaluate how well he or she led the meeting: "Did you 'loosen up' the group before plunging into discussion?," "Did you pose a challenging question to start the discussion?"

Perhaps the best way to keep meeting planning and organization in step with the needs of the school is to have participants evaluate the meeting process at least twice a year. Bradford provides six brief evaluation forms members can complete at meeting's end. The leader and group can use the resulting data in several ways: a summary of the results can be announced at the next meeting; the leader can select themes from the forms and ask for discussion on those topics only; or the group can devote a whole meeting to the maintenance issues that surfaced via the evaluation forms.

Jack Fordyce and Raymond Weil describe several simple techniques for improving meetings. In "Going Around the Room," each participant in turn is asked to state his or her position at that moment. This method is useful "when the group is hung up around the views of those who are dominating the conversation," say Fordyce and Weil, as well as "when the group seems to have run out of solutions." It is also a handy method for quickly evaluating a meeting and for winding up a meeting.

In "Subgrouping," the group is temporarily divided into smaller groups of two to six people to discuss either the same or different topics. In larger groups, subgrouping can keep members involved, allow every participant to be heard, and permit more than one topic to be discussed at once. (A legislature with its committee system is the epitome of subgrouping.) Fordyce and Weil report the success of subgrouping in a meeting that included both professional and clerical workers: "To surface underlying issues for the agenda, the group was divided into homogeneous subgroups. Each subgroup reported its proposed agenda items. For the first time, the voices of the clerical staff were heard."

Publications containing additional evaluation tools and suggestions for improving meetings are *Meetings: Accomplishing More with Better & Fewer* by Robert Maidment and William Bullock, *Taking Your Meetings Out of the Doldrums* by Eva Schindler-Rainman and her colleagues, and *Handbook of Organizational Development in Schools and Colleges* by Richard Schmuck and Philip Runkel.

Conclusion

Meetings can be a drag, or they can be a satisfying, almost magical, interplay of ideas and interactions. Effective planning and techniques go a long way toward creating more of the latter, and less of the former. Education cannot afford the price of unproductive and unsatisfying meetings. Each meeting must become better at grappling with the future, more effective as an arena of controlled change. At the same time, meetings must satisfy personal needs for affiliation, achievement, activity, and power, for the long-term benefit of both the organization and society.

In summation, this chapter has outlined the process of successful meeting management as follows:

At the beginning of the process, the leader's first guides are the goals and purposes he or she wishes to accomplish in the meeting. The leader must then decide what type of leadership style is best suited to his or her own nature, the structure and goals of the school, and the needs and desires of group members. Next, the meeting planner draws up the blueprint for the meeting's action — the agenda. The framework of the meeting takes form as the participants are invited, the seating arrangements are determined, the meeting room is arranged, and background information and agendas are distributed to participants.

As the meeting opens, the interpersonal and discussion skills of the chairperson come to the fore. Using the agenda as a roadmap, the leader guides the group through the chaos of problem-solving and decision-making. At the same time, the leader is alert to the surfacing of negative emotions and maintains the human relations in the group as needed. As decisions are made, the leader makes sure responsibilities are clearly designated and deadlines for action are set. After the meeting, the leader distributes the minutes or executive summary, follows up on the decisions made, and evaluates the effectiveness of the meeting.

Meetings run in this way can't help but be productive. Participants go home feeling good about themselves, their jobs, their coworkers, and their school.

CHAPTER

15

Managing Time, Stress, and Conflict

Sandra Huffstutter, John Lindelow,
James J. Scott, Stuart C. Smith, Jenny Watters

Accomplished executives know how to use time wisely, cope with stress, and resolve conflicts. They are also instinctively aware that these topics interrelate. A problem in one area inevitably affects the others.

Lack of time to carry out all the duties specified in their contracts is a major source of stress for school executives. In turn, stress reduces leaders' capacity for intelligently managing their time. And what could be more stressful—and time-consuming—than having to manage a full-blown conflict in the workplace. Conversely, being under stress can make leaders more vulnerable to conflicts.

Effective management of time, stress, and conflict is an ongoing concern in schools. This chapter examines issues related to time, stress, and conflict management facing the school administrator—from problem origins to solutions.

Time-Management Strategies

Peter Drucker, whose management expertise has made him the patron saint of both MBA students and executives of multinational corporations, says, "Time is the scarcest resource, and unless it is managed, nothing else can be managed." Alan Lakein opens his best-selling *How To Get Control of Your Time and Your Life* with the words: "Time is life. It is irreversible and irreplaceable. To waste your time is to waste your life, but to master your time is to master your life and make the most of it."

Time management may appear to be a mystery, but it is actually quite straightforward. Journal articles and books on the topic are strikingly similar in content, so much so that one can speak of a "classical" approach to time management—a four-part, rather circular process that includes the following:

1. goal-setting, which leads to prioritizing
2. keeping a daily time log, which leads to the identification of time-wasters
3. management of time-wasters, which leads to increased discretionary time
4. wise use of discretionary time, which leads to the accomplishment of those goals identified in step one

Goal-Setting and Prioritizing

Just as the smart teacher does not teach without a course outline, the smart administrator needs a written outline of professional goals to administer *effectively*. Drucker insists that "the executive's job is to be effective," not efficient—which means getting "the right things done," rather than merely doing things right. And those "right things" relate directly to advancing the organization's primary purpose.

For principals, one of the most important "right things" is instructional leadership. Yet this activity is often displaced by other tasks. When Larry Hughes surveyed fifty-one instructional supervisors in medium to very large Texas school systems, they reported, on average, that ideally they would like to allocate 30 percent of their time to classroom observation and work with teachers. But only 10 percent of their actual time was spent on this activity. Heading the list of time constraints were telephone interruptions, preparing "useless" reports and other paperwork, excessive meetings, and spontaneous interruptions.

These instructional supervisors need to reexamine their goals and priorities. "It is possible," Hughes says, "that the supervisor's and organization's expectations may not be the same." Such conflicting expectations happen all too frequently, "even when there are well-written job descriptions." If you experience conflict between your own and others' expectations, Hughes recommends that you seek clarification of your job. Do this by listing both major tasks and less central ones. Next, discuss these lists with your superordinate and colleagues and reach agreement about them.

Through this process you will be sure your goals are consistent with your organization's goals. This being the case, your organization presumably will allow you to clear your job description of all tasks keeping you from accomplishing agreed-upon high-priority goals.

Your goals list can take any number of forms. Lakein recommends identification of lifetime goals, three-year goals, and six-month goals. It is important to put them in writing because writing makes them real.

After listing your goals, the next step is to prioritize them. Not all goals or values are equally important or of the same importance at all times. Prioritize based on your present point of view. You should modify your goals and priorities when your point of view changes—as it inevitably will.

Once you've prioritized, you're ready to identify specific short-term activities that will further your two or three most important goals.

Finally, after listing activities that will move you closer to your three most important goals, prioritize again. This should result in your "A-1" goal and your "A-1" activity to further that goal, as Lakein would say. This activity constitutes your foremost potential contribution to your school district, your primary leadership responsibility.

How are you going to find time to pursue this high-priority activity? You simply identify time-wasters with a daily time log and learn to manage those time wasters that are within your control.

The Daily Time Log

Drucker listed five practices that are characteristic of effective executives. "Effective executives know where their time goes" was no. 1. To know for certain where your time goes, most management consultants recommend documenting your use of time in a daily log for at least a week. The kind of log you use is less important than that you track your time.

To gain maximum benefit from a time log, you must use it again and again at least four times a year, says Ruth Rees, to benefit from "the process of self-awareness, self-monitoring, and hence self-development for a more effective management of time."

When you track your activities, try to evaluate each on the basis of its significance. Michael Sexton and Karen Dawn Dill Switzer recommend the following rating system:

#1 = Professional Goal Function (long-range planning and leadership activities; curriculum planning, for example)

#2 = Critical/Crisis Function (immediate, situational concerns; a student-teacher conflict, for example)

#3 = Maintenance Functions (routine administrative tasks, such as fire drills)

P = Personal Activities (calling home, going to the dentist)

While your primary responsibility as a leader is to engage in #1s, your time log will probably reveal that your workday is consumed by #2s and #3s. Patrick Duignan found that superintendents are often diverted from long-range planning and other leadership functions by the interruption-filled, discontinuous nature of their workday. He observes that, within the superintendent's typical 8.2 hour, work-through-lunch workday, he or she engages in about 38 disparate activities, nearly 40 percent of which last less than five minutes each.

Moreover, Duignan found that 25 percent of an average superintendent's day is spent in unscheduled meetings, including drop-in visitors, and nearly another 25 percent is spent in scheduled meetings. Rather than acting as a decision-maker, then, the superintendent acts as a contact-person, an "information broker."

Does this sound familiar? If so, you, like many leaders, are working in a "reactive" mode, rather than in a self-directed "active" mode. For a more productive balance, you need to recognize and manage time-wasters.

Managing Time Wasters

The time-waster is a two-headed dragon. External time-wasters wear the face of "the other": visitors, phone calls, meetings, paperwork, coworkers' needs. Internal time-wasters wear the face of the self: inability to say "no," inability to schedule and prioritize, inability to delegate, tendency to procrastinate.

Visitors and Telephone Calls

Telephone and visitor interruptions are two of the three worst daily time-wasters (meetings being third). Because they act as interrupters, they destroy concentration and momentum. Management of these time-wasters is first a matter of attitude, then a matter of skill. Administrators must value their own time before expecting others to do the same.

Most time-management experts recommend reducing visitor and telephone interruptions through the use of "buffering" and "limiting" techniques. Buffering is primarily accomplished by the secretary—who screens calls and visitors—while limiting is accomplished by the development of some rather brusque habits, such as not offering coffee and tea to visitors, not offering your visitors a chair, not socializing excessively.

However, these recommendations may be inappropriate in the educational setting, since democratic and open communication with students, parents, colleagues, and staff probably constitutes some of the highest and best uses of your time. Therefore, business-oriented time management requires some tempering here.

It might be more productive to schedule regular blocks of time when you are inaccessible. Because it is commonly accepted that one is unavailable during a meeting, consider this time to be a "meeting with yourself."

During this time, have your calls intercepted. Close the door to your office. Place bookshelves and files adjacent to your desk. Strive to make yourself highly invisible during this time, just as you make yourself highly visible at other times.

Above all, train your staff and colleagues to respect this quiet time, because studies show that it will likely be the only productive work time available to you during the entire day.

When you select the times that you will be inaccessible, be sure to take into account what Rees calls "the ebb and flow of the organization." Consider the times of day when you are least needed by students and colleagues and schedule your quiet time during those periods.

Paperwork

Paperwork is often a frustrating external time-waster. Donna and Merrill Douglass assert that "there are only three kinds of paper": action items, information items, and throw-away items. After your secretary prioritizes your mail accordingly, try some of these methods for effectively dealing with action and information items:

Action Items. ❐ Lakein advises handling each piece of paper only once. The Douglasses estimate that "at least 80 percent of mail could be answered immediately when read." Handle the mail quickly, by priority, at a scheduled time of day.

Action items with low priority may not need attention. Lakein suggests a procrastination drawer: dump low priority items into it and see if they're ever missed.

❐ Gilbert Weldy suggests grouping action items into manila folders with labels such as "urgent," "dictate," "to do," and so forth.

❐ Delegate paperwork to your secretary. Outline a brief response in the margin of incoming correspondence, then let your secretary draft the formal response.

❐ Use paperwork expediters: routing slips, attachment slips, form letters, form paragraphs, handwritten responses, email messages, faxes, and the telephone.

❐ Limit the items on your desk. R. Alec MacKenzie says to limit what is on your desk to the project you are working on and your planner/organizer.

❐ Initiate a "tickler" or "suspense" filing system. Manila folders or accordion files labeled 1 through 31 and January through December will permit you to keep track of upcoming tasks, commitments, or annual responsibilities.

Information Items. ❒ Use a variety of filing systems: desk-top files and ticklers, desk files that include frequently needed information, and cabinet files that are arranged clearly for both you and your secretary.

❒ Invest in good database-management software that will enable you to store, sort, and retrieve personnel, financial, student, and other data.

❒ Recognize this: Some studies estimate that 95 percent of all papers filed are never retrieved again. The Douglasses recommend the following steps for determining whether an item is worth keeping.

1. Have your secretary keep a log, for several months, of items retrieved from files. These items will comprise your "useful filing" list.
2. Before filing an item, ask yourself: "Does this item fit in the 'useful filing' category?" "Could I retrieve this information from someone else's files, if needed?" "What use shall I make of this item within the next year?"

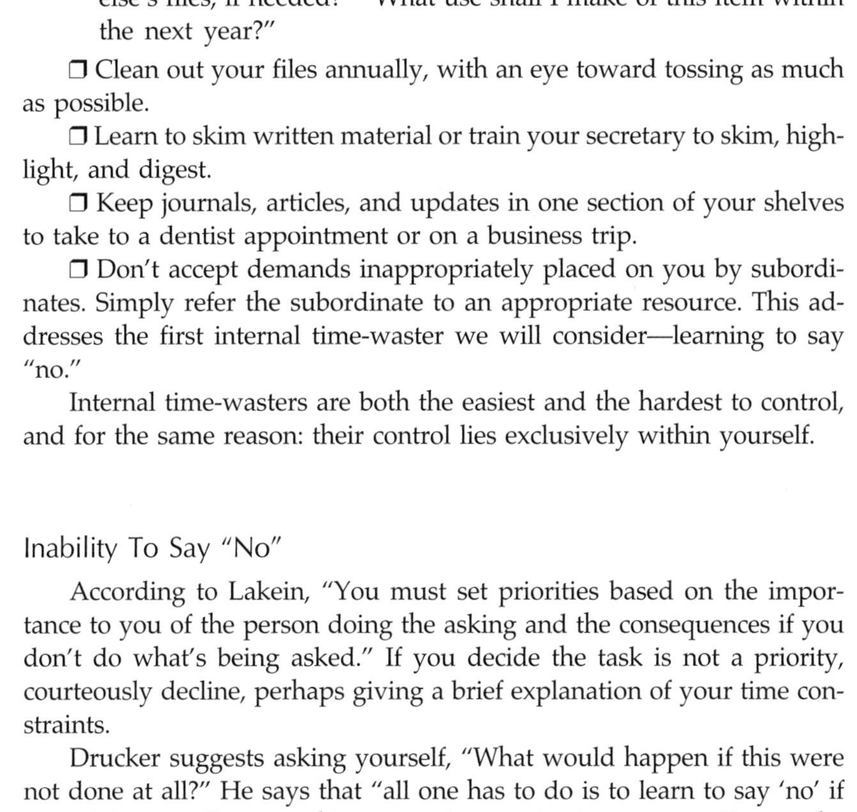

❒ Clean out your files annually, with an eye toward tossing as much as possible.

❒ Learn to skim written material or train your secretary to skim, highlight, and digest.

❒ Keep journals, articles, and updates in one section of your shelves to take to a dentist appointment or on a business trip.

❒ Don't accept demands inappropriately placed on you by subordinates. Simply refer the subordinate to an appropriate resource. This addresses the first internal time-waster we will consider—learning to say "no."

Internal time-wasters are both the easiest and the hardest to control, and for the same reason: their control lies exclusively within yourself.

Inability To Say "No"

According to Lakein, "You must set priorities based on the importance to you of the person doing the asking and the consequences if you don't do what's being asked." If you decide the task is not a priority, courteously decline, perhaps giving a brief explanation of your time constraints.

Drucker suggests asking yourself, "What would happen if this were not done at all?" He says that "all one has to do is to learn to say 'no' if an activity contributes nothing to one's organization, to oneself, or to the organization for which it is to be performed." Similarly, W. A. Mambert recommends the "wash decision"—abondoning a project when complications begin to outweigh the value of the final result.

With your chief contribution to the school district's primary purpose firmly in mind, deciding whether to say "yes" or "no" to any activity should be simplified.

Inability To Schedule

Consciousness of your primary purpose will also enhance your ability to schedule. Scheduling includes planning, prioritizing, clustering, and delegating. All are essential to managing time effectively.

You began to plan when you created and ranked a list of goal statements and activities. Now, you need to narrow your focus. Take fifteen minutes to make a "to do" list. Include the day's chief tasks, including steps toward accomplishment of your A-1 activity. Then prioritize those tasks.

Prioritizing is greatly aided by knowledge of the 80/20 rule. According to Lakein:

> The 80/20 rule suggests that in a list of ten items, doing two of them will yield most (80 percent) of the value. Find these two, label them A, get them done. Leave most of the other eight undone, because the value you'll get from them will be significantly less than that of the two highest-value items.

Next, coordinate your "to dos" with your scheduled appointments, remembering to schedule a block of quiet time for work on your A-1 activity. Weldy estimates that the educational administrator can probably wrest only half an hour of such time from daily demands. Your daily time log should reveal peaks and lulls in external activities and in your internal energy level: schedule this time realistically. Common sense dictates that you schedule your leadership time as close as possible to the intersection of peak-energy and low-activity levels.

After scheduling, attack your "to dos" in order of priority. Delegate whatever you can, and don't fret if lower priority tasks have to wait another day. Cluster similar activities whenever possible and finish each task before going to the next.

Inability To Delegate

For a variety of reasons, most administrators find it difficult to delegate. Again, an attitudinal change must precede learning new skills. Delegation is often perceived as thrusting one's "dirty work" onto others.

Instead, the leader should distinguish between work that advances one's contribution to the organization's primary purpose and work that does not. Once that distinction is made, the leader should retain the former and delegate the latter.

Effective delegation requires clear communication with the one to whom work is being delegated, assignment of authority and decision-making capability to the individual, a system for monitoring and followup, and a relaxed attitude toward the staff member's work procedures.

Weldy suggests thinking of delegation as a time investment that accrues long-term benefits such as invaluable on-the-job training for your staff, whose expertise reflects directly on you. Moreover, your ability to rise to a more challenging position hinges directly on the competence and effectiveness of those you have trained in your current position.

Procrastination

Procrastination is a demon we are all familiar with. Procrastination is professionally debilitating in that we tend to avoid those difficult, challenging, A-1 activities we should be pursuing. Low-priority tasks, on the other hand, are quickly accomplished, provide instant gratification, and are therefore completed with much more regularity.

Lakein suggests a variety of tactics to address procrastination: recognize the consequences of delay and the advantages of action; reduce a large task to small subtasks; work at the task for five minutes per day to initiate involvement; gather additional data; perform a subtask of the A-1 that coincides with your current mood; set deadlines and announce your deadline to someone else; take rest breaks; reward yourself as subtasks are accomplished.

Darrell Lewis and Tor Dahl state: "It is generally accepted that most managers should be able to clear about 25 percent of their time with little or no drop in current output." Having begun the management of time, why not research and implement a program to manage its corollary—stress?

Stress Management

Why should leaders learn to manage their stress? It has been estimated that stress-related dysfunctions cause about twenty billion dollars of losses each year in industrial productivity. Stress hurts workers' performance in several ways. Stressed people lose their concentration and make mistakes, resulting in injury or loss of property. They also are susceptible to illness. Leaders under stress are more likely to make bad decisions. As leadership researchers Kenneth E. Clark and Miriam B. Clark say, "Stress degrades the use of intelligence in leadership performance." Leaders who want to be effective will try to avoid stress, not just because it is unpleasant, but because it is unproductive.

Understanding the commonalities of time and stress management is a first step toward minimizing the negative effects of stress. Specific problem areas in time and stress management are identical. For instance, paperwork, telephone and visitor interruptions, excessive meetings, lack of planning time, and procrastination are both time wasters and stress producers. Mismanagement of one exacerbates mismanagement of the other.

Like time management, the management of stress requires (1) a shift in attitudes and level of awareness, (2) self-analysis and identification of stressors via the daily stress log, and (3) practical techniques for managing those stressors.

What precisely is stress? Walter Gmelch and Wilbert Chan say that "stress is any event that places a demand on your body, mentally or physically." Whether the stress is positive or negative, the physiological response is similar (increase in heart rate, blood pressure, respiration, and levels of adrenaline). Psychological responses to stress include irritability, depression, anxiety, or withdrawal. Further, stress is integrally related to control: the greater one's sense of powerlessness over the stressor, the greater the stress.

Do You Know Your Level of Stress?

Stress is a highly subjective phenomenon. That is, each person perceives a "threatening situation" differently. Consequently, an intellectual awareness of and an adaptive attitude toward stress are important.

Holmes and Rahe's Social Readjustment Rating Scale (see table 1) attempts to quantify the relative stressfulness of various events. The scale lists forty-three different "life events," ranging from "Death of Spouse" to "Minor Violations of the Law" and assigns each event a numerical value that correlates to the stressfulness of the event. The significance of the scale lies in the fact that studies have shown a positive correlation between degrees of stress and the probability of incipient illness or accidents, as Dudley and Welke explain:

> Should you accumulate 150 points on the Social Readjustment Rating Scale within a period of two years, there is a 33 percent probability for you to contract an illness or suffer an accident. When 300 points are accumulated, the probability soars to 66 percent. At 450 points the probability is almost certain—in the 90 percent range.

TABLE 1

Social Readjustment Rating Scale

Rank	*Life Event*	*Mean Value*
1	Death of a Spouse	100
2	Divorce	73
3	Marital Separation	65
4	Jail Term	63
5	Death of Close Family Member	63
6	Personal Injury or Illness	53
7	Marriage	50
8	Fired at Work	47
9	Marital Reconciliation	45
10	Retirement	45
11	Change in Health of Family Member	44
12	Pregnancy	40
13	Sex Difficulties	39
14	Gain of New Family Member	39
15	Business Readjustment	39
16	Change in Financial State	38
17	Death of Close Friend	37
18	Change to Different Line of Work	36
19	Change in Number of Arguments with Spouse	35
20	Mortgage over $10,000	31
21	Foreclosure of Mortgage or Loan	30
22	Change in Responsibilities at Work	29
23	Son or Daughter Leaving Home	29
24	Trouble with In-Laws	29
25	Outstanding Personal Achievement	28
26	Wife Begins or Stops Work	26
27	Begin or End School	26
28	Change in Living Conditions	25
29	Revision of Personal Habits	24
30	Trouble with Boss	23
31	Change in Work Hours or Conditions	20
32	Change in Residence	20
33	Change in Schools	20
34	Change in Recreation	19
35	Change in Church Activities	19
36	Change in Social Activities	18
37	Mortgage or Loan Less than $10,000	17
38	Change in Sleeping Habits	16
39	Change in Number of Family Get-Togethers	15
40	Change in Eating Habits	15
41	Vacation	13
42	Christmas	12
43	Minor Violations of the Law	11

Reprinted with permission from *Journal of Psychosomatic Research,* vol. II, T. H. Holmes, R. H. Rahe, 1967, p. 216, Table III, Pergamon Press, Ltd.

While a personal tally on the rating scale can prove revealing, Walter Gmelch cautions against an overly literal reading of the scale:

> A few points should be kept in mind: first, both pleasant (marriage) and unpleasant (divorce) life events can cause harmful stress; second, no one can escape, nor does anyone necessarily want to escape all these crises, since to some degree stress is life; and third, due to differing abilities to cope, the same event does not have the same impact on all individuals.

Gmelch and Chan offer their own comprehensive stress-assessment exercise. It includes eleven sections on stressors in private life, environmental, role conflict, and interpersonal areas, to name a few.

The ability to cope is a learned set of skills and is central to understanding and managing stress. Most people rely on coping mechanisms that have served them in stressful situations. These coping skills may be adaptive or maladaptive, but they are ingrained. Donald Dudley and Elton Welke offer a coping quiz that asks questions ranging from "Do people who know you well think you get upset easily?" to "Have you set goals for the future that satisfy you and are realistic?"

Another exercise is the "Type 'A' Behaving" questionnaire included in Michael and Dolores Giammatteo's book. A high proportion of yes answers to such questions as "I'm frequently in a hurry," "I really enjoy winning and hate to lose," and "My job is the most important thing in my life" indicates the probability of a "Type A" personality. This personality type is defined as "one who is always pushing, doing, creating, initiating, and who may be headed toward an early death or heart attack."

After becoming more attentive to the subject of stress and your personal triggers, assess your work attitudes. Be aware of attitudes that promote stress: authoritarianism, intolerance, preoccupation with what "should be" rather than with what "is," indecisiveness, worry, perfectionism, "stockpiling hurts," magnifying minor irritants, failing to communicate feelings, believing that you are a victim of fate and of your feelings, and needing and seeking approval from everyone.

Identifying Stressors

As with your use of time, it's important to track sources of stress for several weeks to identify problem areas and patterns.

Gmelch recommends that school leaders tally at the end of each day for one week the most stressful incident, the most stressful series of related incidents, and the approximate level of your stress on a scale from one to ten. As with the daily time log, doing this form of tracking, and doing it in writing, is more critical than following a particular format.

After tracking your sources of stress, you might compare your stressors with Gmelch's administrative index—a list of thirty-five typical stressors identified by educational administrators. The top ten on this list include:

1. Complying with state, federal, and organizational rules and policies
2. Feeling that meetings take up too much time
3. Trying to complete reports and other paperwork on time
4. Trying to gain financial support for programs
5. Trying to resolve personnel conflicts
6. Evaluating staff members' performance
7. Having to make decisions that affect the lives of individual people that I know (colleagues, staff members)
8. Feeling that I have too heavy a workload, one that I cannot possibly finish during the normal work day
9. Imposing excessively high expectations on myself
10. Being interrupted frequently by telephone calls

In another study, Robert Koff and colleagues factored and weighted four areas of stress for elementary, middle, and secondary school principals. Conflicts with teachers were consistently ranked as the highest stressor. Irregular events with severe consequences were ranked the next most stressful, for example, teacher strikes, involuntary transfers, bad publicity, threats and assaults, and legal action against the school. Student conflicts were rated below these, though the stress therein increased significantly from elementary to high school. Finally, routine management tasks were consistently ranked as the lowest, most manageable stressor.

All these findings echo what was noted earlier—that stress is integrally related to feelings of powerlessness. Successful stress management requires not just identifying your stressors but also categorizing them into those that are within your control and those that are not. The distinction will determine your strategy for attacking the stressor.

Managing Controllable Stressors

In discussions of stress management, time management is one strategy always highlighted. But time management can be subsumed by a larger concept of "pacing," of consciously regulating the ebb and flow of your life. Time management will help you do that. So will proper use of the Social Readjustment Rating Scale; for instance, if you are aware that you've recently experienced a high number of life-change events, you should consider forgoing another controllable change—moving to a new neighborhood, for example.

You can also pace yourself by regulating what Dudley and Welke refer to as naturally occurring cycles of "activation and withdrawal." While it's normal to alternate between periods of outward-reaching activity and periods of quiet renewal, the authors caution against abrupt swings from one extreme to the other.

Another strategy for managing stress is timely problem-solving. Delays in confronting problems inevitably magnify them. Such procrastination not only allows the problem to worsen, but also allows mental exaggeration that is disproportionate to the problem's actual severity.

A third stress-management strategy is effective communication. The importance of skillful communication to stress management becomes clearer as one recalls that authoritarianism (excessively directive communication), intolerance (excessively negative communication), and failure to express feelings (excessively repressive communication) are three key promoters of stress. It's important to recognize that the words you use—and choose not to use—don't merely describe reality, they create it.

Job and role clarifications also contribute significantly to stress management. A job can be inherently stressful if one's role is unclear or subject to conflicting expectations, or if the job involves too much work, too little work, too little opportunity for achievement, and/or inadequate performance evaluation. Any process that analyzes and sets out, in writing, the expectations to each job is useful.

Gmelch offers the following systematic procedure for confronting controllable stressors:

1. Identify your most bothersome stressors and select one to resolve.
2. Search for the causes of this stressful event.
3. Generate a set of possible solutions to remedy the causes.
4. Specify a plan of action you will take to alleviate one cause.
5. Develop a time table to implement your plan of action.
6. Set a date and method for how you will follow up and evaluate the effectiveness of your plan.
7. Investigate the potential problems or unintended consequences (additional stress) your action plan may have created.

Finally, remember to ask for help. Management consultants, self-help books, professional associations, central administration, your peer group, the school advisory council or other parent committees, and professional analysts can all help to generate solutions to stressful situations. Don't suffer in silence. Consult with them.

Managing Uncontrollable Stressors

When stressors are beyond your control—for example, statewide budget cuts or a personality conflict with your superior—you must seek to reduce stress in the one area left to you: within yourself. This is accomplished through a series of strategies that build up your resistance to stress and increase your level of tolerance.

General physical health and well-being are fundamental here. Don't overlook the value of regular exercise, good eating habits, and periods of recreation.

Because stress is subjective, a variety of mental skills can be employed to alter one's outlook in the midst of stress. Many of these practices—meditation, prayer, biofeedback, yoga, the relaxation response—increase one's sense of serenity and well-being. Mental imagery—the conscious production of positive mental scenes—is also commonly used to induce a state of relaxation.

James Manuso recommends learning a "quieting response"—a reaction to minor daily irritations in which "one takes two deliberate deep breaths, paying attention to relaxing the jaw, the shoulders and tongue, and one tells himself he will not permit his body to get involved in this. This breaks the sequence of the stress response."

Similarly, "thought stopping" is a means of quieting internal anxiety. In thought stopping, one learns to banish obsessive or worrisome thoughts by mentally shouting "Stop!' and saying to yourself, "I'm not going to think about that now." Next, consciously seek an alternative thought or activity with which to become involved.

Jerry Terrill lists some additional dos and don'ts to help cope with difficult stressors:

1. Work on your attitude. Playing the victim wastes energy.
2. Do a positive inventory. List those things that are going well.
3. Create a new personal focus.
4. Initiate a new professional focus.
5. Be good to yourself. Give yourself permission to take "time out" and pamper yourself.
6. Make sure your support system is established and used.
7. Look at other career options.
8. Don't waste your time trying to fix blame.
9. Don't self-medicate. You are enough. You don't need a chemical or a fix to make you equal to the occasion.
10. Don't ignore the problem. Find a balance.

11. Don't lose your perspective. Humor is a wonderful coping technique.

A tolerant attitude is crucial in combating uncontrollable stressors—tolerance of individuals unlike ourselves and of situations unlike those we desire.

Don't Be a Source of Stress

While attending to their own stress, school administrators would do well to remember that they may also inflict stress on their subordinates. The Clarks report that "over 60% of immediate superiors are the major cause of stress in the workplace.... Only those superiors who have subjected themselves to anonymous evaluation by their subordinates have any right to feel comfortable about this widespread problem." Why is boss stress so prevalent? Many managers "behave in too authoritarian a manner for the circumstances"—a result, the Clarks speculate, of the culture instilling "in them expectancies and stereotypes about boss behavior."

Successful time and stress management cannot be exercised in a vacuum. Programs for time and stress management should encompass the leader, support staff, colleagues, and, better yet, even filter upwards. A similar team approach is often the most successful in resolving conflicts in the school and district.

Managing Conflict

Conflict is an inevitable part of the human experience. It exists on many levels and takes many forms. Conflict is inherent in the role of the public school administrator. As James M. Lipham and James A. Hoeh, Jr. state, "All institutional roles, particularly those in public institutions, are subject to numerous sources and types of disagreement or conflict. But few seem so fraught with conflict potential as that of the public school principal."

Because conflict recurs consistently in the roles of principals and superintendents, they must learn to understand conflict and learn to manage it effectively.

The Value of Conflict

As Stephen Robbins notes, the word *conflict* has a negative connotation for most individuals. Indeed, many situations involving conflict are disturbing to participants and observers alike, and many conflicts are resolved ineffectively. However, conflict can also be a source of creativity and constructive action. Gordon Lippitt lists both negative and positive effects of conflict. On the negative side, it

- diverts energy from the task at hand
- destroys morale
- polarizes individuals and groups
- deepens differences
- obstructs cooperative action
- produces irresponsible behavior
- creates suspicion and distrust
- decreases productivity

But on the positive side, conflict

- opens up an issue in a confronting manner
- develops clarification of an issue
- increases involvement
- improves problem-solving quality
- provides more spontaneity in communication
- is needed for growth
- strengthens a relationship when creatively resolved

Conflict can be a valuable source of organizational renewal. Robbins even suggests stimulating conflict within organizations by disrupting communications and altering organizational structure. "Organizations that do not stimulate conflict," he states, "increase the probability of stagnant thinking, inadequate decisions, and at the extreme, organizational demise."

Conflict in schools can help prevent teachers and administrators from ignoring what is best for students, says Robert Maidment, who advises principals to "encourage legitimate resistance." "When principals fully embrace the notion that teachers have both the right and the responsibility for legitimate resistance, it again places conflict in a proper—and positive—perspective," he says.

Thus, school administrators should not seek to eliminate all conflict; rather, they should attempt to manage conflict by maximizing constructive conflict and minimizing destructive conflict.

Understanding Conflict

Just what is *conflict*? Robbins describes it as "all kinds of opposition or antagonistic interaction." Numerous writers have identified types, sources, and stages of conflict. These characteristics can be applied to social conflict—conflict between individuals and conflict between groups—common to the school environment.

Types of Conflict

One typology already mentioned is that of constructive or "functional" conflict and destructive or "dysfunctional" conflict. Says Robbins: "The demarcation between functional and dysfunctional is neither clear nor precise." He continues:

> No level of conflict can be adopted at face value as acceptable or unacceptable.... The level that creates healthy and positive involvement towards one group's goals, may in another group or in the same group at another time, be highly dysfunctional, requiring immediate conciliatory attention by the administrator.

Warren Schmidt and Robert Tannenbaum classify conflict according to issues of disagreement. Disagreement can occur over *facts, goals, methods,* and *values or ethics.*

Stephen Bailey suggests another way of classifying conflict—by levels of severity or quality. At the first level there is "an endless simmer of petty personality conflicts reflecting the chemistry and foibles of interacting humans." The second level involves differences over program and budget matters. Level three is that of "revolutionary" conflict, which involves "the legitimacy of regime" rather than program priorities.

Sources of Conflict

A more comprehensive understanding of conflict can be gained by considering communication problems, organizational structure, and "human" factors, which are all primary sources of conflict within the school.

Communications Problems. Much of the conflict in organizations can be traced to faulty communication. For instance, staff members who do not receive regular feedback about their performance may experience poor morale, which may manifest itself in negative remarks or unwillingness to follow management's directives. Lack of communication among departments can lead to destructive competition. Ill-defined expectations, hidden agendas, and lack of candor are additional examples of communication breakdowns that can induce conflict.

Organizational communication problems can be difficult to resolve without the assistance of a trained consultant. In cases of interpersonal conflict where communication problems appear to be the source of conflict, bringing the parties together in a problem-solving session can often resolve the conflict.

Organizational Structure. The structure of the organization is another possible source of conflict. One study reported by Robbins found that conflict was more likely when jobs were less structured and routinized.

For instance, when teachers are given considerable latitude in choosing instructional methods, some teachers may adopt methods that provoke debate. Within limits, controversy that is a byproduct of greater autonomy is a reasonable tradeoff for the increased creativity and flexibility such a structure generates within organizations.

The degree to which an organization's structure allows its employees to participate in decisions also has an effect on conflict. As participation increases, the frequency of conflict may rise; however, major incidents of conflict may decrease. As Robbins suggests, participation in decision-making "permits a greater opportunity for the expression of existing disputes and allows more occasions for disagreements to arise"; however, this may also "prevent minor irritations from developing into major incidents."

Joanne Yatvin believes the hierarchical structure inherent in school systems will inevitably produce conflict. As a school superintendent, Yatvin has experienced many more conflicts caused by her superiors or government agencies than by students, parents, or teachers. She states:

> Given the complexity of individuals and institutions, I don't think we will ever all play on the same team. But those of us in education could work toward flattening the structures of our teams, so that the people making the rules and setting the standards are also the ones on the line playing the game: getting dirty, suffering bruises, feeling fear, and tasting their own blood from time to time.

Human Factors. Whereas communications and structural factors can, in part, be controlled by an administrator, human factors are largely beyond his or her control. Personality traits that have been found to correlate with increased conflict are high authoritarianism, high dogmatism, and low self-esteem. Differing value or goal systems are often impossible to change and can only be "managed."

Limited Resources. Another source of conflict is of immediate practical concern to school administrators—competition over limited resources. When the science department needs a new laser disk player and the library needs to replace some books but funds aren't available for both purchases, the principal must decide who gets what. No matter what the principal decides, someone will be dissatisfied. It's the principal's job to ensure that all parties feel they have been treated fairly, even though they may not get what they want.

At the district level, conflict can develop when teachers want a pay increase and taxpayers refuse to provide the necessary funds. Failure to resolve such conflicts can lead to long and costly teachers' strikes.

Cultural Diversity. Demographers project that by the year 2000 one-third of the nation's students wil be members of racial or ethnic minorities. As communities and schools throughout the country become more diverse racially, ethnically, and religiously, many people are being exposed for the first time to cultures other than their own. The potential for conflict, whether from blatant racism or from innocent misunderstanding of another culture's language and mannerisms, is obvious.

Stages of Conflict

Schmidt and Tannenbaum identify the following stages of conflict development:

1. *Anticipation.* For example, a manager knows of an impending change and projects its consequences.
2. *Conscious, but unexpressed, difference.* Word leaks out about the change, and a feeling of tension begins to build in the organization.
3. *Discussion.* Information is formally presented about the change. Differing opinions begin to emerge.
4. *Open dispute.* Differences become more sharply and explicitly defined.
5. *Open conflict.* Each disputant tries to force his or her view on the others. The only possible outcomes now are win, lose, or compromise.

Other authors present different stages, and many include a "relaxation" stage after the conflict has peaked. As conflict passes through different stages, different management techniques become useful. According to Bailey:

> When conflict is incipient, or in early stages of virulence, a sensitive administrator may release dangerous tension with a special meeting or a joke. When the storm is raging, certain types of meetings become impossible, and the very notion of jokes becomes obscene. When exhaustion is followed by a new-found harmony, the administrator's best therapy may be "natural healing," rather than any conscious strategy.

Preventing Conflict

Stopping conflict before it starts is possible at times; minimizing its intensity and impact is another avenue to explore. Patricia Anderson states that if management and labor build an environment that is conducive to teamwork and cooperation, conflict will be less frequent. She advocates steps managers can take to help prevent conflict.

One step is to ensure that all work toward the same goal. Neil Katz and John Lawyer claim that "the lack of clear agreements or the lack of follow-through on agreements made is the cause of a significant amount of conflict in schools." They present an "agreement management model" that works to prevent conflict with individuals and groups. Briefly, the model consists of:

Agreement Setting

1. Say what you want and why.
2. Listen and clarify.
3. Identify and resolve any problems.
4. State the agreement.

Agreement Managing

1. Monitor the agreement.
2. Assert feelings about any proposed solutions for lapsed and broken agreements.
3. Establish and follow through on consequences.

Katz and Lawyer point out that "one of the most effective ways to prevent conflict from emerging in schools is to create a system in which everyone in the school, including the students, has the opportunity to influence the decisions." They present a model for consensus decision-making that can yield positive and effective outcomes.

Katz and Lawyer give the following advice to consensus-building group members:

1. Present your position clearly and logically. Avoid blindly arguing for your own judgments.
2. Reflectively listen to others' reactions and consider them carefully before pressing your point.
3. Only support solutions you're at least somewhat in agreement with. Avoid changing your mind only to reach agreement and to avoid conflict.
4. Seek differences of opinion and avoid "conflict-reducing" procedures such as majority vote, tossing a coin, averaging, or bargaining.
5. Discuss underlying assumptions, listen carefully, and encourage everyone to participate.
6. Look for the next most acceptable alternative when a discussion reaches a stalemate.

Although consensus decision-making fosters involvement and commitment and helps to prevent conflict, Katz and Lawyer point out disadvantages associated with this method: it's time-consuming; it allows less control for those in authority; indecision may be more likely and involve costs; and subtle intimidation of some group members by others may occur and reduce the number of wise decisions or the commitment to the decision.

Techniques for Managing Conflict

There are as many methods for resolving conflict as there are types of conflict. No one method works best in all circumstances. It is important for administrators to be aware of all possible conflict-management techniques, selecting from them as the situation warrants.

Avoiding Conflict

"The most natural manner in which all animals, including man, eliminate conflict is to avoid it," states Robbins. Administrators who do not handle anxiety well may put the most effort into avoiding conflict. Monte Blue says that some administrators will try to reduce the level of organizational conflict—whether it's resolved or not—in an attempt to lessen the anxiety they feel. Avoidance techniques include ignoring conflict, procrastination, isolation, withholding feelings or beliefs, staffing with like-minded people, and "smoothing." Although avoiding conflict may seem like the wrong thing to do, it is often a valuable short-term alternative.

Ignoring and Procrastinating. Whenever possible, humans withdraw from conflict and ignore the situation. Sometimes this instinctive response is the best one available. Events often reach their own state of equilibrium, and intervention may be either unnecessary or counterproductive.

"Deciding not to decide" may also be a valuable short-term management strategy. The administrator may need more information or time to understand a situation or may wait for the situation to take clearer form before taking action. As Maidment puts it, it is "better to regroup than to re-grope."

Deciding when to intervene can be difficult. Administrators must decide whether bringing out a conflict will have destructive or constructive consequences. Low levels of communication, limited problem-solving skills, and lack of trust may well engender destructive outcomes.

Isolating Conflicting Parties. A manager can avoid conflict between two potentially explosive individuals by isolating them from one another in the organization so that they seldom interact. An administrator and subordinate may also use this technique.

Withholding Feelings. When two individuals find it impossible to avoid each other, each may withhold his or her feelings or beliefs about the other. Such behavior conceals differences but it does avoid overt confrontation.

Seeking Like-Minded People. Another means of avoiding conflict is to staff the school with like-minded people. Used consistently, however, this approach reduces creativity, as Schmidt and Tannenbaum state: "When everyone in the room thinks the same thing, no one is thinking very much.

Smoothing. "Smoothing" is the process of playing down differences between conflicting parties while emphasizing their common interests. Although smoothing is often relied on, resolutions are superficial and conflicts are only postponed.

Avoiding conflicts in the above ways can be valuable for managing conflict in some minor conflict situations. When employed to manage major conflicts, however, the same techniques can lead to expansion of the conflict, instead of containment.

Individualizing Conflict

Many potential conflicts between school administrators and members of the general public can be contained by individualizing them. The following example demonstrates this technique: A high school has a mandatory P.E. program that, for a few weeks out of the year, involves boys playing football. Brad broke his leg playing football several years ago, and—despite his doctor's assurances that the injury is completely healed—his parents want to make sure it doesn't happen again. They want Brad held out of the football portion of the P.E. program.

If the principal takes the attitude that rules are rules with no exceptions, Brad's parents may try to enlist citizen support for their side. Eventually, what started off as an individual grievance may blossom into a major conflict over the role P.E. should play in an educational program. However, if the principal agrees that Brad's parents have a point and accommodates their wishes—perhaps by working out an alternative program for Brad during football—then the matter will probably go no further.

Creating Superordinate Goals

Another technique for managing conflict is the creation of a superordinate goal—a highly valued goal that two conflicting parties can reach only by cooperating with each other. Superordinate goals are popular because of their promise of "win-win" solutions.

Given that all the people involved in the school organization share one overriding goal—educating the children—it would appear that using superordinate goals would be an effective conflict-management technique. However, superordinate goals that supersede the conflicting parties' individual goals are difficult to create. The mutual trust and confidence needed for conflicting parties to work together are also often absent.

Creative Problem-Solving

> Had the six blind men who came into contact with different parts of the same elephant pooled their information, they would have arrived at a more accurate description of the animal. In the same way, many problems can be seen clearly, wholly, and in perspective only if the individuals who see different aspects can come together and pool their information. (Schmidt and Tannenbaum)

Mutual problem-solving is often the best means for resolving social conflict, which usually stems from communication problems. Bringing conflicting parties together to discuss their differences can, if properly managed, lead to increased understanding, clarification of differences, and constructive collaboration.

Schmidt and Tannenbaum provide guidelines for conducting an effective problem-solving session. The administrator should:

- welcome the existence of differences within the organization as a valuable resource
- listen with understanding rather than evaluation
- recognize and accept the feelings of the individuals involved
- clarify the nature of the conflict
- indicate who will make the decision being discussed
- suggest procedures and ground rules for resolving differences
- create appropriate vehicles for communication among the disputing parties
- encourage separation of ideas from the people who propose them

In a problem-solving session, facts, goals, and strategies are discussed and clarified. Areas for potential compromise are discovered. Faulty perceptions are corrected.

When group members have varied opinions on some issue yet are not entrenched in their positions, problem-solving sessions can be used to channel the energy generated by conflict into creative solutions. However, forced problem-solving between two parties with incompatible value systems, Robbins observes, "only widens the differences and entrenches each of the participants deeper into his position—for all intents and purposes probably increasing, and certainly not lessening, the level of conflict."

Compromise and Use of a Third Party

Compromise is probably the most widely used technique for resolving conflict. Compromise can be generated internally in a problem-solving session, or externally by a mediator or arbitrator.

Compromise doesn't result in clear winners and losers, and it requires each party to give up something. "The idea is that it is better to have half a loaf than none at all," says Mary Nebgen. She states that compromise works best when "the cooperative interests of the bargainers are stronger than their competitive interests" and when both parties have ample resources with which to bargain.

The principal can act as a mediator, clarifying and facilitating communication between two parties, or can act as an arbitrator, making the final decision after both sides have presented their claims. If the principal is one of the conflicting parties, he or she may call for a neutral third party to help settle the dispute.

Maidment advises administrators to "intervene cautiously" in a dispute between two staff members. "An intervention is appropriate whenever (1) the issue is unduly prolonged, (2) other staff members enter the fray and take sides, or (3) the performance of either disputant is adversely affected." When intervening, the administrator should talk separately with each party—listening carefully and probing for hidden agendas—and then meet again separately to share observations. Only then, says Maidment, should the disputants meet together to attempt a resolution, either by themselves or with the administrator acting as an "observer, mediator, or adjudicator, depending on the complexity, severity, and intensity of the dispute."

If the parties compromise simply because each side recognizes that it lacks the power to impose its will on the other, then the compromise is in danger the moment the balance of power shifts. However, if each believes the compromise is *reasonable,* it may prove to be a long-term solution to the conflict.

The moderator of a dispute should work closely with both sides to develop a compromise that both sides consider to be fair, rather than one that each side grudgingly accepts for lack of an alternative.

Changes in Organizational Structure

Conflicts can often be managed by making changes in the organizational structure. For example, when two departments are in conflict, increasing their contact can reduce communication barriers.

Robbins cites the example of a major company in which two departments were in continual conflict. Management had the two supervisors switch jobs for six months. This "promoted greater understanding and reduced intergroup conflict as the modified views filtered down" through each department.

Another avenue to address departmental conflict is to create a "coordinator" position. The coordinator would perform functions in both departments and integrate their functions.

Improved intraorganizational communications can also be gained by creating a system of interlocking work teams in the school or district (see the discussion of vertical teams in chapter 8).

Grievance and appeal systems can be designed to allow members to challenge the rulings of superiors. Robbins observes that this technique "can act to reduce conflict by requiring the superior to rethink the legitimacy of the demands he makes upon his subordinates."

Too much emphasis on unity and common organizational goals may also be a source of conflict if the philosophies and instructional styles of faculty members are highly varied. In this case, conflict may be managed by allowing for planned diversity, organizing the school into several teams, houses within schools, even schools within schools.

Authoritative Command

"Individuals in organizations, with rare exceptions, recognize and accept the authority of their superiors," states Robbins. "Though they may not be in agreement with these decisions, they will almost always abide by them."

The principal's authoritative command can solve conflicts quickly and neatly. However, the overuse or misuse of power, without meaningful input from subordinates, can foment a more serious kind of conflict—challenge to the legitimacy of authority.

Using force to settle disputes, states Nebgen, "may be most usefully applied to conflicts which arise out of differing goals or values of special interest groups and interpersonal provocation." If the parties are entrenched in their position with little chance for compromise, "only forcing the issue will settle the problem."

The effective leader utilizes a variety of styles in conflict management, including, at times, authoritative command. Whatever course the leader chooses to settle an issue, he or she should clearly communicate how the matter will be settled before the process begins.

When a conflict ends because one side succeeds in imposing its will on the other, a higher authority imposes its will upon both, or both sides compromise through necessity, a substantial residue of ill-feeling and dissatisfaction may remain. Under such circumstances, an administrator should make a conscious effort to reconcile the conflicting parties and create an atmosphere conducive to everyone working together again.

Finding Common Ground

"We are either enriched or divided by our diversity," observes Marjorie A. Ledell. Public schools are increasingly the center of conflicts stemming from a diversity of values in regard to religion, curricula, and educational reform. When parents, community members, and educators focus only on the battle, they catch children in the "cross-fire." Ledell proposes a "common ground" model that encourages schools and communities to engage in conversation, debate, and democratic process for the good of their children's education.

Seeking common ground requires courage and motivation to modify personal agendas without compromising individual liberties. Ledell states that public schools should:

- Respect individual liberties, including religious beliefs, guaranteed in the Constitution and Bill of Rights.
- Always strive to improve learning for all children.
- Honor the individuality and needs of each and every student.
- Comply with laws and regulations at all levels of government.
- Reach out to a wide cross-section of the community, both internally and externally.
- Be honest in all communications.
- Realize all decisions will not please everyone, but that all decisions should ultimately be based on what's best for all students and their respective communities.

Ledell points out that the journey toward common ground takes "a great deal of time, energy, and patience." To succeed on their journey, all parties—administrators, teachers, parents, and community members—must:

- Share a motivation to improve student achievement for all children.
- Commit to reach collective decisions through democratic processes.
- Pledge to honor group decisions while ensuring that the interests of those not in the majority are respected.

Conflict is a constant companion of all human undertakings and should be considered a natural, not an anomalous, phenomenon. For most observers and participants, conflict invokes negative feelings, for it often leads to destructive ends. But conflict can also be a constructive force in organizations, leading to increased creativity and adaptability.

To master the art of conflict management, as with time and stress management, educational administrators must understand the types, sources, and dynamics—and be familiar with numerous techniques for managing all three areas.

But knowledge alone is not enough. Ultimately, administrators must apply their time-, stress-, and conflict-management skills in their day-to-day professional experiences.

Bibliography

Many of the items in this bibliography are indexed in ERIC's monthly catalog *Resources in Education* (*RIE*). Reports in *RIE* are indicated by an "ED" number. Journal articles, indexed in ERIC's companion catalog, *Current Index to Journals in Education*, are indicated by an "EJ" number.

Most items with an ED number are available from ERIC Document Reproduction Service (EDRS), 7420 Fullerton Rd., Suite 110, Springfield, VA 22153-2852.

To order from EDRS, specify the ED number, type of reproduction desired—microfiche (MF) or paper copy (PC), and number of copies. Add postage to the cost of all orders and include check or money order payable to EDRS. For credit card orders, call 1-800-443-3742.

Introduction: Leadership for Excellence

Bennis, Warren, and Burt Nanus. *Leaders: The Strategies for Taking Charge.* New York: Harper and Row, 1985. 244 pages.

Bolman, Lee G., and Terrence E. Deal. "Looking for Leadership: Another Search Party's Report." *Educational Administration Quarterly* 30, 1 (February 1994): 77-96. EJ 477 513.

Bredeson, Paul V. "Letting Go of Outlived Professional Identities: A Study of Role Transition and Role Strain for Principals in Restructured Schools." *Educational Administration Quarterly* 29, 1 (February 1993): 34-68. EJ 457 237.

Brubaker, Dale L. "How the Principalship Has Changed: Lessons from Principals' Life Stories." *NASSP Bulletin* 79, 574 (November 1995): 88-95.

Clark, Kenneth E., and Miriam B. Clark. "Introduction." In *Impact of Leadership*, edited by Kenneth E. Clark, Mariam B. Clark, and David P. Campbell. 1-10. Greensboro, North Carolina: Center for Creative Leadership, 1992. ED 353 421.

Conley, David T., and Paul Goldman. *Facilitative Leadership: How Principals Lead Without Dominating*. Eugene: Oregon School Study Council, University of Oregon, August 1994. OSSC Bulletin Series. 42 pages. ED 379 728.

Edmonds, Ronald. *A Discussion of the Literature and Issues Related to Effective Schooling*. 49 pages. ED 170 394.

Fiedler, Fred E.; Martin M. Chemers; and Linda Mahar. *Improving Leadership Effectiveness: The Leader Match Concept.* New York: John Wiley & Sons, 1976.

Hallinger, Philip, and Ronald H. Heck. "Reassessing the Principal's Role in School Effectiveness: A Review of Empirical Research, 1980-1995." *Educational Administration Quarterly* 32,1 (February 1996): 5-44.

Johnson, Marlene. *Leadership: Review of Selected Research.* Urbana, Illinois: The National Center for School Leadership, 1993. 30 pages. ED 363 964.

Kanungo, Rabindra N., and Manuel Mendonca. *Ethical Dimensions of Leadership.* Thousand Oaks, California: Sage Publications, 1996. 152 pages.

Krug, Samuel E. "Leadership Craft and the Crafting of School Leadership." *Phi Delta Kappan* 75, 3 (November 1993): 240-44. EJ 472 592.

Lipham, James M., and John C. Daresh, eds. *Administrative and Staff Relationships in Education: Research and Practice in IGE Schools.* Madison, Wisconsin: Research and Development Center for Individualized Schooling, University of Wisconsin, 1979. 149 pages. ED 186 448.

Pejza, John P. "The Catholic School Principal: A Different Kind of Leader." Paper presented at annual meeting of the National Catholic Educational Association, St. Louis, April 1985. 21 pages. ED 256 053.

Terry, George R. *Principles of Management.* 3rd edition. Homewood, Illinois: Richard D. Irwin, 1960.

Thomson, Scott D. "Editorial: Effective Leadership." *NASSP Newsletter* 27, 8 (April 1980): 2.

Thomson, Scott D., ed. *School Leadership: A Blueprint for Change.* Newbury Park, California: Corwin Press, Inc., 1992. 52 pages. ED 341 144.

Truman, Harry S. *More Plain Speaking,* edited by Margaret Truman and Scott Meredith. New York: Warner Books.

Welte, Carl E. "Management and Leadership: Concepts with an Important Difference." *Personnel Journal* 57, 11 (November 1978): 630-32, 642. EJ 197 456.

Chapter 1. Portrait of a Leader

Armstrong, Colleen. "How's Your Story Arsenal?" *Principal* 71, 3 (January 1992): 40-41. EJ 437 540.

Autry, James A. *Life and Work: A Manager's Search for Meaning.* New York: William Morrow, 1994.

Bass, Bernard M. *Bass & Stodill's Handbook of Leadership: Theory, Research, and Managerial Applications.* 3rd edition. New York: The Free Press, 1990.

Bennis, Warren. "Transformative Power and Leadership." In *Leadership and Organizational Culture: New Perspectives on Administrative Theory and Practice,* edited by Thomas J. Sergiovanni and John E. Corbally. 64-71. Urbana, Illinois: University of Illinois Press, 1984.

Bennis, Warren, and Burt Nanus. *Leaders: The Strategies for Taking Charge.* New York: Harper & Row, 1985.

Blase, Joseph, and Jo Roberts Blase. *Empowering Teachers: What Successful Principals Do.* Thousand Oaks, California: Corwin Press, 1994. 192 pages. ED 377 576.

Blumberg, Arthur. *School Administration as a Craft: Foundations of Practice.* Boston: Allyn & Bacon, 1989. 238 pages. ED 304 773.

Blumberg, Arthur, and William Greenfield. *The Effective Principal: Perspectives on School Leadership.* 2nd edition. Newton, Massachusetts: Allyn and Bacon, 1986. 253 pages. ED 283 274.

Bolman, Lee G., and Terrence E. Deal. "Leading and Managing: Effects of Context, Culture, and Gender." *Educational Administration Quarterly* 28, 3 (August 1992): 314-29. EJ 447 155.

Clark, Kenneth E., and Miriam B. Clark, eds. *Measures of Leadership.* West Orange, New Jersey: Leadership Library of America, 1990. ED 363 928.

Crowson, Robert, and Van Cleve Morris. *The Superintendency and School Leadership: The National Center for School Leadership Project Report.* Urbana, Illinois: National Center for School Leadership, 1990. 77 pages. ED 328 945.

Duke, Daniel L. "The Aesthetics of Leadership." *Educational Administration Quarterly* 22, 1 (Winter 1986): 7-27. EJ 337 437.

Feistritzer, C. Emily. *Profile of Teachers in the U.S.* Washington, D. C.: National Center for Education Information, 1986.

Foster, William. "Leadership as a Critical Practice." *The Australian Administrator* 6, 2 (April 1985).

Gardner, Howard. *Leading Minds: An Anatomy of Leadership.* New York: Basic Books, 1995.

Gorton, Richard A., and Kenneth E. McIntyre. *The Senior High School Principalship. Volume II: The Effective Principal.* Reston, Virginia: National Association of Secondary School Principals, 1978. 98 pages. ED 158 440.

Gough, Harrison G. "Testing for Leadership with the California Psychological Inventory." In *Measures of Leadership*, edited by Kenneth Clark and Miriam Clark. 355-79. West Orange, New Jersey: Leadership Library of America, 1990.

Hemphill, John K.; Daniel E. Griffiths; and Norman Fredericksen. *Administrative Performance and Personality: A Study of the Principal in a Simulated Elementary School.* New York: Teachers College, Columbia University, 1962.

Hord, Shirley M., and Gene E. Hall. "Principals Use Research-Based Techniques for Facilitating School Effectiveness." Paper presented at annual meeting of the American Educational Research Association, New Orleans, April 1984. 23 pages. ED 258 338.

Jaques, Eliot. *Requisite Organization.* Arlington, Virginia: Cason Hall, 1989.

Kaplan, Robert E. *The Expansive Executive.* 2nd edition. Greensboro, North Carolina: Center for Creative Leadership, June 1991. 76 pages. ED 354 193.

Kouzes, James M., and Barry Z. Posner. *Credibility: How Leaders Gain and Lose It. Why People Demand It.* San Francisco: Jossey-Bass, 1993.

Krug, Samuel E. "Instructional Leadership: A Constructivist Perspective." *Educational Administration Quarterly* 28, 3 (August 1992): 430-43. EJ 447 162

Locke, Edwin A.; Shelley Kirkpatrick; Jill K. Wheeler; Jodi Schneider; Kathryn Niles; Harold Goldstein; Kurt Welsh; and Dong-Ok Chah. *The Essence of Leadership: The Four Keys to Leading Successfully.* New York: Lexington Books, 1991.

Lortie, Dan C. *Schoolteacher: A Sociological Study.* Chicago: The University of Chicago Press, 1975.

Marshall, Catherine. "School Administrators' Values: A Focus on Atypicals." *Educational Administration Quarterly* 28, 3 (August 1992): 368-86. EJ 447 158.

McCaulley, Mary H. "The Myers-Briggs Type Indicator and Leadership." In *Measures of Leadership*, edited by Kenneth Clark and Miriam Clark. 381-418. West Orange, New Jersey: Leadership Library of America, 1990.

Meadows, B. J. "Nurturing Cooperation and Responsibility in a School Community." *Phi Delta Kappan* 73, 6 (February 1992): 480-81. EJ 439 301.

Mendez-Morse, Sylvia. *Leadership Characteristics That Facilitate School Change*. Austin, Texas: Southwest Educational Development Laboratory, 1992. 67 pages. ED 370 215.

Morris, Edmund. *The Rise of Theodore Roosevelt*. New York: Coward, McCann and Geoghegan, 1979.

Palus, Charles J.; William Nasby; and Randolph Easton. *Understanding Executive Performance: Life-Story Perspective. An Exploration of the Foundations of Leadership in Terms of Personal Identity*. Greensboro, North Carolina: Center for Creative Leadership, 1991. 61 pages. ED 354 192.

Prestine, Nona A. "Extending the Essential Schools Metaphor: Principal as Enabler." *Journal of School Leadership* 3, 4 (July 1993): 356-79. EJ 466 823.

Richardson, Michael D., and others. "Teacher Perception of Principal Behaviors: A Research Study." Paper presented at annual meeting of the Mid-South Educational Research Association, Knoxville, Tennessee, November 1992. 15 pages. ED 352 710.

Sergiovanni, Thomas. *Moral Leadership: Getting to the Heart of School Improvement*. San Francisco: Jossey-Bass, 1992. 173 pages. ED 364 965.

Shakeshaft, Charol. *Women in Educational Administration*. Newbury Park, California: Sage Publications, 1987. ED 341 126.

Tye, Kenneth. "The Goal Orientation of the Principal: A Key Factor in the Success or Failure of School Change." Paper presented at the annual meeting of the American Association for Supervision and Curriculum Development, Chicago, March 1994. 15 pages. ED 370 244.

Wagner, Richard K., and Robert J. Sternberg. "Street Smarts." In *Measures of Leadership*, edited by Kenneth Clark and Miriam Clark. 493-504. West Orange, New Jersey: Leadership Library of America, 1990. ED 363 928.

Wilson, Robert E. "The Anatomy of Success in the Superintendency." *Phi Delta Kappan* 62, 1 (September 1980): 20-21. EJ 232 032.

Wright, Peter L., and David S. Taylor. *Improving Leadership Performance: Interpersonal Skills for Effective Leadership*. 2nd edition. London: Prentice Hall, 1994.

Wynne, Edward A., and R. Bruce McPherson. "Good Principals in Public and Church-Related Schools: A Study in Socialization." Paper presented at annual meeting of the American Educational Research Association, Montreal, Quebec, Canada, April 1983. 48 pages. ED 253 921.

Chapter 2. Leadership Styles and Strategies

Bass, Bernard M. *Leadership and Performance Beyond Expectations*. New York: The Free Press, 1985.

_______. *Bass & Stogdill's Handbook of Leadership: Theory, Research, and Managerial Applications.* (3rd edition). New York: The Free Press, 1990.

Beck, Lynn G., and Joseph Murphy. *Understanding the Principalship: Metaphorical Themes 1920s-1990s.* New York: Teachers College Press, 1993.

Benfari, Robert. *Understanding Your Management Style: Beyond the Myers-Briggs Type Indicators.* Lexington, Massachusetts: Lexington Books, 1991.

Blake, Robert R., and Jane S. Mouton. *The Managerial Grid III: The Key to Leadership Excellence.* Houston: Gulf Publishing Company, 1985.

Blase, Joseph, and Jo Roberts Blase. *Empowering Teachers: What Successful Principals Do.* Thousand Oaks, California: Corwin Press, 1994.

Blase, Joseph; Jo Blase; Gary L. Anderson; and Sherry Dungan. *Democratic Principals in Action: Eight Pioneers.* Thousand Oaks, California: Corwin Press, 1995.

Blumberg, Arthur. *School Administration as a Craft: Foundations of Practice.* Boston: Allyn and Bacon, 1989.

Bolman, Lee, and Terry Deal. *Reframing Organizations: Artistry, Choice and Leadership.* San Francisco: Jossey-Bass, 1991. 492 pages. ED 371 457.

_______. "Reframing Leadership: The Effects of Leaders' Images of Leadership." In *Impact of Leadership,* edited by Kenneth E. Clark; Miriam B. Clark; and David P. Campbell. 269-80. Greensboro, North Carolina: Center for Creative Leadership, 1992.

Bridges, Edwin. *The Incompetent Teacher: Managerial Responses.* Washington, D.C.: Falmer Press, 1992.

Burns, James McGregor. *Leadership.* New York: Harper and Row, 1978.

Callahan, Raymond E. *Education and the Cult of Efficiency.* Chicago: The University of Chicago Press, 1962.

Conger, Jay A. *The Charismatic Leader: Behind the Mystique of Exceptional Leadership.* San Francisco: Jossey-Bass, 1989. 231 pages. ED 314 990.

Conley, David T., and Paul Goldman. *Facilitative Leadership: How Principals Lead Without Dominating.* Eugene, Oregon School Study Council, University of Oregon, August 1994. OSSC Bulletin Series. 43 pages. ED 379 728.

Deal, Terrence E., and Kent D. Peterson. *The Leadership Paradox: Balancing Logic and Artistry in Schools.* San Francisco: Jossey-Bass, 1994. 133 pages. ED 371 455..

De Pree, Max. *Leadership Is an Art.* New York: Doubleday, 1989.

Dolan, W. Patrick. *Restructuring Our Schools: A Primer on Systems Change,* edited by Lilot Moorman. Kansas City, Kansas: Systems and Organization, 1994.

Dunlap, Diane, and Paul Goldman. "Power as a System of Authority vs. Power as a System of Facilitation." 1990. 25 pages. ED 325 943.

Eagly, Alice H.; Steven J. Karau; and Blair T. Johnson. "Gender and Leadership Style Among School Principals: A Meta-Analysis." *Educational Administration Quarterly* 28, 1 (February 1992): 76-102. EJ 441 085.

Fiedler, Fred E. *A Theory of Leadership Effectiveness.* New York: McGraw-Hill Book Company, 1967.

Fiedler, Fred E.; Martin M. Chemers; and Linda Mahar. *Improving Leadership Effectiveness: The Leader Match Concept.* New York: John Wiley and Sons, 1976.

Gates, Philip E.; Kenneth H. Blanchard; and Paul Hersey. "Diagnosing Educational Leadership Problems: A Situational Approach." *Educational Leadership* 33, 5 (February 1976): 348-54.

Gerth, H. H., and C. Wright Mills, eds. *From Max Weber: Essays in Sociology*. New York: Oxford University Press, 1946.

Griffin, Gary A. "Influences of Shared Decision Making on School and Classroom Activity: Conversations with Five Teachers." *The Elementary School Journal* 96, 1 (September 1995): 29-45. EJ 510 577.

Hall, Gene; William L. Rutherford; Shirley M. Hord; and Leslie L. Huling. "Effects of Three Principal Styles on School Improvement." *Educational Leadership* 41, 5 (February 1984): 22-29. EJ 293 145.

Heifetz, Ronald A. *Leadership Without Easy Answers*. Cambridge: Belknap Press, 1994.

Helgesen, Sally. *The Female Advantage: Women's Ways of Leadership*. New York: Doubleday, 1990.

Hersey, Paul, and Kenneth Blanchard. *Management of Organizational Behavior: Utilizing Human Resources*. 6th edition. Englewood Cliffs, New Jersey: Prentice-Hall, 1993.

Hord, Shirley M. *Facilitative Leadership: The Imperative for Change*. Austin, Texas: Southwest Educational Development Laboratory, 1992. ED 370 217.

Kirby, Peggy C.; Louis V. Paradise; and Margaret I. King. "Extraordinary Leaders in Education: Understanding Transformational Leadership." *Journal of Educational Research* 85, 5 (May/June 1992): 303-11. EJ 452 326.

Leithwood, Kenneth. "Contributions of Transformational Leadership to School Restructuring." Paper presented at the convention of the University Council for Educational Administration, Houston, October 1993. 58 pages. ED 367 061.

Liontos, Lynn Balster. *Transformational Leadership: Profile of a High School Principal*. Eugene: Oregon School Study Council, University of Oregon, October 1993. OSSC Bulletin Series. ED 363 969.

Lortie, Dan. *Schoolteacher: A Sociological Study*. Chicago: University of Chicago Press, 1975.

McMurry, Robert N. "The Case for Benevolent Autocracy." *Harvard Business Review* 36, 1 (January-February 1958), 82-90.

McNeil, Linda. *Contradictions of Control: School Structure and School Knowledge*. New York: Routledge and Kegan Paul, 1986.

Myers, Isabel Briggs, and Peter B. Myers. *Gifts Differing*. Palo Alto, California: Consulting Psychologists Press, 1980.

Patterson, Jerry L.; Stewart C. Purkey; and Jackson V. Parker. *Productive School Systems for a Nonrational World*. Alexandria, Virginia: Association for Supervision and Curriculum Development,. 1986.

Pittenger, David J. "The Utility of the Myers-Briggs Type Indicator." *Review of Educational Research* 63, 4 (Winter 1993): 467-88. EJ 482 588.

Prestine, Nona. "Extending the Essential Schools' Metaphor: Principal as Enabler." *Journal of School Leadership* 3 (July 1993): 356-79. EJ 466 823.

Roberts, Nancy. "Transforming Leadership: A Process of Collective Action." *Human Relations* 38, 11 (November 1985): 1023-46.

Sergiovanni, Thomas J. *Moral Leadership: Getting To the Heart of School Improvement*. San Francisco: Jossey-Bass, 1992. 173 pages. ED 364 965.

_______. Building Community in Schools. San Francisco: Jossey-Bass, 1994. 219 pages. ED 364 962.

Shedd, Joseph B., and Samuel Bacharach. *Tangled Hierarchies: Teachers as Professionals and the Management of Schools*. San Francisco: Jossey-Bass, 1991.

Tannenbaum, Robert, and Warren H. Schmidt. "How To Choose a Leadership Pattern." *Harvard Business Review* 36, 2 (March-April 1958): 95-101.

Tyack, David, and Elizabeth Hansot. *Managers of Virtue: Public School Leadership in America, 1820-1980*. New York: Basic Books, 1982.

Vroom, Victor H., and Jago. Arthur G. *The New Leadership: Managing Participation in Organizations*. Englewood Cliffs, NJ: Prentice Hall, 1988.

Weber, Max. *From Max Weber: Essays in Sociology*. Translated, edited, and with an introduction by H. H. Gerth and C. Wright Mills. New York: Oxford University Press, 1958.

Chapter 3. Developing School Leaders

Anderson, Mark E. *Principals: How To Train, Recruit, Select, Induct, and Evaluate Leaders for America's Schools*. Eugene, Oregon: ERIC Clearinghouse on Educational Management, 1991. ED 337 843.

Baltzell, D. Catherine, and Robert A. Dentler. *Selecting American School Principals: A Sourcebook for Educators*. Cambridge, Massachusetts: Abt Associates, Inc., January 1983. 68 pages. ED 236 811.

Beckham, Joseph. "Visiting Clinical Professors: Sharing Models of Excellence." *NASSP Bulletin* 78, 559 (February 1994): 38-40. EJ 479 291.

Biklen, Sari Knopp. *School Work: Gender and the Cultural Construction of Teaching*. New York: Teachers College Press, 1995.

Björk, Lars G., and Rick Ginsberg. "Principles of Reform and Reforming Principal Training: A Theoretical Perspective." *Educational Administration Quarterly* 31, 1 (February 1995): 11-37. EJ 499 068.

Blumberg, Arthur. *School Administration as a Craft: Foundations of Practice*. Boston: Allyn and Bacon, 1989. 238 pages. ED 304 773.

Bridges, Edwin M. "The Nature of Leadership." In *Educational Administration*, edited by L. L. Cunningham, W. G. Hack, and R. O. Nystrand. 202-30. Berkeley, California: McCutchan Publishing, 1977.

Bridges, Edwin M., and Philip Hallinger. *Implementing Problem-Based Learning in Leader-ship Development*. Eugene, Oregon: ERIC Clearinghouse on Educational Management, 1995.

Chase, Susan E. *Ambiguous Empowerment: The Work Narratives of Women Superintendents*. Amherst: University of Massachusetts Press, 1995. 272 pages. ED 384 959.

Cordeiro, Paula A.; Jo Ann Krueger; David Parks; Nan Restine; and Peter T. Wilson. "Taking Stock: Learnings Gleaned from Universities Participating in the Danforth Program." In *Changing the Way We Prepare School Leaders: The Danforth Experience*, edited by Mike Milstein and Associates. 17-38. Newbury Park, California: Corwin Press, 1993. ED 362 945.

Daresh, John C. "The Highest Hurdles for the First Year Principal." Paper presented at the annual meeting of the American Educational Research Association. Washington, D. C., April 1987. 27 pages. ED 280 136.

_______. "Questioning the Assumptions of Field-Based Preparation Programs." Paper presented at the annual meeting of the Mid-Western Educational Research Association, Chicago, October 1987. 17 pages.

Daresh, John C., and Marsha A. Playko. "Portfolios for Principals: Planning for Professional Development." *Here's How* 14, 1 (September 1995): 1-4.

Delisle, James R. "'Too Smart To Be a Teacher.'" *Education Week* 15, 2 (September 13, 1995): 32.

Donaldson, Gordon A., Jr., and George F. Marnik. *Becoming Better Leaders: The Challenge of Improving Student Learning*. Thousand Oaks, California: Corwin Press, 1995. 176 pages. ED 383 090.

Duke, Daniel L. "Why Principals Consider Quitting." *Phi Delta Kappan* 70, 4 (December 1988): 308-12. EJ 381 971.

_______. "Setting Goals for Professional Development." *Educational Leadership* 47, 8 (May 1990): 71-75. EJ 410 215.

_______. "Removing Barriers to Professional Growth." *Phi Delta Kappan* 74, 9 (May 1993): 702-4. EJ 463 873.

Duke, Daniel L., and Edward Iwanicki. "Principal Assessment and the Notion of 'Fit'." *Peabody Journal of Education* 68, 1 (Fall 1992): 25-36. EJ 464 836.

Edson, Sakre K. *Pushing the Limits: The Female Administrative Aspirant*. Albany: State University of New York Press, 1988. 299 pages. ED 307 721.

Gordon, Deanna, and Margaret Moles. "Mentoring Becomes Staff Development: A Case of Serendipity." *NASSP Bulletin* 78, 559 (February 1994): 66-70. EJ 479 298.

Hunter-Boykin, Harriet S. "Responses to the African American Teacher Shortage: 'We Grow Our Own' Through the Teacher Preparation Program at Coolidge High School." *Journal of Negro Education* 61, 4 (Fall 1992): 483-95. EJ 456 671.

Jacobson, Stephen L. "Future Educational Leaders: From Where Will They Come?" In *Educational Leadership in an Age of Reform*, edited by Stephen L. Jacobson and James A. Conway. 160-80. New York: Longman, 1990.

Johnson, M. Claradine, and Rex Douglas. "Assessment Centers: What Impact Have They Had on Career Opportunities for Women?" *NASSP Bulletin* 69, 484 (November 1985): 105-11. EJ 326 637.

Jones, Betty B. "Working with the 'Only One' in the Division." Paper presented at the annual International Conference for Community College Chairs, Deans, and Other Instructional Leaders, Phoenix, Arizona, February 1993. 13 pages. ED 354 935.

Kleine, Patricia. "Is a Woman's Place Only in the Classroom?" Paper presented at the annual meeting of the Eastern Educational Research Association, Sarasota, Florida. February 1994. 21 pages. ED 376 601.

Leithwood, Kenneth. "Preparing School Leaders: What Works?" *Connections* 3, 3 (Spring 1995): 1-7. ED 384 963.

Lewis, Anne C. "The South Carolina Teacher Cadet Program." *Phi Delta Kappan* 73, 6 (February 1992): 482-85. EJ 439 302.

Marshall, Catherine, and Katherine Kasten. *The Administrative Career: A Casebook on Entry, Equity, and Endurance*. Thousand Oaks, California: Corwin Press, 1994. ED 377 577.

Metzger, Christa. "Helping Women Prepare for Principalships." *Phi Delta Kappan* 67, 4 (December 1985): 294. EJ 327 988.

Milstein, Mike. "Learnings Across the Terrain." In *Changing the Way We Prepare School Leaders: The Danforth Experience*, edited by Mike Milstein and Associates. 178-218. Newbury Park, California: Corwin Press, 1993.

Murphy, Joseph. *The Landscape of Leadership Preparation: Reframing the Education of School Administrators*. Newbury Park, California: Corwin Press, 1992. 236 pages. ED 352 703

Murray, Gloria J.; William Husk; and Karen Simms. *Minorities in Educational Administration: Issues and Recommendations*. Louisville, Kentucky: University of Louisville, 1993. 17 pages. ED 361 912.

Muse, Ivan D., and E. Vance Randall. "The NASSP-Brigham Young Leader Preparation Program: Partners in Education." *NASSP Bulletin* 78, 559 (February 1994): 4-7. EJ 479 283.

National Association of Secondary School Principals. *Developing School Leaders: A Call for Collaboration. A Special Report of the NASSP Consortium for the Performance-Based Preparation of Principals*. Reston, Virginia: National Association of Secondary School Principals, 1992. 54 pages. ED 351 758.

Nelson, Robert A. "The Organizational Socialization of Public School Administrators." Doctoral Dissertation, University of Oregon, 1986.

Ortiz, Flora Ida. *Career Patterns in Education: Women, Men and Minorities in Public School Administration.* New York: Praeger, 1982.

Parkay, Forrest W.; Gaylon D. Currie; and John W. Rhodes. "Professional Socialization: A Longitudinal Study of First-Time High School Principals." *Educational Administration Quarterly* 28, 1 (February 1992): 43-75. EJ 441 084.

Parks, David. "Three Concepts Shape the New Roles of Principals in Administrator Preparation." *NASSP Bulletin* 75, 539 (December 1991): 8-12. EJ 437 500.

Richardson, M. D., and R. L. Prickett. "Recognizing How Adults Learn: Implications for Principals." *NASSP Bulletin* 78, 558 (January 1994): 85-89. EJ 475 871.

Schmuck, Richard A. "Beyond Academics in the Preparation of Educational Leaders: Four Years of Action Research." *OSSC Report* 33, 2 (Winter 1992): 1-10. Oregon School Study Council. ED 354 610.

Seeley, David. "Needed: A New Kind of Educational Leadership." Urbana, Illinois: National Center for School Leadership, 1992. 19 pages. ED 353 667.

Shakeshaft, Charol. *Women in Educational Administration*. Newbury Park, California: Sage Publications, 1987. ED 341 126.

Thompson, Thomas E. "Increasing the Opportunities for Minorities in School Administration." *NASSP Bulletin* 76, 546 (October 1992): 6-11. EJ 451 445.

U.S. Department of Education. *Principal Selection Guide*. Washington D.C.: Office of Educational Research and Improvement, U.S. Department of Education, June 1987. 43 pages. ED 282 358.

Valentine, Jerry W. "Performance/Outcome Based Principal Evaluation." Paper presented at the annual convention of the American Association of School Administrators, New Orleans, Louisiana, February 1987. 24 pages. ED 281 317.

Von Villas, Barbara A. "Smoothing the Transition for the New Principal: What Can You Do? *NASSP Bulletin* 78, 566 (December 1994): 79-84. EJ 497 490.

Chapter 4. Ethical Leadership

Beck, Lynn G. "Meeting the Challenge of the Future: The Place of a Caring Ethic in Educational Administration." *American Journal of Education* 100, 4 (August 1992): 454-96. EJ 452 424.

Beck, Lynn G., and Joseph Murphy. *Ethics in Educational Leadership Programs: An Expanding Role.* Thousand Oaks CA: Corwin Press, 1994. 137 pages. ED 378 690.

Blase, Joseph; Jo Blase; Gary L. Anderson; and Sherry Dungan. *Democratic Principals in Action: Eight Pioneers.* Thousand Oaks, California: Corwin Press, 1995. 193 pages. ED 380 890.

Block, Peter. *Stewardship: Choosing Service over Self-Interest.* San Francisco: Berrett-Koehler Publishers, 1993.

Blumberg, Arthur, and William Greenfield. *The Effective Principal: Perspectives on School Leadership.* Boston: Allyn and Bacon, 1986. 253 pages. ED 283 274.

Bricker, David. "Character and Moral Reasoning: An Aristotelian Perspective." In *Ethics for Professionals in Education: Perspectives for Preparation and Practice,* edited by Kenneth Strike and P. Lance Ternasky. 13-26. New York: Teachers College Press, 1993.

Bridges, William. *JobShift: How to Prosper in a Workplace without Jobs.* Reading, Massachusetts: Addison-Wesley, 1994.

Bull, Barry L., and Martha M. McCarthy. "Reflections of the Knowledge Base in Law and Ethics for Educational Leaders." *Educational Administration Quarterly* 31, 4 (November 1995): 613-31. EJ 513 436.

Butts, R. Freeman. "The Public School as Moral Authority." In *The School's Role as Moral Authority,* edited by R. Freeman Butts, Donald H. Peckenpaugh, and Howard Kirschenbaum. 5-29. Washington, D. C.: Association for Supervision and Curriculum Development, 1977.

Callahan, Raymond E. *Education and the Cult of Efficiency.* Chicago: The University of Chicago Press, 1962.

Chaleff, Ira. *The Courageous Follower: Standing Up to and for Leaders.* San Francisco: Berrett-Koehler, 1995. 194 pages. ED 387 872.

Colby, Anne, and William Damon. *Some Do Care: Contemporary Lives of Moral Commitment.* New York: The Free Press, 1992.

Etzioni, Amitai. *The Spirit of Community: Rights, Responsibilities, and the Communitarian Agenda.* New York: Crown Publishers, 1993.

Gallagher, Maggie. "Which Way for Education: Process or Performance?" *Seattle Times,* November 7, 1995.

Gardner, Howard. *Leading Minds: An Anatomy of Leadership.* New York: Basic Books, 1995.

Gilligan, Carol. *In a Different Voice: Psychological Theory and Women's Development.* Cambridge, Massachusetts: Harvard University Press, 1982.

Green, Thomas F. "The Conscience of Leadership." In *Leadership: Examining the Elusive,* edited by Linda T. Scheive and Marian B. Schoenheit. 105-15. No Location: Association for Supervision and Curriculum Development, 1987.

Greenfield, William D. Jr. "Rationale and Methods to Articulate Ethics and Administrator Training." Paper presented at the annual meeting of the American Educational Research Association. Chicago, April, 1991a. 32 pages. ED 332 379.

_______. "The Micropolitics of Leadership in an Urban Elementary School." In *The Politics of Life in Schools.* edited by Joseph Blase. 161-84. Newbury Park, California: Sage Publications, 1991b. ED 336 834.

_______. "The Moral Socialization of School Administrators: Informal Role Learning Outcomes." *Educational Administration Quarterly* 21, 4 (Fall 1985): 99-119. EJ 329 616.

Greenleaf, Robert K. *Servant Leadership: A Journey into the Nature of Legitimate Power and Greatness.* New York: Paulist Press, 1977.

Hodgkinson, Christopher. *Educational Leadership: The Moral Art*. Albany: The State University of New York Press, 1991.

Holt, John. *How Children Fail*. New York: Pitman, 1964.

Hostetler, Karl. "Ethics and Power: Implications for the Principal's Leadership." *NASSP Bulletin* 70, 488 (March 1986): 31-16. EJ 334 232.

Huebner, Dwayne. "The Vocation of Teaching." In *Teacher Renewal*, edited by Frances Bolin and J. M. Falk. 17-27. New York: Teachers College Press, 1987.

Kanungo, Rabindra N., and Manuel Mendonca. *Ethical Dimensions of Leadership*. Thousand Oaks, California: Sage Publications, 1996.

Kasten, Katherine L., and Carl R. Ashbaugh. "A Comparative Study of Values in Administrative Decision Making." *Journal of Research and Development in Education* 21, 3 (Spring 1988): 16-23. EJ 377 004.

Kidder, Rushworth M. *How Good People Make Tough Choices*. New York: William Morrow, 1995.

Kirby, Peggy C.; Louis V. Pardise; and Russell Protti. "The Ethical Reasoning of School Administrator: The Principled Principal." Paper presented at the annual meeting of the American Educational Research Association, Boston, April 1990. 11 pages. ED 320 253.

Kouzes, James M., and Barry Z. Posner. *The Leadership Challenge: How to Keep Getting Extraordinary Things Done in Organizations*. San Francisco: Jossey-Bass, 1995.

_______. *Credibility: How Leaders Gain and Lose It, Why People Demand It*. San Francisco: Jossey-Bass, 1993.

Lipsitz, Joan. "Prologue: Why We Should Care About Caring." *Phi Delta Kappa*n 76, 9 (May 1995): 665-66. EJ 502 931.

MacIntyre, Alasdair. *After Virtue: a Study in Moral Theory*. Notre Dame, Indiana: Notre Dame Press, 1981.

Macmillan, C. J. B. "Ethics and Teacher Professionalization." In *Ethics for Professionals in Education: Perspectives for Preparation and Practice*, edited by Kenneth Strike and P. Lance Ternasky. 189-201. New York: Teachers College Press, 1993.

Noddings, Nel. *The Challenge to Care in Schools: An Alternative Approach to Education*. New York: Teachers College Press, 1992. 191 pages. ED 377 590.

Norton, David. "'Character Ethics' and Organizational Life.'" In *Papers on the Ethics of Administration*, edited by N. Dale Wright. 47-66. Provo, Utah: Brigham Young University, 1988.

Osterman, Karen F., and Kottkamp, Robert B. *Reflective Practice for Educators: Improving Schooling through Professional Development*. Corwin Press: Thousand Oaks, California, 1993. 219 pages. ED 370 156.

Purpel, David E., and Svi Shapiro. *Beyond Liberation and Excellence: Reconstructing the Public Discourse on Education*. Westport, Connecticut: Bergin and Garvey, 1995.

Rishel, Kenn C., and Suzanne Tingley. "Lessons in Grace." *Executive Educator* 17, 4 (April 1995): 25-26. EJ 501 239.

Schrader, Dawn E. "Lawrence Kohlberg's Approach and the Moral Education of Education Professionals." In *Ethics for Professionals in Education: Perspectives for Preparation and Practice*, edited by Kenneth Strike and P. Lance Ternasky. 84-101. New York: Teachers College Press, 1993.

Sergiovanni, Thomas J. *Moral Leadership: Getting to the Heart of School Improvement*. San Francisco: Jossey-Bass, 1992. 173 pages. ED 364 965.

Sichel, Betty A. "Ethics Committees and Teacher Ethics." In *Ethics for Professionals in Education: Perspectives for Preparation and Practice,* edited by Kenneth Strike and P. Lance Ternasky. 162-75. New York: Teachers College Press, 1993.

Smith, Arthur E., Paul D. Travers, and George J. Yard. *Codes of Ethics for Selected Fields of Professional Education.* St. Louis, Missouri, 1990. 32 pages. ED 318 736.

Sockett, Hugh. *The Moral Base for Teacher Professionalism.* New York: Teachers College Press, 1993. 194 pages. ED 366 576.

Solomon, Robert C. *A Passion for Justice: Emotions and the Origin of the Social Contract.* Reading, Massachusetts: Addison-Wesley, 1990.

Starratt, Robert J. "Building an Ethical School: A Theory for Practice in Educational Leadership." *Educational Administration Quarterly* 27, 2 (May 1991): 185-202. EJ 425 540.

_______. "Afterword." In *Ethics in Educational Leadership Programs: An Expanding Role,* edited by Lynn Beck and Joseph Murphy. 100-03. Thousand Oaks California: Corwin Press, 1994.

Strike, Kenneth A.; Emil J. Haller; and Jonas F. Soltis. *The Ethics of School Administration.* New York: Teachers College Press, 1988. 137 pages. ED 304 752.

Strike, Kenneth, and P. Lance Ternasky. "Introduction: Ethics in Educational Settings." In *Ethics for Professionals in Education: Perspectives for Preparation and Practice,* edited by Kenneth Strike and P. Lance Ternasky. 1-9 New York: Teachers College Press, 1993.

Thomas, M. Donald. ""How Can School Leaders Be Courageous?" *NASSP Bulletin* 68, 476 (December 1984): 36-40. EJ 311 632.

Tyack, David, and Elizabeth Hansot. *Managers of Virtue: Public School Leadership in America,* 1820-1980. New York: Basic Books, 1982.

Wilson, James Q. *The Moral Sense.* New York: The Free Press, 1993.

Wirth, Arthur G. "The Violation of People at Work in Schools," *Teachers College Record* 90, 4 (Summer 1989): 535-49. EJ 398 402.

Chapter 5. Visionary Leadership

Barth, Roland S. *Improving Schools from Within: Teachers, Parents, and Principals Can Make the Difference.* San Francisco: Jossey-Bass, 1990. 190 pages. ED 319 126.

Bennis, Warren; Jagdish Parikh; and Ronnie Lessem. *Beyond Leadership: Balancing Economics, Ethics, and Ecology.* Cambridge, Massachusetts: Blackwell Publishers, 1994.

Blase, Joseph, and Jo Roberts Blase. *Empowering Teachers: What Successful Principals Do.* Thousand Oaks, California: Corwin Press, 1994. 192 pages. ED 377 576.

Blumberg, Arthur, and William Greenfield. *The Effective Principal: Perspectives on School Leadership.* Newton, Massachusetts: Allyn and Bacon, 1986. 253 pages. ED 283 274.

Bridges, William. *Managing Transitions: Making the Most of Change.* Reading, Massachusetts: Addison-Wesley, 1991.

Chance, Edward W., and Marilyn L. Grady. "Creating and Implementing a Vision for the School." *NASSP Bulletin* 74, 529 (November 1990): 12-18. EJ 418 117.

Collins, James C., and Jerry I. Porras. *Built to Last: Successful Habits of Visionary Companies.* New York: Harper Business, 1994.

Conley, David T.; Diane M. Dunlap; and Paul Goldman. "The 'Vision Thing' and School Restructuring." *OSSC Report* 3, 2 (Winter 1992): 1-8. Eugene: Oregon School Study Council. ED 343 246.

Conley, David T., and Paul Goldman. *Facilitative Leadership: How Principals Lead Without Dominating*. OSSC Bulletin Series. Eugene: Oregon School Study Council, August 1994. 52 pages. ED 379 728.

Cunningham, William G., and Donn W. Gresso. *Cultural Leadership: The Culture of Excellence in Education*. Boston: Allyn and Bacon, 1993. 285 pages. ED 377 582.

Deal, Terry. "Symbols and Symbolic Activity." In *Images of Schools: Structures and Roles in Organizational Behavior,* edited by Samuel B. Bacharach and Bryan Mundell. 108-36. Thousand Oaks, California: Corwin Press, 1995.

Dolan, W. Patrick. *Restructuring Our Schools: A Primer on Systems Change.* Edited by Lilot Moorman. Kansas City, Kansas: Systems and Organization, 1994.

Drucker, Peter F. "The Age of Social Transformation." *Atlantic Monthly* 274, 5 (November 1994): 53-80.

Gardner, Howard. *Leading Minds: An Anatomy of Leadership*. New York: Basic Books, 1995.

Gitlin, Andrew, and Frank Margonis. "The Political Aspect of Reform: Teacher Resistance as Good Sense." *American Journal of Education* 103 (August 1995): 377-405.

Hammer, Michael, and Steven A. Stanton. *The Reengineering Revolution: A Handbook*. New York: Harper Collins Publishers, 1995.

Herman, Jerry J. "Action Plans To Make Your Vision a Reality." *NASSP Bulletin* 74, 523 (February 1990): 14-17. EJ 403 782.

Hoyle, John R. *Leadership and Futuring: Making Visions Happen*. Thousand Oaks, California: Corwin Press, 1995. 83 pages. ED 386 809.

Hurst, David K. *Crisis & Renewal: Meeting the Challenge of Organizational Change*. Boston: Harvard Business School Press, 1995.

Kaufman, Roger. *Mapping Educational Success: Strategic Thinking and Planning for School Administrators*. Thousand Oaks, California: Corwin Press, 1995. ED 351 802.

Kelley, Robert E. *The Power of Followership: How To Create Leaders People Want*. New York: Doubleday, 1992.

Kouzes, James M., and Barry Z. Posner. *The Leadership Challenge: How To Keep Getting Extraordinary Things Done in Organizations*. San Francisco: Jossey-Bass, 1995.

Louis, Karen, and Matthew Miles. *Improving the Urban High School: What Works and Why*. New York: Teachers College Press, 1990. 357 pages. ED 327 623.

Manasse, A. Lorri. "Vision and Leadership: Paying Attention to Intention." *Peabody Journal of Education* 63, 1 (Fall 1986): 150-73. EJ 354 954.

Nanus, Burt. *Visionary Leadership: Creating a Compelling Sense of Direction for Your Organization*. San Francisco: Jossey-Bass, 1992. 237 pages. ED 350 948.

Postman, Neal. *The End of Education: Redefining the Value of School*. New York: Alfred A. Knopf, 1995.

Renchler, Ron. *Leadership with a Vision: How School Principals Develop and Implement Their Visions for School Success*. OSSC Bulletin Series. Eugene: Oregon School Study Council, January 1991. ED 328 976.

Rose, Michael. *Possible Lives: The Promise of Public Education in America.* Boston: Houghton Mifflin, 1995.

Sashkin, Marshall. "Visionary Leadership." In *The Leader's Companion: Insights on Leadership Through the Ages*, edited by J. Thomas Wren. 402-7. New York: The Free Press, 1995.

Schwartz, Peter. *The Art of the Long View*. New York: Doubleday, 1991.

Senge, Peter M. *The Fifth Discipline: The Art and Practice of the Learning Organization*. New York: Doubleday, 1990.

Sergiovanni, Thomas J. *Moral Leadership: Getting to the Heart of School Improvement*. San Francisco: Jossey-Bass, 1992. 173 pages. ED 364 965.

Sheive, Linda Tinelli, and Marian Beauchamp Schoenheit. "Vision and the Work Life of Educational Leaders." In *Leadership: Examining the Elusive*, edited by Linda Scheive and Marian Schoenheit. Alexandria, Virginia: Association for Supervision and Curriculum Development, 1987.

Starratt, Robert J. *Leaders with Vision: The Quest for School Renewal*. Thousand Oaks, California: Corwin Press, 1995.

Tyack, David, and Larry Cuban. *Tinkering Toward Utopia: A Century of Public School Reform*. Cambridge, Massachusetts: Harvard University Press, 1995.

Wagner, Tony. "Seeking Common Ground: Goal-Setting with All Constituencies." *Educational Leadership* 53, 4 (December 1995/January 1996): 40-44.

Wheatley, Margaret J. *Leadership and the New Science: Learning about Organization from an Orderly Universe*. San Francisco: Berrett-Koehler, 1994.

Chapter 6. Cultural Leadership

Arter, Judith A. *Assessing School and Classroom Climate: A Consumer's Guide*. Portland, Oregon: Northwest Regional Educational Laboratory, April 1987. 80 pages. ED 295 301.

Bowers, C. A., and David J. Flinders. *Responsive Teaching: An Ecological Approach to Classroom Patterns of Language, Culture, and Thought*. New York: Teachers College Press, 1990. 271 pages.

Burnham, Joan, and Shirley Hord, eds. *Toward Quality in Education: The Leader's Odyssey*. Washington, D.C.: National LEADership Network Study Group on Restructuring Schools, May 1993. 103 pages.

Cheng, Yin Cheong. "Profiles of Organizational Culture and Effective Schools." *School Effectiveness and School Improvement* 4, 2 (1993): 85-110. EJ 465 332.

Cunningham, William G., and Donn W. Gresso. *Cultural Leadership: The Culture of Excellence in Education*. Needham Heights, Massachusetts: Allyn & Bacon, 1993. 285 pages. ED 377 582.

Deal, Terrence E., and Allan A. Kennedy. *Corporate Cultures: The Rites and Rituals of Corporate Life*. Reading, Massachusetts: Addison-Wesley, 1982. 232 pages.

Deal, Terrence E., and Kent D. Peterson. *The Principal's Role in Shaping School Culture*. Washington, D.C.: Office of Educational Research and Improvement, 1990. 122 pages. ED 325 914.

Firestone, William A., and Bruce L. Wilson. "Bureaucratic and Cultural Linkages: Implications for the Principal." In *Educational Leadership and School Culture*, edited by Marshall Sashkin and Herbert J. Walberg. 19-39. Berkeley, California: McCutchan Publishing, 1993. 182 pages.

Fyans, Leslie J., Jr., and Martin L. Maehr. *"School Culture," Student Ethnicity, and Motivation*. Urbana, Illinois: The National Center for School Leadership, 1990. 29 pages. ED 327 947.

Geertz, Clifford. *The Interpretation of Cultures*. New York: Basic Books, 1973. 470 pages.

Gonder, Peggy Odell, and Donald Hymes. *Improving School Climate and Culture*. Critical Issues Report. Arlington, Virginia: American Association of School Administrators, 1994. 120 pages.

Gottfredson, Denise C., and others. *School Climate Assessment Instruments: A Review*. Baltimore, Maryland: Center for Social Organization of Schools, The John Hopkins University, July 1986. 24 pages. ED 278 702.

Heckman, Paul E. "School Restructuring in Practice: Reckoning with the Culture of School." *International Journal of Educational Reform* 2, 3 (July 1993): 263-72. EJ 465 326.

Keefe, James W. "Leadership for School Restructuring—Redesigning Your School." *High School Magazine* 1, 2 (December 1993): 4-9. EJ 477 437.

Keefe, James W., and Edgar A. Kelley. "Comprehensive Assessment and School Improvement." *NASSP Bulletin* 74, 530 (December 1990): 54-63. EJ 418 214.

Lane, Bruce A. "Cultural Leaders in Effective Schools: The Builders and Brokers of Excellence." *NASSP Bulletin* (February 1992): 85-96. EJ 439 356.

Leithwood, Kenneth; Doris Jantzi; and Alicia Fernandez. "Transformational Leadership and Teachers' Commitment to Changes." In *Reshaping the Principalship: Insights from Transformational Reform Efforts*, edited by Joseph Murphy and Karen Seashore Louis. 77-98. Thousand Oaks, California: Corwin Press, 1994.

Liontos, Lynn Balster. *Transformational Leadership: Profile of a High School Principal*. OSSC Bulletin Series. Eugene: Oregon School Study Council, University of Oregon, July 1993. 57 pages. ED 359 652.

Louis, Karen Seashore; Helen M. Marks; and Sharon Kruse. "Teachers' Professional Community in Restructuring Schools." Madison, Wisconsin: Center on Organization and Restructuring of Schools, December 6, 1994. 58 pages. ED 381 871.

Maehr, Martin, and Rachel Buck. "Transforming School Culture." In *Educational Leadership and School Culture*, edited by Marshall Sashkin and Herbert J. Walberg. 40-60. Berkeley, California: McCutchan Publishing, 1993. 182 pages.

Maxwell, T.W., and A. Ross Thomas. "School Climate and School Culture." *Journal of Educational Administration* 29, 2 (1991): 72-82. EJ 525 826.

Sashkin, Marshall, and Molly G. Sashkin. "Leadership and Culture Building in Schools: Quantitative and Qualitative Understandings." Paper presented at the annual meeting of the American Educational Research Association, Boston, April 16-20, 1990. 41 pages. ED 322 583.

Schein, Edgar H. "Coming to a New Awareness of Corporate Culture." *Sloan Management Review* 25 (1984): 3-16.

_______. *Organizational Culture and Leadership*. San Francisco: Jossey-Bass, 1985. 358 pages.

Witcher, Ann E. "Assessing School Climate: An Important Step for Enhancing School Quality." *NASSP Bulletin* 77, 554 (September 1993): 1-5.

Chapter 7. School-Based Management

American Association of School Administrators, National Association of Elementary School Principals, and National Association of Secondary School Principals. *School-Based Management: A Strategy for Better Learning.* Arlington, Virginia: Author, 1988. Reprinted 1990. 24 pages. ED 300 905.

Bair, Linda H. "What Research Has to Say About School-Based Management." *Catalyst,* 21, 2 (Winter 1992): 17-19. EJ 461 899.

Berry, James E. "Defining Shared Decision-Making." *Catalyst* (Winter 1993): 15-17.

Brown, Daniel J. *A Preliminary Inquiry Into School-Based Management.* Ottawa, Ontario: Social Sciences and Humanities Research Council of Canada, March 1987. 39 pages. 43 pages. ED 284 331.

Caldwell, Sarah D., and Fred H. Wood. "Breaking Ground in Restructuring." *Educational Leadership* 50, 1 (September 1992): 41, 44. EJ 449 918.

Chion-Kenney, Linda. *Site-Based Management and Decision Making: Problems and Solutions,* edited by Donald L. Hymes. Arlington, Virginia: Author. 1994. 89 pages. ED 379 755.

Clune, William H., and White, Paula A. *School-Based Management: Institutional Variation, Implementation, and Issues for Further Research.* Rutgers, New Jersey: Center for Policy Research in Education, The State University of New Jersey at Rutgers, September 1988. 42 pages. ED 300 908.

Committee for Economic Development. *Putting Learning First: Governing and Managing the Schools for High Achievement.* A Statement by the Research and Policy Committee of the CED. New York: Author, 1994.

Drury, William R. "The Principal's Role in Site-Based Management." *Principal* 73, 1 (September 1993): 16-19. EJ 466 871.

Glickman, Carl D. "The Essence of School Renewal: The Prose Has Begun." *Educational Leadership* 50, 1 (September 1992): 24-27. EJ 449 913.

Guskey, Thomas R., and Kent D. Peterson. "The Road to Classroom Change." *Educational Leadership* 53, 4 (December/January 1996): 10-14.

Hansen, Barbara J., and Carl L. Marburger. *School Based Improvement: A Manual for District Leaders.* Columbia, Maryland: The National Committee for Citizens in Education, 1988. ED 301 954.

_______. *School Based Improvement: A Manual for Training School Councils.* Columbia, Maryland: The National Committee for Citizens in Education, 1989. ED 323 654.

Hill, Paul T.; Josephine J. Bonan; and Kelly Warner. "Uplifting Education." *The American School Board Journal* 179, 3 (March 1992): 21-25. EJ 441 134.

Kowalski, Jackie, and Arnold Oates. "The Evolving Role of Superintendents in School-Based Management." *Journal of School Leadership* 3, 4 (July 1993): 380-90. EJ 466 824.

Lynn, Leon. *Brief to Principals: Building Parent Involvement.* Madison, Wisconsin: Center on Organization and Restructuring of Schools, Winter 1994.

Malen, B.; R. Ogawa; and J. Kranz. "What Do We Know About School Based Management? A Case Study of the Literature—A Call for Research." Paper presented at the Conference on Choice and Control in American Education, Madison, Wisconsin, University of Wisconsin, 1989.

Midgley, Carol, and Stewart Wood. "Beyond School-Based Management: Empowering Teachers to Reform Schools." *Phi Delta Kappan* 75, 3 (November 1993): 245-52. EJ 472 593.

Mitchell, James E. "Share the Power." *The American School Board Journal* 177, 1 (January 1990): 42-43. EJ 402 323.

Murphy, Joseph. *Principles of School-Based Management*. Chapel Hill: North Carolina Educational Policy Research Center, University of North Carolina, February 1994.

National School Boards Association. *Shared Decision Making*. NSBA Series on School Board Governance, no date. 8 pages.

Neal, Richard G. "School-Based Management Lets Principals Slice up the Budget Pie." *The Executive Educator* 11, 1 (January 1989): 16-19. EJ 383 853.

Ogawa, R., and P. A. White. "School Based Management: An Overview." In *Site-Based Management: Organizing for High Performance*, edited by S. A. Mohrman and P. Wohlstetter. San Francisco: Jossey-Bass, 1994.

Oregon School Boards Association. *Selected Sample Policies 21st Century Schools Councils. Version 1.* November 2, 1993.

Palanki, Ameetha, and others. *Mapping the Policy Landscape: What Federal and State Governments Are Doing to Promote Family-School-Community Partnerships*. Baltimore, Maryland: Center on Families, Communities, Schools, and Children's Learning, 1992. 82 pages. ED 343 700.

Peterson - del Mar, David. *Building Coalitions to Restructuring Schools*. OSSC Bulletin Series. Eugene: Oregon School Study Council 1993. ED 364 958.

Prasch, John C. *How to Organize for School-Based Management*. Alexandria, Virginia: Association for Supervision and Curriculum Development, 1990. 65 pages. ED 328 944.

Robertson, Peter J.; Priscilla Wohlstetter; and Susan Albers Mohrman. "Generating Curriculum and Instructional Innovations Through School-Based Management." Unpublished article, August 1994.

Schneider, Gail Thierbach. "Teacher Involvement in Decision Making: Zones of Acceptance, Decision Conditions, and Job Satisfaction." *Journal of Research and Development in Education* 18, 1: (Fall 1984): 25-32. EJ 307 690.

Smylie, Mark A. "Teacher Participation in School Decision Making: Assessing Willingness to Participate." *Educational Evaluation and Policy Analysis* 14,1 (Spring 1992): 53-67. EJ 446 665.

Stover, Del. "But Some Principals Feel Threatened." *The Executive Educator* (January 1989): 17. EJ 383 854.

Summers, Anita A., and Amy W. Johnson. "Doubts About Decentralized Decisions." *School Administrator* 52, 3 (March 1995): 24-26, 28, 30, 32.

Walker, Peter A., and Lawrence Roder. "Reflections on the Practical and Legal Implications of School-Based Management and Teacher Empowerment." *Journal of Law & Education* 22, 2 (Spring 1993): 159-75. EJ 470 593.

White, Paula. "Teacher Empowerment Under 'Ideal' School-Site Autonomy." *Educational Evaluation and Policy Analysis* 14, 1 (Spring 1992): 69-82. EJ 446 666.

Wohlstetter, Priscilla. *School-Based Management: Strategies for Success*. Consortium for Policy Research in Education Finance Briefs. New Brunswick, NJ: Eagleton Institute of Politics, Rutgers, The State University of New Jersey, January 1993.

Wohlstetter, Priscilla, and Kerri L. Briggs. "The Principal's Role in School-Based Management." *Principal* (November 1994): 14-17.
Wohlstetter, Priscilla; Roxane Smyer; and Susan Albers Mohrman. "New Boundaries for School-Based Management: The High Involvement Model." Paper presented at the Annual Meeting of the American Educational Research Association, April 4-8, 1994, New Orleans, Louisiana.

Chapter 8. Quality Work Teams

American Association of School Administrators. *Creating Quality Schools.* Arlington, Virginia: Author, 1992. ED 349 698.
_______. *District Continuous Instructional Improvement Teams.* Arlington, Virginia: Author, no date. 10 pages.
Bass, Bernard M., and Bruce J. Avolio, editors. *Improving Organizational Effectiveness Through Transformational Leadership.* Thousand Oaks, California: Sage Publications, 1994. 238 pages. ED 387 944.
Cunningham, William G., and Donn W. Gresso. *Cultural Leadership: The Culture of Excellence in Education.* Needham Heights, Massachusetts: Allyn and Bacon, 1993. 285 pages. ED 377 582.
Deming, W. Edwards. *Out of Crisis.* Cambridge; Massachusetts Institute of Technology, Center for Advanced Engineering Study, 1986. 507 pages.
Elliott, Stephen N., and Susan M. Sheridan. "Consultation and Teaming: Problem Solving among Educators, Parents, and Support Personnel." *The Elementary School Journal* 92, 3 (January 1992): 315-38. EJ 443 453.
Helphand, Margot. *Facilitation for 21st Century School Councils: A Program for Central Oregon.* Sponsored by Oregon Professional Development Center, Deschutes Educational Service District, fall 1994. 44 pages.
Johnson, David W., and Roger T. Johnson. *Leading the Cooperative School.* Edina, Minnesota: Interaction Book Company, 1989.
Kansas State Board of Education. *School Site Councils for Kansas Schools and Districts.* Topeka, Kansas: Author, April 1992. 51 pages.
Kessler, Robert. "Shared Decision Making Works!" *Educational Leadership* (September 1992): 36-38. EJ 449 916.
Maeroff, Gene I. "Building Teams To Rebuild Schools." *Phi Delta Kappan* 47, 7 (March 1993): 512-19. EJ 459 406.
McLagan, Patricia. "The Dark Side of Quality." *Training* 28, 11 (November 1991): 31-33. EJ 435 273.
Melvin III, Charles A. "Translating Deming's 14 Points for Education: A Wisconsin Consortium Turns to Total Quality System Improvements." *The School Administrator* 48, 9 (November 1991): 19-20, 23. EJ 434 406.
Murgatroyd, Stephen, and Colin Morgan. *Total Quality Management and the School.* Philadelphia: Open University Press, 1992.
Pellicer, Leonard O.; Lorin W. Anderson; James W. Keefe; Edgar A. Kelley; and Lloyd E. McCleary. *High School Leaders and Their Schools, Volume III: Profiles of Effectiveness.* Reston, Virginia: National Association of Secondary School Principals, 1990. ED 319 139.
Scarr, L. E. "Using Self-Regulating Work Teams." *Educational Leadership* 50, 3 (November 1992): 68-70. EJ 454 332.
Siu-Runyan, Yvonne, and Sally Joy Heart. "Management Manifesto." *The Executive Educator* 14, 1 (January 1992): 23-26. EJ 439 231.

Snyder, Karolyn J., and Robert H. Anderson. *Managing Productive Schools: Toward an Ecology*. Chicago: Harcourt Brace Jovanovich, Academic Press College Division, 1986. ED 281 269.

Vollmer, Nancy. "Effective, Successful Teams/Groups." Handouts. Corvallis, Oregon: Linn-Benton-Lincoln Educational Service District, no date.

Chapter 9. Shared Decision-Making

Allen, Lew, and Carl D. Glickman. "School Improvement: The Elusive Faces of Shared Governance." *NASSP Bulletin* 76, 542 (March 1992): 80-87. EJ 441 161.

Alvarez, Doris Sanchez. "Professional Growth Seminars Encourage Shared Decision Making, Collaboration." *NASSP Bulletin* 76, 540 (January 1992): 70-75. EJ 437 586.

Bauer, Scott C. "Myth, Consensus, and Change." *Executive Educator* 14, 7 (July 1992): 26-28. EJ 447 135.

Blase, Joseph; Jo Blase; Gary L. Anderson; and Sherry Dungan. *Democratic Principals in Action: Eight Pioneers*. Thousand Oaks, California: Corwin Press, 1995. 193 pages. ED 380 890.

Bradley, Ann. "'Strong Democracy' Yields Improvement in Chicago Reforms." *Education Week* (July 14, 1993).

Daniels, Cecil T. "A Principal's View: Giving Up My Traditional Ship." *School Administrator* 7, 8 (September 1990): 20, 22-24. EJ 413 139.

Frase, Larry E., and Larry Sorensen. "Teacher Motivation and Satisfaction: Impact on Participatory Management." *NASSP Bulletin* 76, 540 (January 1992): 37-43. EJ 437 581.

Goldman, Jay P. "When Participatory Management Attracts No Buyers." *School Administrator* 49, 1 (January 1992): 15. EJ 437 631.

Goldman, Paul, and others. "Administrative Facilitation and Site-Based School Reform Projects." Paper presented at the annual meeting of the American Educational Research Association, Chicago, April 1991. 32 pages. ED 332 334.

Griffin, Gary A. "Influences of Shared Decision Making on School and Classroom Activity: Conversations with Five Teachers." *The Elementary School Journal* 96, 1 (September 1995): 29-45. EJ 510 577.

Hall, Gene, and Gary Galluzzo. *Changing Policy into Practice: School-Based Decisionmaking*. Charleston, West Virginia: Appalachia Educational Laboratory, 1991. 57 pages. ED 346 563.

Hallinger, Philip, and Don Richardson. "Models of Shared Leadership: Evolving Structures and Relationships." Paper presented at the annual meeting of the American Educational Research Association, New Orleans, April 5-9, 1988. 19 pages. ED 310 490.

Horgan, Dianne. "A Training Model for School Based Decision Making." Paper presented at the annual meeting of the American Educational Research Association, Chicago, 1991. 9 pages. ED 332 357.

Huddleston, Judith, and others. "Participative Decision Making Can Capitalize on Teacher Expertise." *NASSP Bulletin* 75, 534 (April 1991): 80-89. EJ 424 394.

Kessler, Robert. "Shared Decision Making Works!" *Educational Leadership* 50, 1 (September 1992): 36-38. EJ 449 916.

Kirby, Peggy C. "Shared Decision Making: Moving from Concerns About Restrooms to Concerns About Classrooms." *Journal of School Leadership* 2, 3 (July 1992): 330-44. EJ 447 131.

Lange, John T. "Site-Based, Shared Decision Making: A Resource for Restructuring." *NASSP Bulletin* 76, 49 (January 1993): 98-107. EJ 457 259.

Levin, Henry M. *Building School Capacity for Effective Teacher Empowerment: Applications to Elementary Schools with At-Risk Students*. New Brunswick, New Jersey: Consortium for Policy Research in Education, September 1991. 35 pages. ED 337 856.

Lifton, Fred B. "The Legal Tangle of Shared Governance." *School Administrator* 49, 1 (January 1992): 16-19. EJ 437 632.

Mayeski, Fran. "Moving Toward Effective Teacher Empowerment Through Improved Decision Making at a Secondary School in Wyoming." Practicum paper. Fort Lauderdale, Florida: Nova University, 1991. 301 pages. ED 336 819.

Meadows, B. J. "The Rewards and Risks of Shared Leadership." *Phi Delta Kappan* 71, 7 (March 1990): 545-48. EJ 403 811.

Miller, Edward. "Shared Decision-Making by Itself Doesn't Make for Better Decisions." *The Harvard Education Letter* 11, 6 (November/December 1995): 1-4.

Mitchell, James E. "Share the Power." *American School School Journal* 177, 1 (January 1990): 42-43. EJ 402 323.

Mutchler, Sue E., and Patricia C. Duttweiler. "Implementing Shared Decision Making in School-Based Management: Barriers to Changing Traditional Behavior." Paper presented at the annual meeting of the American Educational Research Association, Boston, 1990. 47 pages. ED 320 286.

National School Boards Association. *Shared Decision Making*. NSBA Series on School Board Governance. Alexandria, Virginia: Author, December 1994. 8 pages.

Newman, Jay B. "Student Involvement in School Restructuring." *ERS Spectrum* 10, 3 (Summer 1992): 19-22. EJ 448 495.

Prestine, Nona. "Extending the Essential Schools Metaphor: Principal as Enabler." *Journal of School Leadership* 3 (July 1993): 356-79. EJ 466 823.

Robinson, Sharon, and Robert Barkley. "Nine Principles Guide Decentralizing Efforts." *School Administrator* 49, 1 (January 1992): 13-14.

Russell, John J., and others. "How Do You Measure Shared Decision Making?" *Educational Leadership* 50, 1 (September 1992): 39-40. EJ 449 917.

Spaulding, Angela McNabb. "The Politics of the Principal: Influencing Teachers' School Based Decision Making." Paper presented at the annual meeting of the American Educational Research Association, New Orleans, April 1994. 40 pages. ED 374 542.

Stine, David O. "How To Build a Leadership Team for Effective Decision Making." In *Tips for Principals*. Reston, Virginia: National Association of Secondary School Principals, September 1993.

Strusinski, Marianne. "The Continuing Development of Shared Decision Making in School-Based Management." April 1991. 6 pages. ED 331 185.

Wagner, Tony. *How Schools Change: Lessons from Three Communities*. Boston: Beacon Press, 1994. 304 pages. ED 379 741.

Watson, Amie, and others. "A Lab School Explores Self-Governance." *Educational Leadership* 49, 5 (February 1992): 57-60. EJ 439 287.

Weiss, Carol H. "Shared Decision Making about What? A Comparison of Schools with and without Teacher Participation." *Teachers College Record* 95, 1 (Fall 1993): 69-92. EJ 475 129.

_______. "The Four 'I's' of School Reform: How Interests, Ideology, Information, and Institution Affect Teachers and Principals." *Harvard Educational Review* 65, 4 (Winter 1995): 571-92.

Weiss, Carol H.; Joseph Cambone; and Alexander Wyeth. "Trouble in Paradise: Teacher Conflicts in Shared Decision Making." *Educational Administration Quarterly* 28, 3 (August 1992): 350-67. EJ 447 157.

Williams, Sheri. "Before You Begin Shared Decision-Making, Try This" and "Effective Practices in Shared Decision-Making." *School Administrator* 49, 1 (January 1992): 11 and 12.

Chapter 10. Leading the Instructional Program

Acheson, Keith. *The Principal's Role in Instructional Leadership*. OSSC Bulletin series. Eugene: Oregon School Study Council, April 1985. ED 254 960.

Anderson, Lorin W. "Instruction and Time-on-Task: A Review." *Journal of Curriculum Studies* 13, 4 (1981): 289-303.

Bird, Tom, and Judith Warren Little. *Instructional Leadership in Eight Secondary Schools: Final Report*. Boulder, Colorado: Center for Action Research, Inc., June 1985. 281 pages. ED 263 694.

Bolster, Sharon J. "Vision: Communicating It to the Staff. " Paper presented at the annual meeting of the American Educational Research Association, San Francisco, March 30, 1989. 27 pages. ED 304 797.

Brookover, Wilbur B., and others. *Creating Effective Schools: An In-Service Program for Enhancing School Learning Climate and Achievement*. Holmes Beach, Florida: Learning Publications, 1982. 290 pages. ED 229 457.

Carr, Judy F., and Douglas E. Harris. *Getting It Together*. Boston: Allyn and Bacon, 1993. 301 pages. ED 361 909.

English, Fenwick W. "Curriculum Development within the School System." In *Considered Action for Curriculum Improvment*, edited by Arthur W. Foshay. 145-57. Alexandria, Virginia: Association for Supervision and Curriculum Development, 1980. ED 186 428.

Evans, Dennis L. "The 'Instructional Leader' Must Go." 1992. 10 pages. ED 350 649.

Glatthorn, Allan A. *Teachers as Agents of Change: A New Look at School Improvement*. Washington, D.C.: National Education Association, 1992. ED 351 787.

Heck, Ronald H., and George A. Marcoulides. "Examining Contextual Differences in the Development of Instructional Leadership and School Achievement." *Urban Review* 22, 4 (December 1990): 247-65. EJ 422 294.

Hughes, Larry W., and Gerald C. Ubben. *The Elementary Principal's Handbook*. 4th edition Boston: Allyn and Bacon, 1994. 379 pages. ED 368 049.

Kushman, James W. "The Organizational Dynamics of Teacher Workplace Commitment: A Study of Urban Elementary and Middle Schools." *Educational Administration Quarterly* 28, 1 (February 1992): 5-42. EJ 441 083.

Leithwood, Kenneth; Doris Jantzi; and Alicia Fernandez. "Secondary School Teachers' Commitment to Change: The Contributions of Transformational Leadership." Paper presented at the annual meeting of the American Educational Research Association, Atlanta, Georgia, April 1993. 42 pages. ED 360 701.

Lezotte, Lawrence W., and others. *School Learning Climate and Student Achievement*. Tallahassee: National Teacher Corps, Florida State University Foundation, 1980.

Liontos, Lynn Balster. *Transformational Leadership: Profile of a High School Principal*. OSSC Bulletin Series. Eugene: Oregon School Study Council, 1993. ED 359 652.

Little, Judith Warren. "Norms of Collegiality and Experimentation: Workplace Conditions for School Success." *American Educational Research Journal* 19, 3 (Fall 1982): 325-40. EJ 275 511.

Loucks-Horsley, Susan F., and M. Melle. "Evaluation of Staff Development: How Do You Know If It Took?" *Journal of Staff Development* 3, 1 (1982): 102-17.

McCaslin, Mary, and Thomas L. Good. "Compliant Cognition: The Misalliance of Management and Instructional Goals in Current School Reform." *Educational Researcher* 21, 3 (April 1992): 4-17. EJ 445 359.

National Education Commission on Time and Learning (NECTL). *Research Findings*. Report. Washington, DC: Department of Education, Office of Educational Research and Improvement, September 1993.

Niemeyer, Roger, and Robert Hatfield. "Using the Curriculum Process as the Basis for Supervision/Leadership Within a Collegial Environment." Paper presented at the annual meeting of the Association for Supervision and Curriculum Development, March 1989. 22 pages. ED 306 670.

Oswald, Lori Jo. *Priority on Learning: How School Districts Are Concentrating Their Scarce Resource on Academics*. Eugene: Oregon School Study Council, 1994.

Rutherford, William L. "School Principals as Efffective Leaders." *Phi Delta Kappan* 67, 1 (September 1985): 31-34. EJ 326 607.

Sagor, Richard D. "Three Principals Who Make a Difference." *Educational Leadership* 49, 5 (February 1992): 13-18. EJ 439 277.

Senge, Peter. "The Leader's New Work: Building Learning Organizations." *Sloan Management Review* (Fall 1990).

Sergiovanni, Thomas J. "Why We Should Seek Substitutes for Leadership." *Educational Leadership* 49, 5 (February 1992): 41-45. EJ 439 283.

Watts, Gary D., and Shari Castle. "The Time Dilemma in School Restructuring." *Phi Delta Kappan* 75, 4 (December 1993): 306-10. EJ 474 291.

Weick, Karl E. "Administering Education in Loosely Coupled Schools." *Phi Delta Kappan* 63, 10 (June 1982): 673-76.

Weiss, Carol H.; Joseph Cambone; and Alexander Wyeth. "Trouble in Paradise: Teacher Conflicts in Shared Decision Making." *Educational Administration Quarterly* 28, 3 (August 1992): 350-67. EJ 447 157.

Chapter 11. Leading the Instructional Staff

Anderson, Mark E., and John Keiter. "New Kids on the Block: How to Recruit, Select, and Orient School Employees." Paper presented at the annual meeting of the American Association of School Administrators, San Diego, California, February 21-24, 1992. 39 pages. ED 343 238.

Black, Susan. "How Teachers Are Reshaping Evaluation Procedures." *Educational Leadership* 51, 2 (October 1993): 38-42. EJ 470 565.

Bloom, Benjamin S. *Developing Talent in Young People*. New York: Ballantine Books, 1985. 557 pages.

_______. "The Search for Methods of Group Instruction as Effective as One to One Tutoring." *Educational Leadership* 41, 8 (1984): 4-17.

Bolton, Dale. Personal Communication, November, 1995.

Bridges, William. *Managing Transitions: Making the Most of Change.* Reading, Massachusetts: Addison-Wesley, 1991. 130 pages.

Caldwell, Terry G. *Hiring Excellent Teachers: Current Interviewing Theories, Techniques, and Practices.* Master's Thesis. Long Beach, California: California State University, 1993. 58 pages. ED 358 512.

Darling-Hammond, Linda. "Standards for Teachers. 34th Charles W. Hunt Memorial Lecture." Paper presented at the 46th annual meeting of the American Association of Colleges for Teacher Education, Chicago, Illinois, February 17, 1994. 22 pages. ED 378 176.

DeBolt, Gary P. *Teacher Induction and Mentoring: School Based Collaborative Programs.* Albany: State University of New York Press, 1992. 203 pages.

Dietz, Mary E., "Using Portfolios as a Framework for Professional Development." *Journal of Staff Development* 16, 2 (Spring 1995): 40-43. EJ 512 846.

Duke, Daniel L. "Removing Barriers to Professional Growth." *Phi Delta Kappan* 74, 9 (May 1993): 702-04, 710-12. EJ 463 873.

Ellis, Arthur K. and Jeffrey T. Fouts. *Research on Educational Innovations.* Princeton Junction, New Jersey: Eye on Education, 1993. 203 pages.

Frase, Larry E. *Maximizing People Power in Schools: Motivating and Managing Teachers and Staff.* Newbury Park, California: Corwin Press, 1992. 137 pages. ED 351 806.

Gall, Meredith D., and Roseanne O'Brien Vojtek. *Planning for Effective Staff Development: Six Research Based Models.* Eugene, Oregon: ERIC Clearinghouse on Educational Management, University of Oregon, 1994. 52 pages. ED 372 464.

Glatthorn, Allan A. *Differentiated Supervision.* Alexandria, Virginia: Association for Supervision and Curriculum Development, 1984. 100 pages. ED 245 401.

Glickman, Carl D. *Supervision of Instruction: A Developmental Approach.* 2nd edition. Boston: Allyn and Bacon, 1990. 471 pages.

Good, Thomas, and Mary M. McCaslin. "Teaching Effectiveness." In *Encyclopedia of Education Research*, 6th edition, volume 4, edited by Marvin C. Alkin. 1373-88. New York: Macmillan, 1992.

Grote, Richard C. *Discipline Without Punishment.* New York: AMACOM, 1995. 243 pages.

Guskey, Thomas R. "Integrating Innovations," *Educational Leadership* 47, 5 (February 1990): 11-15. EJ 482 392.

Haefele, Donald L. "Evaluating Teachers: An Alternative Model." *Journal of Personnel Evaluation in Education* 5, 4 (June 1992): 335-45. EJ 448 012.

Hanson, Marjorie K. "Peer Evaluation Among Teachers: Acceptance of Alternative Roles." Paper presented at the annual meeting of the American Educational Research Association, San Francisco, April 20-24, 1992. 13 pages. ED 347 662.

Herman, Douglas. *Remediating Marginal Teachers: What Makes Plans of Assistance Work?* Oregon School Study Council Bulletin Series. Eugene: Oregon School Study Council, 1993. 13 pages. ED 364 935.

Huling-Austin, Leslie. "Research on Learning To Teach: Implications for Teacher Induction and Mentoring Programs." *Journal of Teacher Education* 43, 3 (May-June 1992): 173-80. EJ 455 171.

Iwanicki, Edward F. "Contract Plans." In *Handbook of Teacher Evaluation*, edited by J. Millman. Beverly Hills, California: Sage Publications, 1981.

Jensen, Mary C. "Leading the Instructional Staff." In *School Leadership: Handbook for Excellence*, Second Edition, edited by Stuart C. Smith and Philip K. Piele. Eugene, Oregon: ERIC Clearinghouse on Educational Management, 1989. 407 pages. ED 309 504.

Joyce, Bruce, and Beverly Showers. *Student Achievement Through Staff Development*. White Plains, New York: Longman, 1988. 190 pages. ED 283 817.

Latham, Gary. "Job Performance and Appraisal," In *International Review of Industrial and Organizational Psychology*, edited by C. L. Cooper and I. T. Robertson. New York: John Wiley and Sons, 1986.

Lieberman, Ann, and Lynne Miller. "Teacher Development in Professional Practice Schools." *Teacher's College Record* 92, 1 (Fall 1990): 105-22. EJ 415 847.

Locke, Edwin; K. N. Shaw; L. M. Saari; and G. P. Latham. "Goal Setting and Task Performance: 1969-1980." *Psychological Bulletin* 90, 1 (1981): 125-52.

McGreal, Thomas L. *Successful Teacher Evaluation*. Alexandria, Virginia: Association for Supervision and Curriculum Development, 1983. 161 pages. ED 236 776.

McMurtry, John. "Evaluating Teaching by Evaluating Learning." *Canadian Social Studies* 27, 2 (Winter 1993): 55-56. EJ 464 754.

Moore, Janet R. "Guidelines Concerning Adult Learning," *Journal of Staff Development* 9, 3 (Summer 1988): 2-5. EJ 388 000.

National Staff Development Council. *Standards for Staff Development*. High School, Middle School, and Elementary Editions. Oxford, Ohio: Author, 1995.

Robbins, Pamela, and Harvey B. Alvy, *The Principal's Companion: Strategies and Hints to Make the Job Easier*. Thousand Oaks, California: Corwin Press, 1995. 282 pages. ED 385 915.

Rosenholtz, Susan J. *Teachers' Workplace: The Social Organization of Schools*. New York: Longman, 1989. 238 pages.

Saphier, Jon, and Matthew King. "Good Seeds Grow in Strong Cultures." *Educational Leadership* 42, 6 (March 1985): 67-74. EJ 315 265.

Schlechty, Phillip C. "A Framework for Evaluating Induction into Teaching." *Journal of Teacher Education* 36, 1 (January-February 1985): 37-41. EJ 314 618.

Showers, Beverly; Bruce Joyce; and Barrie Bennett. "Synthesis of Research on Staff Development: A Framework for Future Study and a State-of-the-Art Analysis." *Educational Leadership* 45, 3 (November 1987): 77-87. EJ 367 365.

Smith, Wilma F., and Richard L. Andrews. *Instructional Leadership: How Principals Make a Difference*. Alexandria, Virginia: Association for Supervision and Curriculum Development, 1989. 155 pages. ED 314 826.

Spady, William G. *Outcome Based Education: Critical Issues and Answers*. Arlington, Virginia: American Association of School Administrators, 1994. 212 pages. ED 380 910.

Sparks, Dennis. "Six Predictions for Staff Development." *The Developer* (September 1990): 7.

Sparks, Dennis, and Stephanie Hirsh. "Staff Development Programs for the 1990's." *Education Week* 9, 33 (May 9, 1990): 40-41, 56.
Starratt, Robert J. "After Supervision." *Journal of Curriculum Supervision* 8, 1 (Fall 1992): 77-86. EJ 452 792.
Walen, Elizabeth, and Mimi DeRose. "The Power of Peer Appraisals." *Educational Leadership* 51, 2 (October 1993): 45-48. EJ 470 568.
Waxman, Hersholt C., and Herbert J. Walberg, eds. *Effective Teaching: Current Research.* Berkeley, California: McCutchan Publishing Corporation, 1991. 314 pages.

Chapter 12. Communicating

Amundson, Kristen. *Speaking and Writing Skills for Educators.* Arlington, Virginia: American Association of School Administrators, 1993. 20 pages.
Armistead, Lew. "A Four-Step Process for School Public Relations." *NASSP Bulletin* 73, 513 (January 1989): 6-8, 10-13. EJ 382 015.
_______. *Building Confidence in Education: A Practical Approach for Principals.* Reston Virginia: National Association of Secondary School Principals, 1982. 55 pages. ED 213 129.
_______. "A Practical and Positive Approach to Public Relations." *School Business Affairs* 54, 12 (December 1988): 15-19. EJ 383 821.
Armstrong, Coleen. "How's Your Story Arsenal?" *Principal* 71, 3 (January 1992): 35-36. EJ 437 540.
Bagin, Don; Donald R. Gallagher; and Leslie W. Kindred. *The School and Community Relations.* 5th edition. Needham Heights, Massachusetts: Allyn and Bacon, 1994. 330 pages. ED 385 391.
Bergman, Abby Barry. "Lessons for Principals from Site-Based Management." *Educational Leadership* 50, 1 (September 1992): 48-51. EJ 449 920.
Covey, Stephen R. *The Seven Habits of Highly Effective People.* New York: Fireside Books, Simon and Schuster, 1990.
Criscuolo, Nicholas P. "Enhance Your Press Rapport." *Executive Educator* 4, 6 (June 1982): 24, 36. EJ 263 085.
Dahlinger, Philip J. "Community Relations in Small School Districts." Paper presented at the annual meeting of the American Association of School Administrators, New Orleans, Louisiana, February 26-March 1, 1982. 8 pages. ED 224 677.
First, Patricia F., and David S. Carr. "Removing Barriers to Communication Between Principals and Teachers." *Catalyst for Change* 15, 3 (Spring 1986): 5-7. EJ 337 454.
Freshour, Frank W. "Listening Effectively." *Streamlined Seminar* 6, 2 (November 1987). Alexandria, Virginia: National Association of Elementary School Principals. 7 pages. ED 291 137.
Frohlichstein, Tripp. "Dealing Successfully with Media Inquiries." *NASSP Bulletin* 77, 555 (October 1993): 82-88. EJ 470 538.
Geddes, Doreen S. *Keys to Communication. A Handbook for School Success.* The Practicing Administrator's Leadership Series, edited by Jerry J. and Janice L. Herman. Thousand Oaks, California: Corwin Press, 1995. 59 pages. ED 377 575.
Gemmet, Richard. *A Monograph on Interpersonal Communications.* Redwood City, California: San Mateo County Superintendent of Schools, 1977. 48 pages. ED 153 323.

Glaser, Susan, and Anthony Biglan. *Increase Your Confidence and Skill in Interpersonal Situations: Instructional Manual*. Eugene, Oregon: Authors, 1977.

Glaser, Susan R., and Anna Eblen. "Organizational Communication Effectiveness: The View of Corporate Administrators." *Journal of Applied Communication Research* 14, 2 (Fall 1986): 119-32. EJ 357 948.

Glaser, Susan, and Peter Glaser. *Letting Go: Power Through Your People*. Forthcoming.

Griffin, Mary Alice. "Say It Like You Mean It." *School Business Affairs* 59, 9 (September 1993): 15-19. EJ 470 518.

Hughes, Larry W., and Gerald C. Ubben. *The Elementary Principal's Handbook, A Guide to Effective Action*. 4th edition Needham Heights, Massachusetts: Allyn and Bacon, 1994. ED 368 049.

Jung, Charles, and others. *Interpersonal Communications: Participant Materials and Leader's Manual*. Portland, Oregon: Northwest Regional Educational Laboratory, 1973. 935 pages. ED 095 127.

Major, Robert L. "Praise—An Often Overlooked Tool of Internal Communication." *Journal of Educational Public Relations* 7, 1 (March 1984): 28-29. EJ 299 496.

Ordovensky, Pat, and Gary Marx. *Working with the News Media*. Arlington. Virginia: American Association of School Administrators, 1993. 32 pages. ED 359 629.

Osterman, Karen F. "Communication Skills: A Key to Caring, Collaboration, and Change." Paper presented at the annual meeting of the University Council for Educational Administration, Houston, Texas, October 29-31, 1993. 23 pages. ED 363 973.

Pierson, Patricia R., and Paul V. Bredeson. "It's Not Just a Laughing Matter: School Principals' Use of Humor in Interpersonal Communications with Teachers." *Journal of School Leadership* 3, 5 (September 1993): 522-33. EJ 466 909.

Schmuck, Richard A., and Philip Runkel. *Handbook of Organization Development in Schools and Colleges*. 4th edition Prospect Heights, Illinois: Waveland Press, 1994. 486 pages. ED 386 817.

Turner, David. "Building Legislative Relationships: A Guide for Principals." Springfield: Illinois Principals Association, April 1995.

Vann, Allan S. "Ten Ways to Improve Principal-Parent Communication." *Principal* 71, 3 (January 1992): 30-31. EJ 437 537.

_______. "That Vision Thing." *Principal* 74, 2 (November 1994): 25-26. EJ 492 877.

Warner, Carolyn. *Promoting Your School: Going Beyond PR*. Thousand Oaks, California: Corwin Press, 1994. 206 pages. ED 378 664.

Chapter 13. Building Coalitions

Armistead, Lew. *Building Confidence in Education: A Practical Approach for Principals*. Reston, Virginia: National Association of Secondary School Principals, 1982. 55 pages. ED 213 129.

Bagin, Don; Donald Ferguson; and Gary Marx. *Public Relations for Administrators*. Arlington, Virginia: American Association of Secondary School Principals, 1985. 125 pages. ED 282 356.

Black, Terry R. "Coalition Building—Some Suggestions." *Child Welfare* 62, 3 (May-June 1983): 263-68. EJ 281 559.

California State Department of Education. *A Guide to School and Community Action*. Sacramento: Author, 1981. ED 208 316.

Conley, David T. *Roadmap to Restructuring: Policies, Practices, and the Emerging Visions of Schooling*. Eugene, Oregon: ERIC Clearinghouse on Educational Management, 1993. 430 pages. ED 359 593.

Davies, Don. "Testing a Strategy for Reform: The League of Schools Reaching Out." Paper presented for a symposium at the American Educational Research Association annual meeting in Chicago, April 1991. 28 pages. ED 331 178.

Edelstein, Frederick S., Esther F. Schaeffer; and Richard J. Kenney. *A Blueprint for Business on Restructuring Education*. Washington, D.C.: The National Alliance of Business, 1989. 38 pages. ED 312 486.

Green, David. "How a Principal Can Make the P.T.O. a Gold Mine." *Executive Educator* 5, 12 (December 1983): 23-24. EJ 291 431.

Hughes, Larry W., and Gerald C. Ubben. *The Elementary Principal's Handbook: A Guide to Effective Action*. 4th edition. Needham Heights, Massachusetts: Allyn and Bacon, Inc., 1994. 379 pages. ED 368 049.

Liontos, Lynn Balster. *Social Services and Schools: Building Collaboration That Works*. OSSC Bulletin Series. Eugene: Oregon School Study Council, 1991. 42 pages. ED 343 264.

Martin-McCormick, Lynda, and others. *Organizing for Change: PEER's Guide to Campaigning for Equal Education*. Washington, D.C.: National Organization for Women, Project on Equal Education Rights, 1982. 196 pages. ED 240 183.

Melaville, Atelia I., and Martin J. Blank. *What It Takes: Structuring Interagency Partnerships To Connect Children and Families with Comprehensive Services*. Washington, D.C.: Education and Human Services Consortium, 1991. 57 pages. ED 330 748.

Michigan State Board of Education. *Mapping Your Millage*. Lansing, Michigan: Author, 1984. 187 pages. ED 251 925.

Palanki, Ameetha; Patricia Burch; and Don Davies. *Mapping the Policy Landscape: What Federal and State Governments Are Doing to Promote Family-School-Community Partnerships*. Baltimore, Maryland: Center on Families, Communities, Schools and Children's Learning, 1992. 82 pages. ED 343 700.

Steffy, Betty E., and Jane Clark Lindle. *Building Coalitions: How To Link TQE Schools with Government, Business, and Community*. Thousand Oaks, California: Corwin Press, Inc., 1994. 107 pages. ED 378 646.

Stone, Calvin. "School-Community Collaboration: Comparing Three Initiatives." Madison, Wisconsin: Center on Organization and Restructuring of Schools, 1993. 15 pages. ED 358 549.

Wilson, Bruce L., and Gretchen B. Rossman. "Collaborative Links with the Community: Lessons from Exemplary Secondary Schools." *Phi Delta Kappan* 67, 10 (June 1986): 708-11. EJ 345 223.

Chapter 14. Leading Meetings

Blanchard, Ken. "Meetings That Work." *Today's Office* 22, 1 (June 1987): 9-11.

Bormann, Ernest G., and Nancy C. Bormann. *Effective Small Group Communications*. 5th edition Edina, Minnesota: Burgess Publishing Co., 1992. 262 pages.

Bradford, Leland P. *Making Meetings Work: A Guide for Leaders and Group Members*. La Jolla, California: University Associates, 1976. 121 pages.

Covey, Steven. *The 7 Habits of Highly Effective People: Powerful Lessons in Personal Change*. New York: Simon & Schuster, 1990. 358 pages.

Criscuolo, Nicholas P. "Staff Meetings: Meaningful or Meaningless?" *NASSP Bulletin* 68, 471 (April 1984): 134-36. EJ 298 017.

DeLuca, Nicholas. "Meetings: With Effective Leadership, They Can Work." *NASSP Bulletin* 67, 464 (September 1983): 114-17. EJ 286 646.

Doyle, Michael, and David Straus. *How To Make Meetings Work: The New Interaction Method.* New York: Jove Books, 1983. 299 pages.

Fordyce, Jack K., and Raymond Weil. *Managing WITH People: A Manager's Handbook of Organization Development Methods.* 2nd edition Reading, Massachusetts: Addison-Wesley Publishing Co., 1983. 206 pages.

Gorton, Richard A., and James Burns. "Faculty Meetings: What Do Teachers Really Think of Them?" *Clearing House* 59, 1 (September 1985): 30-32. EJ 325 148.

Jay, Antony, "How To Run a Meeting." *Harvard Business Review* 54, 2 (March-April 1976): 43-57. EJ 134 472.

Jones, Rebecca. "Meetings Without Tedium." *The Executive Educator* 17, 9 (September 1995): 18-20. EJ 511 681.

Maidment, Robert, and William Bullock, Jr. *Meetings! Accomplishing More with Better & Fewer.* Reston, Virginia: National Association of Secondary School Principals, 1985. ED 252 950.

Maude, Barry. *Managing Meetings.* London: Business Books Limited, 1975. 70 pages.

Moore, Kermit. "How Seating Can Determine Your Standing." *Executive Educator* 7, 4 (April 1985): 22-23. EJ 315 281.

Morley, Cindy Lakin. *How To Get the Most out of Meetings.* Alexandria, Virginia: Association for Supervision and Curriculum Development, 1994. 31 pages. ED 374 535.

Palmer, Barbara C., and Kenneth R. Palmer. *The Successful Meeting Master Guide for Business and Professional People.* Englewood Cliffs, New Jersey: Prentice Hall, 1983. 277 pages.

Ratteray, Oswald M.T. "After the Meeting, Then What?" *Successful Meetings* (February 1984): 76-77. ED 242 013.

Schindler-Rainman, Eva; Ronald Lippitt; and Jack Cole. *Taking Your Meetings out of the Doldrums.* Revised edition. San Diego, California: University Associates, 1988. 123 pages.

Schmuck, Richard A., and Philip Runkel. *Handbook of Organizational Development in Schools and Colleges.* 4th edition. Prospect Heights, Illinois: Waveland Press, Inc., 1994. 486 pages. ED 386 817.

Shelton, Maria M., and Laurie K. Bauer". *Secrets of Highly Effective Meetings*." In *The Practicing Administrator's Leadership Series,* edited by Jerry J. and Janice L. Herman. Thousand Oaks, California: Corwin Press, 1994. 54 pages. ED 378 662.

3M Meeting Management Team. *How to Run Better Business Meetings: A Reference Guide for Managers.* New York: McGraw-Hill Book Company, 1987. 216 pages.

Whitehead, Jack L., Jr. "Improving Meeting Productivity." In *Professional Communication in the Modern World: Proceedings of the Southeast Convention of the American Business Communication Association,* Hammond, Louisiana, April 5-7, 1984. 185-91. ED 262 402.

Chapter 15. Managing Time, Stress, and Conflict

Anderson, Patricia L. "Conflict: How To Beat the Odds." *School Business Affairs* 59, 9 (September 1993): 4-8. EJ 478 516.

Bailey, Stephen K. "Preparing Administrators for Conflict Resolution." *Educational Record* 52, 3 (Summer 1971): 223-39. EJ 045 040.

Blue, Monte. "Conflict: Educational Administrators Must Learn To Manage It." *Thrust for Educational Leadership* 17, 4 (January 1988): 46-48.

Clark, Kenneth E., and Miriam B. Clark. "Introduction." In *Impact of Leadership*, edited by Kenneth E. Clark; Miriam B. Clark; and David P. Campbell. 1-10. Greensboro, North Carolina: Center for Creative Leadership, 1992. ED 353 421.

Douglass, Donna Niksch, and Merrill E. Douglass. "Timely Techniques for Paperwork Mania." *Personnel Administrator* 24, 9 (September 1979): 19-22. EJ 206 368.

Drucker, Peter F. *The Effective Executive.* New York: Harper & Row, 1966. 178 pages.

Dudley, Donald L., M.D., and Elton Welke. *How to Survive Being Alive.* Garden City, New York: Doubleday & Co., 1977. 179 pages.

Duignan, Patrick. "Administration Behavior of School Superintendents: A Descriptive Study." *Journal of Educational Administration* 18, 1 (July 1980): 5-26. EJ 236 676.

Giammatteo, Michael C., and Dolores M. Giammatteo. *Executive Well-Being: Stress and Administrators.* Reston, Virginia: National Association of Secondary School Principals, 1980. 67 pages. ED 180 134.

Gmelch, Walter H. "The Principal's Next Challenge: The Twentieth Century Art of Managing Stress." *NASSP Bulletin* 62, 415 (February 1978): 5-12. EJ 173 486.

_______. *Release from Stress.* Eugene: Oregon School Study Council, University of Oregon, May/June 1981. 75 pages.

Gmelch, Walter H., and Wilbert Chan. *Thriving on Stress for Success.* Thousand Oaks, California: Corwin Press, Inc., 1994. 132 pages. ED 378 660.

Hughes, Larry W. "Time Management Problems of Instructional Supervisors." *Catalyst for Change* 13, 1 (Fall 1983): 21-25. EJ 289 708.

Katz, Neil H., and John W. Lawyer. *Preventing and Managing Conflict in Schools.* Thousand Oaks, California: Corwin Press, Inc., 1994. 72 pages.

Koff, Robert; James Laffey; George Olson; and Donald Cicon. "Stress and the School Administrator." *Administrator's Notebook* 28, 9 (1979-80): 1-4. EJ 242 356.

Lakein, Alan. *How To Get Control of Your Time and Your Life.* New York: Signet, The New American Library, 1974. 160 pages.

Ledell, Marjorie A. *How To Avoid Crossfire and Seek Common Ground: A Journey for the Sake of Children.* Arlington, Virginia: American Association of School Administrators, 1995. 32 pages. ED 380 907.

Lewis, Darrell R., and Tor Dahl. "Time Management in Higher Education Administration: A Case Study." Paper presented at annual meeting of American Educational Research Association, Washington D.C., January 1975. 25 pages. ED 104 239.

Lipham, James M., and James A. Hoeh., Jr. *The Principalship: Foundations and Functions.* New York: Harper and Row, 1974.

Lippitt, Gordon L. "Can Conflict Resolution Be Win-Win?" *School Administrator* 40, 3 (March 1983): 20-22. EJ 278 026.

MacKenzie, R. Alec. "Plan Your Work and Work Your Plan." *School Business Affairs* 51, 1 (January 1985): 48-49. EJ 311 727.

Maidment, Robert. *Conflict! A Conversation about Managing Differences.* Reston, Virginia: National Association of Secondary School Principals, 1987. 48 pages. ED 289 252.

Mambert, W.A. "Busy, Busy, Busy—and Promises To Keep." *Credit* 6, 6 (November/December 1980): 25-27.

Manuso, James S. "Executive Stress Management." *Personnel Administrator* 24, 11 (November 1979): 23-26. EJ 210 942.

Nebgen, Mary K. "Conflict Management in Schools." *Administrator's Notebook* 26, 6 (1978): 1-4. EJ 183 246.

Rees, Ruth. *SOS: A Time Management Framework.* Ontario, Canada: Queen's University at Kingston, November 1985. 23 pages. ED 263 681.

Robbins, Stephen P. *Managing Organizational Conflict. A Nontraditional Approach.* Englewood Cliffs, New Jersey: Prentice-Hall, 1974. 156 pages.

Schmidt, Warren H., and Robert Tannenbaum. "Management of Differences." In *The Social Technology of Organization Development,* compiled by W. Warner Burke and Harvey A. Hornstein. 127-40. La Jolla, California: University Associates, 1972. 340 pages.

Sexton, Michael J., and Karen Dawn Dill Switzer. "The Time Management Ladder." *Educational Leadership* 35, 6 (March 1978): 482-83, 485-86. EJ 175 684.

Terrill, Jerry L., "Coping with Stress in Difficult Times." *NASSP Bulletin* 77, 550 (February 1993): 89-93. EJ 459 356.

Weldy, Gilbert R. *TIME: A Resource for the School Administrator.* Washington, D.C.: National Association of Secondary School Principals, 1974. 63 pages. ED 094 475.

Yatvin, Joanne. "Memoir of a Team Player." *Educational Leadership* 49, 5 (February 1992): 50-52. EJ 439 285.

Interviews

Chapter 7. School-Based Management

Kearns, Homer H. Superintendent. Salem-Keizer School District. Telephone interview. January 2, 1995.

Wohlstetter, Priscilla. Director of the University of Southern California's Center on Educational Governance and Associate Professor in the School of Education. University of Southern California. Los Angeles, California. Telephone Interviews. January 26, 1995.

Chapter 8. Quality Work Teams

Chan, Carmen, Principal, Robert Frost Elementary School, Lake Washington School District, Kirkland, Washington. Telephone interview September 7, 1995.

Davis, Carol, Deputy Superintendent, Salem-Keizer School District, Salem, Oregon. Telephone interview September 7, 1995.

Keller, Ernie R., Ed.D, Wasco-Region 9 Education Service District, The Dalles, Oregon. Telephone interview August 15, 1995.

Miller, Winston, McKay Area Operations Director, Salem-Keizer School District, Salem, Oregon. Telephone interview January 2, 1995.

Mutchie, Scott, Superintendent, Bend-LaPine School District, Bend, Oregon. Telephone interview February 7, 1995.

Scarr, L. E. "Bud," Superintendent, Lake Washington School District, Kirkland, Washington. Telephone interview September 5, 1995.

Vollmer, Nancy, School Improvement Specialist, Linn-Benton-Lincoln Education Service District, Corvallis, Oregon. Telephone interview August 14, 1995.

Chapter 13. Building Coalitions

Billie Bagger, Adult and Family Services Representative for Service Integration, Salem, Oregon. Telephone interview September 28, 1993.

Jan Baxter, Principal, Hollydale School, Gresham, Oregon. Telephone interview September 27, 1993.

Wendy del Mar, Social Worker, Centennial School District, Portland, Oregon. Interview September 27, 1993.

George Dyer, Principal, South Salem High School, Salem, Oregon. Telephone interview September 22, 1993.

Twila Schell, Volunteer Program Manager, Department of Human Resources, Pendleton, Oregon. Telephone interview September 29, 1993.

Other Publications Available from ERIC/CEM

Measuring Leadership A Guide to Assessment for Development of School Executives

Larry Lashway • 1999 • 6x9 inches • viii + 117 pages • perfect bind • ISBN 0-86552-140-9 •$9.75.Code: EMOMLG.

Student Motivation: Cultivating a Love of Learning

Linda Lumsden • 1999 • 6x9 inches • vi + 113 pages • perfect bind • ISBN 0-86552-141-7 •$9.50. Code: EMOSMC.

Leading with Vision

Larry Lashway • 1997 • 6 x 9 inches • xii + 148 pages • perfect bind • ISBN: 0-86552-138-7 • $13.50. Code: EMOLWV

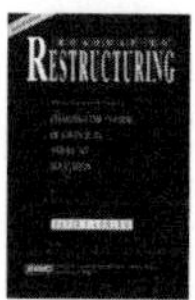

Roadmap to Restructuring: Charting the Course of Change in American Education

David T. Conley • Second Edition • 1997 • 6 x 9 inches • xvi + 571 pages • Cloth ISBN: 0-86552-136-0 ($34.95) Code: EMORMC • Paper ISBN 0-86552-137-9 ($23.95) Code: EMORMP

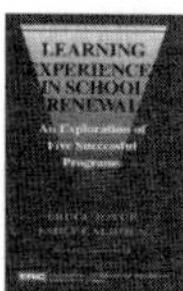

Learning Experiences in School Renewal: An Exploration of Five Successful Programs

Bruce Joyce and Emily Calhoun • 1996 • 6 x 9 inches • viii + 208 pages • perfect bind • ISBN: 0-86552-133-6 • $14.50. Code: EMOLES

How to Order: You may place an order by sending a check or money order, mailing or faxing a purchase order, or calling with a Visa or MasterCard number. Add 10% for S&H (minimum $4.00). Make payment to University of Oregon/ERIC and mail to ERIC/CEM, 5207 University of Oregon, Eugene, Oregon 97403-5207. Shipping is by UPS ground or equivalent.

Telephone (800) 438-8841
Fax (541) 346-2334

You can also order online (with Visa or MasterCard) from our website—your gateway to information about educational policy and management.

http://eric.uoregon.edu